A Modern Introduction to International Law

A MODERN INTRODUCTION TO INTERNATIONAL LAW

MICHAEL AKEHURST

M.A., LL.B.(Cantab.),
Docteur de l'Université de Paris,
of the Inner Temple, Barrister-at-Law,
Reader in Law at the University of Keele

FIFTH EDITION

London
GEORGE ALLEN AND UNWIN
Boston   Sydney

George Allen & Unwin (Publishers) Ltd,
40 Museum Street, London WC1A 1LU, UK

George Allen & Unwin (Publishers) Ltd,
Park Lane, Hemel Hempstead, Herts HP2 4TE, UK

Allen & Unwin, Inc.,
9 Winchester Terrace, Winchester, Mass. 01890, USA

George Allen & Unwin Australia Pty Ltd,
8 Napier Street, North Sydney, NSW 2060, Australia

A Modern Introduction to International Law was first published as
No. 25 in the Minerva Series of Student's Handbooks.

First published in 1970
Second edition 1971
Third edition 1977
Fourth impression 1980
Fourth edition 1982
Second impression 1983
Fifth edition 1984

British Library Cataloguing in Publication Data

Akehurst, Michael, 1940–
    A modern introduction to international
law – 5th ed.
1. International law
I. Title
341   JX3091
ISBN 0–04–341025–1
ISBN 0–04–341026–X Pbk

Library of Congress Cataloging in Publication Data

Akehurst, Michael Barton.
    A modern introduction to international law.
Includes bibliographical references and index.
1. International law.   I. Title.
JX1308.A43   1984   341   84–9195
ISBN 0–04–341025–1 (alk. paper)
ISBN 0–04–341026–X (pbk. : alk. paper)

Set in 11 on 12 point Times
and printed in Great Britain
by Mackays of Chatham

Contents

To My Students
Past, Present and Future

A Modern Introduction to International Law

Chapter 1

Is International Law Really Law?

International law (otherwise known as public international law or the law of nations) is the system of law which governs relations between states. At one time states were the only bodies which had rights and duties under international law, but nowadays international organisations, companies and individuals also sometimes have rights and duties under international law; however, it is still true to say that international law is *primarily* concerned with states.

English textbooks on international law usually discuss not only international law, but also certain rules of English law, such as the British Nationality Act, which are relevant to international relations; and this is a practice which the present book will also follow.

Popular Scepticism about International Law

The initial reaction of law students and laymen alike, when they are first told about international law, is usually highly sceptical. They believe that states have little respect for international law, and have no incentive to obey it in the absence of a supranational system of sanctions capable of being enforced against the lawbreaker. In short, the popular belief is that international law is not really law.

The question whether international law is really law cannot be dismissed as a purely verbal question. If cabinet ministers and diplomats shared the popular scepticism about international law, then international law would be broken far more often than it is. Even if they regarded international law as a form of morality rather than law, respect for it would still be weakened; it is significant that those who regard international law as a form of morality usually speak of it as *'mere* morality'. Although experienced diplomats do not often share the popular scepticism about international law, there is a danger that the popular attitude may affect inexperienced officials and pressure groups within a state, and that the state may, as a result, be pushed into breaking international law.

In fact, however, states do accept that international law is law; and, what is more, they usually obey it. It is true that international law is sometimes broken with impunity; but the same could be said of any legal system. In English law, for instance, the cost of bringing a civil action is often greater than the amount of damages which can be recovered; and many people never even think of going to court, because they are ignorant of their rights. Even in English criminal law, where prosecutions are normally brought by the police, about 59 per cent of the serious crimes known to the police are never solved. In some other countries the position is even worse. If war is taken as the supreme example of a breakdown of law and order, it is significant that in many states civil wars and rebellions have been far more frequent (and often more devastating) than international wars.

International law is not broken more often than any other system of law. But people imagine that it is constantly broken. Why has this impression arisen? There are, I think, two explanations.

In the first place, it is only the violations of the law that get into the newspapers. When people are robbed or murdered, or when states attack one another, it is news; if the law is obeyed, it is not reported, but taken for granted. A visitor from another planet, picking up one of our newspapers and finding it full of accounts of robberies and murders, might be forgiven for thinking that life was not safe; we, who live on this planet, can tell from our own experience of everyday life that what is reported in the newspapers is the exception, not the rule. But most people have no similar experience of international relations to set against what they read in the newspapers, and so they think that the reported breaches of international law are typical instead of being exceptional.

Secondly, people tend to imagine that the mere existence of an international dispute proves that at least one state has broken the law. But international disputes are not necessarily caused by breaches of international law, just as disputes between individuals are not necessarily caused by breaches of national law. International law does not provide an answer to all international disputes, just as English law does not provide an answer to all quarrels between Englishmen. It is worth listing some of the other factors which can cause international disputes.

(1) There may be a genuine uncertainty about the facts. For instance, before one can decide whether United States participation in the Vietnam fighting was legal or illegal, one has to decide whether the National Liberation Front (Vietcong) in South Vietnam represented spontaneous internal revolt or whether it represented subversion from North Vietnam. In the former case,

American intervention was probably unlawful; in the latter case, it was probably lawful (see below, pp. 242–6). But opinions and evidence about the nature of the NLF differ, and one has to know the facts before one can apply the law.

(2) There may be genuine uncertainty about the law. For instance, some states think it is lawful to nationalise foreign property without compensation; others disagree. When a dispute arises between a state in the first group and a state in the second group, each will be convinced that it is in the right, and it is difficult to predict how an international court would decide the case (see below, pp. 91–6).

(3) An international dispute may be caused by a demand for a change in the law, just as strikes and other types of industrial dispute are often caused by a demand for alterations in the workers' contracts of employment. One cannot solve such a dispute by telling states what the existing law is, any more than one can persuade strikers to go back to work by telling them that Professor X says in his book on industrial law that wages are fixed by the contract of employment and that Professor Y says in his book on the law of contract that contracts can only be altered by mutual agreement.

(4) An international dispute may be caused by an unfriendly but legal act. The duties which international law places on states are often limited, and it may therefore be possible to injure another state severely without breaking the law. For instance, apart from special treaty provisions, international law does not prevent a state increasing its tariffs on goods coming from another state, even though the result may be to cause severe unemployment in the other state.

(5) An international dispute may arise from a violation of a body of rules which does not form part of international law. Just as societies of individuals have rules of morality, good manners, and so on, which are not part of the law, so the international society of states has rules of conduct which do not form part of international law. Some of these rules may be briefly mentioned.

(a) There are rules of courtesy, for example, saluting the flags of foreign warships at sea. There is an obvious similarity between such rules and the rules of courtesy which individuals observe in a national society (for example, taking your hat off in church).

(b) There are certain ideals which are regarded as desirable but not always practicable, such as human rights, and self-determination of peoples. It is precisely because they are not always practicable that they have often not been treated as rules of law; for law demands 100 per cent compliance.[1] They bear some resemblance to moral ideals like truthfulness, which national law does not seek to enforce, because violations are too common to make enforcement practicable.

(c)   Under the doctrine of spheres of influence, a major power adopts the policy of defending smaller powers within its sphere of influence against outside attacks (to this extent the doctrine serves to strengthen international law); the major power also claims the right to intervene in the affairs of the smaller powers within its sphere of influence (and here the doctrine runs counter to international law). The world received a grim reminder of the continuing existence of this doctrine at the time of the Soviet invasion of Czechoslovakia in August 1968, which the Soviet Union publicly justified by reference to the concept of spheres of influence. The doctrine mercifully has no exact parallel in national societies, but something like it may be seen in those unspoken patterns of segregation which exist in societies where there are deep racial or religious differences; a Catholic who buys a house in a Protestant area of Belfast will soon be made to feel a trespasser, even though he may have an impeccable legal title to the property.

There is really only one way of distinguishing international law from non-legal rules applicable to international relations, and that is to ask: 'Do states regard this particular rule as a rule of international law, or not?' The question is important and needs to be asked, because two significant consequences depend on the answer.

In the first place, when a non-legal rule is turned into a legal rule, it acquires a vigour which it never had before. An immoral or discourteous act is regarded as worse if it is illegal as well. For instance, Argentina reacted sharply to the Israeli abduction of the Nazi war criminal Eichmann from Argentina in 1960, not because they had any interest in protecting Eichmann from punishment, but because the abduction constituted an infringement of Argentina's rights under international law; if Argentina had merely regarded the abduction as discourteous or immoral, her reaction would probably not have been as sharp. Similarly, a sphere of influence is strengthened if it is placed on a legal basis. Thus, the fact that America has promised *by treaty* to defend the

---

[1] Such ideals are gradually becoming rules of law; see below, pp. 74–81 and 248–55. But the process is gradual, because states require time to get used to such stringent ideals.

European members of NATO against Soviet attack means that America is more likely to honour her promise than she would have been in the absence of a *legally* binding promise; as a result NATO's effectiveness as a deterrent is greatly increased.

Second, when a non-legal rule is turned into a legal rule, arguments about the scope of that rule take on a new character. Lawyers are trained not only to know (or to know where to find) the law when the law is clear, but also how to argue a case when the law is not clear – how to interpret or distinguish previous authorities, how to make use of analogies, how to deduce general principles from more detailed rules, and vice versa. Legal argument is a distinctive form of argument, just as literary criticism is a distinctive form of argument. The applicability of legal argument to particular rules is both a consequence and a proof of the legal character of those rules; to argue about rules of morality or of courtesy in the same way that one argues about rules of law would clearly be grotesque:

> What predominate in the arguments, often technical, which states address to each other over disputed matters of international law, are references to precedents, treaties and juristic writings; often no mention is made of moral right or wrong . . . Hence the claim that the Peking Government has or has not a right under international law to expel the Nationalist forces from Formosa, is very different from the question whether this is fair, just, or a morally good or bad thing to do, and is backed by characteristically different arguments. (H. L. A. Hart, *The Concept of Law*, 1961, p. 223)

The Problem of Sanctions

In a modern state we are accustomed to find a legislature which enacts the law; a judiciary which tries violations of the law; and an executive body which, among other things, enforces the decisions of the legislature and the judiciary. In international law, these features are almost wholly lacking. To a large extent, states create international law for themselves and need not accept a new rule unless they agree to it; they need not appear before an international tribunal unless they agree to do so; and there is no centralised executive body with the task of enforcing the law.

The absence of a legislature in international law led some nineteenth-century philosophers to deny that international law was law, but this defect is not regarded as crucial nowadays. What contemporary sceptics seize on is the absence of sanctions – that is to say, the absence of obligatory judicial settlement, and the absence of a centralised executive authority to enforce judgments.

If one state commits an illegal act against another state, and refuses to make reparation or to appear before an international tribunal, there is (or was until recently) only one sanction in the hands of the injured state: self-help. Self-help exists as a sanction in all legal systems. In primitive law (for example, English law before the Norman Conquest) most sanctions involved the use of self-help in one form or another. Even in modern English law an individual may defend himself against assaults, retake property which has been stolen from him, evict trespassers from his land and terminate a contract if the other party has broken a major term of the contract. But in modern societies self-help has become the exception rather than the rule, whereas in international law it has remained the rule.

At one time states could even go to war to enforce their legal rights. However, this is no longer lawful, with certain exceptions such as self-defence against armed attack. The remaining forms of self-help are retorsion and reprisals.

Retorsion is a lawful act which is designed to injure the wrong-doing state, for example, cutting off economic aid (this is lawful because there is no legal obligation to give economic aid, apart from special treaty provisions).

Reprisals are acts which would normally be illegal but which are rendered legal by a prior illegal act committed by the other state. For instance, if state A expropriates property belonging to state B's citizens without compensation, state B can retaliate by doing the same to property of state A's citizens. Reprisals need not take exactly the same form as the original illegal act; for instance, in the example just given, state B could, instead of expropriating the property of state A's citizens, repudiate a loan which it had borrowed from state A's citizens. But reprisals must be proportionate to the original wrong; for instance, state B could not expropriate property worth several times the value of the property which its citizens had lost; still less would it be entitled to kill or imprison state A's citizens.

One disadvantage of retorsion and reprisals is that the state imposing them may injure itself as much as the state against which they are directed; this is particularly true when one state cuts off trade with another state. But other types of sanctions share the same defect; for instance, in English law, a businessman who sues a customer to recover a debt may face a bill from his lawyers which is greater than the value of the original debt. A more serious disadvantage of self-help is that it only works effectively if the injured state is in some way more powerful or more determined than the wrong-doing state.

Not surprisingly, therefore, there has been a recent tendency for sanctions to be imposed by large groups of states, working through international organisations such as the United Nations. But the United Nations Security Council can impose sanctions only in limited circumstances, and is often paralysed by the power of veto possessed by each of its five permanent members. The United Nations General Assembly is not subject to the veto, but its resolutions are usually not legally binding (although they are an institutionalised form of public opinion and can exercise great political pressure). Both the Security Council and the General Assembly, being political and not judicial bodies, base their decisions on political considerations and sometimes pay little attention to the legal rights and wrongs of a dispute.

International organisations with more specialised functions may exercise a more effective control over their members, especially if they provide essential services, like the International Monetary Fund: a state which was excluded from membership of the Fund would be unable to borrow gold and foreign currency from the Fund to meet a balance of payments crisis. And regional organisations may exercise an even stricter discipline over their members; for instance, the Court of Justice of the European Communities has compulsory jurisdiction over member-states which are accused of breaking the rules of the EEC.

However, it must be confessed that sanctions work less effectively in international law than in national law. States are few in number and unequal in strength, and there are always one or two states which are so strong that other states are usually too weak or too timid or too disunited to impose sanctions against them. But this does not mean that international law as a whole works less effectively than national law – only that it works in a different way. The importance of sanctions must not be exaggerated. They are not the main reason why the law is obeyed in any legal system. People do not refrain from committing murder because they are afraid of being punished, but because they have been brought up to regard murder as unthinkable – habit, conscience, morality, affection and tolerance play a far more important part than sanctions. Sanctions are only effective if the law-breaker is in a small minority; if he is not, sanctions are powerless to secure compliance with the law, as is shown by widespread violation of speed limits on English roads. It is unsound to study any legal system in terms of sanctions. It is better to study law as a body of rules which are usually obeyed, not to concentrate exclusively on what happens when the rules are broken. We must not confuse the pathology of law with law itself.

Reasons Why States Obey International Law

States obey international law far more often than most people suppose. Fear of sanctions has very little to do with this obedience. There are other factors inherent in the very nature of international law and of international society which induce states to obey international law. These factors more than compensate for the weakness of sanctions, but few people are aware of them, because they have no counterpart in national systems of law. Not all of these factors may operate at the same time, but compliance with international law will usually be secured even if only one of them operates in a particular case.

(1) *The absence of a legislature* is paradoxically a source of strength for international law. All legal systems correspond to some extent to the prevailing climate of opinion in the society in which they operate, but in national legal systems the concentration of legislative power in the hands of a small number of individuals may result in the enactment of rules which most people do not want and are reluctant to obey. In international law the absence of a legislature means that states very largely create law for themselves, and it is unlikely that they will create law which is not in their interests or which they will be tempted to break. Of course, it is possible that a state may be forced to agree to a rule under duress, or that the interests of states may change, or that a change of circumstances may render a rule burdensome; but international law provides at least a partial solution to these problems (see below, pp. 132-9).

It is not difficult to see why it is in the interests of states to agree to rules of international law. States are naturally interdependent in many ways (for example, international trade), and international law facilitates international co-operation; states have a common interest in preventing pollution of the sea, for instance, but prevention of pollution requires detailed rules about such things as the discharge of oil from ships, and a treaty or some other legal instrument is the obvious way of laying down the necessary rules. Similarly, when a particular problem is constantly arising (for example, do aircraft from one state have a right to fly through the air space above another state?), it is in everyone's interests to have an agreed rule to deal with all such cases, instead of leaving every individual case to be decided by a trial of strength between the particular states concerned. Even when the relevant rule of international law is imprecise, it still performs a useful function; it may not eliminate the area of disagreement between states, but at least it reduces that area, and thus makes it easier for disputes to be settled without friction.

The fact that international law largely reflects the interests of states does not justify the conclusion that states would act in the same way even if there were no law; still less does it justify the cynical view that states only obey international law when it is in their interests to do so. In the first place, as we shall see, the mere fact that a rule is a rule of international law provides states with reasons for obeying it even when there appear to be short-term gains to be derived from breaking it. Second, as I have already tried to show (above, pp. 4–5), a rule acquires a life of its own when it becomes a rule of international law. Out of habit, states obey the rule even when it goes against their interests, and claim their legal rights even when their interests are not involved. And legal arguments as well as political arguments are used in disputes about applications of the rule.

(2) *International law is largely based on custom.* By obeying a customary rule, states strengthen the rule. By breaking it, they weaken it and, so to speak, cast a vote in favour of its repeal. Customary law has a built-in mechanism of change. Thus, a state which breaks a rule of customary law may find that it has created a precedent which can be used against it, not only by the original victim, but also by third states, when the wrong-doing state wants to claim the benefit of that rule in the future. Realisation of this possibility often deters states from breaking international law.

However, the application of this factor is subject to three disadvantages:

(a) When states break rules of international law, they often attempt to justify their conduct by suggesting a narrow exception to the original rule, in the hope that a narrow exception will not constitute a dangerous precedent. But sometimes this hope is not fulfilled. For instance, when India invaded Goa in 1961, she argued that the liberation of territories seized in the past by colonial powers constituted an exception to the general prohibition against the use of force. A year later China invaded some areas held by India in the Himalayas, arguing that these areas had originally been seized from China by a colonial power (Britain) and that China was therefore entitled to use force to recover them, just as India had done in Goa.

(b) A state may deliberately try to undermine a rule if that rule generally works against the state's interests. However, in some cases it may be difficult to undermine a particular rule without undermining the law as a whole, and a realisation of this may act as a deterrent on the state concerned.

(c)   Many diplomats may not be sophisticated enough to weigh the long-term disadvantages of violating a rule against the short-term gains of violation. At times of great tension, it may be difficult to look beyond the immediate crisis. The cynical view is that states will always violate international law when their vital (short-term) interests are in danger. This view is only partly true, because violations, when they do occur, are more often unconscious than conscious. It often happens that there is no absolutely right answer to a legal problem; instead, there are answers of varying degrees of legal soundness and unsoundness. In times of crisis, when a state's vital interests are in danger, the state's legal advisers may lose their usual calmness and impartiality and be content with a lower degree of legal soundness than they would normally have required. The danger is that what seems reasonably sound to one side will not seem reasonably sound to the other side, particularly if the other side is equally inflamed. Consequently each side may genuinely believe that *it* is obeying the law and that the other side is the law-breaker.

(3) *States are few in number and are composed of territory.* The fact that states are few in number means that every state comes into frequent contact with every other state. The fact that states are composed of territory means that a state cannot choose its neighbours; it is forced to live with the states near it. Occasionally a state is able to live in virtual isolation from the rest of the world, as Japan did for over two centuries before 1854. But normally a state is driven by economic and other needs to seek benefits from other states. If it tries to take those benefits by force, it will unite other states against it in a defensive alliance. If it tries to obtain benefits by peaceful means, it will have to give something in return. And, in order to induce other states to 'do business' with it, it will have to acquire the reputation of being trustworthy and law-abiding. This applies particularly to its relations with its neighbours, with whom it is likely to have the most frequent dealings. In national societies, an individual who acquires a reputation for lawlessness in his home-town can move to another town where he is unknown and find anonymity in a large crowd. But states cannot move from one continent to another; even if they could, they would find that their reputation was known all over the world, simply because the international society of states is so much smaller than a national society of individuals.

It is frequently supposed that only small states need to worry about acquiring a reputation for being law-abiding. But such a reputation is an indispensable asset for the foreign policy of even the strongest states. For instance, under the North Atlantic Treaty, which is a cardinal feature of United States foreign policy, the USA undertakes to defend its European allies against Soviet attack. In order to make the alliance an effective deterrent in Soviet eyes, and in order to encourage the European allies to remain in the alliance, the USA has to convince both the Soviet Union and the European members of NATO that it is a state which keeps its promises.

Suggestions for Further Reading

M. A. Kaplan and N. de B. Katzenbach, *The Political Foundations of International Law*, 1961, especially chs 1, 2 and 13.

L. Henkin, 'International law and the behaviour of nations', *Recueil des cours de l'Académie de droit international de La Haye*, vol. 114, 1965, pp. 171–276.

L. Henkin, *How Nations Behave*, 2nd ed., 1979.

A. James, *The Bases of International Order*, 1973, pp. 60–84.

J. G. Merrills, *Anatomy of International Law*, 2nd ed., 1981.

Roger Fisher, *Points of Choice*, 1978.

John A. Perkins, *The Prudent Peace: Law as Foreign Policy*, 1981.

Chapter 2

Historical and Political Factors

Whenever independent political communities have come into peaceful contact with one another, they have felt the need for some sort of international law to govern their relations, even though the rules may have been very rudimentary, for example, that treaties should be obeyed and that envoys should not be harmed. Thus, there were systems of international law in force between the city-states of classical Greece and between the Hindu kingdoms of ancient India. Even during the Middle Ages in Western Europe international law existed. But medieval Europe was not very suitable for the development of international law, because it was not divided into states in the modern sense. Nowadays we think of states as having undisputed political control over their own territory, and as being independent of external political control. Medieval kings were not in this position; internally, they shared power with their barons, each of whom had a private army; externally, they acknowledged some sort of allegiance to the pope and to the Holy Roman emperor.

Modern international law began to develop at the same time as the modern system of states, in the sixteenth and seventeenth centuries. It originated in Western Europe, but at first Europeans were prepared to admit that non-European states had at least limited rights under the European system of international law. Non-European states were also often prepared to admit that European states had at least limited rights under their various non-European systems of international law, and so legal relations between European and non-European states became possible. By about 1880, however, Europeans had conquered most of the non-European states, which was interpreted in Europe as conclusive proof of the inherent superiority of the white man, and the international legal system became a white man's club, to which non-European states would be elected only if they produced evidence that they were 'civilised'.

It was not until after the First World War that international law rid itself of this racialist bias and became truly universal. Since 1945 so many colonies have become independent that the majority of states are now non-European. But the separate systems of international law which had once existed between non-European states had been destroyed during the period of European domination, and non-European peoples had been subjected to a long period of European cultural and technological influence. Consequently, instead of seeking the re-establishment of traditional non-European systems of international law, non-European states have accepted the system which had originally been developed by Europeans, and have merely tried to obtain revision of individual rules which are contrary to their interests (see below, pp. 19–22).

Naturalists and Positivists

During the formative period of international law, academic writers exercised a much greater influence than they do nowadays. Since they have, to some extent, left a mark on the modern law, it is necessary to say something about them, and in particular to describe the two main schools of thought – naturalists and positivists.

The leading naturalist writer was the Dutchman Hugo Grotius (1583–1645), who is often regarded as the founder of modern international law; other important naturalist writers were the Spaniards Vitoria (1480–1546) and Suárez (1548–1617), Gentili, an Italian protestant who fled to England (1552–1608), and the Englishman Zouche (1590–1660). Although disagreeing about many things, all these writers agreed that the basic principles of all law (national as well as international) were derived, not from any deliberate human choice or decision, but from principles of justice which had a universal and eternal validity and which could be discovered by pure reason; law was to be found, not made.

These basic principles of law were called natural law. Natural law was originally regarded as having a divine origin, but Grotius wrote that natural law would still have existed even if God had not existed; instead, Grotius considered that the existence of natural law was the automatic consequence of the fact that men lived together in society and were capable of understanding that certain rules were necessary for the preservation of society. According to this line of argument, the prohibition of murder, for instance, was a rule of natural law, independently of any legislation forbidding murder, because every intelligent man would realise that such a rule was just and necessary for the preservation of human society.

The theory of natural law has a long tradition, going back to Roman times, and is still the official philosophy of law accepted by the Roman Catholic Church. But nowadays it is not accepted by many people outside the Roman Catholic Church. Having religious overtones and being incapable of verification, the theory is suspect in a scientific and secular age. The essence of the theory was that law was derived from justice, and, although lawyers and judges often appeal to justice in order to fill gaps or to resolve uncertainties in the law, the theory of natural law must logically lead to a much more radical conclusion, namely, that an unjust rule is not law at all and can be disregarded by the judge; but this is a conclusion which no modern legal system would accept. Even the supporters of the theory have been unable to state principles of natural law with any precision; for instance, 'Thou shalt not kill' may be accepted as a universally valid rule, necessary for the maintenance of human society, but writers on natural law do not agree about the number of exceptions to the rule which ought to be recognised.

However, in the sixteenth and seventeenth centuries the theory was universally accepted, and it performed a very useful function by encouraging respect for justice at a time when the collapse of the feudal system and the division of Europe between Catholics and Protestants might otherwise have led to complete anarchy. It is hard to think of any other foundations on which a system of international law could have been built at that time. Even the vagueness of the natural law theory, which is such a defect in it nowadays, was less apparent in the time of Grotius, who illustrated his arguments with biblical quotations, references to Greek and Roman history and – above all – analogies drawn from Roman private law, which at that time was admired as a fairly accurate reflection of natural law and was therefore copied by many European countries.

After Grotius's death the intellectual climate became more sceptical, and international law would have lost respect if it had remained based on the theory of natural law. Men were beginning to argue by 1700 that law was largely positive, that is, man-made; consequently, law and justice were not the same thing, and laws might vary from time to time and from place to place, according to the whim of the legislator. Applied to international law, positivism (as this new theory was called) regarded the actual behaviour of states as the basis of international law. The first great positivist writer on international law was another Dutchman, Cornelis van Bynkershoek (1673–1743), who was to some extent ahead of his time; positivism had its roots in the eighteenth century but was not fully accepted until the nineteenth century. Unfortunately, apart from collecting the texts of treaties, little attempt was made to study the practice of states scientifically until the twentieth century.

An attempt to combine naturalism and positivism was made by

the Swiss writer Emerich de Vattel (1714–69). He emphasised the *inherent rights* which states derived from natural law, but said that they were accountable only to their own consciences for the observance of the *duties* imposed by natural law, unless they had expressly agreed to treat those duties as part of positive law. Vattel exercised a strong and pernicious influence on many writers and states during the eighteenth, nineteenth and early twentieth centuries; even today his influence is still sometimes felt. An intellectual climate which encourages states to assert their rights and to ignore their duties is a sure recipe for disorder.

The Theory of Sovereignty

One word which recurs frequently in the writings of Vattel's followers is 'sovereignty', and it is doubtful whether any single word has ever caused so much intellectual confusion and international lawlessness.

The theory of sovereignty began as an attempt to analyse the internal structure of a state. Political philosophers taught that there must be, within each state, some entity which possessed supreme legislative power and/or supreme political power.[1] It was easy to argue, as a corollary to this theory, that the sovereign, possessing supreme power, was not himself bound by the laws which he made.

Then, by a shift of meaning, the word came to be used to describe, not only the relationship of a superior to his inferiors *within* a state, but also the relationship of the ruler or of the state itself towards *other* states. But the word still carried its emotive overtones of unlimited power above the law, and this gave a totally misleading picture of international relations. The fact that a ruler can do what he likes to his own subjects does not mean that he can – either as a matter of law or as a matter of power politics – do what he likes to other states.

When international lawyers say that a state is sovereign, all that they really mean is that it is independent, that is, that it is not a dependency of some other *state*. They do not mean that it is in any

---

[1] The theory dates back to the sixteenth century, but its best known exponent, as far as lawyers are concerned, was John Austin (1790–1859), who defined law as the general commands of a sovereign, supported by the threat of sanctions. Since international law did not fit his theory, he said that international law was not law. In fact, it is hard to find any legal system which does fit his theory. In federal states like the USA, legislative power is divided by the constitution between the federation and the member-states, neither of which has supreme legislative power. Even in England, where the queen in Parliament has supreme legislative power, legislation is not the only source of law, nor the oldest source of law.

way above the *law*. It would be far better if the word 'sovereignty' were replaced by the word 'independence'. In so far as 'sovereignty' means anything in addition to 'independence', it is not a legal term with any fixed meaning, but a wholly emotive term. Everyone knows that states are powerful, but the emphasis on sovereignty exaggerates their power and encourages them to abuse it; above all, it preserves the superstition that there is something in international co-operation as such which comes near to violating the intrinsic nature of a 'sovereign' state.

At the end of the nineteenth century, many international lawyers, particularly in Germany, developed the doctrine of sovereignty to the point where it threatened to destroy international law altogether. Since 1914 there has been a reaction. International lawyers in the Western world have rejected the old dogmas about sovereignty and the inherent rights of states; indeed, scientific examinations of the practice of states, which were carried out for the first time in the twentieth century, have shown that those dogmas were never taken half as seriously by states as they were by theorists.

In 1923 the Permanent Court of International Justice said: 'The Court declines to see, in the conclusion of any treaty by which a state undertakes to perform or refrain from performing a particular act, an abandonment of its sovereignty . . . [T]he right of entering into international engagements is an attribute of state sovereignty' (*Wimbledon* case, PCIJ, series A, no. 1, p. 25). Of course, one can imagine treaties containing such far-reaching obligations as to deprive a state of its independence – for instance, a treaty whereby one state becomes a protectorate of another state (see below, p. 56). But there is no fixed dividing-line between independence and loss of independence; it is a matter of degree and opinion; even 'independence' shares some of the emotive qualities of the word 'sovereignty'. For instance, the idea of joining a supranational organisation like the European Economic Community (Common Market), which would have been regarded as an intolerable restriction upon independence a century ago, is nowadays discussed in more realistic terms of economic advantages and disadvantages.

In the Western world, sovereignty is no longer worshipped as it used to be. However, when we examine the attitudes of communist countries and of Afro-Asian countries, a rather different picture emerges.

The Communist Theory of International Law

A central article of Marxist faith is that economics is the determining force in society. Law and political institutions are merely the 'superstructure', reflecting the will of the ruling class (that is, of the class which controls the means of production, distribution and exchange). Since there are different ruling classes in different states, one might imagine that there could be no international law of universal validity. But communist theory is unanimously of the opinion that an international law of universal validity does exist; indeed, to read some Russian writers, one might be forgiven for thinking that the Soviet Union had invented international law. The efforts to reconcile this position with the general Marxist theory of law have been long and tortuous.

Immediately after the Russian revolution, it was suggested that there were two systems of international law – one applying among 'capitalist' states, and the other applying between 'capitalist' states and 'socialist' states. But this idea was soon discarded, and since the 1920s the orthodox communist view has been that there is only one system of international law; this system is said to reflect a compromise or coincidence of interests between different ruling classes in different states.

Originally the Soviet communists expected that the 'capitalist' countries would soon launch an all-out war against the Soviet Union in the hope of eradicating communism, which would emerge from this war triumphant throughout the world; pending the final conflict, international law existed as a temporary arrangement, limited in scope to trade treaties and the like. Later, as the final conflict became a remoter prospect, a wider scope was attributed to international law. Finally, in 1956 Khrushchev proclaimed that war between 'capitalist' and 'socialist' states was not inevitable, and that communism would triumph throughout the world by peaceful means and/or internal revolts, which would not necessarily lead to international war. The new doctrine was described as peaceful coexistence between states with different economic systems. Since then 'peaceful coexistence' has been incorporated into every Soviet definition of international law.

One striking characteristic of communist thinking about international law is the emphasis on sovereignty and the pre-eminence of the state. The idea of a world government, which is popular among progressive thinkers in the West, is anathema to the true communist; as long as states have different ruling classes, it is unthinkable that they will surrender their sovereignty; the only true world community will be a communist one, when states and law have both withered away; a 'world state' or 'world government' is a contradiction in terms.

More specifically, communist writers say that international law can be derived only from an agreement between states (see below, pp. 31 and 36, n. 2).

In principle, when a state has agreed to a rule of international law, it cannot revoke its consent unilaterally. But communist countries maintain that there is an exception to this principle; they claim that, when a class revolution takes place within a state, the new ruling class is not bound by rules accepted on behalf of the state by the old ruling class, if those rules existed solely for the benefit of the old ruling class. No list has ever been given of such rules, but they obviously include the rule requiring compensation for expropriation, together with the majority of loans raised by the old government. It is doubtful whether the list extends far beyond these obvious examples; indeed, with the passage of time, Russian writers have regarded the 1917 revolution as constituting less and less of a break in the continuity of Russia's rights and obligations.

Similarly, the orthodox communist view used to be that only states enjoyed rights under international law. This has now been modified so as to allow international organisations (which are established by agreement between states) to enjoy rights under international law; but communist lawyers refuse to follow Western lawyers in recognising that individuals can enjoy rights under international law (see below, pp. 71–2). Further evidence of communist determination to establish the pre-eminence of the state over the individual may be seen in the strictness with which communist writers uphold the view that individuals cannot sue a state in the courts of another state (see below, p. 110). Similarly, communist practice is opposed to allowing individuals (other than state officials, of course) to play any part in settling disputes between states. This is one of the reasons for communist opposition to judicial settlement of international disputes (see below, pp. 210 and 211), and for their desire to minimise the powers of the United Nations Secretariat (see below, pp. 179 and 190).

However, a careful reading of communist writers shows that sovereignty is not regarded as a dogma, as an end in itself; it is a means towards the end of protecting 'socialist' states against 'capitalist' states.[1] 'Socialist' states are very conscious of being in a minority; indeed, for many years the Soviet Union was the only 'socialist' state in the world. Marxist theory had always taught that the 'capitalist' countries would attack a 'socialist' country, in order

---

[1] An extreme example of this approach can be seen in the Soviet attempt to distort the concept of sovereignty so as to give the impression that the Soviet invasion of Czechoslovakia in 1968 was designed to defend the sovereignty of Czechoslovakia; see Hazard, 'Renewed emphasis upon a socialist international law', *American Journal of International Law*, vol. 65, 1971, p. 142 (but cf. the comment by Butler, ibid., p. 796), and Ginsburgs, 'Socialist internationalism and state sovereignty', *Year Book of World Affairs*, vol. 25, 1971, p. 39.

to prevent its example influencing their own working classes; and the Allied intervention in Russia in 1919–21, and the American policy concerning Formosa from 1950 onwards, were taken as confirming the Marxist prediction.

A reliance on state sovereignty is a natural defensive reaction of a minority of states facing a hostile majority. Erosion of sovereignty might lead to majority rule, and the 'socialist' countries would be outvoted. It is significant that the only United Nations organ where the Soviet Union really feels at ease is the Security Council, which is the only organ where it cannot be outvoted (thanks to the veto); that is why the Soviet Union interprets the Charter so as to give the maximum amount of power to the Security Council and the minimum amount to other organs. As peaceful coexistence becomes more of a reality, and as the Soviet Union realises that it has less to fear from the West, we may hope that the Soviet Union will feel less need of its defensive approach to international law.

One final point needs to be stressed. Communist writings about international law are often on an extremely theoretical level. The practice of communist states can reveal a different picture – not only brutal violations, like the invasion of Czechoslovakia in 1968, but also a readiness to forget theoretical differences and to accept compromises on practical problems. For instance, improbable though it may seem, the majority of communist countries have entered into compromise agreements with Western countries providing for the payment of compensation representing part of the value of Western-owned property nationalised by the communist countries (see below, p. 94).

Attitudes of Afro-Asian States

It is much less easy to generalise about Afro-Asian states than about communist states. They do not form a bloc in any real sense. They have no common ideology. Their governments vary from the far right to the far left of the political spectrum. However, there are certain facts which are true of the vast majority of Afro-Asian states, and these facts tend to make most of those states adopt a distinctive attitude towards international law.

(1) *Afro-Asian states value their independence*; this is natural, since most of them have gained their independence since 1945. They therefore tend to be suspicious of rules which limit their independence, and they are glad of opportunities to demonstrate their independence – for instance, by expelling European residents

for minor indiscretions (see, for example, the story of the woman lecturer from Yorkshire who was expelled from Malawi for wearing a miniskirt at a party, reported in *The Times*, 15 February 1969). 'Sovereignty' is a favourite word in their vocabulary. It may be that this truculent attitude will wear off as they learn to take independence for granted; but, unless something radical is done to improve their standard of living, there is a danger that demonstrations of *political* independence will become more frequent as a sort of psychological compensation for their sense of *economic* impotence.

However, Afro-Asian countries have not generally carried their fondness for sovereignty to extreme lengths. They have been eager to co-operate in the United Nations and other organisations, and they have set up regional organisations of their own, such as the Organisation of African Unity.

(2) *Afro-Asian countries were mostly under alien rule during the formative period of international law*, and therefore played no part in shaping that law. Occasionally their leaders argue that they are not bound by rules which they did not help to create. However, this argument is only used in relation to rules which go against the interests of Afro-Asian states, and the argument that those states played no part in shaping the rules is only a subsidiary argument designed to strengthen the main contention that the rules are outmoded. Afro-Asian states have never dreamt of rejecting *all* rules of international law which were laid down before they became independent; to do so would mean rejecting many rules which operate to the advantage of Afro-Asian states. All the same, Western lawyers would be well advised to be tactful in dealing with Afro-Asian countries, and to stress the benefits which those countries receive from rules of international law, instead of relying mechanically on old authorities. It is also desirable to ask Afro-Asian countries to help in codifying the law, so as to give them a sense of participation.

The fact that Afro-Asian countries are non-European and mainly non-Christian has had very little effect on their attitudes to international law. They have shown no desire to revive their local systems of international law which existed before the coming of Europeans, or to mould international law in accordance with analogies drawn from their pre-European systems of internal law. The reason is clear – their pre-European conceptions of law were usually highly conservative and designed to perpetuate inequalities of wealth. Nothing could be farther from the interests of states which are generally poor and dissatisfied.

It is unfortunate that some Western international lawyers are still prepared to risk alienating Afro-Asian countries by stressing the early history of international law and its European, Christian and naturalist origins. In addition to being politically unfortunate, such attitudes misrepresent the nature of modern international law. Whatever its historical origins, there is scarcely any rule of international law at the present day which can be described as peculiarly European or Christian. English law developed in a feudal, agricultural society, but has outgrown its origins; and so has international law.

(3) *Most Afro-Asian countries are poor* (with a few exceptions, such as some of the oil-exporting countries) and are anxious to develop their economies. Those which wish to develop their economies along socialist lines are therefore opposed to the traditional rule of international law which forbids expropriation of foreign-owned property without compensation; but other countries are prepared to accept the traditional rule as a means of encouraging foreign private investment (see below, pp. 91-6). The economic interests of Afro-Asian countries also affect their attitudes to other rules of international law; for instance, if their fishing fleets are dependent on *local* fisheries (because they cannot afford the large trawlers and refrigerating equipment which are needed for fishing in *distant* waters), they may try to gain exclusive rights to local fisheries by claiming a wide territorial sea, exclusive fishery zone or exclusive economic zone (see below, pp. 265-72).

Since 1973 Afro-Asian states have demanded the establishment of a new international economic order, which would entail a legal obligation for richer states to help the economic development of poorer states. On the whole, Western states have not accepted these demands; Western states have helped the economic development of poorer states in many ways, but are usually reluctant to recognise or undertake any legal obligation to help poorer states (see below, pp. 198-9).

(4) *Many Afro-Asian states have a feeling of resentment about past exploitation*, real or imagined. That is one reason why they usually claim that they have not succeeded to obligations accepted on their behalf by the former colonial powers before they became independent (see below, pp. 157-63). Almost all of them are strongly opposed to all remaining forms of colonialism and apartheid, although their reactions to violations of the principle of self-determination in other contexts are much weaker (see below, pp. 250-9).

(5) For the reasons stated above, *Afro-Asian states often feel that international law sacrifices their interests to the interests of Western states*. They therefore demand changes in the law. Unfortunately, if there is no consensus, it is often difficult to change international law without breaking it. States may refuse to alter a

treaty unless they are forced to do so. States which are dissatisfied with an existing rule of customary law may start following a new custom, but, until the new custom is widely established, they may be denounced as law-breakers by states adhering to the old custom. One solution of this problem has been the multilateral treaty; conferences called to draw up a treaty codifying the existing law can slip imperceptibly into amending the law (see below, p. 33). Another solution favoured by Afro-Asian states has been to try to use the United Nations General Assembly as if it were a legislature; but the General Assembly is not really a legislature, and it is doubtful whether its resolutions can be used as evidence of international law against states which voted against them (see below, pp. 27, 32 and 37–8).

Nevertheless, major changes in international law have occurred since 1945. Western states are anxious not to drive the Afro-Asian states into the arms of the communist states, and have therefore agreed to many of the changes sought by Afro-Asian states. Most of the rules which Afro-Asian states used to regard as contrary to their interests have been changed, or are in the process of being changed (for instance, see below, pp. 157–63, 250–9 and 265–72). The accusation that international law is biased against the interests of Afro-Asian states is, on the whole, no longer true.

Suggestions for Further Reading

Rosalyn Higgins, *Conflict of Interests: International Law in A Divided World*, 1965.

Arthur Nussbaum, *A Concise History of the Law of Nations*, rev. ed., 1947.

Bernard A. Ramundo, *Peaceful Co-existence*, 1967.

Ivo Lapenna, 'The legal aspects and political significance of the Soviet conception of co-existence', *International and Comparative Law Quarterly*, vol. 12, 1963, p. 737.

G. I. Tunkin, *Theory of International Law*, 1974.

F. I. Kozhevnikov (ed.), *International Law*, Foreign Languages Publishing House, Moscow, 1957(?).

Hungdah Chiu, 'Communist China's attitude towards international law', *American Journal of International Law*, vol. 60, 1966, p. 245.

R. P. Anand, 'Attitude of the Afro-Asian states toward certain problems of international law', *International and Comparative Law Quarterly*, vol. 15, 1966, p. 55.

T. O. Elias, *New Horizons in International Law*, 1980, especially ch. 2.

Chapter 3

Sources of International Law

Article 38(1) of the Statute of the International Court of Justice provides:

> The Court, whose function is to decide in accordance with international law such disputes as are submitted to it, shall apply:
> (*a*) international conventions, whether general or particular, establishing rules expressly recognized by the contesting states;
> (*b*) international custom, as evidence of a general practice accepted as law;
> (*c*) the general principles of law recognized by civilized nations;
> (*d*) . . . judicial decisions and the teachings of the most highly qualified publicists of the various nations, as subsidiary means for the determination of rules of law.

This provision is usually accepted as constituting a list of the sources of international law. Some writers have criticised it on the grounds that it does not list all the sources of international law, or that it includes things which are not genuine sources, but none of the alternative lists which have been suggested has won general approval. It is therefore proposed to examine the sources listed in the Court's Statute before considering other possible sources of international law.

Treaties

The Statute of the International Court of Justice speaks of 'international conventions, whether general or particular, establishing rules expressly recognized by the contesting states'. The word 'convention' means a treaty,[1] and that is the only meaning which the world possesses in international law, and in international relations

---

[1] Other words used as a synonym for treaties, or for particular types of treaty, are agreement, pact, protocol, charter, statute, act, covenant, declaration, engagement, arrangement, accord, regulations, provisions, and so on. Some of these words have alternative meanings (that is, they can also mean something other than treaties), which makes the problem of terminology even more confusing.

generally. This is a point worth emphasising, because students have been known to confuse conventions with conferences, or to confuse conventions in international law with conventions of the constitution in English law.

Treaties are the maids of all work in international law. Very often they resemble contracts in national systems of law, but they can also perform functions which in national systems would be carried out by Acts of Parliament, by conveyances, or by the memorandum of association of a company. In English law, Acts of Parliament are regarded as sources of law, but contracts are not; contracts are merely legal transactions. (Contracts create rights and duties only for the contracting parties, who are very few in number, and it is generally agreed that a 'source of law' means a source of rules which apply to a very large number of people.) Some writers have tried to argue that treaties should be regarded as sources of international law only if they resemble Acts of Parliament in content, that is, if they impose the same obligations on all the parties to the treaty and seek to regulate the parties' behaviour over a long period of time; such treaties are called law-making treaties. According to this theory, 'contract-treaties', that is, treaties which resemble contracts (for instance, a treaty whereby one state agrees to lend a certain sum of money to another state) are not sources of law, but merely legal transactions. However, the analogy between Acts of Parliament and law-making treaties is misleading for two reasons.

(1) In national systems of law anyone can make a contract, but Acts of Parliament are passed by a small group of people. In international law, any state can enter into a treaty, including a law-making treaty.
(2) In national systems of law contracts create rights and duties only for the contracting parties, who are very few in number, whereas Acts of Parliament apply to a very large number of people. In international law all treaties, including law-making treaties, apply only to states which agree to them. Normally the parties to a law-making treaty are more numerous than the parties to a 'contract-treaty', but there is no reason why this should always be so.

The only distinction between a law-making treaty and a 'contract-treaty' is one of content. As a result, many treaties constitute borderline cases, which are hard to classify. A single treaty may contain some provisions which are 'contractual', and others which are 'law-making'. The distinction between law-making treaties and 'contract-treaties' is not entirely useless – for instance, a 'contract-treaty' is more likely to be terminated by the outbreak of war between the parties than a law-making treaty – but it is too slight and imprecise to justify regarding law-making treaties as the only treaties which are a source of international law. The better view is to regard all treaties as a source of law.

Treaties are of growing importance in international law. The official published version of treaties entered into by the United Kingdom in 1892 (the UK Treaty Series) filled 190 pages; the treaties entered into by the United Kingdom in 1960 filled 2,500 pages in the same series. As collectivism has replaced *laissez-faire*, a large number of questions have become subject to governmental regulation – and to intergovernmental regulation when they transcend national boundaries. Modern technology, communications and trade have made states more interdependent than ever before, and more willing to accept rules on a vast range of problems of common concern – extradition of criminals, safety regulations for ships and aircraft, economic aid, copyright, standardisation of road signs, and so on. The rules in question are usually laid down in treaties, with the result that international law has expanded beyond all recognition in the last 130 years (although it must be pointed out that most of the rules are too specialised to be dealt with in ordinary textbooks on international law). Treaties are the major instrument of co-operation in international relations, and co-operation often involves a change in the relative positions of the states involved (for example, rich countries give money to poor countries). Treaties, therefore, are often an instrument of change – a point which is forgotten by those who regard international law as an essentially conservative force.

To some extent treaties have begun to replace customary law. Where there is agreement about rules of customary law, they are codified by treaty; where there is disagreement or uncertainty, states tend to settle disputes by *ad hoc* compromises – which also take the form of treaties.

Custom

The second source of international law listed in the Statute of the International Court of Justice is 'international custom, as evidence of a general practice accepted as law'.

Where to look for evidence of customary law
The main evidence of customary law is to be found in the actual practice of states, and a rough idea of a state's practice can be gathered from published material – from newspaper reports of actions taken by states, and from statements made by government

spokesmen to Parliament, to the press, at international conferences and at meetings of international organisations; and also
from a state's laws and judicial decisions, because the legislature
and the judiciary form part of a state just as much as the executive
does. At times the Foreign Ministry of a state may publish extracts
from its archives; for instance, when a state goes to war or gets
involved in a particularly bitter dispute, it may publish documents
to justify itself in the eyes of the world. But the vast majority of
the material which would throw light on a state's practice concerning, questions of international law – correspondence with other
states, and the advice which each state receives from its own legal
advisers – is normally not published; or, to be more precise, it is
only recently that efforts have been made to publish digests of the
practice followed by different states.

Evidence of customary law may sometimes also be found in the
writings of international lawyers, and in judgments of national and
international tribunals, which are mentioned as subsidiary means
for the determination of rules of law in Article 38(1)(d) of the
Statute of the International Court of Justice (see below, p. 36–7,
and cf. also *The Paquete Habana* (1900), 175 U.S. 677, 700–1).

Similarly, treaties can be evidence of customary law; but great
care must be taken when inferring rules of customary law from
treaties. For instance, treaties dealing with a particular subject-
matter may habitually contain a certain provision; thus, extradition treaties almost always provide that political offenders shall not
be extradited. It has sometimes been argued that a standard
provision of this type has become so habitual that it should be
regarded as a rule of customary law, to be inferred even when a
treaty is silent on that particular point. On the other hand, why
would states bother to insert such standard provisions in their
treaties if the rule existed already as a rule of customary law? The
problem is a difficult one, and one needs to know more about the
intentions of the parties to the treaties in question before one is
safe in invoking a standard treaty provision as evidence of
customary law.

However, there is another way in which a treaty can definitely
constitute evidence of customary law – if the treaty claims to be
declaratory of customary law, or is intended to codify customary
law, it can be quoted as evidence of customary law even against a
state which is not a party to the treaty.[1] Such a state is not bound

---

[1] This is so even if the treaty has not received enough ratifications to come into force (for
an example, see below, p. 238, and on ratification and entry into force of treaties generally,
see below, pp. 123–7). It may be asked why states should be unwilling to ratify a treaty if it
merely restates customary law. Explanations include inertia and lack of parliamentary time
(if ratification requires the participation of the legislature, as it does in many countries).
Moreover, only part of the treaty may codify customary law, and a state may refuse to
ratify because it objects to other parts.

by the treaty, but by customary law; therefore, if it can produce other evidence to show that the treaty misrepresents customary law, it can disregard the rule stated in the treaty. This possibility is not open to states which are parties to the treaty, since they are bound by the treaty, regardless of whether it accurately codifies customary law or not.

Finally, there is the possibility that customary law may change so as to conform with an earlier treaty. For instance, the Declaration of Paris 1856 altered certain rules about the conduct of war at sea; as a treaty, it only applied between the parties to it - Austria, France, Prussia, Russia, Sardinia, Turkey and the United Kingdom. Subsequently, however, the rules contained in the Declaration were accepted by a large number of other states as rules of customary law.

Similar problems arise with resolutions passed at meetings of international organisations, particularly resolutions of the United Nations General Assembly (cf. below, pp. 37-8). Most resolutions have nothing to do with international law; an obvious example would be a resolution recommending research into the causes of cancer. Even when resolutions do have something to do with international law, they may simply be recommending changes, and the text of such a resolution clearly cannot be interpreted as representing the existing law; a resolution declaring that X *ought* to be the law is obviously not evidence that X *is* the law. If a resolution declares that X *is* the law, it can be used as evidence of customary law. But the value of such a resolution varies in proportion to the number of states voting for it; if many states vote against it, its value as evidence of customary law is correspondingly reduced.

A resolution passed at a meeting of an international organisation is never *conclusive* evidence of customary law. It has to be examined in conjunction with all the other available evidence of customary law, and it may thus be possible to prove that the resolution is not a correct statement of customary law.

For further discussion of resolutions of international organisations as evidence of customary law, see Akehurst, 'Custom as a source of international law', *British Year Book of International Law*, vol. 47, 1974-5, pp. 1, 5-7.

The problem of repetition

It has sometimes been suggested that a single precedent is not enough to establish a customary rule, and that there must be a degree of repetition over a period of time; thus, in the *Asylum* case the International Court of Justice suggested that a customary rule must be based on 'a constant and uniform usage' (*ICJ Reports*, 1950, pp. 266, 276-7). However, this statement must be seen in the light of the facts of the *Asylum* case, where the Court said: 'The facts . . . disclose so much uncertainty and contradiction, so much fluctuation and discrepancy in the exercise of diplomatic asylum and in the official views expressed on various occasions . . . that it has not been possible to discern . . . any constant and uniform usage, accepted as law' (ibid.). In other words, what prevented the formation of a customary rule in the *Asylum* case was not the absence of repetition, but the presence of major inconsistencies in the practice.

Major inconsistencies in the practice (that is, a *large* amount of practice which goes against the 'rule' in question) prevent the creation of a customary rule. *Minor* inconsistencies (that is, a *small* amount of practice which goes against the rule in question) do not prevent the creation of a customary rule (*Fisheries* case, *ICJ Reports*, 1951, pp. 116, 138), although in such cases the rule in question probably needs to be supported by a *large* amount of practice, in order to outweigh the conflicting practice (Akehurst, 'Custom as a source of international law', *British Year Book of International Law*, vol. 47, 1974–5, pp. 1, 12–21). On the other hand, where there is *no* practice which goes *against* an alleged rule of customary law, it seems that a *small* amount of practice is sufficient to create a customary rule, even though the practice involves only a small number of states and has lasted for only a short time (Akehurst, loc. cit.).

What states say and what states do

It is sometimes suggested that state practice consists only of what states do, not of what they say. For instance, in his dissenting opinion in the *Fisheries* case, Judge Read argued that claims made to areas of the sea by a state could not create a customary rule unless such claims were enforced against foreign ships.[1] But in the later *Fisheries Jurisdiction* case ten of the fourteen judges inferred the existence of customary rules from such claims, without considering whether they had been enforced.[2] Similarly, the Nuremberg Tribunal cited resolutions passed by the League of Nations Assembly and a Pan-American Conference as authority for its finding that aggressive war was criminal according to the 'customs and practices of states'.[3] The better view therefore appears to be that state practice consists not only of what states do, but also of what they say.

State practice also includes omissions; many rules of inter-

---

[1] *ICJ Reports*, 1951, pp. 116, 191.
[2] *ICJ Reports*, 1974, pp. 3, 47, 56–8, 81–8, 119–20, 135, 161. The remaining four judges did not deal with this issue.
[3] *American Journal of International Law*, vol. 41, 1947, pp. 172, 219–20.

national law forbid states to do certain acts, and, when proving such a rule, it is necessary to look not only at what states do, but also at what they do not do.

The psychological element in the formation of customary law

When inferring rules of customary law from the conduct of states, it is necessary to examine not only *what* states do, but also *why* they do it. In other words, there is a psychological element in the formation of customary law. For instance, suppose it could be proved that states habitually wrote to one another on white paper. The most that could be inferred from this fact alone would be that international law did not forbid states to write to one another on white paper; one could not infer that writing on white paper was legally obligatory unless there was some evidence that states felt a sense of legal obligation to use white paper.

The technical name given to this psychological element is *opinio iuris sive necessitatis* (*opinio iuris* for short). It is usually defined as a conviction felt by states that a certain form of conduct is required by international law. This definition presupposes that all rules of international law are framed in terms of duties. But that is not so; in addition to rules laying down duties, there are also permissive rules, which permit states to act in a particular way (for example, to prosecute foreigners for crimes committed within the prosecuting state's territory) without making such actions obligatory. In the case of a rule imposing a duty, the traditional definition of *opinio iuris* is correct; in the case of a permissive rule, *opinio iuris* means a conviction felt by states that a certain form of conduct is *permitted* by international law.

There is clearly something artificial about trying to analyse the psychology of collective entities such as states. Indeed, the modern tendency is not to look for direct evidence of a state's psychological convictions, but to infer *opinio iuris* indirectly from the actual behaviour of states. For these purposes, it must be remembered that rules of international law govern the behaviour of states in their relations with other states; it is therefore necessary to examine not only what one state does or refrains from doing, but also how other states react. If conduct by some states provokes *protests* from other states that such conduct is *illegal*, the protests can deprive such conduct of any value as evidence of customary law.

Permissive rules can be proved by showing that some states have acted in a particular way (or have claimed that they are entitled to act in that way) and that other states, whose interests were affected by such acts (or claims), have not protested that such acts (or claims) are illegal.

In the case of rules imposing duties, it is not enough to show that states have acted in the manner required by the alleged rule, and that other states have not protested that such acts are illegal. It also needs to be proved that states regard the action as *obligatory*. Recognition of the obligatory character of particular conduct can be proved by pointing to an express acknowledgement of the obligation by the states concerned, or by showing that failure to act in the manner required by the alleged rule has been condemned as illegal by other states whose interests were affected.

The difference between permissive rules and rules imposing duties can be clearly seen in the *Lotus* case. The facts of the case were as follows: a French merchant ship collided with a Turkish merchant ship on the high seas, as a result (allegedly) of negligence on the part of Lieutenant Demons, an officer on the French ship, and several people on the Turkish ship were drowned. France had jurisdiction to try Lieutenant Demons for manslaughter, but the question was whether Turkey also had jurisdiction to try him. Turkey argued that there was a permissive rule empowering her to try him; France argued the exact opposite, namely, that there was a rule imposing a duty on Turkey not to try him. The Permanent Court of International Justice accepted the Turkish argument and rejected the French argument because (*a*) although there were only a few cases in which states in Turkey's position had instituted prosecutions, the other states concerned in those cases had not protested against the prosecutions; and (*b*) although most states in Turkey's position had refrained from instituting prosecutions, there was no evidence that they had done so out of a sense of legal obligation (1927, PCIJ, series A, no. 10, pp. 28 ff.).

Opinio iuris is sometimes interpreted to mean that states must believe that something is already law before it can become law. However, that is probably not true; what matters is not what states believe, but what they say. If some states claim that something is law and other states do not challenge that claim, a new rule will come into being, even though all the states concerned may realise that it is a departure from pre-existing rules (for an example, see below, pp. 278–9).

Customary law has a built-in mechanism of change. If states are agreed that a rule should be changed, a new rule of customary international law based on the new practice of states can emerge very quickly; thus the law on outer space developed very quickly after the first artificial satellite was sent up (see below, p. 287, and cf. *ICJ Reports*, 1969, pp. 3, 42–3, 230). If the number of states supporting a change, or the number of states resisting a change, is small, they will probably soon fall into line with the practice of the majority. The real difficulty comes when the states supporting the change and the states resisting the change are fairly evenly balanced. In this case change is hard and slow, and disagreement and uncertainty about the law may persist for a long time until a new consensus emerges (the controversy about the width of the territorial sea is a good example; see below, pp. 265–8).

Universality and the consensual theory of international law

It has already been suggested that the practice followed by a small number of states is sufficient to create a customary rule if there is no practice which conflicts with that rule (see above, p. 28). But what if some states oppose the alleged rule? Can the opposition of a single state prevent the creation of a customary rule? If so, there would be very few rules, because state practice differs from state to state on many topics. On the other hand, to allow the majority to create a rule against the wishes of the minority would lead to insuperable difficulties. How large must the majority be? In counting the majority, must equal weight be given to the practice of Guatemala and the practice of the USA? If, on the other hand, some states are to be regarded as more important than others, on what criteria is importance to be based? – population? area? wealth? military power?

In the *Lotus* case, the Permanent Court of International Justice said: 'The rules of law binding upon states . . . emanate from their own free will as expressed in conventions or by usages generally accepted as expressing principles of law' (1927, PCIJ, series A, no. 10, p. 18). This consensual theory, as it is called, has been criticised in the West, but it has been accepted with enthusiasm by Soviet lawyers. Soviet doctrine teaches that international law is the result of an agreement between states, and that the only difference between treaties and custom is one of form, treaties representing an express agreement and custom representing an implied agreement. The merit of this approach is that it explains divergences in state practice; just as different treaties can be in force between different groups of states, so different rules of customary law can apply between different groups of states. The International Court of Justice came some way towards the Soviet approach in the *Asylum* case, where it recognised the existence of regional customs applying among groups of states in Latin America (*ICJ Reports*, 1950, pp. 266, 277, 293–4, 316).

The consensual theory explains divergences in state practice, but it is rather unconvincing when it is applied to new states. The orthodox rule is that new states are automatically bound by generally accepted international law. Tunkin, the leading Soviet international lawyer, tries to reconcile this rule with the consensual theory by saying:

As regards new states, they are legally entitled not to recognize particular customary rules of general international law. However, entry into official relations with other countries without reservations means that the new state accepts a certain body of principles and rules of existing international law which form the basis of relations between states.[1]

This analysis reduces the element of consent to a fiction; the new state is bound, not because it has consented, but because it has failed to object to the rules.

The element of consent can also become fictitious when one is dealing with the emergence of new rules of customary law among existing states. The International Court of Justice has emphasised that a claimant state which seeks to rely on a customary rule must prove that the rule has become binding on the defendant state.[2] The obvious way of doing this is to show that the defendant state has recognised the rule in its own state practice (although recognition for this purpose may amount to no more than failure to protest when other states have applied the rule in cases affecting the defendant's interests). But it may not be possible to find any evidence of the defendant's attitude towards the rule, and so there is a second – and more frequently used – way of proving that the rule is binding on the defendant: by showing that the rule is accepted by other states. (Tunkin himself writes that 'the recognition of a particular rule as a rule of international law by a large number of states raises a presumption that the rule is generally recognized'.[3]) In these circumstances the rule in question is binding on the defendant state unless the defendant state can show that it has expressly and consistently rejected the rule since the earliest days of the rule's existence; dissent expressed after the rule has become well established is too late to prevent the rule binding the dissenting state. Thus, in the *Fisheries* case, the International Court of Justice held that a particular rule was not generally recognised, but added: '*In any event*, the . . . rule would appear to be inapplicable as against Norway, in as much as she has *always* opposed any attempt to apply it to the Norwegian coast' (*ICJ Reports*, 1951, pp. 116, 131 (italics added)).

---

[1] G. I. Tunkin, *Droit international public: problèmes théoriques*, 1965, p. 87 (translation). Tunkin does not follow his theory to its logical conclusion. If relations between a new state and old states are wholly consensual, and if the new state can withhold consent from certain rules in its relations with the old states, surely the old states must have an equal right to withhold consent from other rules in their relations with the new state.

[2] *Asylum* case, *ICJ Reports*, 1950, pp. 266, 276-7; *Rights of Nationals of the USA in Morocco, ICJ Reports*, 1952, pp. 176, 200.

[3] op. cit., p. 87 (translation). See also the *North Sea Continental Shelf* cases, *ICJ Reports*, 1969, pp. 3, 28, 130. Maybe Tunkin is too severe in requiring that the rule be recognised by a *large* number of states; cf. above, p. 28.

Codification of customary law

In recent years there has been a tendency to codify customary law. Four conventions on the law of the sea were signed at Geneva in 1958; a convention on diplomatic relations and immunities was signed at Vienna in 1961; a convention on consular relations and immunities was signed at Vienna in 1963; a convention on the law of treaties was signed at Vienna in 1969; and a convention on succession of states in respect of treaties was signed at Vienna in 1978.

There are obvious advantages to be gained from codifying customary law in a treaty – the rules become more precise and more accessible; and new states are more willing to accept rules which they themselves have helped to draft. But, in view of the divergences between the practice of different states, codification often means that a compromise is necessary, and there is a limit to the number of compromises that states are willing to accept at any one time. Consequently, codification will succeed only if it proceeds slowly; acceleration produces the risk of failure, as happened at the codification conference organised by the League of Nations in 1930, and the failure of a codification scheme may cast doubt on customary rules which were previously well established. (This is what happened to the three-mile rule concerning the width of the territorial sea after the failure of the 1930 conference.)

The preparatory work for the Geneva and Vienna conventions was carried out by the International Law Commission, a body of thirty-four (originally fifteen) international lawyers elected by the United Nations General Assembly. It is entrusted not only with the codification of international law, but also with its progressive development (that is, the drafting of rules on topics where customary law is non-existent or insufficiently developed); in practice the distinction between codification and progressive development is often blurred. Sometimes the Commission seeks to codify the law, not by preparing a draft convention, but simply by summarising the law in a report to the General Assembly. Such reports are not binding in the same way as treaties, but they do constitute valuable evidence of customary law; the Commission's members are distinguished scholars, and they base their work on extensive research and on an attempt to ascertain and reconcile the views of the member-states of the United Nations (for example, by circulating questionnaires and by inviting states to comment on their draft reports – the same procedure is followed during the preliminary work on draft conventions).

Unofficial bodies have also tried their hand at codification. For instance, the Harvard Law School has produced a number of draft conventions; these are not intended to be ratified by states, but are simply used as a convenient means of restating the law. They derive their value from the eminence of the professors who have helped to draw them up.

General Principles of Law

The third source of international law listed in the Statute of the International Court of Justice is 'the general principles of law recognized by civilized nations'. This phrase was inserted in the Statute of the Permanent Court of International Justice, the forerunner of the International Court of Justice, in order to provide a solution in cases where treaties and custom provided no guidance; otherwise, it was feared, the Court might be unable to decide some cases because of gaps in treaty law and customary law. However, there is little agreement about the meaning of the phrase. Some say it means general principles of international law; others say it means general principles of national law. Actually, there is no reason why it should not mean both; the greater the number of meanings which the phrase possesses, the greater the chance of finding something to fill gaps in treaty law and customary law – which was the reason for listing general principles of law in the Statute of the Court. Indeed, international tribunals had applied general principles of law in both these senses for many years before the PCIJ was set up in 1920.

General principles of international law
According to this definition, general principles of law are not so much a source of law as a method of using existing sources – extending existing rules by analogy, inferring the existence of broad principles from more specific rules by means of inductive reasoning, and so on. English judges develop English law in this way without needing any statutory authorisation, and English lawyers therefore have difficulty in understanding why an international court should need statutory authorisation before it can do the same thing. However, in continental countries with a detailed written code, it is popularly supposed that the function of judges is to apply the law, and not to develop it; consequently, continental statesmen might have accused the PCIJ of exceeding its jurisdiction if it had sought to develop the law without being expressly authorised to do so.

General principles of national law
According to this second definition of general principles of law,

gaps in international law may be filled by borrowing principles which are common to all or most national systems of law; specific rules of law usually vary from country to country, but the basic principles are often similar.

The difficulty of proving that a principle is common to most or all legal systems is not as great as might be imagined. Legal systems are grouped in families; the law in most English-speaking countries is very similar, just as the law in most Latin American countries is very similar. Once one has proved that a principle exists in English law, one is fairly safe in assuming that it also exists in New Zealand and Australia. In fact, what sometimes happens in practice is that an international judge or arbitrator makes use of principles drawn from the legal system in his own country, without examining whether they are also accepted by other countries. The practice is obviously undesirable, but it is too common to be regarded as illegal.

General principles of law have proved most useful in 'new' areas of international law. When the modern system of international law was beginning to develop in the sixteenth and seventeenth centuries, writers like Grotius drew heavily on Roman law, and a Roman ancestry can still be detected in many of the rules which have now been transformed into customary law (for example, concerning the acquisition of title to territory). In the nineteenth century international arbitration, which had previously been rare, became common, and the need for rules of judicial procedure was met by borrowing principles from national law (for example, the principle that a tribunal is competent to decide whether or not it has jurisdiction in cases of doubt, and the principle that claims brought before a tribunal after an unreasonable delay must be dismissed as inadmissible). In the present century international law, or something closely resembling international law (see below, pp. 73–4), has come to regulate certain contracts made by individuals or companies with states or international organisations, for example, contracts of employment in international organisations, and oil concessions. Treaties and customary law contain few rules applicable to such topics, and the gap has been filled by recourse to general principles of commercial and administrative law, borrowed from national legal systems. For instance, international administrative tribunals, which try disputes between international organisations and their staff, have consistently applied the principle, borrowed from national law, that an official must be informed of criticisms made against him and must be given an opportunity to reply to those criticisms before the international organisation employing him takes a decision to his detriment on the basis of those criticisms.

However, it must be remembered that the environment in which international law operates is very different from the environment in which national law operates, and principles of national law can be used to fill gaps in international law only if they are suited to the international environment (cf. the unhappy attempts to equate law-making treaties with Acts of Parliament, above, p. 24).

Judicial Decisions

Article 38(1)(*d*) of the Statute of the International Court of Justice directs the Court to apply 'judicial decisions . . . as subsidiary means for the determination of rules of law'. This direction is made 'subject to the provisions of Article 59', which state that 'the decision of the Court has no binding force except between the parties and in respect of that particular case'. In other words, international courts are not obliged to follow previous decisions, although they almost always take previous decisions into account.

We have already seen that judicial and arbitral decisions can be evidence of customary law.[1] But it is probably true to say that judges can also create new law. The International Court of Justice is particularly important in this respect. Many of its decisions introduced innovations into international law which have subsequently won general acceptance – for instance, the *Reparation for Injuries* case, the *Genocide* case and the *Fisheries* case.[2] There is a very strong probability that the International Court (and other tribunals) will follow such decisions in later cases, since judicial consistency is the most obvious means of avoiding accusations of bias.

Judgments of national courts are also covered by Article 38(1)(*d*); many of the rules of international law on topics such as diplomatic immunity have been developed by judgments of national courts. But judgments of national courts need to be used with caution; the judges may look as if they are applying international law (and may actually believe that they are doing so), when in fact all that they are applying is some peculiar rule of their own national law (for examples, see below, pp. 48–52 and 66–8).

[1] See above, p. 26. Judicial and arbitral decisions may conveniently be considered together, because there is little difference between judicial settlement and arbitration in international law (see below, p. 204–5).

[2] See below, pp. 70–1, 128 and 268–9. The necessity for subsequent acceptance by states is stressed by Soviet lawyers, who regard treaties and custom as the only true sources of international law. According to them, other so-called sources represent only a halfway stage in the development of rules of international law; the development is not complete until the 'rules' suggested by judges, writers, and so on, have been adopted in treaties or in state practice.

Learned Writers

Article 38(1)(*d*) also directs the Court to apply 'the teachings of the most highly qualified publicists of the various nations, as subsidiary means for the determination of rules of law'. The word 'publicists' means 'learned writers'. Like judicial decisions, learned writings can be evidence of customary law, but they can also play a subsidiary role in developing new rules of law.

In the past, writers like Grotius exercised influence of a sort which no writer could hope to exercise nowadays. But writers have not entirely lost their influence. They still continue to provide the sort of conceptual framework which is necessary for any legal discussion; for instance, states had been claiming limited rights in areas adjacent to their territorial sea long before Gidel started writing about such claims, but it was Gidel who produced the concept of the contiguous zone as a framework for discussing the validity of these claims (see below, p. 270). Moreover, one finds that states in diplomatic controversies still quote profusely from writers (although the quotations are not always acknowledged), because writers provide a comprehensive, succinct and (with luck) impartial summary of state practice. (A summary which is deliberately made as brief as possible, like the Harvard draft conventions, is particularly useful for purposes of quotation.) In a nutshell, writers quote states and states quote writers.

Other Possible Sources of International Law

Having completed our examination of the list of sources in the Statute of the International Court of Justice, we must now examine whether there are any other sources which are omitted from that list.

Acts of international organisations

The growth of international organisations since the First World War has been accompanied by suggestions that the acts of international organisations should be recognised as a source of international law. But most of the organs of international organisations are composed of representatives of member-states, and very often the acts of such organs are merely the acts of the states represented in those organs. For instance, a resolution of the United Nations General Assembly can be evidence of customary law because it reflects the views of the states voting for it; it would probably have exactly the same value if it had been passed at a conference outside the framework of the United Nations, and, if many states vote against it, its value as evidence of customary law is correspondingly reduced.

However, international organisations usually have at least one organ which is not composed of representatives of member-states, and the practice of such organs is capable of constituting a source of law. For instance, the United Nations Secretariat often acts as a depositary of treaties (see below, p. 123, n. 1) and its practice as depositary has already affected the law of treaties on such topics as reservations (see below, p. 127-8). Similarly, it is possible that in the future the practice of United Nations forces will influence the evolution of the laws of war. But, in both the examples cited, the United Nations is performing functions which are normally performed by states – acting as a depositary and waging war – so it is only natural that the practice of the United Nations should play the same part as the practice of states in creating customary law.

Sometimes an international organisation is authorised to take decisions (often by majority vote) which are binding on member-states. Apart from 'internal' questions relating to the budget, the admission and expulsion of members, and so on, the only clear example in the United Nations Charter is in Chapter VII, which empowers the Security Council to give orders to states as part of its action to deal with threats to the peace, breaches of the peace and acts of aggression. In some other organisations powers to take binding decisions can be exercised more frequently; this is particularly true of the European Economic Community (Common Market). But it is questionable whether such decisions should be treated as a separate source of law, because the power to take such decisions is conferred by the constituent *treaty* of the organisation concerned.

Equity and natural law

Equity, in the present context, is used not in the technical sense which the word possesses in English law, but as a synonym for justice. Moreover, those who look to equity as a source of international law often appeal to natural law (see above, p. 13) in order to strengthen their arguments and to escape accusations of subjectivism. Thus the three terms – equity, justice and natural law – tend to merge into one another.

During the sixteenth and seventeenth centuries natural law was a major source of international law. In the nineteenth and twentieth centuries arbitrators have often been authorised to apply justice and equity as well as international law (such authorisations were commoner before 1920 than they are today); even in the absence of such authorisation, judges and arbitrators sometimes invoke equitable considerations.[1]

Whatever the position may have been in the past, it is doubtful whether equity forms a source of international law today. It cannot be assumed that a judge is using equity as a source of law every time he describes a rule as equitable or just. Counsel and judges in national courts frequently appeal to considerations of equity and justice when the authorities are divided on a point of law, but that does not lead to equity being regarded as a source of national law; nor should appeals by international lawyers to considerations of equity be interpreted to mean that equity is a source of international law.

One of the problems about equity is that it can often be defined only by reference to a particular ethical system. Consequently, although references to equity are meaningful in a national society which can be presumed to hold common ethical values, the position is entirely different in the international arena, where the most mutually antagonistic philosophies meet in head-on conflict.

See Akehurst, 'Equity and general principles of law', *International and Comparative Law Quarterly*, vol. 25, 1976, p. 801.

The Hierarchy of the Sources

What happens if a rule derived from one source of international law conflicts with a rule derived from another source? Which prevails over the other?

The relationship between treaties and custom is particularly difficult. Clearly a treaty, when it first comes into force, over-rides customary law as between the parties to the treaty; one of the main reasons why states make treaties is because they regard the relevant rules of customary law as inadequate. But treaties can come to an end through desuetude – a term used to describe the situation in which the treaty is consistently ignored by one or more parties, with the acquiescence of the other party or parties. Desuetude often takes the form of the emergence of a new rule of customary law, conflicting with the treaty. Thus treaties and custom are of

---

[1] A judge or arbitrator can always use equity to *interpret* or *fill gaps* in the law, even when he has not been expressly authorised to do so. But he may not give a decision *ex aequo et bono* (a decision in which equity *over-rides* all other rules) unless he has been expressly authorised to do so. Article 38(2) of the Statute of the International Court of Justice provides that the list of sources in Article 38(1) 'shall not prejudice the power of the Court to decide a case *ex aequo et bono*, if the parties agree thereto'. Article 38(2) has never been applied, but other tribunals have occasionally been authorised to decide *ex aequo et bono*; for instance, two Latin American boundary disputes were decided in this way by arbitrators in the 1930s (*UN Reports of International Arbitral Awards* II 1307 and III 1817).

equal authority; the later in time prevails.

Since the main function of general principles of law is to fill gaps in treaty law and customary law, it would appear that general principles of law are subordinate to treaties and custom (that is, treaties and custom prevail over general principles of law in the event of conflict).

Judicial decisions and learned writings are described in Article 38(1)(d) as 'subsidiary means for the determination of rules of law', which suggests that they are subordinate to the other three sources listed – treaties, custom and general principles of law. Judicial decisions usually carry more weight than learned writings, but there is no hard-and-fast rule; much depends on the quality of the reasoning which the judge or writer employs.

It is doubtful whether equity is a source of international law at all; even if it is, the existence of such doubts would appear to indicate that it is, at most, a very low-ranking source. (However, when a tribunal is authorised to decide *ex aequo et bono*, the tribunal is allowed to substitute its own ideas of equity for any and every rule of international law.)

As for the acts of international organisations, a distinction must be made between the practice of international organisations (which has the same force as state practice, and is therefore evidence of customary law) and binding decisions of international organisations (which are taken under powers conferred by treaty and which therefore have almost the same authority as a treaty).

'Ius Cogens'

Some of the early writers on international law said that a treaty would be void if it was contrary to morality or to certain (unspecified) basic principles of international law. The logical basis for this rule was that a treaty could not over-ride natural law. With the decline of the theory of natural law, the rule was largely forgotten, although some writers continued to pay lip-service to it.

Recently there has been a tendency to revive the rule, although it is no longer based on natural law; the state most in favour of the rule is the Soviet Union, which would never support the semi-religious theory of natural law! Moreover, the rule is now said to limit the liberty of states to create local custom, as well as their liberty to make treaties; the rule thus acts as a check on the tendency of international law to disintegrate into different regional systems – a tendency which would otherwise be the inevitable consequence of the Soviet definition of custom as an implied agreement.

The technical name now given to the basic principles of international law, which states are not allowed to contract out of, is 'peremptory norms of general international law', otherwise known as *ius cogens*.

Article 53 of the Convention on the Law of Treaties, signed at Vienna in 1969, provides as follows:

A treaty is void if, at the time of its conclusion, it conflicts with a peremptory norm of general international law. For the purposes of the present Convention, a peremptory norm of general international law is a norm accepted and recognized by the international community of states as a whole as a norm from which no derogation is permitted and which can be modified only by a subsequent norm of general international law having the same character.

(What is said about treaties being void would also probably apply equally to local custom. The reason why local custom is not mentioned is because the purpose of the Convention was to codify the law of *treaties* only.)

Although cautiously expressed to apply only 'for the purposes of the present Convention', the definition of a 'peremptory norm' is probably valid for all purposes. Moreover, the definition is more skilful than appears at first sight. A rule cannot become a peremptory norm unless it is 'accepted and recognized [as such] by the international community of states *as a whole*' – a requirement which is too logical and reasonable to be challenged, but which is well worth stating expressly, because there have already been cases of states trying to evade rules of international law which they found inconvenient by arguing that those rules were contrary to some exotic examples of *ius cogens*; this danger should, with luck, be averted by requiring such states to prove that the alleged rule of *ius cogens* has been 'accepted and recognized [as such] by the international community of states *as a whole*'.

At present very few rules pass this test. Many rules have been suggested as candidates, but the only one which at present receives anything approaching general acceptance is the rule against aggression.

Although the question is controversial, the better view appears to be that a rule of *ius cogens* can be derived from custom and possibly from treaties, but probably not from other sources (Akehurst, 'The hierarchy of the sources of international law', *British Year Book of International Law*, vol. 47, 1974–5, pp. 273, 281–5).

Suggestions for Further Reading

Clive Parry, *The Sources and Evidences of International Law*, 1965.

Michael Akehurst, 'Custom as a source of international law', *British Year Book of International Law*, vol. 47, 1974–5, p. 1.

Gutteridge, Cheng and Adamkiewicz, 'The meaning and scope of Article 38(1)(c) of the Statute of the International Court of Justice', *Transactions of the Grotius Society*, vol. 38, 1952, p. 125.

Michael Akehurst, 'Equity and general principles of law', *International and Comparative Law Quarterly*, vol. 25, 1976, p. 801.

Jorge Castañeda, *Legal Effects of United Nations Resolutions*, 1969.

Michael Akehurst, 'The hierarchy of the sources of international law', *British Year Book of International Law*, vol. 47, 1974–5, p. 273.

Chapter 4

International Law and Municipal Law

'Municipal law' is the technical name given by international lawyers to the national or internal law of a state. The question of the relationship between international law and municipal law can give rise to many practical problems, especially if there is a conflict between international law and municipal law.

The Attitude of International Law to Municipal Law

International law does not entirely ignore municipal law. For instance, as we have seen, municipal law may be used as evidence of international custom or of general principles of law, which are both sources of international law (see above, pp. 26 and 34-6). Moreover, international law leaves certain questions to be decided by municipal law; thus, in order to determine whether an individual is a national of state X, international law normally looks at the law of state X, provided that the law of state X is not wholly unreasonable.

However, the general rule of international law is that a state cannot plead a rule or a gap in its own municipal law as a defence to a claim based on international law. Thus, in the *Free Zones* case, the Permanent Court of International Justice said: 'It is certain that France cannot rely on her own legislation to limit the scope of her international obligations' (1932, PCIJ, series A/B, case no. 46, p. 167). This is particularly true when, as often happens, a treaty or other rule of international law imposes an obligation on states to enact a particular rule as part of their own municipal law.

The Attitude of English Law to International Law

The attitude of municipal law to international law is much less easy to summarise than the attitude of international law to municipal law. For one thing, the laws of different countries vary greatly in this respect. Consequently, for purposes of simplicity, discussion here will be mainly confined to the attitude of English law towards international law.

Treaties

In the United Kingdom the power to make or ratify treaties belongs to the queen, acting on the advice of her ministers; Parliament plays no part in the making or ratifying of treaties. Consequently, a treaty does not automatically become part of English law;[1] otherwise the queen could alter English law without the consent of Parliament, which would be contrary to the basic principle of English constitutional law that Parliament has a monopoly of legislative power. If a treaty requires changes in English law, it is necessary to pass an Act of Parliament in order to bring English law into conformity with the treaty. If the Act is not passed, the treaty is still binding on the United Kingdom from the international point of view, and the United Kingdom will be guilty of breaking the treaty.

An Act of Parliament giving effect to a treaty in English law can be repealed by a subsequent Act of Parliament; in these circumstances there is a conflict between international law and English law, since international law regards the United Kingdom as still bound by the treaty, but English courts cannot give effect to the treaty.[2] However, English courts usually try to interpret Acts of Parliament so that they do not conflict with earlier treaties made by the United Kingdom.[3]

As far as the United Kingdom is concerned, there is a very clear difference between the effects of a treaty in international law and the effects of a treaty in municipal law; a treaty becomes effective in international law when it is ratified by the queen, but it usually

---

[1] With the exception of treaties regulating the conduct of warfare: see McNair, *The Law of Treaties*, 1961, pp. 89–91, and *Porter* v. *Freudenberg*, [1915] 1 K.B. 857, 874–80. This exception is probably connected with the rule of English constitutional law which gives the queen, acting on the advice of her ministers, the power to declare war without the consent of Parliament.

[2] *Inland Revenue Commissioners* v. *Collco Dealings Ltd,* [1962] A.C. 1. Would English courts apply subsequent Acts of Parliament which conflicted with the European Communities Act 1972? See Trindade, 'Parliamentary sovereignty and the primacy of European Community law', *Modern Law Review*, 1972, p. 375; E. C. S. Wade and G. G. Phillips, *Constitutional and Administrative Law*, 9th ed., 1977, pp. 126–33; and the notes by Hood Phillips in the *Law Quarterly Review*, 1979, p. 167, and 1980, p. 31.

[3] *Inland Revenue Commissioners* v. *Collco Dealings Ltd,* [1962] A.C. 1 (*obiter*). This rule is not limited to treaties which have been given effect in English law by previous Acts of Parliament. See *R.* v. *Secretary of State for Home Affairs, ex p. Bhajan Singh*, [1975] 2 All E.R. 1081; *R.* v. *Chief Immigration Officer, Heathrow Airport, ex p. Salamat Bibi*, [1976] 3 All E.R. 843, 847; and *Pan-American World Airways Inc.* v. *Department of Trade* (1975), *International Law Reports*, vol. 60, pp. 431, 439. See also Duffy, 'English law and the European Convention on Human Rights', *International and Comparative Law Quarterly*, 1980, p. 585.

has no effects in municipal law until an Act of Parliament is passed to give effect to it. In other countries this distinction tends to be blurred. In the vast majority of democratic countries outside the Commonwealth, the legislature, or part of the legislature, participates in the process of ratification, so that ratification becomes a legislative act, and the treaty becomes effective in international law and in municipal law simultaneously. For instance, the Constitution of the USA provides that the President 'shall have power, by and with the advice and consent of the Senate, to make treaties, provided two-thirds of the Senators present concur'. Treaties ratified in accordance with the Constitution automatically become part of the municipal law of the USA.

Custom

The traditional rule is that customary international law automatically forms part of English law; this is known as the doctrine of incorporation. Lord Chancellor Talbot said in *Barbuit's* case in 1735 that 'the law of nations in its fullest extent is and forms part of the law of England' (25 E.R. 777). Strictly speaking, this statement is too wide, because it is not true of treaties; but, as far as customary international law is concerned, it was repeated and applied in a large number of cases between 1764 and 1861, and was reaffirmed by Lord Denning in *Trendtex Trading Corporation* v. *Central Bank of Nigeria*, [1977] Q.B. 529, 553–4.

However, it is possible to interpret some recent cases as discarding the doctrine of incorporation in favour of the doctrine of transformation, that is, the doctrine that rules of customary international law form part of English law only in so far as they have been accepted by English Acts of Parliament and judicial decisions. A remark made by Lord Justice Atkin in *Commercial and Estates Co. of Egypt* v. *Board of Trade* is sometimes regarded as supporting this doctrine: 'International law as such can confer no rights cognisable in the municipal courts. It is only in so far as the rules of international law are recognized as included in the rules of municipal law that they are allowed in municipal courts to give rise to rights and obligations' ([1925] 1 K.B. 271, 295).

Other judgments emphasise the difficulty of discovering what are the rules of customary international law on any given subject,[1] and it is here that we can find an explanation of the apparent conflict between the incorporation doctrine and the transformation doctrine. Most English barristers and judges know very little about international law, and therefore tend to overlook much of the

---

[1] *R.* v. *Keyn* (1876), 2 Ex. D. 63, 202–3; *West Rand Central Gold Mining Co.* v. *R.*, [1905] 2 K.B. 391, 407–8.

evidence of customary international law. They usually seek evidence of customary international law only in the sources which are most familiar to them – in judicial decisions of English courts or of the courts in other common law countries; if such judicial decisions provide no answers, they look at textbooks. Textbooks are not a bad place to look for evidence of customary international law, provided they are reliable and up to date; it is the heavy reliance on judicial decisions which is dangerous, because the most recent judicial decision may have been decided a long time ago, and customary international law may have changed since then. There is thus a danger that English courts may apply obsolete rules of international law instead of modern international law. Moreover, if there are no relevant judicial decisions, English courts may wrongly assume that there is no rule of customary law, and may invent a new rule which conflicts with customary international law.[1]

In short, the theory of English law is in favour of the incorporation doctrine, but, since English courts look to English judgments as the main evidence of customary international law, practice approximates to the transformation theory.

Quite apart from the problem of ascertaining the content of customary international law, there are a number of situations which constitute exceptions to the general rule, and in which English courts cannot apply customary international law:

(1) If there is a conflict between customary international law and an Act of Parliament, the Act of Parliament prevails.[2] However, where possible, English courts will interpret Acts of Parliament so that they do not conflict with customary international law (*Maxwell's Interpretation of Statutes*, 12th ed., 1969, pp. 183–6).
(2) If there is a conflict between customary international law and a binding judicial precedent laying down a rule of *English* law, the judicial precedent prevails (*Chung Chi Cheung* v. *R.*, [1939] A.C. 160, 168; *Trendtex Trading Corporation* v. *Central Bank of Nigeria*, [1977] Q.B. 529, 557). But English courts are probably free to depart from earlier judicial precedents laying down a rule of *international* law if international law has changed in the meantime (*Trendtex Trading Corporation* v. *Central Bank of*

---

[1] For an example, see Akehurst, 'Uganda Asians and the *Thakrar* case', *Modern Law Review*, vol. 38, 1975, pp. 72–7.

[2] *Mortensen* v. *Peters* (1906), 8 F. (J.C.) 93. For an account of the background and sequel of this case, see H. W. Briggs, *The Law of Nations*, 2nd ed., 1953, pp. 52–7. The case is not absolutely conclusive, because the Court doubted the scope of the relevant rule of customary international law.

Nigeria, [1977] Q.B. 529, 554, 557, 576–9, rejecting the contrary view in *The Harmattan*, [1975] 1 W.L.R. 1495, 1493–5).

(3) Under the so-called 'act of state' doctrine in English constitutional law, an alien, who is injured abroad by an act authorised or subsequently approved by the Crown, has no remedy in English courts; his only remedy is to try to get his own state to make an international claim against the United Kingdom (*Buron* v. *Denman* (1848), 145 E.R. 450).

(4) There are certain questions about which English courts accept a certificate signed by the Foreign Secretary as conclusive. Foreign Office certificates, as they are called, are most often used in connection with the recognition of states and governments (see below, pp. 66–8), but they can also deal with other questions, such as the extent of British territory (or territorial sea) or of the territory of another country, the existence of a state of war (whether or not the United Kingdom is engaged in the war) and entitlement to diplomatic status. The element common to all these questions is that they involve recognition of a particular status; and the courts treat the Foreign Office certificate as binding because they realise that the Foreign Office would be embarrassed in its handling of foreign affairs if, for instance, the courts recognised a foreign government and the Foreign Office did not, or vice versa. On the other hand, the certificate is only binding as regards the existence of a particular status; the legal effects of that status are determined by the court. Thus, a certificate stating that X is a diplomat prevents the courts from deciding that he is not a diplomat, but it is for the courts to determine whether X and other diplomats are immune from a particular type of tax. If the certificate said that X was not a diplomat, although in fact he was, the court would be forced to decide the case in a manner contrary to international law; but this is unlikely to happen, since the Foreign Office is advised by lawyers who understand international law far better than many English judges do.

Other sources

There are no English cases dealing with rules of international law derived from sources other than treaties and custom. But it is probable that such rules would be treated in the same way as customary rules. The dictum in *Barbuit's* case, that 'the law of nations in its fullest extent is and forms part of the law of England', appears to represent the general theory of English law, and its application is not limited to customary law; the fact that treaties do not form part of English law is simply an isolated exception, to be explained by reference to special doctrines of English constitutional law.[1]

Conclusions

From what has been said above, it is clear that English law will sometimes fail to reflect the correct rule of international law. But this does not necessarily mean that the United Kingdom will be breaking international law. Very often the divergence between English law and international law simply means that the United Kingdom is unable to exercise rights which international law entitles (but does not require) the United Kingdom to exercise. Even when a rule of municipal law is capable of resulting in a breach of international law, it is the application of the rule, and not its mere existence, which normally constitutes the breach of international law; consequently, if the enforcement of the rule is left to the executive, which enforces it in such a way that no breach of international law occurs, all is well. For instance, there is no need to pass an Act of Parliament in order to exempt foreign diplomats from customs duties; the government can achieve the same result by *instructing* customs officers not to levy customs duties on the belongings of foreign diplomats.

The legal advisers to the Foreign Office keep English law under constant review to make sure that it does not violate international law. For instance, if a proposed treaty is likely to necessitate changes in English law, the requisite legislation is always passed *before* the treaty is ratified, so that the United Kingdom may not be accused of committing even a temporary violation of the treaty.

Public International Law and Private International Law

Laws are different in different countries. If a judge in state X is trying a case which has more connection with state Y than with state X, he is likely to feel that the case should have been tried in state Y, or (since some judges are reluctant to forgo the sense of self-importance which comes from trying cases) that he himself

---

[1] But the rule about treaties also applies to binding decisions taken by international organisations under powers derived from treaties. There was a crisis in 1968 when the House of Lords temporarily withheld its consent to a statutory instrument designed to bring English law into line with a Security Council resolution imposing mandatory sanctions against the Smith régime in Rhodesia. If the House of Lords had persisted in its refusal to approve the statutory instrument, the United Kingdom would have been in breach of its obligations under the United Nations Charter. See *Keesing's Contemporary Archives*, 1967–8, pp. 22922–4.

Regulations and certain other rules made by the EEC Council and Commission are made part of English law by section 2(1) of the European Communities Act 1972.

should try the case in accordance with the law of state Y. Feelings of this sort have produced a complicated set of rules in almost every country, directing the courts (*a*) when to exercise jurisdiction in cases involving a foreign element, (*b*) when to apply foreign law in cases involving a foreign element, (*c*) when to recognise or enforce the judgments of foreign courts. These rules are known as private international law, or the conflict of laws. (The type of international law to which this book is mainly devoted is often called public international law, in order to distinguish it from private international law; the expression 'international law', used without any qualification, almost always means public international law, not private international law.)

There appears to be little connection between public international law and the various municipal systems of private international law. Private international law originated from a belief that in certain circumstances it would be appropriate to apply foreign law or to let a foreign court decide the case. The trouble is that each state has its own idea of what is appropriate. For instance, English courts are very ready to enforce foreign judgments; the courts in the Netherlands and several other countries seldom do so, unless there is a treaty to that effect. The rules determining the jurisdiction of a state's own courts in civil cases involving a foreign element differ so much that it is impossible to discern any common pattern. Even the rules about the application of foreign law differ. For instance, before 1800 a man's 'personal law' (that is, the law governing legitimacy, capacity to marry and other questions of family law) was the law of his religion in Muslim countries, and the law of his domicile (permanent home) in Western countries; one reason for this difference was that there was more religious tolerance in Muslim countries than in Christian countries. After 1800 France, in Napoleon's time, went through an intensely nationalistic phase, and decided that French law should be the personal law of all French *nationals*; after some hesitation, French courts inferred from this rule, by way of analogy, that *everyone's* personal law should be his *national* law, not the law of his domicile. The same thing happened in other continental countries at a slightly later date. England adhered to the old rule of domicile, but a series of nineteenth-century judicial decisions introduced a lot of artificiality and complexity into the rules about acquisition and loss of domicile. The consequence is extreme diversity between the rules of private international law in different countries, with resulting hardship; for instance, if a Spanish national domiciled in England gets an English divorce, it will be recognised in most English-speaking countries but not in most continental countries. The significant thing, however, is that no country protested when France and other countries started abandoning the old rule of domicile – and it is submitted that the absence of protest constitutes a tacit admission that states are free to alter their rules of private international law at will.

Admittedly the differences between the rules of private international law in different countries must not be exaggerated; there *are* rules which are more or less the same in the vast majority of countries. An example is the rule concerning transfers of property; the validity of the transfer depends on the law in force at the place where the property was at the time of the alleged transfer (*lex situs* or *lex rei sitae*). But this similarity could be due to coincidence or to commercial convenience rather than to any rules of public international law. Similarity between the laws in different countries does not necessarily reflect a rule of public international law; for instance, the law of contract is much the same in most English-speaking countries – simply because the original settlers in most English-speaking countries came from England. In order to prove that public international law requires states to incorporate a particular rule in their municipal laws, it is not enough to show that that rule does in fact exist in their municipal laws; it is also necessary to show an *opinio iuris*, a *conviction* that public international law requires states to incorporate the rule in question in their municipal laws (see above, pp. 29–31). This is what is lacking. When judges apply the *lex situs*, or any rule of private international law, they do not ask what the practice is in other countries, or attempt to bring their decisions into line with it; nor do they suggest that their actions are governed by any rule of public international law.[1] When a state departs from a generally accepted rule of private international law, it is not denounced as a law-breaker by judges or diplomats in other countries.

It is therefore submitted that the rules of private international law do not form part of public international law, or vice versa. However, it should be noted that states sometimes make treaties to unify their rules of private international law; and, when this happens, the content of private international law does come to be regulated by public international law.

---

[1] English judges sometimes say that their actions are dictated by 'comity'. This is an unusual word, and therefore gives the impression of being a technical term; but it is unclear what, if anything, English judges mean when they use it. Its literal meaning is 'courtesy', and in this sense comity is regarded as something different from law of any sort (see above, pp. 3–4); rules of comity are customs which are normally followed but which are not legally obligatory. At other times it is used as a synonym for private international law; as a synonym for public international law; or as a totally meaningless expression. It is a wonderful word to use when one wants to blur the distinction between public and private international law, or to eliminate clarity of thought.

The Act of State Doctrine

Under the so-called 'act of state' doctrine, the acts of a state, carried out within its own territory, cannot be challenged in the courts of other states (not even if the acts are contrary to international law, according to the most extreme version of the doctrine). The doctrine overlaps with private international law, and there have been cases in which English courts have applied the doctrine and private international law as alternative grounds for their decision,[1] with the result that private international law and the act of state doctrine are sometimes confused with one another. But there is a difference; the act of state doctrine is wider than private international law, because it covers acts performed by a foreign state within its own territory *which are contrary to its own law*; but the doctrine is also much narrower than private international law, because it only covers acts of a *state* and not, for instance, a sale of goods between two private individuals.

Opinions differ as to whether the act of state doctrine is a rule of public international law. The disagreement is probably caused by a failure to perceive that the doctrine really covers two very different types of situation:

(1) The first situation is where an individual is sued or prosecuted in the courts of one state for acts which he performed as a servant or agent of another state. In this situation the act of state doctrine is a sort of corollary to the principle of sovereign immunity, and is an established rule of international law (see below, p. 117).
(2) The second situation is where a state expropriates property situated within its territory and sells it to a private individual, who is then sued by the original owner in the courts of another state. Different considerations apply here; the purchaser is not forced to buy the property in the same way that a servant or agent is forced to carry out the orders of the state. Many of the cases applying the act of state doctrine in this situation are American, and the leading American case[2] regards the doctrine, not as a rule of public inter-

---

[1] If Ruritania expropriates property situated in Ruritania, do English courts accept the expropriation as legal because it is legal under the laws of the place where the property is situated (private international law), or because the expropriation has been carried out by a foreign state (act of state doctrine)? See Lipstein, 'Recognition of governments and the application of foreign laws', *Transactions of the Grotius Society*, vol. 35, 1949, p. 157.

[2] *Banco Nacional de Cuba* v. *Sabbatino* (1964), 376 U.S. 398, which held that American courts could not challenge the Cuban nationalisation of American-owned sugar plantations. The effect of this decision was subsequently reversed by an Act of Congress. See the case-note by K. R. Simmonds in *International and Comparative Law Quarterly*, vol. 14, 1965, p. 452.

The act of state doctrine has a different meaning in English constitutional law; see above, p. 47.

national law, but as a rule of American constitutional law, derived from the principle of the separation of powers – the courts should not embarrass the executive in its conduct of foreign relations by questioning the acts of foreign states.

Suggestions for Further Reading

D. J. Harris, *Cases and Materials on International Law*, 3rd ed., 1983, ch. 3.
Akehurst, 'Jurisdiction in international law', *British Year Book of International Law*, vol. 46, 1972–3, pp. 145, 170–7, 179–90, 212–40 (on the relationship between public international law and private international law) and 240–57 (on the act of state doctrine).

Chapter 5

States and Governments

States

Since international law is primarily concerned with the rights and duties of states, it is necessary to have a clear idea of what is a state for the purposes of international law. The answer to this question is less simple than one might suppose.

It is usually agreed that a state must satisfy three conditions:

(1) It must have territory. But absolute certainty about a state's frontiers is not required; many states have long-standing frontier disputes with their neighbours.
(2) A state must have a population.
(3) A state must have a government capable of maintaining effective control over its territory, and of conducting international relations with other states. This requirement is not always applied strictly; thus, a state does not cease to exist when it is temporarily deprived of an effective government as a result of civil war or similar upheavals. Even when all of its territory is occupied by the enemy in wartime, the state continues to exist, provided that its allies continue the struggle against the enemy (see below, p. 146).

The requirement of government is, however, strictly applied when part of the population of a state tries to break away to form a new state. There is no rule of international law which forbids secession from an existing state; nor is there any rule which forbids the mother-state to crush the secessionary movement, if it can. Whatever the outcome of the struggle, it will be accepted as legal in the eyes of international law.[1] But, so long as the mother-state is still struggling to crush the secessionary movement, it cannot be said that the secessionary authorities are strong enough to maintain control over their territory with any certainty of permanence. Traditionally, therefore, states refrained from recognising the

[1] These propositions (and some others in the present chapter) may need modification when one side is acting contrary to the principle of self-determination, but the principle of self-determination has a limited scope, and the propositions stated in the text remain true in most cases. See below, pp. 253-9; and see James Crawford, *The Creation of States in International Law*, 1979, pp. 103-6 and 247-68.

secessionary movement as an independent state until its victory was assured; for instance, no country recognised the independence of the southern states during the American Civil War (1861–5). In recent years, however, states have used (or abused) recognition as a means of showing support for one side or the other in civil wars of a secessionary character; thus in 1968 a few states recognised 'Biafra' as an independent state *after* the tide of war had begun to turn *against* 'Biafra' – recognition was intended as a sign of sympathy. See also p. 255, below.

Indeed, some writers treat recognition as a fourth condition which has to be satisfied before a state exists for the purposes of international law. But, for reasons which will be explained later, the better view appears to be that recognition is usually no more than evidence that the three requirements listed above are satisfied. In most cases the facts will be so clear that recognition will not make any difference, but in borderline cases recognition can have a decisive effect. For instance, recognition of very small states such as Monaco and the Vatican City State is important, because otherwise it might be doubted whether the territory and popula- tion of such states are large enough to make them states in the eyes of international law. Similar considerations apply in the case of secessionary struggles; outright victory for one side or the other will create a situation which international law cannot ignore, and no amount of recognition or non-recognition will alter the legal position; but in borderline cases such as Rhodesia, where the mother-state's efforts to reassert control are rather feeble, recogni- tion or non-recognition by other states may have a decisive effect on the legal position (see below, pp. 59–61 and 63).

Federal States

Unions of states can take several forms, but the only form which has much importance nowadays is the federal state (or federation). It has been calculated that half the world's population lives under a federal form of government. The basic feature of a federal state is that authority over internal affairs is divided by the constitution between the federal authorities and the member-states of the federation, while foreign affairs are normally handled solely by the federal authorities. International law is concerned only with states capable of carrying on international relations; consequently the federal state is regarded as a state for the purposes of international law, but the member-states of the federation are not. If a member- state of the federation acts in a manner which is incompatible with the international obligations of the federal state, it is the federal state which is regarded as responsible in international law. For instance, when a mob lynched some Italian nationals in New Orleans in 1891, the USA admitted liability and paid compensation to Italy, even though the prevention and punishment of the crime fell exclusively within the powers of the State of Louisiana, and not within the powers of the federal authorities (J. B. Moore, *A Digest of International Law*, 1906, Vol. 6, pp. 837–41).

Although the normal practice is for foreign affairs to be handled solely by the federal authorities, there are a few federal constitutions which give member-states of the federation a limited capacity to enter into international relations. For instance, in 1944 the constitution of the USSR was amended so as to allow the Ukraine and Byelo-Russia (two member-states of the USSR) to become members of the United Nations alongside the USSR; the purpose and effect of this device was to give the USSR three votes instead of one. In recent years the province of Quebec has signed treaties on cultural questions with France and other French-speaking countries, under powers reluctantly delegated by the federal authorities of Canada.

Independent and Dependent States

In international law the distinction between independent and dependent states is based on external appearances and not on the underlying political realities of the situation; as long as a state appears to perform the functions which independent states normally perform (sending and receiving ambassadors, signing treaties, making and replying to international claims, and so on), international law treats the state as independent and does not investigate the possibility that the state may be acting at the direction of another state. An independent state becomes a dependent state only if it enters into a treaty or some other legal commitment whereby it agrees to act at the direction of another state or to assign the management of most of its international relations to another state. It may seem artificial to describe Czechoslovakia, for instance, as an independent state, when everybody knows that Czechoslovakia is forced to follow Soviet policy on all important questions; however, if international law tried to take all the political realities into account, it would be impossible to make a clear distinction between dependent and independent states, because all states, even the strongest, are subject to varying degrees of pressure and influence from other states.

A state is a state in the eyes of international law only if it has capacity to enter into international relations. The vast majority of such states are independent, in the sense explained in the previous paragraph. But there are several examples of dependent states, which have only a limited capacity to enter into international relations:

(1) One example may occasionally be found among the member-states of a federation, as explained above.

(2) Colonies in the process of becoming independent often have a limited capacity to enter into international relations. In the case of Canada, Australia, New Zealand and South Africa, the process of gaining independence was so gradual that it is impossible to point to any single date as the date of independence, and, while this process was taking place, the four dominions gradually acquired a greater and greater degree of capacity to conduct international relations. Even today, when independence is normally granted at a specific point in time, the formal grant of independence is usually preceded by a period of training, during which the colonial power delegates certain international functions to the colony, in order to give the local leaders experience of international relations. For instance, when Singapore was still a British colony, it was authorised to enter into commercial treaties and to join inter-national organisations of a technical character, subject to the veto of the United Kingdom.

(3) Protectorates are another example. The basic feature of a pro-tectorate is that it retains control over most of its internal affairs, but agrees to let the protecting state exercise most of its inter-national functions as its agent. However, the exact relationship depends on the terms of the instrument creating the relationship, and no general rules can be laid down. Protectorates were generally a by-product of the colonial period, and most of them have now become independent.

Governments

A state cannot exist for long, or at least cannot come into existence, unless it has a government. But the state must not be identified with its government; the state's international rights and obligations are not affected by a change of government. Thus the postwar govern-ments of West Germany and Italy have paid compensation for the wrongs inflicted by the Nazi and Fascist régimes. The same principle is also illustrated by the *Tinoco* case.[1] Tinoco, the dictator

[1] (1923), *UN Reports of International Arbitral Awards* I 375. But see above, p. 18, for the communist theory about class revolutions. For further discussion of the *Tinoco* case, see below, pp. 60–1.

of Costa Rica, acting in the name of Costa Rica, granted concessions to British companies and printed banknotes, some of which
were held by British companies. After his retirement, Costa Rica
declared that the concessions and banknotes were invalid. The
United Kingdom protested on behalf of the British companies, and
the two states referred the case to arbitration. The arbitrator held
that Tinoco had been the effective ruler of Costa Rica, and that his
acts were therefore binding on subsequent governments; the fact
that his régime was unconstitutional under Costa Rica law, and that
it had not been recognised by several states, including the United
Kingdom, was dismissed as irrelevant.

Recognition of States and Governments in International Law

Recognition is one of the most difficult topics in international law.
It is a confusing mixture of politics, international law and
municipal law. The legal and political elements cannot be disen-
tangled; when giving or withholding recognition, states are
influenced more by political than by legal considerations, but their
acts do have legal consequences. What is not always realised, however, is that the legal effects of recognition in international law are
very different from the legal effects of recognition in municipal law
(or at any rate English law).[1] Once this distinction is grasped, the
whole topic of recognition should become easier to understand;
apparent conflicts between two sets of cases will be easily resolved
when it is realised that one set is concerned with international law
and the other with English law.

Another reason why recognition is a difficult subject is because it
deals with a wide variety of factual situations; in addition to recognition of states and governments, there can also be recognition of
territorial claims (see below, pp. 148-50). In the present section of
the book it is proposed, for purposes of simplicity, to concentrate
on recognition of states and governments and to make only
passing references to recognition of territorial claims.

When a new state comes into existence, or when a new government comes into power in an existing state by violent means,[2] other

[1] In other countries the legal effects of recognition are not the same as in England: D. P.
O'Connell, *International Law*, 2nd ed., 1970, Vol. 1, pp. 172-83. The legal effects of
recognition in English law are dealt with below, pp. 66-8.

[2] Recognition is accorded to the head of state, and so no problem of recognition arises
when a revolution does not affect the head of state (for example, the military coup in Greece
in April 1967, which overthrew the Prime Minister but not the king). Nor does any problem
of recognition arise when there is a constitutional change in the head of state, for example,
when an English king dies and is succeeded by his eldest son, or when a new President of the
USA is elected.

states are confronted with the problem of deciding whether or not to recognise the new state or government. Recognition means a willingness to deal with the new state as a member of the international community, or with the new government as the representative of the state. A refusal to recognise is sometimes based on a belief that the new state or government is not in effective control of the territory which it claims, but a refusal to recognise can also be based on other factors; for instance, the USA at one time refused to recognise foreign governments simply because it disapproved of them; in the eyes of the USA, recognition was a mark of approval. The United Kingdom, on the other hand, usually recognised all governments which were in actual control of their territory, without necessarily implying any approval of such governments.

Because non-recognition of foreign governments has often been used as a mark of disapproval, recognition of a foreign government has sometimes been misinterpreted as implying approval, even in cases where no approval was intended. In order to avoid such misinterpretations, some states have adopted the policy of never recognising *governments* (although they continue to grant or withhold recognition of foreign *states*). This policy originated in Mexico, where it is known as the Estrada doctrine, and has been applied in recent years by several other states, including France, Spain and the USA; on 10 October 1977 the Department of State *Bulletin* noted that 'in recent years United States practice has been to deemphasize and avoid the use of recognition in cases of changes of governments and to concern ourselves [instead] with the question of whether we wish to have diplomatic relations with the new governments' (John A. Boyd, *Digest of United States Practice in International Law 1977*, p. 19). On 28 April 1980 the British Foreign Secretary announced that the United Kingdom would adopt this policy:

we have decided that we shall no longer accord recognition to *governments*.
   The British government recognise *states* . . .
   Where an unconstitutional change of régime takes place in a recognised state, governments of other states must necessarily consider what dealings, if any, they should have with the new régime, and whether and to what extent it qualifies to be treated as the government of the state concerned. Many of our partners and allies take the position that they do not recognise governments and that therefore no question of recognition arises in such cases. By contrast, the policy of successive British governments has been that we should make and announce a decision formally 'recognising' the new government.
   This practice has sometimes been misunderstood, and, despite explanations to the contrary, our 'recognition' interpreted as implying

approval. For example, in circumstances where there may be legitimate public concern about the violation of human rights by the new régime . . . it has not sufficed to say that an announcement of 'recognition' is simply a neutral formality.

We have therefore concluded that there are practical advantages in following the policy of many other countries in not according recognition to governments. Like them, we shall continue to decide the nature of our dealings with régimes which come to power unconstitutionally in the light of our assessment of whether they are able . . . to exercise effective control of the territory of the state concerned, and seem likely to continue to do so.

(*House of Lords Debates*, vol. 408, cols 1121–2 (italics added))

At first sight the Estrada doctrine appears to abolish the entire system of recognition of governments. In practice, however, it probably merely substitutes implied recognition for express recognition; recognition is not announced expressly, but can be implied from the existence of diplomatic relations or other dealings with a foreign government (the Foreign Secretary seems to have adopted this interpretation in his subsequent statement on 23 May 1980, quoted on pp. 67–8 below; as regards the circumstances in which recognition can be implied, see pp. 65–6 below).

Most states which have adopted the Estrada doctrine in the past have not applied it consistently; sooner or later they succumb to the temptation of announcing recognition of a foreign government, in order to demonstrate their support for it or in the hope of obtaining its good will (Charles Rousseau, *Droit international public*, Vol. 3, 1977, pp. 555–7). It will be interesting to see whether the United Kingdom will be able to show greater consistency.

Legal effects of recognition

The question of the legal effects of recognition has given rise to a bitter theoretical quarrel. According to the constitutive theory, a state or government does not exist for the purposes of international law until it is recognised; recognition thus has a constitutive effect in the sense that it is a necessary condition for the 'constitution' (that is, establishment or creation) of the state or government concerned. The constitutive theory is opposed by the declaratory theory, according to which recognition has no legal effects; the existence of a state or government is a question of pure fact, and recognition is merely an acknowledgment of the facts.

Historically, the constitutive theory has more to be said for it than one might suppose. During the nineteenth century, international law was often regarded as applying mainly between states with a European civilisation; other countries were admitted to the 'club' only if they were 'elected' by the other 'members' – and the 'election' took the form of recognition. There were also occasions (for example, during the period of the Holy Alliance, immediately after 1815) when some states tended to treat revolutionary governments as outlaws, who were likewise excluded from the 'club' until they were recognised.

Even today, recognition can sometimes have a constitutive effect, although state practice is not always consistent. If the establishment of a state or government is a breach of international law, the state or government is often regarded as having no legal existence until it is recognised. For instance, for many years the Western powers refused to recognise the existence of the German Democratic Republic (East Germany), mainly because they considered that the establishment of the German Democratic Republic by the Soviet Union was a breach of the Soviet Union's obligations under treaties made between the allies concerning the administration of Germany after the Second World War. The recognition of the German Democratic Republic by the Western powers in 1973 had a constitutive effect as far as the Western powers were concerned; recognition cured the illegality of the German Democratic Republic's origins, and converted it from a legal nullity into a state (and see below, pp. 255–6, on the 'Bantustans' created by South Africa).

However, in most cases the establishment (even the violent establishment) of a new state or government is not a breach of international law; there is no general rule of international law which forbids a group of people to overthrow the government of their state, or to break away and form a new state, if they have the strength to do so. In such cases the existence of a state or government is simply a question of fact, and recognition and non-recognition usually have no legal effects. For instance, in the *Tinoco* case, Chief Justice Taft, the arbitrator, held that Tinoco's régime was the government of Costa Rica because it was clearly in effective control of Costa Rica, and the fact that it had not been recognised by several states, including the United Kingdom, made no difference. Nevertheless, Chief Justice Taft indicated that recognition or non-recognition would have assumed greater importance if the effectiveness of Tinoco's control over Costa Rica had been less clear, because 'recognition by other powers is an important evidential factor in establishing proof of the existence of a government'.[1] Where the facts are clear, as in the *Tinoco* case, the evidential value of recognition or non-recognition is not strong enough to affect the outcome; in such circumstances recognition is declaratory. But in

---

[1] (1923), *UN Reports of International Arbitral Awards* I 375, 380. (For the facts of the *Tinoco* case, see above, pp. 56–7). Similarly, recognition can play an evidential role when it is uncertain whether a body claiming to be a state fulfils the factual requirements of statehood; see above, p. 54.

borderline cases, where the facts are unclear, the evidential value of recognition can have a decisive effect; in such circumstances recognition is semi-constitutive.

On the other hand, recognition has little evidential value if the granting or withholding of recognition by other nations is not based on an assessment of the government's control over the country.

> When recognition *vel non* of a government is by such nations determined by inquiry, not into its . . . governmental control, but into its illegitimacy or irregularity of origin [as in the *Tinoco* case], their non-recognition loses something of evidential weight on the issue with which those applying the rules of international law are alone concerned (*Tinoco* case, *loc. cit.*, at p. 381).

The discretionary character of recognition

International law allows states to exercise great discretion when granting or withholding recognition. States have often used recognition as an instrument of policy; for instance, the USA has often regarded recognition as a mark of approval, and in President Wilson's time it withheld recognition from Latin American régimes which had come to power by unconstitutional means, such as Tinoco's régime in Costa Rica.

A number of limitations on the discretion of states in matters of recognition have been suggested. Some of these suggestions have been made for quite a long time; others are of more recent origin; but few of them are firmly established.

(1) *Premature recognition*. If rebels are recognised as a new government or as a new state before they have established permanent control over the territory in question, the government which is attempting to crush the rebellion will regard such recognition as a very unfriendly act. Academic opinion is virtually unanimous in condemning premature recognition as illegal, but states seldom invoke legal considerations when condemning premature recognition. It is true that premature recognition is rare, but infrequency is not necessarily a proof of illegality; it is a general feature of recognition that states are generally too slow and cautious in granting recognition, rather than being too fast and impetuous. In any case, premature recognition is not as rare now as it used to be (see above, pp. 53–4, and below, p. 255).

(2) *Premature withdrawal of recognition* is the opposite side of the coin to premature recognition; premature recognition of rebels is accompanied by premature withdrawal of recognition from the old régime. What has been said about premature recognition is equally true of premature withdrawal of recognition, that is, it is

rare, but not as rare as it used to be; it is regarded as an unfriendly act; writers condemn it as illegal, but states seldom invoke legal considerations when condemning it.

Withdrawal of recognition from a state or government whose authority is not contested by a rival authority (that is, premature withdrawal of recognition unaccompanied by premature recognition of another entity) is very rare indeed. It serves no useful purpose; if a state or government is firmly established, recognition and non-recognition are irrelevant in determining its status; nor does withdrawal of recognition in such circumstances undermine the evidential value of previous recognition.

Severence of diplomatic relations does not constitute withdrawal of recognition.

(3) *The Stimson doctrine.* In 1931 Japanese troops set up the puppet state of Manchukuo in Manchuria, which had until then formed part of China. Almost all states considered that Japan was guilty of aggression, and the American Secretary of State, Stimson, announced that his government would not recognise situations brought about by aggression. The following year the Assembly of the League of Nations passed a resolution stating that 'it is incumbent upon the members of the League of Nations not to recognize any situation, treaty or agreement which may be brought about by means contrary to the Covenant of the League of Nations or to the Pact of Paris' (cf. below, pp. 218–19). In 1970 the United Nations General Assembly declared that it was a basic principle of international law that 'no territorial acquisition resulting from the threat or use of force shall be recognized as legal'.[1] These resolutions suggest that there is a duty to withhold recognition, but states have not always acted in accordance with them. For instance, three years after the Italian conquest of Ethiopia in 1936, the conquest was recognised *de jure* by the United Kingdom; and the United Kingdom has also recognised (although only *de facto*) the Soviet conquest of the Baltic republics in 1940. The only effect of the Stimson doctrine seems to have been to delay the grant of recognition, not to prevent it.

(4) *The Lauterpacht doctrine.* The late Sir Hersch Lauterpacht argued that states were under a duty to recognise entities which fulfilled the factual requirements of a state or government.[2] This doctrine has been accepted by British governments since the Second World War, maybe because it was a useful means of

---

[1] Ian Brownlie, *Basic Documents in International Law,* 3rd ed., 1983, pp. 35, 39. See above, p. 60 and below, pp. 65 (n. 1) and 147–50.

[2] Lauterpacht, *Recognition in International Law,* 1947, p. 74. Lauterpacht recognised an exception to his doctrine where the state or government had come into being as a result of a breach of international law.

fending off criticism from the USA about British recognition of communist governments in China and elsewhere.

But the vast majority of state practice constitutes a tacit rejection of the Lauterpacht doctrine. Many states have frequently used recognition as an instrument of policy, by withholding recognition from states or governments which they did not like. Recognition is often conditional, that is, a state will agree to recognise a foreign government only if the foreign government is prepared to make certain promises about its future behaviour. In the past the United Kingdom itself has acted inconsistently with the Lauterpacht doctrine; for instance, it withheld recognition from the Tinoco régime in 1917–19 out of deference to the USA, although the Tinoco régime was the effective government of Costa Rica.

(5) *The Charter of the United Nations* authorises the Security Council to *order* member-states to impose non-military sanctions. In 1970 the Security Council ordered member-states not to recognise the Smith régime in Rhodesia (*International Legal Materials*, 1970, pp. 636, 637; cf. below, pp. 181–4).

De jure *and* de facto *recognition*[1]

One of the most confused aspects of recognition is the distinction between *de jure* and *de facto* recognition. For a start, the expressions '*de jure* recognition' and '*de facto* recognition', although commonly used, are technically incorrect; '*de jure* recognition' really means recognition of a *de jure* government; the words '*de jure*' or '*de facto*' describe the government, not the act of recognition.

The terminology implies that a *de facto* government does not have the same sound legal basis as a *de jure* government. But it is difficult to find any body of legal rules by which this legal basis can be determined.

(1) One cannot base the distinction between *de jure* and *de facto* governments on the law of the country where the change of

---

[1] The distinction between *de jure* and *de facto* recognition usually arises in the case of governments. It is sometimes said that a state can only be recognised *de jure*, but there are a few examples of states being recognised *de facto*; for instance, Indonesia was recognised *de facto* by several states while it was fighting for its independence against the Dutch in 1945–9. Similarly there are a few examples of territorial claims being given only *de facto* recognition; the United Kingdom, for example, has only given *de facto* recognition to the Soviet annexation of Estonia, Latvia and Lithuania in 1940. *De facto* recognition of states and territorial claims is governed by roughly the same rules, and gives rise to roughly the same problems, as *de facto* recognition of governments.

When recognition is granted by an express statement, it should probably always be treated as *de jure* recognition, unless the recognising state announces that it is granting only *de facto* recognition. When recognition is not express, but implied (see below, p. 65), there will often be uncertainty as to the intentions of the recognising state – did it intend to grant *de jure* recognition, or did it intend to grant *de facto* recognition?

government has occurred. Revolutionary governments are often described as *de facto* governments, but a successful revolution brings about a change in the constitutional law of the country concerned. The present system of government in England is based on the Glorious Revolution of 1688; it is undoubtedly illegal under pre-1688 law, but, in order to determine the legality of post-1688 governments, one has to apply the post-1688 law, not the pre-1688 law. To put it crudely, it is the government which makes the law, not the law which makes the government.

(2) Nor are *de jure* governments more lawful than *de facto* governments if international law is taken as the criterion of legality. International law does not require states to adopt any particular form of government; as long as a government is in effective control of a country, it constitutes the government of that country for the purposes of international law, however revolutionary or undemocratic it may be. (Occasionally a state may agree by treaty to adopt a particular form of government – for instance, as a means of protecting its racial minorities. In these circumstances a government set up in violation of the treaty may sometimes only be recognised *de facto* by other countries, and here '*de facto* government' carries an implication of illegality under international law. But such cases are exceptional; normally the words '*de facto* government' do not imply that the government is in any way illegal under international law.)

(3) Sometimes the distinction between *de jure* and *de facto* government is based on the idea of *legitimacy*; and legitimacy in this context is defined in terms of political ideology, not in terms of law. Thus, the communist government in Russia had defeated all rivals to its authority in 1921, but the Liberal–Conservative coalition government in the United Kingdom only recognised it *de facto*; however, ten days after the Labour Party formed a British government in 1924, the communist government of Russia was recognised *de jure*. When *de facto* recognition is used in this way as a mark of disapproval, it is not surprising that relations between the recognising state and the *de facto* government are not very cordial.

(4) Most often, the distinction between *de jure* and *de facto* governments is based on the degree of effectiveness of the control which they exercise. The British Foreign Secretary said, in answer to a question in the House of Commons on 21 March 1951:

The conditions under international law for the recognition of a new régime as the *de facto* government are that the new régime has in fact effective control over most of the state's territory and that this control seems likely to continue. The conditions for the recognition of a new régime as the *de jure* government of a state are that the new régime should not merely have effective control over most of the state's territory, but that it should in fact be firmly established.

In other words, *de facto* recognition is more provisional and is used in unstable situations.

Whatever the basis for the distinction between *de jure* and *de facto* recognition, the effects of the two types of recognition are much the same.[1] If, like Chief Justice Taft in the *Tinoco* case, one thinks of recognition as having an evidential value, then presumably *de jure* recognition would have a greater evidential force than *de facto* recognition; but the difference is probably not very great.

Express and implied recognition

Normally, when a state recognises another state or government, it says so expressly. But in some circumstances recognition can be implied from conduct. It is sometimes said that recognition cannot be implied from a state's conduct unless the state intends that it should be implied; but the law may deduce intentions from behaviour which are different from a state's real intentions, just as a person who signs a contract without reading it will be deemed by the law to have intended all sorts of things which he never intended in fact. The fear of inadvertently recognising an unrecognised government is a recurrent nightmare for diplomats. For instance, during the Second World War, General de Gaulle sent a gorilla from French Equatorial Africa as a present to President Roosevelt. The news that the gorilla was on its way across the Atlantic caused consternation in the State Department, because the USA had not at that time recognised de Gaulle's government in exile, and accepting the gift might have constituted implied recognition; on the other hand, refusing the gift would have mortally offended the General. Fortunately the gorilla, who was evidently a born diplomat, solved the problem by dying when halfway across the Atlantic.

If a state is in the habit of making an express announcement whenever it wants to recognise another state or government, there is a presumption that it does not intend to recognise another state or government in the absence of such an announcement. In these circumstances recognition will not readily be implied.[2] Entry into

---

[1] However, if a state or government has been established (or a territorial change brought about) in violation of international law, it seems that only *de jure* recognition can cure the illegality; *de facto* recognition is insufficient to cure the illegality, cf. above, pp. 60 and 62, and below, pp. 147–50.

[2] Lachs, 'Recognition and modern methods of international cooperation', *British Year Book of International Law*, vol. 35, 1959, p. 252. If a state does *not* normally make an express announcement whenever it wants to recognise a foreign government (see above, p. 58, on the Estrada doctrine), recognition of a foreign government can probably be implied more readily.

diplomatic relations will constitute implied recognition, but the exchange of trade missions (even permanent trade missions) will not; nor will presentation of an international claim, or payment of compensation. Entering into a treaty with an unrecognised state or government will probably not constitute implied recognition; for instance, the Arab states (except Egypt, since 1979) do not recognise Israel, although both Israel and the Arab states are members of the United Nations. (In all these cases, where there is a presumption against implied recognition, that presumption can be strengthened if the state which wishes to withhold recognition announces expressly that a particular act should not be interpreted as implying recognition.) So it seems that the State Department should not have been so scared of accepting General de Gaulle's gorilla.

In any case, if one follows the *Tinoco* case in treating recognition as having an evidential effect, the choice between non-recognition and implied recognition is a false dilemma; informal dealings with unrecognised governments, it is submitted, have varying degrees of evidential value lying somewhere between the effects of full recognition and the effects of total non-recognition.

Recognition of States in English Law

There is a major difference between the effects of recognition in English law and the effects of recognition in international law. In most cases recognition does not have a constitutive effect in international law, but it usually does have a constitutive effect in English law. In most cases, when English courts have to decide whether a foreign state exists, they regard themselves as bound by the Foreign Office certificate (see above, p. 47) and they will treat the foreign state as non-existent unless the Foreign Office certifies that it has been recognised by the British government.

Recognition has several important effects in English law:

(1) A recognised state has sovereign immunity and cannot be sued in English courts without its consent (*The Annette*, [1919] P. 105; *Duff Development Co.* v. *Kelantan Government*, [1924] A.C. 797; see below, p. 109).
(2) Since an unrecognised state is regarded as non-existent by English courts, it cannot sue in an English court (by analogy from *City of Berne* v. *Bank of England* – see below, p. 67).
(3) The English rules of private international law frequently direct English courts to apply foreign laws (see above, pp. 48–50). In such

cases, they can apply only the laws of *recognised* states (*Carl Zeiss Stiftung* v. *Rayner & Keeler Ltd*, [1965] Ch. 596, C.A.; but see also the decision of the House of Lords in the same case, [1967] 1 A.C. 853, especially the *obiter dicta* on pp. 907-8 and 954 which criticise this rule).

(4) When a legal document uses words like 'state', the author of the document may have intended the words to refer to states recognised by the British government, in which case the courts will interpret the words in that sense. On the other hand, he may have intended the words in a wider and less technical sense, in which case the courts will regard recognition as irrelevant – and this is the interpretation which has been adopted in the majority of cases. But it is essentially a question of discovering the intended meaning of the document, and no general rules can be laid down; words used in one sense in one document can be used in another sense in another document (Merrills, *International and Comparative Law Quarterly*, 1971, p. 476).

Recognition of Governments in English Law

In the past, English courts approached recognition of governments in the same way as recognition of states, and treated a foreign government as non-existent unless the Foreign Office certified that it had been recognised by the United Kingdom. Unless a government was recognised, it was not entitled to sovereign immunity (*The Arantzazu Mendi*, [1939] A.C. 256), it could not sue in an English court (*City of Berne* v. *Bank of England* (1804), 32 E.R. 636), its laws were not applied in English courts (*Luther* v. *Sagor*, [1921] 1 K.B. 456 and [1921] 3 K.B. 532) and it was not entitled to the property of the state which it claimed to govern (*Haile Selassie* v. *Cable & Wireless Ltd*, [1939] Ch. 182).

The British government's decision in 1980 to abandon the practice of (expressly) recognising foreign governments (see above, pp. 58-9) has thrown the whole of this area of the law into uncertainty. When the Foreign Secretary was asked 'how in future, for the purposes of legal proceedings, it may be ascertained whether, on a particular date, Her Majesty's Government regarded a new régime as the government of the state concerned', he replied: 'In future cases where a new régime comes to power unconstitutionally our attitude to the question whether it qualifies to be treated as a government will be left to be inferred from the nature of the dealings, if any, which we may have with it, and in particular on whether we are dealing with it on a normal government-to-government basis.'[1] But even if the Foreign Office supplies judges with details of its dealings with foreign governments, it may be difficult for judges to infer *from the nature of those dealings* whether or not the foreign government 'qualifies to be treated as a government'; how can a judge, who has no experience of diplomacy, decide which types of negotiations between the British government and the foreign government justify the inference that the foreign government 'qualifies to be treated as a government', and which types of negotiations do not justify that inference? In any case, the extent of a government's control over its territory provides a better test of its status than the extent of its dealings with the British government; if a government is in firm control of a country, it is artificial and unjust to refuse to apply its laws in an English court solely because the British government refuses to have any dealings with it. If the Foreign Office will not provide judges with information about the control exercised by a foreign government, the judges should decide for themselves whether a foreign government is in control of a foreign country; the difficulties which English judges would experience in making such decisions would probably be less than the difficulties which they would experience in deciding which were the correct inferences to be drawn from the nature of that government's dealings with the British government.

[1] *House of Lords Debates*, 23 May 1980, vol. 409, cols. 1097–8. But the old practice of issuing a binding Foreign Office certificate stating expressly that a government is recognised will still be followed for the purposes of sovereign immunity; section 21 of the State Immunity Act 1978 provides that 'a certificate by or on behalf of the Secretary of State shall be conclusive evidence . . . as to the . . . persons to be regarded for those purposes as the . . . government of a state'.

Suggestions for Further Reading

James Crawford, 'The criteria for statehood in international law', *British Year Book of International Law*, vol. 48, 1976–7, p. 93.

D. J. Harris, *Cases and Materials on International Law*, 3rd ed., 1983, ch. 4.

Chapter 6

International Organisations, Individuals and Companies

When lawyers say that an entity is a legal person, or that it is a subject of the law (these two terms are interchangeable), they mean that it has a capacity to enter into legal relations and to have legal rights and duties. In modern systems of municipal law all individuals have legal personality, but in former times slaves had no legal personality; they were simply pieces of property. Companies also have legal personality, but animals do not; although rules are made for the *benefit* of animals (for example, rules against cruelty to animals), these rules do not confer any *rights* on the animals (for instance, animals cannot start judicial proceedings if the rules are broken).

In the nineteenth century states were the only legal persons in international law; international law regarded individuals in much the same way as municipal law regards animals. The position has changed in the last century, and international organisations, individuals and companies have acquired some degree of international legal personality; but when one tries to define the precise extent of the legal personality which they have acquired, one enters a very controversial area of the law.

International Organisations

The term 'international organisation' is usually used to describe an organisation set up by agreement between two or more *states*. It is different from a 'non-governmental organisation', which is set up by individuals or groups of individuals, although some non-governmental organisations are entrusted with certain functions by states; the outstanding example is the International Committee of the Red Cross, which plays an important role in supervising the application of the Geneva Conventions on the laws of war.

International organisations, in the sense of interstate organisations, have existed since 1815, if not earlier, but it is only since the First World War that they have acquired much political importance. The idea that they have international legal personality is even more recent.

Treaties setting up international organisations often provide, as Article 104 of the United Nations Charter does, that 'the organization shall enjoy in the territory of each of its members such legal capacity as may be necessary for the exercise of its functions and the fulfilment of its purposes'. All that this means is that the organisation enjoys legal personality under the *municipal* laws of its member-states; it can own property, enter into contracts, and so on. There is no corresponding article in the Charter expressly giving the United Nations personality under *international* law. Nevertheless, it is generally agreed that the United Nations does have at least some degree of international personality; for instance, Article 43 of the Charter empowers the United Nations to make certain types of treaty with member-states – a power which could not exist if the United Nations had no international personality.

When states create an international organisation, they set it up for specific purposes and give it limited powers. For this reason, legal personality must be treated as a relative concept, not as an absolute concept. One cannot ask whether an international organisation has legal personality in the abstract; one should ask, 'What specific rights, duties and powers is it capable of exercising?' An organisation may have a power to make treaties about one topic, for instance, but not about others. Similarly, powers may vary from organisation to organisation. The United Nations can take military action (in certain circumstances) but the World Health Organisation cannot.

The leading judicial authority on the personality of international organisations is the advisory opinion given by the International Court of Justice in the *Reparation for Injuries* case. The case arose out of the murder of Count Bernadotte, the United Nations mediator in Palestine, in 1948. The United Nations considered that Israel had been negligent in failing to prevent or punish the murderers, and wished to make a claim for compensation under international law. There was uncertainty over the preliminary problem of whether the United Nations had the legal capacity to make such a claim, and so the following question was put to the Court:

In the event of an agent of the United Nations in the performance of his duties suffering injury in circumstances involving the responsibility of a state, has the United Nations, as an organization, the capacity to bring an international claim against the responsible *de jure* or *de facto* government with a view to obtaining the reparation due in respect of the damage caused (*a*) to the United Nations, (*b*) to the victim . . .?

The Court answered both halves of the question in the affirmative.[1] The Court began by saying that the United Nations organisation had international personality *in principle*; its functions were so important that the organisation could not carry them out unless it had some degree of international personality. The Court then went on to advise that the organisation's personality included the capacity to bring the type of claim mentioned in the request to the Court. It decided without much argument that the organisation could claim for the loss suffered by the organisation itself as a result of the breach of an international obligation owed to it. The capacity to claim for the loss suffered by the organisation's agents raised a more difficult problem, but the Court nevertheless advised that the organisation had an *implied power* to make such a claim, because the organisation could not work effectively without the help of loyal and efficient agents, who would not serve it loyally and efficiently unless they were sure of its protection.

The Court's reasoning is of the utmost importance for the law of international organisations generally, because it shows that the powers of international organisations need not necessarily be conferred expressly in the organisation's constituent treaty; an organisation also has such implied powers as are necessary for the most efficient performance of its functions.

Individuals and Companies

In the seventeenth century, when all law was regarded as derived from natural law, a sharp distinction was not made between international law and municipal law, and it was easy to assume that individuals had legal personality under international law. But in the nineteenth century, when positivism was the dominant philosophy, states were usually regarded as the only subjects of international law.

The present century has seen a growing tendency to admit that individuals – and companies – have some degree of international personality, but the whole subject is extremely controversial. Soviet international lawyers admit that individuals can be guilty of crimes (for example, war crimes) against international law, but usually deny that individuals and companies have any *rights* under

[1] *ICJ Reports*, 1949, p. 174. The Court dealt with the abstract question of the capacity to claim, not with the facts of the Bernadotte case. Although the UN has capacity to make a claim, it cannot enforce that claim through the ICJ, since Article 34 of the Statute of the ICJ provides that only states may be parties in contentious cases before the Court (on the difference between contentious and advisory proceedings, see below, pp. 209-210). In the end the Bernadotte case was settled by negotiation; Israel agreed to pay compensation, while denying that she was under an obligation to do so.

international law; they probably fear that such rights would undermine the powers of states over their own nationals. In Western countries writers and governments are usually prepared to admit that individuals and companies have some degree of international legal personality; but the personality is usually seen as something limited – much more limited than the legal personality of international organisations. Individuals and companies may have various rights under special treaties, for instance, but it has never been suggested that they can imitate states by acquiring territory, appointing ambassadors, or declaring war. As in the case of international organisations, it is useless to treat legal personality as an absolute concept; one must break it down into specific rights and duties.

Very many rules of international law exist for the *benefit* of individuals and companies, but that does not necessarily mean that the rules create *rights* for individuals and companies, any more than municipal rules prohibiting cruelty to animals confer *rights* on animals. Even when a treaty expressly says that individuals and companies shall enjoy certain rights, one has to read the treaty very carefully to ascertain whether the rights exist directly under international law, or whether the states parties to the treaty are merely under an obligation to grant municipal law rights to the individuals or companies concerned.

One way of proving that the rights of the individuals or companies exist under international law is to show that the treaty conferring the rights gives the individuals or companies access to an international tribunal in order to enforce their rights.[1] Most international tribunals are not open to individuals or companies; for instance, Article 34 of the Statute of the International Court of Justice provides that only states may be parties to contentious cases before the Court. But there are exceptions; thus, the International Bank for Reconstruction and Development has set up an international arbitral tribunal to hear disputes arising out of investments between states and the nationals of other states (see below, p. 96). Similarly, in the European Communities individuals and companies can bring claims before the Court of Justice of the European Communities; but this is not a very good example, because the powers exercised by the Communities over the governments and nationals of the member-states are so extensive that

---

[1] Judicial protection of rights is much more necessary for individuals than it is for states. States can and often do refuse to accept the jurisdiction of international tribunals, but they have other reasons for obeying international law in their dealings with *other states* – reasons which have nothing to do with sanctions imposed by courts (see above, pp. 8–11). These other reasons for obeying international law do not apply to the dealings of states with *individuals*.

'Community law' is almost a hybrid between international law and federal law.

Some other treaties provide for a different means of enforcement; individuals take their complaints, not to an international tribunal, but to a political organ of an international organisation, which investigates the complaint and takes such action as it considers necessary and feasible against the offending state. (For instance, the 1919 peace treaties allowed members of certain racial minorities in Central and Eastern Europe to complain to the Council of the League of Nations if they considered that they were victims of racial discrimination.) The individual initiates the proceedings, but thereafter has no control over them and plays no active part in the proceedings. If the political organ refuses to take up his case, he has no remedy; but if it does take up his case, it may be able to protect his interests more effectively than he could ever hope to do by appealing to an international tribunal – apart from anything else, this indirect system of enforcement spares the individual the costs of litigation. Moreover, the system is popular with states, because it provides a speedier means of rejecting frivolous claims. However, it is doubtful whether the individual's interests which are protected by such a system can be regarded as rights conferred on him by international law; there is room for argument about what is meant by a legal right, but most lawyers would probably agree that in such cases the rights are vested in the political organ and not in the individual.

It has sometimes been suggested that individuals (or companies) can acquire rights under international law by making agreements with states (or international organisations) containing a provision that the agreements should be governed by international law. This suggestion has given rise to considerable controversy, especially in connection with oil concessions. Since the quadrupling of the price of oil in 1973 oil-producing states have been in a strong bargaining position, and oil concessions granted since 1973 are generally governed by the law of the state granting the concession. But before 1973 the oil companies were in a stronger bargaining position, and were often reluctant to allow their oil concessions to be governed by the law of the state granting the concession. On the other hand, the state granting the concession might have felt humiliated if it had allowed the concession to be governed by the law of a foreign country. The obvious answer was for the state and the company to agree that the concession should be governed by international law or (more commonly) by general principles of law. General principles of law are a source of international law (see above, pp. 34–6), but some writers have suggested that general principles of law can also constitute a legal system in their own right, distinct from municipal law and from international law. For instance, McNair (*British Year Book of International Law*, vol. 33, 1957, p. 1) followed the old-fashioned view that states were the only subjects of international law; he therefore argued that contracts between a state and a company could not be governed by international law, but that they could be governed by general principles of law as a separate system of law. McNair's views were criticised by Mann (ibid., vol. 35, 1959, pp. 34, 35), who argued that general principles of law were not a legal system in their own right, and that contractual provisions specifying that a contract is governed by general principles of law should be interpreted to mean it is governed by international law.

Similar problems arise in connection with employment in international organisations, which is generally not governed by municipal law, but by an elaborate set of rules enacted by the organisation and interpreted in the light of general principles of administrative law. International administrative tribunals, which decide disputes between organisations and their officials, have sometimes described this body of law as the 'internal law of the organisation', without saying whether the 'internal law' represents part of international law or a separate system of law. See Michael Akehurst, *The Law Governing Employment in International Organizations*, 1967, especially pp. 3–10, 249–63.

In conclusion, it should be noted that the international legal personality of individuals and companies (and, indeed, of international organisations) is still comparatively rare and limited. Moreover, it is *derivative*, in the sense that it can only be conferred by states – it is states which set up international organisations; it is states which make treaties or adopt customary rules giving international rights to individuals and companies; it is only states (or international organisations, created by states) which can make contracts with individuals or companies governed by international law. Consequently, when some states say that individuals are subjects of international law, and when other states disagree, both sides may be right; if states in the first group confer international rights on individuals, then individuals are subjects of international law as far as those states are concerned; states in the second group can, for practical purposes, prevent individuals from acquiring international personality, by refraining from giving them any rights which are valid under international law.

Human Rights

The international rules concerning the protection of human rights are a good example of the difficulty of deciding whether individuals derive rights from international law, or whether they merely derive benefits. Indeed, there is an even greater problem of classification in this context, since many of the commitments undertaken by states are expressed in such vague and idealistic language that it is uncertain whether they enunciate legal obligations at all, as distinct from merely moral aspirations.

The United Nations Charter

International protection of what we nowadays call human rights is nothing new; as early as 1815 the United Kingdom tried to persuade states to make treaties for the suppression of the slave trade. During the following century treaties were made to protect individuals against various forms of injustice. A big step forward came with the peace treaties of 1919, which provided guarantees of fair treatment for the inhabitants of mandated territories (see below, p. 248) and for certain racial minorities in Eastern and Central Europe, and which set up the International Labour Organisation to promote improvements in working conditions throughout the world. However, until 1945 international action tended to concentrate on remedying particular abuses or on protecting particular groups; it was only after the United Nations Charter was signed in 1945 that any attempt was made to provide comprehensive protection for all individuals against all forms of injustice.

Article 55 of the United Nations Charter says that 'the United Nations shall promote . . . universal respect for, and observance of, human rights and fundamental freedoms for all without distinction as to race, sex, language or religion'. In Article 56, 'all members pledge themselves to take joint and separate action in cooperation with the organization for the achievement of the purposes set forth in Article 55'. The use of the word 'pledge' ('*s'engagent*' in the French text) implies a legal obligation, but the obligation is probably not to observe human rights *now* (the rights are not defined or listed in any case), but to work towards their fulfilment in the *future*; the vagueness of the language probably leaves a wide discretion to states about the speed and means of carrying out their obligations, and it is notorious that in many countries no perceptible progress, and little imperceptible progress, have been made towards the realisation of human rights. On the other hand, a state which deliberately moved *backwards* as far as human rights are concerned would probably be regarded as having broken Article 56; certainly this is the attitude of most members of the United Nations towards the South African policy of apartheid, although it is only natural that coloured countries tend to feel more bitter about apartheid than they would about other forms of discrimination.

In 1946 the United Nations set up a Commission on Human Rights, to carry out research and to draft treaties implementing Articles 55 and 56 of the Charter. Many individuals have an exaggerated idea of the Commission's powers, and send it all sorts of complaints about alleged violations of human rights. The Commission has adopted the practice of forwarding such complaints (but not revealing the name of the complainant) to the state concerned, which is sometimes moved by its own conscience to take remedial action. Since 1971 the Commission has been able to debate complaints which reveal gross and persistent violations of human rights, and to make recommendations concerning such complaints; but so far the Commission has made little use of these powers, limited though they are.

Whatever legal obligations may or may not be imposed by Articles 55 and 56 of the Charter, it is clear that these provisions confer no *international* rights on individuals, but only benefits. In countries, such as the USA, where the ratification of the Charter has the effect of transforming it into municipal law, courts have generally held that Articles 55 and 56 are too imprecise to confer any rights on individuals – not even rights under *municipal* law.

The Universal Declaration of Human Rights

The Universal Declaration of Human Rights is a resolution passed by the UN General Assembly on 10 December 1948, by forty-eight votes to nil, with eight abstentions (the communist countries, plus Saudi Arabia and South Africa). Its provisions fall into two main categories.

First, there are provisions enunciating what have subsequently come to be known as civil and political rights. They prohibit slavery, inhuman treatment, arbitrary arrest and arbitrary interference with privacy, together with discrimination on grounds of race, colour, sex, language, religion, political or other opinion, national or social origin, property, birth, or other status. They also proclaim the right to a fair trial, freedom of movement and residence, the right to political asylum, the right to have and change nationality, the right to marry, the right to own property, freedom of belief and worship, freedom of opinion and expression, freedom of peaceful assembly and association, free elections and equal opportunities for access to public positions.

The second group of provisions is concerned with what have subsequently come to be known as economic, social and cultural rights – the right to social security, to full employment and fair conditions of work, to an adequate standard of living, to education and to participation in the cultural life of the community.

After the preamble, the opening words of the resolution are as follows:

The General Assembly proclaims this Universal Declaration of Human Rights as a common standard of achievement [*l'idéal commun à atteindre*] for all peoples and all nations, to the end that every individual and every organ of society, keeping this Declaration constantly in mind, shall strive by teaching and education to promote respect for these rights and freedoms and by progressive measures, national and international, to secure their universal and effective recognition and observance . . .

Many laymen imagine that states are under a legal obligation to respect the rights listed in the Declaration. But most of the states which voted in favour of the Universal Declaration regarded it as a statement of a relatively distant ideal, which involved little or nothing in the way of legal obligations. The Declaration merely recommends states to keep it in mind and to 'strive . . . by progressive [not immediate] measures . . . to secure . . . universal and effective recognition and observance' of its provisions. At the most, the Declaration is simply a list of the human rights which member-states 'pledge' themselves to 'promote' under Articles 55 and 56 of the Charter; but, as we have seen, the Charter leaves a wide discretion to states concerning the speed and means of fulfilling their pledge.

It is possible, however, that the Universal Declaration of Human Rights may *subsequently* have become binding as a new rule of customary international law. For instance, the United Nations Conference on Human Rights at Teheran in 1968 passed a resolution proclaiming *inter alia* that 'the Universal Declaration of Human Rights . . . constitutes an obligation for the members of the international community' (text in *American Journal of International Law*, 1969, p. 674). See also *Filartiga* v. *Pena-Irala* (*International Legal Materials*, 1980, pp. 966, 971, 973) and *USA* v. *Iran* (*ICJ Reports*, 1980, pp. 3, 42).

The European Convention for the Protection of Human Rights and Fundamental Freedoms

Conflicting ideologies and interests make it difficult to reach agreement at the United Nations about human rights. Western countries tend to emphasise civil and political rights, while communist and developing countries tend to emphasise economic and social rights.

Agreement is easier to reach at the regional level, where states are more likely to have common values and interests. In 1950 the Council of Europe, an international organisation comprising almost all the non-communist states in Europe, drafted the European Convention for the Protection of Human Rights and Fundamental Freedoms, which entered into force on 3 September 1953 (text in Ian Brownlie, *Basic Documents in International Law*, 3rd ed., 1983, p. 320). Almost all the non-communist states in Europe are now parties to the Convention. A number of protocols (that is, supplementary agreements) were added later.

The European Convention, plus the protocols, cover much the same ground as the Universal Declaration of Human Rights;[1] one revealing difference is that Article 1 of the first protocol goes much further than. Article 17 of the Universal Declaration in underlining the sanctity of property. Since the Convention and protocols are legally binding on the states parties to them, they are drafted in much more detail than the Universal Declaration – as one would expect in the case of a legal document. Some of the details have the effect of restricting the force of the Convention. In particular, Article 15 provides: 'In time of war or other public emergency threatening the life of the nation any . . . party may take measures derogating from its obligations under this Convention' (subject to certain conditions and exceptions – see the article by Rosalyn Higgins in the *British Year Book of International Law*, 1976–7, pp. 301–7, 319–20).

The Convention set up a Commission of Human Rights, composed of individuals elected by the Committee of Ministers of the Council of Europe (the Committee of Ministers is a political body roughly corresponding to the General Assembly in the UN). The Commission hears complaints against state parties to the Convention who are accused of breaking it. Complaints may be made by any other state party to the Convention, although experience has shown that states have little inclination to protect other states' nationals except when their own interests are involved (thus, Austria has a political interest in protecting German-speaking Italians in the South Tyrol). In addition, states have the option of empowering the Commission to hear complaints from individuals; most states parties to the Convention have accepted this right of

---

[1] There is nothing corresponding to Articles 22–5 of the Universal Declaration, which deal with social security, full employment, fair conditions of work and adequate standards of living. These are covered in detail by a separate treaty, the European Social Charter, which was opened for signature in 1961 and entered into force in 1965. The semi-judicial enforcement machinery of the European Convention would be inappropriate for the European Social Charter, which uses a less 'legal' and more 'political' system of enforcement. See D. J. Harris, 'The European Social Charter', *International and Comparative Law Quarterly*, vol. 13, 1964, p. 1076.

individual petition, as it is called, although the United Kingdom did not accept it until 14 January 1966. There are, however, a number of obstacles to be overcome before the Commission can hear a complaint, and the obstacles are particularly severe in the case of individual petitions. For instance, if local remedies exist, they must be exhausted before the individual concerned or a state party to the Convention can refer the case to the Commission (the local remedies rule is discussed in more detail on p. 100, below); individual petitions may also be rejected for other reasons, for example, if they are anonymous or an abuse of the right of petition.

The Commission investigates the complaint and tries to solve the dispute by conciliation (for a definition of conciliation, see below, p. 202). If conciliation fails, the Commission draws up a report on the case and refers it to the Committee of Ministers, which may, by a two-thirds majority, decide that there has been a breach of the Convention and order the defaulting state to rectify the situation. In extreme cases, the ultimate sanction is expulsion from the organisation – a threat which forced Greece to withdraw from the Council of Europe in 1969 (Greece was readmitted to the Council of Europe in 1974, after the restoration of democratic government in Greece).

After the case has been heard by the Commission, the Commission or (in certain circumstances) a state party to the Convention may refer the case to the European Court of Human Rights, if the defendant state has accepted the jurisdiction of the Court. Acceptance of the Court's jurisdiction is optional for states parties to the Convention; most of them have accepted it, although the United Kingdom did not accept it till 14 January 1966. The Court's decision is binding and may be enforced by the Committee of Ministers.

Some anomalies in the functioning of the Court were demonstrated in the *Lawless* case. Lawless, an Irishman and an alleged member of the Irish Republican Army, complained to the Commission that Ireland had interned him without trial. The Commission referred the case to the Court. Before the Court, the parties to the proceedings, from a formal point of view, were the Commission and Ireland. But the Commission, like the Court, was supposed to be an independent and impartial body of experts. After acting in a quasi-judicial capacity during its own investigations and attempts at conciliation, it could hardly change its character overnight and appear as an advocate for Lawless before the Court. Moreover, Lawless, whose interests formed the subject-matter of the dispute, was not technically a party to the proceedings before the Court. The Commission overcame these difficulties by presenting an impartial report to the Court and allowing Lawless to add his own arguments as an annex to the report. The Court, over-ruling the Irish government's objections, held that this device was legitimate. A procedural injustice was thus avoided – but in a rather clumsy way (see the case-note by Robertson in the *British Year Book of International Law*, 1960, p. 343).

In countries where ratification of the European Convention has the effect of transforming it into municipal law, the Convention clearly gives *municipal* law rights to individuals. Whether it gives them international law rights is less certain. The position is complicated by the fact that some states accept the right of individual petition, or the jurisdiction of the Court, or both, while other states accept neither. But, even when the defendant state has accepted both the right of individual petition and the jurisdiction of the Court, difficulties of classification remain. The individual is a party to the proceedings before the Commission, but the Commission is only a semi-judicial body; the Court is clearly a judicial body, but the individual is not technically a party to the proceedings before the Court. Of course, it can be argued that access to an international tribunal is not the only criterion of the international personality of individuals, but an analysis of the European Convention does demonstrate the difficulties of deciding whether individuals have rights under international law, or whether they merely have benefits (see above, pp. 72–3).

Further developments at the United Nations

The European Convention has been copied in regional treaties and municipal enactments in other parts of the world; and, on 16 December 1966, after twelve years of discussion, the United Nations completed the drafting of two treaties designed to transform the principles of the Universal Declaration of Human Rights into binding, detailed rules of law – the International Covenant on Civil and Political Rights, and the International Covenant on Economic, Social and Cultural Rights (text in Ian Brownlie, *Basic Documents in International Law*, 3rd ed., 1983, pp. 270, 258). Both Covenants came into force in 1976. In 1981 sixty-eight states were parties to the International Covenant on Economic, Social and Cultural Rights and sixty-six states were parties to the International Covenant on Civil and Political Rights; the UK and the USSR are parties to both Covenants, but the USA and China are parties to neither.

In many of their articles, the two Covenants closely follow the European Convention for the Protection of Human Rights and the European Social Charter. But there are some differences: the UN Covenants say nothing about property, for instance. The biggest difference concerns the machinery for enforcement, which is much weaker than in the European Convention. There is an optional protocol to the Covenant on Civil and Political Rights, which provides for individual petitions; but all that the Human Rights Committee (the equivalent of the European Commission of Human Rights) can do is to call upon the state concerned for explanations, and make recommendations. In 1981 twenty-five states were parties to the optional protocol.

Other machinery for the enforcement of the Covenants, not involving petitions from individuals, is contained in Articles 40-2 of the Covenant on Civil and Political Rights and in Articles 16-23 of the Covenant on Economic, Social and Cultural Rights.

Nationality

Individuals do not often have rights and duties under international law, but many rules of international law create benefits and burdens for individuals. The factor which usually connects an individual with those burdens and benefits is nationality, which may be defined as the status of belonging to a state for certain purposes of international law. Each state regards itself as having certain rights and duties vis-à-vis other states in respect of its own nationals. For instance:

(1) A state is under a duty not to ill-treat the nationals of other states (see below, pp. 87-101).

(2) A state may prosecute its own nationals, but not (according to some states) the nationals of other states, for crimes committed abroad (see below, pp. 103-4).

(3) A state may not impose compulsory military service on the nationals of other states (although there may be an exception in the case of foreigners who are permanent residents of the con-scripting state).

(4) Treaties often provide for special benefits or burdens to be conferred on nationals of a particular state. For instance, extradition treaties often provide that a state need not extradite its own nationals.

(5) When a national of state A is expelled from state B, state A is obliged to receive him, unless he is willing to go to another state which is willing to admit him (see below, pp. 85-6).

Nationality may also have important effects in municipal law. In most states foreigners are not allowed to vote or to hold certain jobs (particularly posts in the civil service). This use of nationality in municipal law is a pure coincidence and does not reflect any rule of international law; international law does not forbid a state to give voting rights to foreigners, nor (apart from treaties on human rights) does it forbid a state to deprive its own nationals of the right to vote.

As a general rule, international law leaves it to each state to define who are its nationals, but the nationality laws of different states often have certain features in common.

Thus, the commonest ways in which nationality may be acquired are:

(1) By birth. Some countries confer their nationality on children born on their territory (*ius soli*), others confer their nationality on children born of parents who are nationals (*ius sanguinis*); in the United Kingdom and some other states nationality may be acquired in either way (subject to certain exceptions).

(2) By marriage.

(3) By adoption or legitimation.

(4) By naturalisation. Technically, this refers to the situation where a foreigner is given the nationality of another state upon his request, but the word is sometimes used in a wider sense to cover any change of nationality after birth (cf. below, p. 98, on 'involuntary naturalisation'). The willingness of states to grant naturalisation varies very much from state to state; states like Switzerland, which wish to discourage foreigners from settling permanently, insist on a very long residence qualification, but in Israel any Jew is entitled to apply for naturalisation without needing to fulfil any residence or other qualification.

(5) As a result of the transfer of territory from one state to another (see below, p. 160).

The commonest ways in which nationality may be lost are:

(1) If a child becomes a dual national at birth, as a result of the cumulative applications of the *ius soli* and *ius sanguinis* by different states, he is sometimes allowed to renounce one of the nationalities upon attaining his majority.

(2) Acquisition of a new nationality was often treated by the state of the old nationality as automatically entailing loss of the old nationality. Nowadays some states, including the United Kingdom, merely give such people the option of renouncing their old nationality; many loyal Britons resident abroad acquire foreign nationality solely for purposes of business convenience.

(3) By deprivation. In the United Kingdom only naturalised citizens may be deprived of their nationality, and on very limited

grounds. Other countries apply the concept of deprivation more widely; in particular, totalitarian states like Nazi Germany deprived vast numbers of people of their nationality on racial or political grounds.

(4) As a result of the transfer of territory from one state to another (see below, p. 160).

Because of the difference between nationality laws in different states, some people have dual or multiple nationality, while others are stateless.

Dual or multiple nationality was regarded as undesirable at one time – hence the rule that acquisition of a new nationality automatically entailed loss of the old. The fact that that rule is being abandoned by many states reflects a realisation that dual or multiple nationality is not as undesirable as people used to believe, and dual or multiple nationality is likely to become more common in future.

Statelessness used to be uncommon, but is becoming much more frequent now as a result of legislation by totalitarian countries depriving people of their nationality on racial or political grounds (though it can, of course, arise in other ways also). It is very unpleasant. Being aliens wherever they go, stateless persons have no voting rights, are frequently excluded from many types of work and are often liable to deportation. States usually issue passports only to their own nationals,[1] and this makes it difficult for stateless people to travel when they want to. In recent years states have entered into treaties to reduce the hardships of statelessness (for example, by providing special travel documents for stateless persons), or to eliminate it altogether by altering their nationality laws.

As a general rule, international law leaves it to each state to define who are its nationals, but the state's discretion can be limited by treaties, such as treaties for the elimination of statelessness. Even under customary law, a state's discretion is not totally unlimited; for instance, it is obvious that international law would not accept as valid a British law which imposed British nationality on all the inhabitants of France. Indeed, the modern tendency is for international law to be increasingly stringent in restricting the discretion of states in matters of nationality (see below, pp. 97–9).

Companies, ships and aircraft possess nationality, as well as individuals; but the nationality of companies, ships and aircraft tends to be relevant only in special contexts, and discussion may

---

[1] It is popularly believed that a passport creates a right to a nationality. In fact, the truth is the other way round; it is nationality which creates a right to a passport.

therefore be conveniently postponed to those sections of the present book which deal with those contexts (see below, pp. 99, 272-3 and 286).

British Nationality

Nationality must not be confused with race. During the colonial period, there was a common nationality for the whole British Empire, and all British subjects (that is, nationals) resident in the United Kingdom had the right to vote, regardless of race.

The idea of a common nationality for the whole British Empire broke down when the dominions became independent and started enacting their own nationality laws. Accordingly, the British Nationality Act 1948 reorganised the law by dividing British subjects (or Commonwealth citizens – the two terms have the same meaning) into two classes:

(1) Citizens of the United Kingdom and colonies, who continued to have a common nationality, regardless of race, and who were United Kingdom nationals for the purposes of international law.
(2) Citizens of independent Commonwealth countries, who are not United Kingdom nationals for the purposes of international law, but who continue to enjoy voting rights and certain other rights in the United Kingdom which are denied to nationals of non-Commonwealth countries.

The British Nationality Act of 1981 created three new categories of British nationals, to replace the old category of citizens of the United Kingdom and colonies:

(1) British citizens, that is, persons who 'belong' to the United Kingdom. There are about 57 million British citizens.
(2) Citizens of British dependent territories, that is, persons who 'belong' to a British colony or other dependent territory. There are about 3 million citizens of British dependent territories, of whom roughly 2,600,000 live in Hong Kong.
(3) British overseas citizens, that is, persons who 'belong' to a territory which used to be under British rule, and who retained British nationality when that territory became independent. When colonies become independent they usually enact their own nationality laws, and corresponding amendments are made to British law on nationality, so that people who 'belong' to the former colony lose their British nationality and become nationals of the newly independent country instead. But in some ex-colonies there were

racial minorities who wished to retain British nationality, so that they could obtain British protection against the local government (see below, p. 87), and so that they could flee to Britain if local conditions became intolerable. The most famous examples are the Asian communities in Uganda, Kenya, Tanzania, Malawi and Zambia. When these countries became independent in 1961–4, Asians resident there were given the choice of acquiring local nationality or of retaining their British nationality. Similar arrangements were made for some people of Chinese or Indian descent living in Malaysia. There are more than 1,500,000 British overseas citizens. About 1,300,000 of them (mostly of Chinese descent) live in Malaysia and also have Malaysian nationality; a further 130,000 (mostly of Indian descent) live in Malaysia but do not have any nationality except British nationality; a further 75,000 (mostly of Indian descent) acquired British nationality through their connections with territories in Africa which used to be under British rule, and most of them do not have any nationality except British nationality (about 36,000 of them still live in Africa and about 39,000 have emigrated to India). There are also small numbers of British overseas citizens in other countries.

All persons in all of these three categories are United Kingdom nationals for the purposes of international law. The big difference between the three categories concerns immigration; British citizens have an absolute right to live in the United Kingdom, but citizens of British dependent territories and British overseas citizens are not normally allowed to live in the United Kingdom. However, restrictions on immigration into the United Kingdom by those citizens of the United Kingdom and colonies who were regarded as 'belonging' to British colonies and ex-colonies (that is, by those persons who are now known as citizens of British dependent territories and British overseas citizens) existed ever since the Commonwealth Immigrants Act of 1962, and were extended by the Commonwealth Immigrants Act of 1968 and the Immigration Act of 1971. The Nationality Act of 1981 does not introduce any new restrictions on immigration; it simply brings the law on nationality into line with the law on immigration.

According to international law, when a national of state A is expelled from state B, state A is obliged to receive him, unless he is willing to go to another state which is willing to admit him. There is thus a possibility of a conflict between international law and the Acts passed by the British Parliament in 1962, 1968, 1971 and 1981, which restricted immigration into the United Kingdom by certain groups of United Kingdom nationals. But fortunately the British government seems willing to apply these Acts in a way which avoids any breach of international law. For instance, when

Asians holding United Kingdom nationality were expelled from Uganda in 1972, the British government waived the restrictions imposed by the 1968 Act and allowed them to enter the United Kingdom; the government stated publicly that it was allowing them to enter the United Kingdom because international law required it to do so (*House of Lords Debates*, vol. 335, col. 497; see also *Keesing's Contemporary Archives*, 1967–8, pp. 22678–82).

Suggestions for Further Reading

H. G. Schermers, *International Institutional Law*, 2nd ed., 1980, pp. 770–86.

C. A. Nórgaard, *The Position of the Individual in International Law*, 1962.

A. D. McNair, 'The general principles of law recognised by civilised nations', *British Year Book of International Law*, vol. 33, 1957, p. 1.

L. B. Sohn, 'The improvement of the United Nations machinery on human rights', *International Studies Quarterly*, vol. 23, 1979, p. 186.

D. J. Harris, *Cases and Materials on International Law*, 3rd ed., 1983, ch. 9.

F. G. Jacobs, *The European Convention on Human Rights*, 1975.

P. Weis, *Nationality and Statelessness in International Law*, 2nd ed., 1979.

P. Sieghart, *The International Law of Human Rights*, 1983.

Chapter 7

Treatment of Aliens

As we saw in the previous chapter, the modern rules concerning human rights (which prohibit ill treatment of *all* individuals, regardless of their nationality) are of fairly recent origin. But for more than 200 years international law has laid down a *minimum international standard* for the treatment of aliens (that is, nationals of other states). States are not obliged to admit aliens to their territory, but, if they permit aliens to come, they must treat them in a civilised manner.[1] To put it in technical terms, failure to comply with the minimum international standard 'engages the international responsibility' of the defendant state, and the national state of the injured alien may 'exercise its right of diplomatic protection', that is, may make a claim, through diplomatic channels, against the other state, in order to obtain compensation or some other form of redress. Such claims are usually settled by negotiation; alternatively, if both parties agree, they may be dealt with by arbitration or judicial settlement.

The defendant state's duties are owed, not to the injured alien, but to the alien's national state. The theory is that the claimant state itself suffers a loss when one of its nationals is injured. Consequently, the claimant state has complete liberty to refrain from making a claim or to abandon a claim; it may agree to settle the claim at a fraction of its true value; and it is under no duty to pay the compensation obtained to its national (although it usually does). In these respects, the injured individual is at the mercy of his national state. However, international law does not entirely disregard the individual; the compensation obtained by the claimant state is usually calculated by reference to the loss suffered by the individual, not by reference to the loss suffered by the claimant state.[2]

---

[1] *A fortiori*, a state is guilty of a breach of international law if it inflicts an injury on aliens at a time when they are *outside* its territory (for example, if Utopia orders Utopian servicemen, stationed in Ruritania, to beat up residents of Ruritania). Indeed, a state may not perform any governmental act in the territory of another state without the latter's consent; see Akehurst, 'Jurisdiction in international law', *British Year Book of International Law*, vol. 46, 1972–3, pp. 145–51.

[2] But not always. For instance, in the *I'm Alone* case (1935), *UN Reports of International Arbitral Awards* III 1609, the United States sank a British ship smuggling liquor into the United States. Although the arbitrators held that the sinking was illegal, they awarded no damages for the loss of the ship, because she was owned by United States citizens and used for smuggling. But they ordered the USA to apologise and to pay $25,000 to the United Kingdom as compensation for the insult to the British flag.

'Imputability'

A state is liable only for its own acts and omissions; and, in this context, the state is identified with its governmental apparatus, not with the population as a whole. If the police beat up a foreigner, the state is liable; if private individuals beat up a foreigner, the state is not liable. The governmental apparatus of the state includes the legislature and the judiciary, as well as the executive; and it includes local authorities as well as central authorities.

A state is liable for the acts of its officials only if those acts are 'imputable' (that is, attributable) to the state. The idea of 'imputability' creates problems when officials exceed or disobey their instructions. Obviously it would be unjust if a state could limit its liability simply by giving restrictive instructions to its officials (for example, if it could escape liability for road accidents merely by telling its chauffeurs to drive carefully); and the cases indicate that a state is liable for the acts of its officials, even when they exceed or disobey their instructions, provided that they are acting with *apparent* authority or that they are abusing *powers or facilities* placed at their disposal by the state. *Youman's* claim (1926, *UNRIAA* IV 110) is a striking example of the law's willingness to make the defendant state liable. In that case, Mexico sent troops to protect Americans from a mob; but, instead of protecting the Americans, the troops, led by a lieutenant, opened fire on them. Mexico was held liable, because the troops had been acting as an organised military unit, under the command of an officer. On the other hand, if the troops had been off duty, their acts would probably have been regarded merely as the acts of private individuals (cf. *Morton's* claim (1929), *UNRIAA* IV 428).

A state is never liable for the acts of private individuals. But the acts of private individuals may be accompanied by some act or omission on the part of the state, for which the state *is* liable. Such act or omission may take one of six forms:

(1) Encouraging individuals to attack foreigners.
(2) Failing to take reasonable care to prevent the individuals, for example, failing to provide police protection when a riot against foreigners is imminent. For instance, early in 1969 the United Kingdom compensated South Africa for damage done to the South African Embassy in London by demonstrators; the demonstration had been advertised several days in advance, and an attack on the South African embassy was foreseeable, even though the demonstrators' main target was Rhodesia House – and there was only one policeman on duty outside the Embassy (*The Times*, 14 January 1969). What constitutes 'reasonable care' will depend on

the circumstances – foreigners who remain in remote areas of the countryside in times of unrest cannot expect the same police protection as foreigners in a peaceful capital city[1] – but special care must be taken to prevent injury to diplomats.

(3) Obvious failure to punish the individuals.[2]

(4) Failure to provide the injured foreigner with an opportunity of obtaining compensation from the wrong-doers in the local courts. This is an example of what is called 'denial of justice' – a term which is used in a bewildering variety of different meanings.

(5) Obtaining some benefit from the individual's act, for example, keeping looted property (*Mazzei's* claim (1903), UNRIAA X 525).

(6) Express ratification of the individual's act, that is, expressly approving it and stating that he was acting in the name of the state (J. B. Moore, *A Digest of International Law*, 1906, vol. 6, p. 989).

The Minimum International Standard

When someone resides or acquires property in a foreign country, he is deemed to accept the laws and customs of that country; his national state cannot base a claim on the fact that he would have been better treated in his home country. But the majority of states accept that the national state *can* claim if the foreign country's laws or behaviour fall below the minimum international standard. During the nineteenth and early twentieth centuries, the USA and the Western European states upheld the idea of the minimum international standard, in opposition to the Latin American countries, which argued that a state's only duty was to treat foreigners in the same way as it treated its own nationals ('national standard'). In arbitrations between the two groups of countries the minimum international standard was usually applied. However, history is now repeating itself, with certain lawyers from Afro-Asian countries arguing in favour of the national standard as opposed to the minimum international standard (for example, Guha Roy, *American Journal of International Law*, 1961, p. 863).

Application of the national standard would simultaneously give the alien too much and too little. Carried to its logical extreme, it would mean that aliens could not be excluded from voting, from entering certain professions, or from enjoying welfare benefits –

[1] *Home Missionary Society* claim (1920), *UNRIAA* VI 42. This case concerned injuries caused by rebels, a topic which gives rise to special problems. See Michael Akehurst, 'State responsibility for the wrongful acts of rebels – an aspect of the Southern Rhodesian problem', *British Year Book of International Law*, vol. 43, 1968-9, p. 49.

[2] J. L. Brierly, 'The theory of implied state complicity in international claims', *British Year Book of International Law*, vol. 9, 1928, p. 42. Compare *Neer's* claim (1926), *UNRIAA* IV 60, with *Janes's* claim (1926), *UNRIAA* IV 82.

rights which states are not obliged to grant to aliens. Conversely, it would also mean that a state would be entitled to torture foreigners to death provided that it also tortured its own nationals to death – a conclusion which would be repugnant to common sense and justice. If the minimum international standard appears to give aliens a privileged position, the answer is for states to treat their own nationals better, not for them to treat aliens worse; indeed, the whole human rights movement may be seen as an attempt to extend the minimum international standard from aliens to nationals, even though the detailed rules in declarations and conventions on human rights sometimes differ slightly from those in the traditional minimum international standard.

What critics of the minimum international standard are really opposed to is not the *principle* of having such a standard, but the *content* of some of the rules which are alleged to form part of the standard. They might be reassured by reading the following quotation from the judgment in the *Neer* claim (1926, *UNRIAA* IV 60, 61-2):

> The treatment of an alien, in order to constitute an international delinquency, should amount to an outrage, to bad faith, to wilful neglect of duty, or to an insufficiency of governmental action so far short of international standards that every reasonable and impartial man would readily recognize its insufficiency.

Some of the rules comprised in the minimum international standard are more widely accepted than others. For instance, few people would deny that a state's international responsibility will be engaged if an alien is killed,[1] imprisoned,[2] or physically ill-treated,[2] or if his property is looted or damaged[3] – unless, of course, the state can rely on some circumstance justifying the act, such as the fact that it was necessary as a means of maintaining law and order (arrest and punishment of criminals, use of force to stop a riot, and so on). On the other hand, *excessive* severity in maintaining law and order will also fall below the minimum international standard (punishment without a fair trial, excessively long detention before trial, fatal injuries inflicted by policemen dispersing a peaceful demonstration, very severe punishment for a trivial offence, and so on).

There are also other ways in which the maladministration of justice can engage a state's responsibility – for instance, if the courts are corrupt, biased, or guilty of excessive delay, or if they follow an

---

[1] *Youman's* claim, above, p. 88.

[2] *Roberts's* claim (1926), *UNRIAA* IV 77; J. C. Hsiung, *Law and Policy in China's Foreign Relations*, 1972, pp. 184-6; *USA* v. *Iran*, *ICJ Reports*, 1980, pp. 3, 42.

[3] *Zafiro* case (1925), *UNRIAA* VI 160; Hsiung, op. et loc. cit. (previous note).

unfair procedure; these rules apply to civil proceedings brought by or against a foreigner, as well as to criminal proceedings.

In other areas the content of the minimum international standard is much more controversial. Deportation is an example. Since 1914 most states have claimed wide powers of deportation. The United Kingdom recognises that other states have a general right to deport United Kingdom citizens without stating reasons (*British Practice in International Law*, 1964, p. 210). On the other hand, the United Kingdom has stated that the right to deport 'should not be abused by proceeding arbitrarily' (ibid., 1966, p. 115) – a rather vague restriction on the right of deportation. It is often hard to prove that a deportation is arbitrary if no reasons are stated for it, but a statement of reasons given voluntarily by the deporting state may reveal that the deportation was arbitrary and therefore illegal (this is what happened when the Asians were expelled from Uganda in 1972 – see Akehurst, 'The Uganda Asians', *New Law Journal*, 8 November 1973, p. 1021).

Expropriation

The rules about expropriation comprised in the minimum international standard are even more controversial than the rules about deportation. The question is of enormous political importance. In 1978 the net book value of British direct investments overseas was £24,900 million. In many underdeveloped countries the economy is dominated by foreign companies, and this problem is not limited to underdeveloped countries; about half of Canadian manufacturing industry, and about 14 per cent of British manufacturing industry, are controlled by United States companies.

According to Western countries, the minimum international standard contains two rules of customary law concerning expropriation. First, expropriation must be for a public purpose (that is, it must not be an act of spite, or a means of adding to the ruler's private fortune).[1] Second, even when expropriation is for a public purpose, it must be accompanied by payment of compensation for the full value of the property – or, as it is often expressed, 'prompt,

---

[1] See the authorities cited by O'Keefe in the *Journal of World Trade Law*, vol. 8, 1974, pp. 257–62. Expropriation is also illegal if it is forbidden by a treaty. The United Kingdom argued that the Egyptian nationalisation of the Suez Canal in 1956 was illegal because it was contrary to the Constantinople Convention of 1888, but the United Kingdom probably misinterpreted the Convention. See R. Delson, 'Nationalization of the Suez Canal Company', *Columbia Law Review*, vol. 57, 1957, p. 755; G. Schwarzenberger, *Foreign Investments and International Law*, 1969, pp. 84–9.

adequate and effective compensation'.[1] (Of course, no compensation need be paid when property is seized as a penalty for breaking an obligation imposed by the local law, provided that the local law does not fall below the minimum international standard by virtue of its excessive harshness.)

Communist countries, on the other hand, believe that states may expropriate the means of production, distribution and exchange without paying compensation. But their practice is not entirely consistent. Among themselves they have concluded treaties providing for a mutual waiver of claims and obligations arising out of one another's expropriation programmes, which implies that claims and obligations existed until waived; even the payment of compensation between communist countries is not entirely unknown (Drucker, *Law Times*, vol. 229, 1960, pp. 279–80, 293–4).

The developing countries hold the balance between the Western countries and the communist countries. Most of them could gain a large short-term benefit by expropriating foreign-owned property without compensation, but in the long term they would lose by doing so, because they would attract no private investments in the future (or, alternatively, they would have to pay a much higher price for private investments, in order to compensate for political risks). Developing countries with left-wing régimes tend to support the communist attitude towards the legality of expropriation. Other developing countries often enter into *treaties* for the protection of investments (see below, p. 96), in order to attract further foreign investment; but they show an increasing reluctance to accept the Western view of *customary* international law about expropriation.

Some of these conflicts and contradictions are reflected in resolution 1803 (XVII) on 'permanent sovereignty over natural resources', passed by the United Nations General Assembly on 14 December 1962 (text in Ian Brownlie, *Basic Documents in International Law*, 3rd ed., 1983, p. 230). The very title of the resolution is peculiar, and is designed to emphasise that foreign *ownership* of the means of production should not deprive a state of its *sovereignty* or, more specifically, of its power of economic planning. The resolution also provides, *inter alia*, that states are free to restrict or prohibit the import of foreign capital. These are principles which Western lawyers might forget, but would never

---

[1] *Norwegian Ships* case (1921), *UNRIAA* I 307, 338; *Spanish Zone of Morocco* case (1925), ibid. II 615, 647; *Shufeldt's* claim (1930), ibid. II 1079, 1095; *Mariposa's* claim (1933), ibid. VI 338; *de Sabla's* claim (1933), ibid. VI 358, 366; *Arabian-American Oil Co. v. Saudi Arabia, International Law Reports*, vol. 27, 1958, pp. 117, 144, 168, 205. See also Bin Cheng, 'The rationale of compensation for expropriation', *Transactions of the Grotius Society*, vol. 44, 1958–9, p. 267.

deny. Western lawyers are mainly interested in paragraph 4 of the resolution, which provides:

> Nationalization, expropriation or requisitioning shall be based on grounds or reasons of public utility, security or the national interest which are recognized as overriding purely individual or private interests, both domestic and foreign. In such cases the owner shall be paid appropriate compensation, in accordance with the rules in force in the state taking such measures . . . and in accordance with international law.

This corresponds to the Western position, apart from the deliberate ambiguity of the phrase 'appropriate compensation' (it is true that compensation is to be paid 'in accordance with international law', but that begs the question as to the content of the relevant rules of international law). As evidence of customary law, the value of the resolution is diminished by the fact that a Soviet amendment, stating that 'the question of compensation . . . shall . . . be decided in accordance with the national law of the [expropriating] state' (without mentioning international law), was defeated by only 39 votes to 28, with 21 abstentions.

Resolutions passed by the General Assembly in the 1970s have moved further away from the Western position. In particular, Article 2(2)(c) of resolution 3281 (XXIX), adopted on 12 December 1974, says that 'appropriate compensation should be paid by the [expropriating] state . . . taking into account its relevant laws and regulations and all circumstances that the state considers pertinent' (text in *International Legal Materials*, 1975, pp. 251, 255; this resolution is known as the Charter of Economic Rights and Duties of States). Resolution 3281 (XXIX), unlike the Soviet amendment of 1962, acknowledges that appropriate compensation should be paid; but what is appropriate is to be determined by the law of the expropriating state (the resolution makes no express mention of international law in this context), and therefore compensation is likely to be very low. However, it is doubtful whether Article 2(2)(c) can be invoked as evidence of customary law against Western states, which voted against it (Article 2(2)(c) was adopted by 104 votes to 16, with 6 abstentions; on the legal position of states which dissent from a new rule of customary law, see the *Fisheries* case, above, p. 32). Indeed, it could be argued that resolution 3281 (XXIX) is not evidence of customary law at all, since it does not claim to declare what the law *is* (the General Assembly deleted a passage in the original draft of the resolution which said that the resolution was intended to codify international law); it merely says what many states think the law *ought* to be (on the significance of this distinction, see above,

p. 27). See also *Texaco* v. *Libya* (*International Legal Materials*, 1978, pp. 1, 27–31, or *International Law Reports*, vol. 53, pp. 389, 483–495) and Brownlie, 'Legal status of natural resources in international law', in *Recueil des cours de l'Académie de droit international de La Haye*, vol. 162, 1979, pp. 245, 255–71.

When disputes arise between states which believe that full compensation must be paid for expropriation and states which think otherwise, they are usually settled by a compromise – the expropriating state pays *part* of the value of the expropriated property. The compromise usually takes the form of a global settlement, so called because it covers *all* the claims made by one state arising out of a particular nationalisation programme of the other state, instead of dealing with each individual's claim separately. The United Kingdom has concluded global settlements with most of the communist countries, and also with Egypt; the global settlement often forms part of a 'package deal', which also includes trade and cultural agreements. The money received under the global settlement is distributed among the former owners in the United Kingdom by an administrative tribunal called the Foreign Compensation Commission.

A disadvantage of global settlements, in the eyes of Western countries, is that only a fraction of the property's value is recovered; on the other hand, if claims were settled in the old way, by arbitration, many of them would be lost through lack of proof, and the expense of proving hundreds of separate claims would be enormous. In any case, even an arbitral tribunal would often find it difficult to define the true value of expropriated property; the value of a productive enterprise, for instance, is based on its profit-earning capacity, which depends on local factors and varies from year to year. Share prices could theoretically be used in assessing compensation, but everyone knows how share prices fluctuate.

Disguised expropriation

States often try to avoid unfavourable reactions from other states by carrying out expropriation in a disguised manner, for example, by placing a company under 'temporary' government control and by maintaining the 'temporary' control indefinitely. Such subterfuges are seldom successful; any act which deprives a foreigner indefinitely of all benefit from his property is regarded by international law as an expropriation, even though a formal change of ownership may not have occurred. The position is less certain as regards acts which diminish the value of property but which do not deprive the owner of its use, for example, devaluation, exchange controls, restrictions on the remittance of profits, increases in taxation, and refusal to issue import licences, trading permits, or building permits. Such acts are permitted by international law, provided that they are not done for an improper motive. The easiest way of proving improper motives is to show that the acts in question discriminate against foreigners, or against a particular group of foreigners.

See Christie, 'What constitutes a taking of property under international law?', *British Year Book of International Law*, 1962, p. 307.

Expropriation of contractual rights

So far we have been concerned only with expropriation of property, but there is no logical reason why the same principles should not apply to other forms of 'acquired rights', such as rights created by contracts between an alien and the defendant state. However, such contracts are usually subject to the law of the defendant state, and it has been argued that the alien, by entering into a contract governed by the law of the defendant state, must take the risk of unfavourable amendments to that law, just as he takes the benefit of favourable amendments. This argument is fallacious; when an alien buys property in the defendant state, his title to the property is governed by the law of the defendant state, just as contracts made with the defendant state are governed by its own law, but few people would accept that the defendant state has an unlimited power to take away property rights; why, then, should it have an unlimited power to take away contractual rights? The idea that an alien voluntarily assumes the risk of unfavourable amendments to the law governing the contract has seldom been pushed to its logical conclusion, but it has exercised a limited influence on the law; breach of contract by a state does not engage the state's international responsibility unless it constitutes an abuse of *governmental* power. For instance, if a state makes a contract of sale and delivers goods of bad quality, that is not a breach of international law, because it is something which a private individual could have done. But if a state does not provide adequate remedies in its own courts for its breach of contract, or if it passes legislation annulling the contract, then it is abusing its governmental power and commits a breach of international law.

Historically, this branch of the law has been greatly influenced by the fact that most of the southern states of the USA have a bad record of default on loans. Other states were not slow to profit from this precedent, and as a result the rule grew up that states are not liable for contracts made by their political subdivisions (this is an exception to the general rule which makes the state liable for all acts of its political subdivisions; see above, pp. 54–5 and 88).

See Jennings, 'State contracts in international law', *British Year*

Book of International Law, 1961, p. 156; Randolph, 'Foreign bondholders and repudiated debts of southern states', *American Journal of International Law*, 1931, p. 63.

Investment protection

In recent years, both developed and developing countries have taken various steps to protect foreign investments in developing countries, in order to attract new investments to those countries. Many developing countries have passed laws – or even inserted provisions in their constitutions – guaranteeing foreign investors against expropriation for a certain number of years, or providing for the payment of compensation in the event of expropriation. But such provisions do not provide much protection, because they can be repealed. Consequently, several developing countries have supplemented such provisions by entering into *treaties*, drafted in similar terms, with developed countries (particularly the USA and West Germany). The increasing uncertainty of the customary rules concerning expropriation makes such treaties increasingly valuable for the developed countries.

The USA also encourages its nationals to invest in developing countries by insuring its nationals, in return for a premium, against political and other risks; but the United States government screens the country and the investment concerned very carefully before agreeing to act as insurer. There are similar schemes in several Western countries, including the United Kingdom.

In 1965 the International Bank for Reconstruction and Development (the 'World Bank', a specialised agency of the UN) drafted a Convention on the Settlement of Investment Disputes between States and Nationals of Other States (text in *International Legal Materials*, 1965, p. 532). The Convention set up an international centre for settling investment disputes by conciliation or arbitration, to which contracting states and the nationals (including companies) of other contracting states may agree to refer disputes arising out of investments. In 1981 eighty-three states were parties to the Convention; they include the USA, the UK, most Western countries, fifty-three Afro-Asian states, but no Latin American states and no communist states (except Romania and Yugoslavia).

See P. F. Sutherland, 'The World Bank Convention on the Settlement of Investment Disputes', *International and Comparative Law Quarterly*, vol. 28 (1979), p. 367, or P. J. O'Keefe, 'The International Centre for Settlement of Investment Disputes', *Year Book of World Affairs*, vol. 34 (1980), p. 286.

Preliminary Objections

When a case involving the treatment of aliens is brought before an international tribunal, it may be lost on a preliminary objection, before the tribunal is able to deal with the substantive issue of whether there has been a violation of the minimum international standard. Although the term 'preliminary objection' is a term of judicial procedure, the rules giving rise to preliminary objections are so well established that they tend to be observed in diplomatic negotiations as well as in proceedings before international tribunals. The principal factors which can give rise to a preliminary objection are as follows: non-compliance with the rules concerning nationality of claims; failure to exhaust local remedies; waiver; unreasonable delay; improper behaviour by the injured alien.

Nationality of claims

A claim will fail unless it can be proved that the injured individual is a national of the claimant state. This basic principle is clear, but the detailed rules flowing from the principle are not.

The position is complicated by the existence of statelessness and dual nationality. The position concerning stateless persons is simple; no state may claim on their behalf. In the case of a person who is a dual national of two states, A and B, two problems arise – first, which state can claim against a third state, C? Second, can one of the national states claim against the other? As regards claims against third states, the most widely held view is that both states can claim,[1] although this view has not gone unchallenged.[2] As regards claims by one national state against the other, the orthodox view is that all such claims are inadmissible,[3] but there have been cases, particularly in recent years, which indicate that the state of the master nationality (that is, the state with which the individual has the closer ties) can protect the individual against the other national state.[4] The United Kingdom still accepts the orthodox rule.[5]

It is in the context of the nationality of claims that international

---

[1] *Salem* case, *Annual Digest of Public International Law Cases*, vol. 6, 1931–2, p. 188.

[2] *Yearbook of the International Law Commission*, 1958, vol. 2, pp. 66–7. A report drawn up by a member of the Commission suggested that claims could be brought only by the state of the master nationality (that is, the state with which the individual had the closer ties).

[3] *Reparation for Injuries* case, *International Court of Justice Reports*, 1949, pp. 174, 186 (*obiter*).

[4] *Mergé* case, *International Law Reports*, vol. 22, 1955, p. 443. This is the rule followed by the USA (*American Journal of International Law*, 1980, p. 163).

[5] *British Practice in International Law*, 1963, p. 120.

law has gone farthest in limiting the discretion of states concerning the nationality of individuals. The orthodox rule applicable to dual nationals was that one national state could not protect the dual national against the other national state, and some Latin American states tried to abuse this rule by imposing their nationality on all persons in respect of whom a claim was likely to be brought. For instance, the Mexican Constitution used to impose Mexican naturalisation on all foreigners who acquired land in Mexico or who became fathers of children born in Mexico. The USA protested against this rule in 1886, arguing that naturalisation 'must be by a distinctly voluntary act' – which it was not, under the Mexican Constitution. The United States contention was supported by several decisions of international arbitral tribunals, and in 1934 Mexico altered the relevant rules of her constitutional law. It was explained that henceforth becoming the father of illegitimate children born in Mexico was to be regarded as *un accidente en la vida de los hombres* ('an accident in the life of mankind') and not as evidence of permanent affection for the Mexican nation.

It was not until many years later that international law began to limit the power of states to turn themselves into claims agents by conferring their nationality on individuals who had no genuine link with them. The leading case is the *Nottebohm* case (*ICJ Reports*, 1955, p. 4). Nottebohm, a German national, owned land in Guatemala, and realised in 1939 that his German nationality would be an inconvenience to him if Guatemala entered the war on the Allied side. Therefore, in 1939 he went to stay for a few weeks with his brother in Liechtenstein and acquired Liechtenstein nationality, thereby automatically losing his German nationality under German law as it stood at that time; he then returned to Guatemala. When Guatemala later declared war on Germany, he was interned and his property confiscated. Liechtenstein brought a claim on his behalf against Guatemala before the International Court of Justice, but failed. The Court held that the right of protection arises only when there is a genuine link between the claimant state and its national, and that there was no genuine link between Nottebohm and Liechtenstein. The effect of the decision is not altogether certain; the Court did not say that Nottebohm's Liechtenstein nationality was invalid for all purposes, only that it gave Liechtenstein no right to protect Nottebohm against Guatemala.

It is significant that the *Nottebohm* case, like the Mexican law mentioned above, was concerned with *change* of nationality, or, more specifically, with *naturalisation*. It is uncertain whether international law would apply the same tests to acquisition of nationality at birth, for instance, or upon marriage. It is possible to acquire the nationality of a country by virtue of being born there, without having any genuine link with that country; is such a nationality caught by the rule in the *Nottebohm* case? Maybe it would be better to think, not in terms of genuine links, but in terms of what is *normal* in nationality laws. Thus it is perfectly normal to acquire nationality at birth under the *ius soli* principle, but the Mexican and Liechtenstein laws on naturalisation were regarded as suspect by the relevant courts because they were abnormal.

Claims may also be made on behalf of companies possessing the nationality of the claimant state. For these purposes, a company is regarded as having the nationality of 'the state under the laws of which it is incorporated and in whose territory it has its registered office'. Even if the company operates in a foreign country and is controlled by foreign shareholders, the state whose nationality the company possesses still has a right to make claims on its behalf.[1]

As a rule, a state is not allowed to make claims on behalf of its nationals who have suffered losses as a result of injuries inflicted on foreign companies in which they own shares. The decision of the International Court of Justice in the *Barcelona Traction* case recognised one exception to this rule – when the company has gone into liquidation, the national state of the shareholders may make a claim in respect of the losses suffered by them as a result of injuries inflicted on the company.[2] In fact, the *Barcelona Traction* case concerned injuries allegedly inflicted by Spain on a Canadian company allegedly controlled by Belgian shareholders; where the injury is inflicted by the state whose nationality the company possesses, it may be that the national state of the shareholders is in a more favourable position as regards making claims.[3] But even in these circumstances it is probably necessary to prove either that the company has gone into liquidation or that the injury in question has deprived it of so many of its assets that it can no longer operate effectively.[4]

[1] *Barcelona Traction* case, *International Court of Justice Reports*, 1970, pp. 3, 42. The Court thus distinguished the *Nottebohm* case (see above, p. 98). If there is no 'genuine link' between the company and the state whose nationality the company possesses, it may be that the national state would have no right to make claims on the company's behalf. What the Court was really saying in the *Barcelona Traction* case was that the mere fact that a company operated abroad and was controlled by foreign shareholders did not, *by itself*, prevent the existence of a genuine link between the company and the state whose nationality it possessed.

[2] ibid., pp. 3, 31–50. In this case the claim failed because the company had not gone into liquidation. See the comments by F. A. Mann in the *American Journal of International Law*, vol. 67, 1973, p. 259.

[3] The International Court of Justice left this point open in the *Barcelona Traction* case (op. cit., p. 48), and the *obiter dicta* of individual judges reached conflicting conclusions (ibid., pp. 72–5, 191–2, 240–1, 257).

[4] See Mervyn Jones, 'Claims on behalf of nationals who are shareholders in foreign companies', *British Year Book of International Law*, vol. 26, 1949, p. 225.

Exhaustion of local remedies

An injured individual (or company) must exhaust remedies in the courts of the defendant state before an international claim can be brought on his behalf. Many reasons have been suggested for this rule; the best is probably that it prevents friendly relations between states being threatened by a vast number of trivial disputes – it is a serious thing to accuse a state of breaking international law. However, when the injury is inflicted directly on a state (for example, when its warships or its diplomats are attacked), there is probably no need to exhaust local remedies; the damage to friendly relations has already been done, and it is beneath the dignity of a state to be required to sue in the courts of another state.

Of course, local remedies do not need to be exhausted when it is clear in advance that the local courts will not provide redress for the injured individual (for example, *Brown's* claim (1923), *UNRIAA* VI 120). But, apart from cases where local remedies are obviously futile, the rule is applied very strictly. For instance, in the *Ambatielos* case (*International Law Reports*, vol. 23, 1956, p. 306), a Greek shipowner, Ambatielos, contracted to buy some ships from the British government and later accused the British government of breaking the contract. In the litigation which followed in the English High Court, Ambatielos failed to call an important witness and lost; his appeal was dismissed by the Court of Appeal. When Greece subsequently made a claim on his behalf, the arbitrators held that Ambatielos had failed to exhaust local remedies because he had failed to call a vital witness and because he had failed to appeal from the Court of Appeal to the House of Lords. Similar conclusions may be drawn from the *Interhandel* case (*ICJ Reports*, 1959, pp. 6, 26–9), where a Swiss company had its assets in the United States seized during the Second World War, on the grounds of its connection with the German company I. G. Farben. After nine years of unsuccessful litigation in American courts, the Swiss company was told by the State Department that its case in the American courts was hopeless. Switzerland started proceedings against the USA in the International Court of Justice; but, while the case was pending before the ICJ, the United States Supreme Court ordered a new trial of the Swiss company's action against the United States authorities. The International Court dismissed the Swiss government's claim on the grounds that local remedies had not been exhausted. It is sometimes said that local remedies need not be exhausted when they are excessively slow; one wonders what, if anything, the words 'excessively slow' mean after the *Interhandel* case.

Waiver

If a state has waived its claim, it cannot change its mind and put the claim forward again. The claim belongs to the state, not to the injured individual; therefore waiver by the individual does not prevent the state pursuing the claim (*Barcelona Traction* case, *ICJ Reports*, 1964, pp. 6, 22–3).

At one time contracts between Latin American states and foreigners frequently contained a 'Calvo clause' (named after the Argentinian lawyer and statesman who invented it), in which the foreigner agreed in advance not to seek the diplomatic protection of his national state. International tribunals generally disregarded such clauses, on the grounds that the right of diplomatic protection was a right which belonged to the state, not to the individual, and that the state was not bound by the individual's renunciation of rights which did not belong to him. For once, the individual's lack of rights works to his advantage.

Unreasonable delay

A claim will fail if it is presented after an unreasonable delay by the claimant state (*Gentini's claim* (1903), *UNRIAA* X 552–5).

Improper behaviour by the injured alien

It is sometimes said that a state cannot make a claim on behalf of an injured national if he suffered injury as a result of engaging in improper activities – or, as the graphic phrase puts it, if his hands are not clean. This is probably true, but only if the injury suffered by the national is roughly proportionate to the impropriety of his activities (as in the *I'm Alone* case, above, p. 87, n. 2); a state cannot, for instance, be allowed to put a foreign national to death for committing a parking offence.

Suggestions for Further Reading

I. Brownlie, *Principles of Public International Law*, 3rd ed., 1979, chs 20, 21 and 23 (especially ch. 23).

D. J. Harris, *Cases and Materials on International Law*, 3rd ed., 1983, ch. 8.

R. B. Lillich, 'Duties of states regarding the civil rights of aliens', *Recueil des cours de l'Académie de droit international de La Haye*, vol. 161, 1978, p. 329.

Chapter 8

Jurisdiction

'Jurisdiction' is a word which must be used with extreme caution. It has an impressively technical sound, and yet many people think that they have a vague idea of what it means; there is therefore a temptation to use the word without stopping to ask what it means. In fact, it can have a large number of different meanings. Sometimes it simply means territory; for instance, in cases concerning the custody of children, English courts may tell a party not to take the child 'out of the jurisdiction of the court', which means 'out of England'. The phrase 'domestic jurisdiction', as used in the United Nations Charter, has a specialised meaning (see below, pp. 168–70). But most often 'jurisdiction' refers to powers exercised by a state over persons, property, or events. But, here again, the word is ambiguous, for the powers under consideration may be powers to legislate in respect of the persons, property, or events in question, powers of physical interference exercised by the executive (arrest of persons, seizure of property, and so on), or powers of a state's courts to hear cases concerning the persons, property, or events in question. It is essential to distinguish between these three groups of powers, particularly between the second and third groups. For instance, if a man commits a murder in England and escapes to France, the English courts have jurisdiction to try him, but the English police cannot enter French territory and arrest him there; they must ask the French authorities to arrest him and to surrender him for trial in England (see above, p. 87, n. 1). This distinction between the right to arrest and the right to try is fairly obvious in the case of crimes committed on land, but can be easily overlooked in the case of crimes committed on ships (see below, pp. 264 and 273–8).

The remainder of this chapter is concerned with the limitations imposed by international law on the jurisdiction of municipal *courts*. It is comparatively rare for international law to *require* a municipal court to hear a case; most of the relevant rules of international law consist of *prohibitions*. If a municipal court exercises jurisdiction in violation of one of these prohibitions, the national state of the injured individual adversely affected by the decision may make an international claim, and it is no excuse for the defendant state to plead that the exercise of jurisdiction was lawful under municipal law, or that the trial was fair and just. But in most cases international law neither forbids nor requires municipal courts to hear cases; it makes an *offer* of jurisdiction, so to speak, which municipal courts need not accept if they do not want to. The jurisdiction of municipal courts is determined mainly by municipal law, and international law confines itself to placing a few limits on the discretion of states.

Apart from cases of sovereign and diplomatic immunity, and so on, which will be dealt with in the next chapter, international law does not seem to impose any restrictions on the jurisdiction of courts in civil cases;[1] it restricts jurisdiction only in criminal cases.

As far as criminal trials are concerned, the bases of jurisdiction most frequently invoked by states are as follows (some of them are more widely accepted than others):

(1) *Territorial principle.* Every state claims jurisdiction over crimes committed in its own territory. Sometimes a criminal act may begin in one state and be completed in another; for instance, a man may shoot across a frontier and kill someone on the other side. In such circumstances both states have jurisdiction; the state where the act began has jurisdiction under the subjective territorial principle, and the state where the act is completed has jurisdiction under the objective territorial principle.[2]

(2) *Nationality principle.* A state may prosecute its nationals for crimes committed anywhere in the world. This rule is universally accepted, and continental countries make extensive use of it. English courts only claim jurisdiction on this ground over a few crimes, such as treason, murder and bigamy, but the United Kingdom does not challenge the extensive use of this principle by other countries.[3]

(3) *Protective principle.* This allows a state to punish acts prejudicial to its security, even when they are committed by foreigners abroad, for example, plots to overthrow its government, spying, forging its currency and plots to break its immigration regulations. Most countries use this principle to some extent, and it therefore seems to be valid, although there is a danger that some states might try to interpret their 'security' too broadly. For instance, if a newspaper published in state A criticises state B, it would be unreason-

---

[1] See Akehurst, 'Jurisdiction in international law', *British Year Book of International Law*, vol. 46, 1972–3, pp. 145, 170–7.

[2] For examples, see the *Lotus* case (1927), Permanent Court of International Justice, series A, no. 10 (above, p. 30, and below, pp. 277–8); Akehurst, loc. cit. (previous note), pp. 152–6.

[3] Some countries claim jurisdiction on the basis of some personal link other than nationality (for example, long residence by the accused in the state exercising jurisdiction), and other states have not protested against such jurisdiction.

able to suggest that state B has jurisdiction to try the editor for sedition.

(4) *Universality principle*. Some states claim jurisdiction over *all* crimes, including all crimes (or at least serious crimes) committed by foreigners abroad (universality principle).[1] English-speaking countries consider that such jurisdiction is normally forbidden by international law. The Permanent Court of International Justice refrained from discussing the validity of such jurisdiction in the *Lotus* case (see above, pp. 30 and 103, n. 2), but individual judges declared that it was normally contrary to international law. The universality principle can obviously lead to unjust results when an individual is punished for doing an act which was lawful under the law of the place where it was done. The universality principle is less objectionable when it is applied to acts which are regarded as crimes in all countries; indeed, even English-speaking countries, which consider that the universality principle is normally contrary to international law, accept that international law allows states to exercise a universal jurisdiction over certain acts which threaten the international community as a whole and which are criminal in all countries, such as war crimes (see below, p. 237), piracy (see below, pp. 275–6), hijacking (*British Year Book of International Law*, 1972–3, pp. 161–2) and various forms of international terrorism (Stanbrook and Stanbrook, *The Law and Practice of Extradition*, 1980, pp. 98–103; see also the International Convention against the Taking of Hostages, 1979, Article 8 (text in *American Journal of International Law*, 1980, p. 277)).

The existence of different grounds of jurisdiction means that several states may have concurrent jurisdiction, that is, the criminal may be tried and punished by several different countries. A conviction or acquittal in a foreign country is treated as a bar to a subsequent prosecution in some countries, but not in all. International law is silent on this point, and the result may be great hardship.

Extradition

A criminal may take refuge in a state which has no jurisdiction to try him, or in a state which is unable or unwilling to try him

---

[1] Some of these states restrict their jurisdiction to cases where the victim of the crime was a national of the state claiming jurisdiction. This is known as the *passive personality principle*. On the universality and passive personality principles generally, see Akehurst, 'Jurisdiction in international law', *British Year Book of International Law*, vol. 46, 1972–3, pp. 145, 160–6.

because all the evidence and witnesses are abroad. To meet this problem, international law has evolved the practice of extradition; individuals are extradited (that is, handed over) by one state to another state, in order that they may be tried in the latter state for offences against its laws. Extradition also includes the surrender of convicted criminals who have escaped before completing their punishment.

Despite occasional statements to the contrary, there is no duty to extradite in the absence of a treaty.[1] On the other hand, there is no rule of international law which prevents states from extraditing in the absence of a treaty.

Extradition treaties are usually bilateral and usually impose the same obligations on both parties. Certain provisions are common to most extradition treaties:

(1) *Definition of extraditable offences.* Extradition is usually confined to serious crimes, which must also be crimes under the laws of both of the states concerned (double criminality principle). This object can be met in one of two ways. First, the treaty may apply to all crimes which are punishable in both countries by so many months or years of imprisonment. Alternatively, the treaty may list the extraditable offences by name. This second alternative, which is used in British extradition treaties, is clumsy; the list becomes out of date as new types of crime emerge (for example, narcotics offences and hijacking of aircraft).

Extradition treaties often provide that the crime must have been committed on the territory of the state requesting extradition. Commission of part of the crime on the requesting state's territory is usually interpreted to be sufficient.[2]

(2) *Definition of extraditable persons.* Extradition treaties may apply to all persons accused or convicted of an extraditable crime; alternatively, they may provide that a state shall not (or need not) extradite its own nationals. The exclusion of nationals is particularly common in treaties concluded by continental countries, most of which claim a very extensive jurisdiction over crimes committed

---

[1] It is sometimes said that asylum ends where extradition begins, that is, a state has a right to grant asylum (that is, refuge) to fugitive criminals unless it has bound itself by treaty to extradite them. The right of asylum means the right of a *state* to *grant* asylum; an *individual* has no right to *demand* asylum. See Weis, 'The Draft UN Convention on Territorial Asylum', *British Year Book of International Law*, vol. 50, 1979, p. 151. For the special problems of asylum in embassies and warships, see D. P. O'Connell, *International Law*, 2nd ed., 1970, Vol. 2, pp. 734–40.

[2] In order to give maximum effect to extradition treaties, English courts have interpreted territory to include ships (*R.* v. *Governor of Brixton Prison, ex p. Minervini*, [1959] 1 Q.B. 155) and territory which the British government recognises to be under a state's *de facto* control but not under its *de jure* sovereignty (*Schtraks* v. *Government of Israel*, [1964] A.C. 556).

by their nationals abroad; but such provisions are also frequently inspired by an often unjustified suspicion of foreign courts. Unfortunately, such provisions often result in criminals escaping punishment, because experience indicates that states show little zeal in prosecuting their own nationals for crimes committed abroad; the difficulties of collecting evidence are too great, and the crime does not affect the interests of the national state. There is much to be said for following the practice of extradition treaties between Latin American states, which provide that states *must* prosecute their own nationals if they refuse to extradite them.

(3) *Offences of a political, military, or religious character are usually excluded.* The definition of political offences has given rise to difficulties of interpretation, which different countries have tried to solve in different ways.[1] In recent years there has been a tendency to exclude acts of terrorism from the category of political offences. This, subject to certain loop-holes, is the approach adopted by the European Convention on the Suppression of Terrorism (text in *International Legal Materials*, 1976, p. 1272; see also ibid., 1980, p. 325); the Suppression of Terrorism Act 1978 (ibid., 1978, p. 1130) gives effect to the Convention in English law.

(4) *Specialty principle.* This means that an extradited person cannot be tried for a crime other than that for which he was extradited, until he has been given a chance to leave the country to which he was extradited.

(5) Prima facie *evidence of guilt.* Extradition treaties made by English-speaking countries usually provide that the courts of the extraditing state must satisfy themselves that there is *prima facie* evidence of guilt before ordering extradition for purposes of trial. Such provisions are unknown in treaties between continental countries, and their insertion in treaties between English-speaking and continental countries has led to difficulties, because continental courts, being unfamiliar with such provisions, have sometimes misinterpreted them to mean that the extraditing state should actually try the case.

Extradition in English law

In English law extradition requires authorisation by an Act of Parliament, otherwise it would constitute a serious offence under the Habeas Corpus Amendment Act 1679. The most important Act is the Extradition Act 1870 which empowers the Crown to

---

[1] I. A. Shearer, *Extradition in International Law*, 1971, ch. 7. See also *R. v. Governor of Pentonville Prison, ex p. Cheng*, [1973] A.C. 931; *R. v. Governor of Winson Green Prison, ex p. Littlejohn*, [1975] 3 All E.R. 208; *R.v. Governor of Pentonville Prison, ex p. Budlong*, [1980] 1 All E.R. 701, 712–14; I. Stanbrook and C. Stanbrook, *The Law and Practice of Extradition*, 1980, pp. 105–13.

make Orders in Council to give effect to extradition treaties.

There are separate Acts dealing with extradition to or from Commonwealth countries (Fugitive Offenders Act 1967) and Ireland (Backing of Warrants (Republic of Ireland) Act 1965). Such extradition is not covered by treaties, but only by parallel municipal legislation in the United Kingdom and the other countries concerned; this is a relic of the days when the Dominions had no treaty-making power.

Conclusion

Extradition is of declining importance throughout the world. Many extradition treaties were terminated by the outbreak of the First or Second World Wars and have not been renewed subsequently; it is uncertain whether extradition treaties made by colonial powers remain binding on their former colonies; surviving extradition treaties are often out of date (for example, they contain a list of crimes which does not include 'new' offences like narcotics offences); and few new extradition treaties have been made in recent years. At the beginning of this century the United Kingdom extradited dozens of people every year under the Extradition Act 1870; now the United Kingdom extradites only two or three people a year under the 1870 Act. (On the other hand, about twenty-eight people are surrendered every year to the Republic of Ireland under the Backing of Warrants (Republic of Ireland) Act 1965. This demonstrates another feature of extradition – it is used principally between countries with a common land boundary. France extradites about 150 people a year, 90 per cent of them to adjacent countries.)

In practice, modern statutory powers to deport aliens are often used as a means of disguised extradition; in this way the safeguards created for the individual in legislation and treaties relating to extradition are evaded (for example, *Soblen's* case, [1963] 2 Q.B. 243). It is probably this use of deportation which explains why there are now fewer extradition treaties and fewer extradition cases than there used to be; deportation, to a considerable extent, is used as a substitute for extradition.

Suggestions for Further Reading

Harvard Research Draft Convention on Jurisdiction with Respect to Crime, *American Journal of International Law*, vol. 29, 1935, supplement, p. 435.

F. A. Mann, 'The doctrine of jurisdiction in international law', *Recueil des cours de l'Académie de droit international de La Haye*, vol. 111, 1964, p. 9, especially pp. 82–95.

M. B. Akehurst, 'Jurisdiction in international law', *British Year Book of International Law*, vol. 46, 1972–3, p. 145, especially pp. 152–69.

D. W. Bowett, 'Jurisdiction: Changing Patterns of Authority over Activities and Resources', *British Year Book of International Law*, vol. 53, 1982, p. 1.

I. A. Shearer, *Extradition in International Law*, 1971.

I. Stanbrook and C. Stanbrook, *The Law and Practice of Extradition*, 1980.

Chapter 9

Immunity from Jurisdiction

There are certain categories of persons and bodies which, by international law, are immune from the jurisdiction of municipal courts. The two principal categories are foreign states (sovereign immunity) and their diplomatic agents (diplomatic immunity); but other categories are of growing importance and need to be noted.

Sovereign Immunity

Since states are independent and equal, no state may exercise jurisdiction over another state without its consent; in particular, the courts of one state may not assume jurisdiction over another state. Historically, the ruler was equated with the state, and to this day the head of a foreign state possesses complete immunity, even for acts done by him in a private capacity.[1]

The question of what constitutes a state for the purposes of this rule is a difficult one. If the British government certifies that it recognises a particular entity as a sovereign state, then English courts will grant immunity to that entity (State Immunity Act 1978, s. 21; see also above, pp. 47 and 66). But the difficulties do not stop there. For instance, the fact that Ruritania is recognised as a sovereign state does not help us to decide whether the political subdivisions of Ruritania, such as provinces and town councils, form part of the state for the purposes of entitlement to sovereign immunity; the cases on this point conflict (Brownlie, *Principles of Public International Law*, 3rd ed., 1979, pp. 341-2; State Immunity Act 1978, s. 14). Again, should nationalised industries and similar bodies in Ruritania be treated as part of the state for the purposes of entitlement to sovereign immunity? Here, too, the cases conflict (Brownlie, op. cit., pp. 342-3; State Immunity Act 1978, s. 14).

[1] *Mighell* v. *Sultan of Johore*, [1894] 1 Q.B. 149 (breach of promise of marriage). If the sultan had abdicated or had been deposed, he could probably have been sued for private (that is, non-official) acts done by him during his reign; see the analogous case of former diplomats, below, p. 115. English law on the legal position of foreign heads of state is now contained in the State Immunity Act 1978, sections 14(1)(*a*) and 20 (text in *International Legal Materials*, 1978, p. 1123).

Nationalised industries raise a further problem: does immunity apply to the commercial activities of states? During the nineteenth century states rarely engaged in trading activities, and it was assumed that states were always immune from the jurisdiction of foreign courts. During the present century, when state trading has become more common, an increasing number of states have abandoned the old rule of absolute immunity, in favour of a rule of qualified immunity, as it is called; they grant immunity only in respect of governmental acts (acts *iure imperii*), not in respect of commercial acts (acts *iure gestionis*). The rule of qualified immunity is accepted by the majority of states in Western Europe and (since 1952) by the USA, while the communist countries and some countries in the British Commonwealth follow the old rule of absolute immunity. For many years English courts followed the old rule of absolute immunity, out of deference to earlier English cases applying the old rule; in the mid-1970s they began moving towards the rule of qualified immunity, but the resulting conflict between the old cases and the new cases made English law very uncertain. In 1978 the British Parliament intervened and passed the State Immunity Act (text in *International Legal Materials*, 1978, p. 1123), section 3 of which provides that foreign states do not enjoy immunity in respect of their commercial transactions. (The Act also provides for various other exceptions to sovereign immunity; see sections 3–11.)

It is sometimes suggested that the rule of qualified immunity somehow implies that it is improper for states to engage in commercial activities. This is not so. From the policy point of view, the distinction between governmental and commercial activities is not based on the propriety of state acts, but on the appropriateness of municipal courts for deciding disputes arising out of those acts. Acts which, by their nature, can only be performed by states, such as expropriating property or testing nuclear weapons, are likely to involve delicate issues of international politics, which make them unsuitable for adjudication by municipal courts. On the other hand, acts which can be performed equally well by states or by private individuals, such as making contracts for the purchase of wheat, are clearly suitable for adjudication by municipal courts, and it would cause unjustified hardship for the other contracting party if municipal courts refused to hear such cases.

A more serious objection to the qualified immunity rule is that the distinction between governmental and commercial acts is not always precise. Some states base the distinction on the nature of the act,[1] others base it on the purpose of the act; for instance, the

[1] This is the approach adopted in the USA (Foreign Sovereign Immunities Act 1976, s. 1603(*d*)) and in the UK (*Trendtex Trading Corporation* v. *Central Bank of Nigeria*, [1977] Q.B. 529, 558, 579; *I Congreso del Partido*, [1981] 3 W.L.R. 328, 335, 337, 345, 349, 350, 351; State Immunity Act 1978, s. 3(3)).

purchase of boots for the army would be regarded as a commercial act under the first test and as a governmental act under the second test. But such borderline cases are exceptional. In any case, under the absolute immunity rule, the question whether nationalised industries form part of the state gives rise to just as many borderline cases, most of which would be avoided if the qualified immunity rule were applied, because the vast majority of the acts of nationalised industries would then be regarded as commercial and not covered by immunity, thus making it unnecessary to decide whether the nationalised industries form part of the state.

So far we have only been considering cases in which legal proceedings are brought against the foreign state. But immunity also applies to proceedings involving property in which the foreign state has an interest, even though the foreign state may not necessarily be a party to the proceedings.[1] For instance, if A sues B, disputing B's title to property which a foreign state has hired from B, the foreign state may intervene to have the proceedings stopped, because judgment in A's favour would deprive the foreign state of its interest in the property. This rule applies if the foreign state claims to own the property,[2] or if it claims some right less than ownership, such as possession[3] or the right to immediate possession.[4]

Clearly a court cannot allow a foreign state to stop proceedings between two private individuals by simply asserting an interest in property, unsupported by evidence. On the other hand, to require the foreign state to prove its title would make nonsense of the idea of immunity, because it would mean forcing the state to submit to the court's jurisdiction on the merits of the case. English courts take the middle course of requiring the foreign state to prove that its alleged interest in the property has a *prima facie* validity; the foreign state must 'produce evidence to satisfy the court that its claim is not merely illusory nor founded on a title manifestly defective'.[5]

Diplomatic Immunity

The rules of diplomatic immunity sometimes arouse indignation from the man in the street, but are almost always observed by

---

[1] Under the qualified immunity rule, no immunity applies if the foreign state is using the property for commercial purposes. For other exceptions to the general principle stated in the main text, see Ian Brownlie, *Principles of Public International Law*, 3rd ed., 1979, pp. 340–1; State Immunity Act 1978, sections 6 and 7.

[2] *The Parlement Belge* (1880), 5 P.D. 197.

[3] *The Cristina*, [1938] A.C. 485; *The Arantzazu Mendi*, [1939] A.C. 256.

[4] *U.S.A. and France* v. *Dollfus Mieg et Compagnie*, [1952] A.C. 582.

[5] *Juan Ysmael & Co.* v. *Republic of Indonesia*, [1955] A.C. 72.

states, because states have a common interest in preserving the rules. A state may be under pressure from its internal public opinion to limit the immunity of foreign diplomats, but it usually resists the pressure, because otherwise it would create a precedent which would be used against its own diplomats in foreign countries. All states are both 'sending states' (that is, states which send diplomatic missions to foreign countries) and 'receiving states', and consequently the rules on diplomatic immunity work much more smoothly than the rules on expropriation, for instance, which are sometimes regarded as favouring the rich states at the expense of the poor states. The rules of diplomatic immunity are 'essential for the maintenance of relations between states and [are] accepted throughout the world by nations of all creeds, cultures and political complexions' (*USA* v. *Iran, ICJ Reports*, 1980, pp. 3, 24). Major breaches of these rules, such as Iran's behaviour towards the United States diplomats who were held as hostages in 1979–81, are extremely rare (but receive disproportionate publicity because of their rarity).

Most of the modern law on diplomatic immunity is contained in the Vienna Convention on Diplomatic Relations 1961 (text in Ian Brownlie, *Basic Documents in International Law*, 3rd ed., 1983, p. 212). In 1981 137 states (including the USA, USSR, UK and China) were parties to the Convention. Most of the provisions of the Convention seek to codify customary law, and can therefore be used as evidence of customary law even against states which are not parties to the Convention.

The Diplomatic Privileges Act 1964 gives effect to the Convention in English law. Section 4 of the Act provides that a Foreign Office certificate shall be conclusive evidence that an individual is a diplomat (cf. above, p. 47).

Diplomatic relations are established by mutual consent between the two states concerned (Article 2 of the Vienna Convention). However, they may be broken off unilaterally (often as a mark of disapproval of an illegal or unfriendly act by the other state); when state A breaks off diplomatic relations with state B, it not only withdraws its own diplomatic mission from state B, but also requires state B to withdraw its mission from state A. The receiving state's consent is necessary for the selection of the head of mission (who nowadays usually has the title of ambassador) but not for the selection of his subordinates (although there are exceptions). The receiving state may at any time declare a diplomat *persona non grata* or not acceptable, which forces the sending state to withdraw him; this is a step which can be employed as a sanction if immunities are abused, although the receiving state has a complete discretion and can take this step in other circumstances also. Article 11 of the Vienna Convention provides that 'the receiving state may require that the size of a mission be kept within limits considered by it to be reasonable and normal' – a desirable innovation.

Article 3(1) of the Convention states:

The functions of a diplomatic mission consist *inter alia* in:
(*a*) representing the sending state in the receiving state;
(*b*) protecting in the receiving state the interests of the sending state and of its nationals, within the limits permitted by international law;
(*c*) negotiating with the government of the receiving state;
(*d*) ascertaining by all lawful means conditions and developments in the receiving state, and reporting thereon to the government of the sending state;
(*e*) promoting friendly relations between the sending state and the receiving state, and developing their economic, cultural and scientific relations.

In modern times, promotion of exports has become a major function of diplomatic missions. So, too, have public relations (less euphemistically known as propaganda) – a practice which occasionally degenerates into interference in the internal affairs of the receiving state (such interference is forbidden by Article 41(1) of the Convention).

Throughout history diplomats and other envoys have needed privileges and immunities for the effective performance of their functions in the receiving state. The preamble to the Vienna Convention recites that 'the purpose of such privileges and immunities is not to benefit individuals but to ensure the efficient performance of the functions of diplomatic missions *as representing states*'. There is thus a double basis for diplomatic immunities; they are needed for the efficient performance of diplomatic functions, and they are also given because diplomats are representatives of states. The 'representative basis', although accepted as the basis of diplomatic immunities in previous centuries, is nowadays rather doubtful; it would suggest that diplomats, like states, are not immune from suit in respect of the commercial activities of states, whereas in fact diplomats *are* immune from suit in respect of such activities. The modern view is to treat immunities as having a 'functional basis', that is, as being necessary 'to ensure the efficient performance of the functions of diplomatic missions'.

Immunity from the jurisdiction of courts
Article 31(1) of the Vienna Convention provides:

A diplomatic agent shall enjoy immunity from the criminal jurisdiction of the receiving state. He shall also enjoy immunity from its civil and administrative jurisdiction, except in the case of:

(a)   a real action relating to private immovable property situated in the territory of the receiving state, unless he holds it on behalf of the sending state for the purposes of the mission;

(b)   an action relating to succession in which the diplomatic agent is involved . . . as a private person . . .;

(c)   an action relating to any professional or commercial activity exercised by the diplomatic agent in the receiving state outside his official functions.

(These exceptions are new, as far as English law is concerned, although they had been recognised previously in some other countries.) The same immunity is enjoyed by a diplomat's family, if they are not nationals of the receiving state.

The existence of immunity does not mean that people injured by diplomats are wholly without a remedy. A diplomat's hopes of promotion are usually dependent on scrupulous good behaviour, and this will induce him not to abuse his immunity; he will probably be willing to settle private claims against him before they come to the attention of his superiors. Alternatively, the injured individual or the government of the receiving state can ask the ambassador to waive his subordinate's immunity, which often happens. Most claims arise out of road accidents, and in England, at least, diplomats are expected to insure their vehicles and the insurance companies do not try to hide behind their clients' immunity (*British Practice in International Law*, 1964, p. 74). In extreme cases of abuse a diplomat can be declared *persona non grata* or not acceptable (see above, p. 112).

One of the most striking features of the Vienna Convention is that it does not grant full immunity to *all* staff of a diplomatic mission. In addition to diplomatic agents, the Convention speaks of administrative and technical staff (for example, clerical assistants, archivists and wireless technicians) and of service staff (for example, drivers, receptionists, and so on). These two categories of subordinate staff have complete immunity from criminal jurisdiction, but their immunity from civil and administrative jurisdiction is limited to their official acts.[1] The limitation is an innovation as far as English law is concerned, although it was not unknown in some other countries. It demonstrates the functional character of immunities; since the functions of subordinate staff are less important than those of diplomats, there is less need for the interests of private litigants in the receiving state to be sacrificed in order to

----

[1] The same is true of diplomatic agents who are nationals or permanent residents of the receiving state (and see Article 38(2) concerning other members of the staff who are nationals or permanent residents of the receiving state).

enable the subordinate staff of the diplomatic mission to carry out their duties efficiently.

When an individual ceases to be a member of the staff of a diplomatic mission, his immunity continues for a reasonable time thereafter, in order to give him time to leave the country. After that, he may be sued for private acts done during his period of office, but not for official acts (Article 39(2) of the Vienna Convention).

Other privileges and immunities

In addition to immunity from the jurisdiction of courts, diplomats possess other privileges and immunities[1] (the meanings of the words 'privilege' and 'immunity' overlap so much that it is impracticable to distinguish between them).

Thus, the premises of a diplomatic mission and the private residence of a diplomat are inviolable; agents of the receiving state are not allowed to enter such places without the permission of the sending state, and must take appropriate steps to protect them from harm (see above, pp. 88-9). On the other hand, diplomatic premises are not extraterritorial; acts occurring there are regarded as taking place on the territory of the receiving state, not on that of the sending state, and criminals who take refuge there must be handed over to the police of the receiving state (see above, p. 105, n. 1). The sending state is not allowed to imprison people on diplomatic premises.

Archives, documents and other property belonging to a diplomatic mission or diplomat are inviolable. The mission must have unimpeded communication with the sending state by all appropriate means, including diplomatic couriers and messages in code or cipher (but it cannot use a wireless transmitter without the receiving state's consent). The mission's official correspondence is inviolable, and the diplomatic bag must not be opened or detained (the diplomatic bag ought to contain only diplomatic documents or articles intended for official use). 'Bugging' of diplomatic premises, which is not mentioned in the Vienna Convention, is contrary to the spirit of the Convention, but is probably too widespread to be regarded as illegal.

The premises of the mission are exempt from all taxes, except those which represent payment for specific services rendered (for example, water rates) (Article 23). Diplomats are also exempt from all taxes, with certain exceptions (Article 34). The receiving state must allow the importation, free of customs duties, of articles for

---

[1] In the interests of simplicity, discussion will be confined to diplomatic agents *stricto sensu* who are not nationals or permanent residents of the receiving state. For the more limited immunities of other persons attached to a diplomatic mission, see Articles 37 and 38 of the Vienna Convention.

the official use of the mission and of articles for the personal use of a diplomat or his family (Article 36); before 1961 this rule was generally observed, but was regarded as a rule of comity, not of law. If exemptions from taxes did not exist, sending states would in effect be contributing to the budgets of the receiving states, which would give an unfair advantage to those states which had the highest rates of tax.

Article 29 of the Vienna Convention provides that diplomats shall not be liable to any form of arrest or detention, and that appropriate steps must be taken to protect them from attack. Terrorists often attack diplomats, but receiving states almost always do their best to protect diplomats in such circumstances. The approval given by Iran to the 'militants' who seized United States diplomats in Iran in November 1979 was correctly described by the International Court of Justice as 'unique' (*USA* v. *Iran, ICJ Reports*, 1980, pp. 3, 42), and was condemned unanimously by the Court and the Security Council (ibid., pp. 29–45, and *UN Chronicle*, 1980, no. 1, p. 13).

Iran tried to excuse its behaviour by claiming that the USA and its diplomats had acted unlawfully towards Iran (for example, by intervening in Iran's internal affairs), but the Court held that these charges, even if they had been proved, would not have justified Iran's violation of diplomatic immunity; the obligation to respect the rules of diplomatic immunity is an absolute obligation which must be obeyed in all circumstances (*ICJ Reports*, 1980, pp. 38–41).

Consular Immunity

Consuls, like diplomats, represent their state in another state, but, unlike diplomats, they are not concerned with political relations between the two states. They perform a wide variety of non-political functions – issuing passports and visas, looking after the shipping and commercial interests of their states, and so on. Consulates often exist in provincial towns as well as in capital cities.

In 1963 the United Nations convened a conference at Vienna, which drew up the Vienna Convention on Consular Relations; in 1981 ninety-eight states (including the USA, China and the UK) were parties to the Convention. According to the International Court of Justice, the 1963 Convention codified the law on consular relations (*USA* v. *Iran, ICJ Reports*, 1980, pp. 3, 24); but some writers have argued that the immunities conferred on consuls by the Convention are wider than the immunities enjoyed by consuls under customary law. However, one may get a rather distorted view by looking at this subject from a British point of view, because, before the 1960s, the United Kingdom was exceptionally ungenerous as regards consular immunity. Moreover, even when the Convention does not reflect the customary law relating to consuls, it often does reflect postwar bilateral consular conventions. This is particularly true of Article 36, which gives consuls a right to communicate with nationals of the sending state in the territory of the receiving state, especially when those nationals are in prison before trial or after conviction in a criminal case.

To a large extent the Convention assimilates the status of consuls to that of diplomats, but this is not surprising, because it is becoming increasingly common nowadays for a state to amalgamate its diplomatic and consular services. People who act simultaneously as diplomats and as consuls have diplomatic immunity. Consuls who do not act as diplomats have many of the same privileges and immunities as diplomats, according to the Convention, but they are immune from the civil or criminal jurisdiction of the receiving state's courts only in respect of official acts. In addition, they may import articles for their personal use, free of duty, only at the time of their first appointment.

The Act of State Doctrine

The rule that former diplomats cannot be sued for acts performed by them in the exercise of their official functions (see above, p. 115) appears to reflect a much wider principle: all servants or agents (or former servants or agents) of a foreign state are immune from legal proceedings in respect of acts done by them on behalf of the foreign state. This act of state doctrine, as it is called, is a corollary of sovereign immunity; such proceedings indirectly implead the state, because the state would probably feel in honour bound to stand behind the individual concerned and to indemnify him for any damages which he had to pay. Also, such proceedings would be likely to involve delicate issues of international politics, which would make them unsuitable for adjudication by municipal courts. However, there are various exceptions to the immunity conferred by the act of state doctrine (Akehurst, *British Year Book of International Law*, vol. 46, 1972-3, pp. 145, 240-4); for instance, it cannot be pleaded as a defence to charges of war crimes, crimes against peace, or crimes against humanity (see below, pp. 237-9).

Immunities of International Organisations

It is uncertain to what extent international organisations enjoy immunities under customary law; in practice the matter is usually regulated by treaties, such as the General Convention on the Privileges and Immunities of the UN 1946. It may be instructive to summarise the provisions of the General Convention, as an example of the immunities enjoyed by international organisations.

The UN has complete immunity from all legal process (section 2); otherwise a combination of eccentric litigants and biased courts could interfere with the performance of its functions. Its premises, assets, archives and documents are inviolable (sections 3 and 4). It is exempt from direct taxes and customs duties (s. 7), and its staff are exempt from income tax on their salaries (s. 18); otherwise income tax would be levied on staff members' salaries by the states where those staff members worked, and states contributing to the UN's budget would in effect be making indirect payments to the states in which the UN had its principal offices (the USA and Switzerland). The Secretary-General and the Assistant Secretaries-General have diplomatic immunity (s. 19); the member-states were not prepared to go as far as this in the case of other staff members, who only have limited immunities, such as immunity from legal process in respect of their official acts, and exemption from military service (s. 18). The Secretary-General must waive a staff member's immunity if in his opinion immunity would impede the course of justice and can be waived without prejudice to the interests of the UN (s. 20). The UN must 'make provisions for appropriate modes of settlement of' claims against it (s. 29); it has done so by insuring itself against tortious liability, entering into arbitration agreements, and so on.

Representatives of member-states attending UN meetings get almost the same privileges and immunities as diplomats, except that their immunity from legal process applies only to their official acts, and they are immune from customs duties only in respect of their personal baggage (sections 11–16).

Waiver of Immunity

Immunity from the jurisdiction of courts does not mean that the holder of the immunity is above municipal law. The obligations of municipal law remain binding on him, but are unenforceable.[1]

---

[1] This is true as regards immunity from the jurisdiction of courts. However, some of the other immunities discussed in the present chapter (for example, immunities from tax) are immunities from obligations, not merely immunities from enforcement.

Consequently, both sovereign and diplomatic immunity can be waived;[1] the effect is to change an unenforceable obligation into an enforceable one. The immunity is conferred in the interests of the state, and can be waived only by the state. A state may waive the immunity of one of its diplomats against the diplomat's wishes (*R.* v. *Kent*, [1941] 1 K.B. 454). Conversely, waiver by a diplomat is ineffective unless authorised by his superiors (*R.* v. *Madan*, [1961] 2 Q.B. 1; see also State Immunity Act 1978, s. 2(7)).

Immunity can be waived either 'in the face of the court' (that is, after proceedings have been started), or by an agreement made before proceedings are started (State Immunity Act 1978, sections 2(2) and 17(2)).

Waiver 'in the face of the court' can take two forms – express (that is, expressly stating to the court that immunity is waived) or implied (that is, defending the action without challenging the jurisdiction of the court). Article 32(2) of the Vienna Convention 1961 says that waiver must always be express, but it is doubtful whether this provision reflects customary law, so it cannot necessarily be applied by analogy to sovereign immunity.

If states or diplomats appear as plaintiffs, they are deemed to waive their immunity in respect of counter-claims arising out of the same subject-matter. For instance, in the days when states enjoyed immunity in respect of their commercial activities, if a state sold goods to an individual and sued him for not paying the price, the state was deemed to have waived its immunity from a counter-claim by the individual that the goods were defective. But a claim by a state for repayment of money lent did not constitute an implied waiver of immunity from a counter-claim for slander, because the counter-claim was entirely unrelated to the original claim (*High Commissioner for India* v. *Ghosh*, [1960] 1 Q.B. 134; see also Article 32(3) of the Vienna Convention 1961, and section 2(6) of the State Immunity Act 1978).

Waiver of immunity in a court of first instance also covers appeals from the judgment of that court; if a state wins on the merits in a court of first instance, it cannot revive its immunity in order to prevent the other party appealing to a higher court (State Immunity Act 1978, s. 2(6)). But waiver of immunity from the jurisdiction of courts does not entail waiver of immunity from execution; a separate act of waiver of immunity from execution is necessary before execution can be levied against the property of a

---

[1] Discussion will be confined to sovereign and diplomatic immunity, since the rules are more clearly established with regard to these types of immunity than with regard to other types. However, the rules governing sovereign and diplomatic immunity are probably applicable by analogy to other types of immunity from the jurisdiction of courts.

foreign state or diplomat in order to satisfy an unpaid judgment debt.[1]

[1] Vienna Convention 1961, Article 32(4); State Immunity Act 1978, s. 13(3). In most cases a state which waives its immunity from jurisdiction will be prepared to carry out an adverse judgment; otherwise it would not have waived its immunity from jurisdiction.

In most countries where foreign states do not enjoy sovereign immunity in respect of their commercial activities, property which foreign states use for commercial purposes does not usually enjoy immunity from execution, and in such cases the question of waiving immunity from execution does not arise. See Sinclair, 'The law of sovereign immunity: recent developments', *Recueil des cours de l'Académie de droit international de La Haye*, vol. 167, 1980, pp. 113, 218–42 (especially p. 242), 255–7 and 263–5, and for British law see State Immunity Act 1978, s. 13(2)(*b*) and (4).

Suggestions for Further Reading

Ian Brownlie, *Principles of Public International Law*, 3rd ed., 1979, chs 15 and 16.

Sompong Sucharitkul, 'Immunities of foreign states before national authorities', *Recueil des cours de l'Académie de droit international de La Haye*, vol. 149, 1976, p. 87.

Sir Ian Sinclair, 'The law of sovereign immunity: recent developments', ibid., vol. 167, 1980, p. 113.

F. A. Mann, 'The State Immunity Act 1978', *British Year Book of International Law*, vol. 50, 1979, p. 43.

Michael Hardy, *Modern Diplomatic Law*, 1968.

Eileen Denza, *Diplomatic Law*, 1976.

Chapter 10

Treaties

States make treaties about every conceivable topic. By and large, all treaties, regardless of their subject-matter, are governed by the same rules, and the law of treaties therefore tends to have a rather abstract and technical character; it is a means to an end, not an end in itself. For the same reasons, the greater part of the law of treaties is not affected by conflicts of interests between states; every state is a party to hundreds of treaties and has an interest in ensuring that treaties work effectively, just as all states have a common interest in preserving the rules of diplomatic immunity in order to facilitate diplomatic relations.

A convenient starting-point for discussing treaties is the Vienna Convention on the Law of Treaties 1969.[1] The Vienna Convention came into force on 27 January 1980; in 1981 thirty-nine states (including the UK, but not the USA, USSR, or China) were parties to it. However, the Convention applies only to treaties made after its entry into force (Article 4). *As a Convention*, therefore, its value is rather limited. Its importance lies in the fact that most of its provisions attempt to codify the customary law relating to treaties, although there are other provisions which represent a 'progressive development' rather than a codification of the law. Unless otherwise stated, the provisions mentioned in this chapter codify the pre-existing law.

[1] Text in Ian Brownlie, *Basic Documents in International Law*, 3rd ed., 1983, p. 349. The preliminary research and drafting were carried out by the International Law Commission, whose commentary (text in *American Journal of International Law*, vol. 61, 1967, p. 285) is a useful guide to the interpretation of the Convention, and indicates the extent to which different articles of the Convention reflect the pre-existing customary law and the agreed views of states. See also I. M. Sinclair, *The Vienna Convention on the Law of Treaties*, 1973. Since 1969 many provisions of the Convention have been frequently cited in judgments and in state practice as accurate statements of the customary rules relating to treaties.

On the interpretation of treaties, which is dealt with briefly in Articles 31-3 of the Vienna Convention, see below, pp. 164-8. See also above, p. 25, concerning the importance of treaties in international law.

A treaty is not the only means by which a state can enter into a legal obligation. A unilateral promise is binding in international law on the state making the promise, if that state intended its promise to be legally binding: *Nuclear Tests case, ICJ Reports*, 1974, pp. 253, 267-8 (although it is submitted that the Court was wrong in holding that France's statement that France would conduct no more nuclear tests in the atmosphere was intended to be a legally binding promise). Similarly a state can lose a legal right by unilaterally waiving it, provided its intention to do so is sufficiently clear.

Article 2(1)(*a*) of the Vienna Convention defines a treaty, for the purposes of the Convention, as 'an international agreement concluded between states in written form and governed by international law, whether embodied in a single instrument or in two or more related instruments, and whatever its particular designation'. This definition excludes agreements between states which are governed by municipal law and agreements between states which are not intended to create legal relations at all. The exclusion of these two types of agreement from the definition of treaties is fairly orthodox, but the definition given in the Vienna Convention is more controversial in so far as it excludes oral agreements between states, and agreements of any sort between international organisations or between states and international organisations. Such agreements are usually called treaties, and the only reason why they are not regarded as treaties *for the purposes of the Convention* is that the rules of international law governing them differ in a few respects from the rules governing written treaties between states; they were therefore not covered by the Convention, in order to prevent the Convention becoming too complicated. In any case, treaties made by international organisations are more usefully studied as part of the law of international organisations, and oral treaties are extremely rare nowadays.

Conclusion and Entry into Force of Treaties

When lawyers talk about the conclusion of a treaty, they are not talking about its termination, but about its making or formation.

Adoption of the text of a treaty
Article 9 of the Vienna Convention provides:

1. The adoption of the text of a treaty takes place by the consent of all the states participating in its drawing up except as provided in paragraph 2.
2. The adoption of the text of a treaty at an international conference takes place by the vote of two-thirds of the states present and voting, unless by the same majority they shall decide to apply a different rule.

Article 9(2) describes what actually happens at most modern conferences (in earlier times unanimity was the normal practice), but each conference adopts its own rules concerning voting procedure, and there is no general rule of customary law governing voting procedure; Article 9(2) therefore represents progressive development rather than codification.

The adoption of the text does not, by itself, create any obligations. A treaty does not come into being until two or more states consent to be bound by it, and the expression of such consent usually comes after the adoption of the text and is an entirely separate process.

Consent to be bound by a treaty

Article 11 of the Vienna Convention provides:

> The consent of a state to be bound by a treaty may be expressed by signature, exchange of instruments constituting a treaty, ratification, acceptance, approval or accession, or by any other means if so agreed.

The multiplicity of methods of expressing consent has unfortunately introduced a good deal of confusion into the law.

Traditionally, *signature* and *ratification* are the most frequent means of expressing consent. In some cases the diplomats negotiating the treaty are authorised to bind their states by signing the treaty; in other cases their authority is more limited, and the treaty does not become binding until it is ratified (that is, approved) by the head of state. In some countries (including the USA but not the United Kingdom), the constitution requires the head of state to obtain the approval of the legislature, or of part of the legislature (for example, the Senate in the USA), before ratifying a treaty.[1]

The relationship between signature and ratification can only be understood in the light of history. In days when slow communications made it difficult for a diplomat to keep in touch with his sovereign, ratification was necessary to prevent diplomats exceeding their instructions; after receiving the text of the treaty and checking that his representatives had not exceeded their instructions, the sovereign was obliged to ratify their signatures. By 1800, however, the idea of a duty to ratify was obsolete, and ratification came to be used for a different purpose – to give the head of state time for second thoughts. With the rise of democracy, the delay between signature and ratification also gave a chance for public opinion to make itself felt; this was particularly true if important

---

[1] See above, pp. 44–5. Strictly speaking, ratification only occurs when instruments of ratification are exchanged between the contracting states, or are deposited with the depositary; see Articles 2(1)(*b*) and 16 of the Vienna Convention. In the case of a multilateral treaty, it is obviously impractical to exchange instruments of ratification between a large number of states, and so, instead, the treaty usually provides that instruments of ratification shall be deposited with a state or international organisation which is appointed by the treaty to act as depositary. Ratifications, accessions, reservations, denunciations (when the treaty provides for a right of denunciation) and similar communications from states concerning the treaty must be sent to the depositary, who notifies the other states concerned whenever such a communication is received.

negotiations had been conducted secretly, or if the treaty necessitated changes in municipal law, or if the constitution of the state concerned required the consent of the legislature for ratification.

During the nineteenth century a further change occurred. By this time many states had adopted constitutions requiring the consent of the legislature for ratification, but states also began to conclude an increasing number of routine treaties which legislatures had no time to discuss. The modern practice therefore grew up of treating many treaties as binding upon signature alone. There is much to be said for this practice. Even in the United Kingdom, where the consent of the legislature is not needed for ratification, many treaties which are subject to ratification are never ratified, simply as a result of the inertia inherent in any large administrative machine; treaties are negotiated in a spirit of popular enthusiasm which soon wanes afterwards, so that there is no pressure for ratification.

The subject-matter of a treaty has little bearing on the question whether it requires ratification. One might have imagined that politically important treaties would always require ratification, but practice is not consistent; for instance, in urgent cases ratification is sometimes dispensed with, because there is no time for it. Treaties usually say expressly whether or not ratification is necessary, and this makes it difficult to know what rule to apply if the treaty is silent. Some writers say the general rule is that treaties need ratification; other writers say the general rule is that treaties do *not* need ratification. But each group of writers recognises that there are many exceptions to the general rule, and so in practice the effects of the difference between the two theories are comparatively slight. The Vienna Convention adopts a 'neutral' attitude; everything depends on the intentions of the parties, and Articles 12(1) and 14(1) of the Convention provide guidelines for ascertaining the intentions of the parties. Article 12(1) provides:

The consent of a state to be bound by a treaty is expressed by the signature of its representative when:
  (a) the treaty provides that signature shall have that effect;
  (b) it is otherwise established that the negotiating states were agreed that signature should have that effect;[1] or
  (c) the intention of the state to give that effect to the signature appears from the full powers[2] of its representative or was expressed during the negotiations.

[1] This can be readily inferred if the treaty provides that it shall come into force at once, or on a fixed date in the very near future.
[2] See below, p. 131, n. 1.

Article 14(1) provides:

> The consent of a state to be bound by a treaty is expressed by ratification when:
>
> (a) the treaty provides for such consent to be expressed by ratification;
>
> (b) it is otherwise established that the negotiating states were agreed that ratification should be required;
>
> (c) the representative of the state has signed the treaty subject to ratification; or
>
> (d) the intention of the state to sign the treaty subject to ratification appears from the full powers of its representative or was expressed during the negotiations.

It should also be added that performance of a treaty can constitute tacit ratification. In particular, if a state successfully claims rights under an unratified treaty, it will be estopped from alleging that it is not bound by the treaty.

In addition to signature and ratification, a state can also become a party to a treaty by *accession* (otherwise known as adhesion or adherence). The difference between accession, on the one hand, and signature or ratification, on the other, is that the acceding state did not take part in the negotiations which produced the treaty, but was invited by the negotiating states to accede to the treaty. Accession is possible only if it is provided for in the treaty, or if all the parties to the treaty agree that the acceding state should be allowed to accede. Accession has the same effects as signature and ratification combined.

These, then, were the traditional methods of expressing consent to a treaty – signature, ratification and accession. However, modern developments have complicated the situation in several different ways.

In the first place, treaties are nowadays often concluded by an exchange of correspondence (usually called an exchange of notes) between the two states. Each note is signed by a representative of the state sending it, and the two signatures are usually enough to establish the consent of the states to be bound; however, exchanges of notes require ratification in the few cases where it can be proved that that was the intention of the states concerned.

Second, the modern practice of leaving certain treaties open for long periods for signature by states which may or may not have participated in the drafting of the treaty has blurred the distinction between accession, on the one hand, and signature and ratification, on the other. For instance, Article 81 of the Vienna Convention provides that the Convention shall be open for nearly a year for signature by certain categories of states, not all of whom attended the Vienna Conference; Article 83 provides that the Convention 'shall [thereafter] remain open for accession by any state belonging to any of the categories mentioned in Article 81'.

Third, *acceptance* or *approval* are sometimes used nowadays in place of ratification (or, alternatively, in place of accession). This innovation is more a matter of terminology than of substance. Acceptance and approval perform the same function on the international plane as ratification and accession; in particular, they give a state time to consider a treaty at length before deciding whether to be bound. The main reason for the popularity of these terms is that they enable a state to evade provisions in its own constitution requiring the consent of the legislature for ratification. Article 14(2) of the Vienna Convention recognises the similarity between ratification and acceptance and approval by providing that 'the consent of a state to be bound by a treaty is expressed by acceptance or approval under conditions similar to those which apply to ratification'.

Finally, it sometimes happens that the text of a treaty is drawn up by an organ of an international organisation (for example, the UN General Assembly) and that the treaty is then declared open for 'accession', 'ratification', 'acceptance', or 'approval' by member-states. The terminological confusion here becomes complete, because 'accession', 'ratification', 'acceptance', or 'approval' are used interchangeably; different terms are used in different treaties to describe a process which is absolutely identical.

Entry into force
A treaty normally enters into force as soon as all the negotiating states have expressed their consent to be bound by it (Article 24 of the Vienna Convention). But the negotiating states are always free to depart from this general rule, by inserting an appropriate provision in the treaty itself.

Thus, the entry into force of a treaty may be delayed by a provision in the treaty, in order to give the parties time to adapt themselves to the requirements of the treaty (for example, in order to enable them to make the necessary changes in their municipal laws). The treaty may provide for its entry into force on a fixed date, or a specified number of days or months after the last ratification.

When very many states participate in drafting a treaty, it is unlikely that they will all ratify it, and it is therefore unreasonable to apply the normal rule that the treaty does not enter into force until all the negotiating states have ratified it. Accordingly, such a treaty often provides that it shall enter into force when it has been ratified by a specified number of states (the number is frequently as high as a third of the number of the negotiating states, because the treaty might not be any use if it were only ratified by a very small number of states). Even when the minimum number of ratifications is reached, the treaty is, of course, only in force between those states which have ratified it; it does not enter into force for other states until they in turn have ratified it.

A treaty can apply retroactively, but only if the contracting states clearly intend it to do so. In the same way, the contracting states may agree to apply a treaty provisionally between its signature and entry into force; this is a useful device when a treaty deals with an urgent problem but requires ratification. However, 'unless . . . the negotiating states have otherwise agreed, the provisional application of a treaty . . . with respect to a state shall be terminated if that state notifies the other states between which the treaty is being applied provisionally of its intention not to become a party to the treaty' (Article 25(2) of the Vienna Convention).

Article 18 of the Vienna Convention provides:

A state is obliged to refrain from acts which would defeat the object and purpose of a treaty when:
(a) it has signed the treaty or has exchanged instruments constituting the treaty subject to ratification, acceptance or approval, until it shall have made its intention clear not to become a party to the treaty; or
(b) it has expressed its consent to be bound by the treaty, pending the entry into force of the treaty and provided that such entry into force is not unduly delayed.

There is some authority for this rule in customary law, but the matter is controversial.

Reservations

A state may be willing to accept most of the provisions of a treaty, but it may, for various reasons, object to other provisions of the treaty. In such cases states often make reservations when they become parties to a treaty. Article 2(1)(d) of the Vienna Convention defines a reservation as 'a unilateral statement . . . made by a state, when signing, ratifying, accepting, approving or acceding to a treaty, whereby it purports to exclude or to modify the legal effect of certain provisions of the treaty in their application to that state'. The effect of a reservation depends on whether it is accepted or rejected by the other states concerned. A reservation to a bilateral treaty presents no problems, because it is, in effect, a new proposal reopening the negotiations between the two states concerning the terms of the treaty; and, unless agreement can be reached about the terms of the treaty, no treaty will be concluded.

In the case of a multilateral treaty the problem is more complicated, because the reservation may be accepted by some states and
rejected by others.

The traditional rule was that a state could not make a reservation to a treaty unless the reservation was accepted by all the states
which had signed (but not necessarily ratified) or adhered to the
treaty. However, this rule was undermined by the advisory opinion
of the International Court of Justice in the *Genocide* case (*ICJ
Reports*, 1951, p. 15). The Court said that the traditional theory
was of 'undisputed value', but was not applicable to certain types
of treaty. More specifically, it was not applicable to the Genocide
Convention, which sought to protect individuals, instead of conferring reciprocal rights on the contracting states. The Court
therefore advised that 'a state which has made . . . a reservation
which has been objected to by one or more of the parties to the
(Genocide) Convention but not by others, can be regarded as a
party to the Convention if the reservation is compatible with the
object and purpose of the Convention'. Since different states may
reach different conclusions about the compatibility of a reservation, the practical effect of the Court's opinion is that a state
making a reservation is likely to be regarded as a party to the treaty
by some states, but not by others.

Articles 19–21 of the Vienna Convention follow the principles
laid down by the Court in the *Genocide* case, but make a concession to the supporters of the traditional rule by recognising that
every reservation is incompatible with *certain types* of treaty unless
accepted unanimously. The International Law Commission's proposals to this effect met a favourable response from member-states
of the United Nations, and it is probable that the rules contained
in Articles 19–21 will be followed in the future, even by states
which are not parties to the Vienna Convention on the Law of
Treaties.

Registration

Article 102 of the United Nations Charter provides that 'every
treaty . . . entered into by any member of the United Nations after
the present Charter comes into force shall as soon as possible be
registered with the Secretariat and published by it'. Treaties
between non-member states are not covered by Article 102, but are
often transmitted voluntarily to the Secretariat for 'filing and
recording'; Article 80 of the Vienna Convention seeks, for the first
time, to make such transmission obligatory.

Article 102 was intended to prevent states entering into secret
agreements without the knowledge of their nationals, and without
the knowledge of other states, whose interests might be affected by

such agreements. An additional advantage of Article 102 is that treaties are published in the United Nations Treaty Series, which is a useful work of reference.

If states fail to register a treaty, as sometimes happens, the treaty is not void; but 'no party to any such treaty . . . may invoke that treaty . . . before any organ of the United Nations' (Article 102(2) of the United Nations Charter).

Application of Treaties

Territorial scope of treaties
'Unless a different intention appears from the treaty or is otherwise established, a treaty is binding upon each party in respect of its entire territory' (Article 29 of the Vienna Convention). This general rule is often altered by a specific provision in a treaty. For instance, treaties often contain a 'colonial clause', which provides that the treaty shall apply automatically only to each party's metropolitan (that is, non-colonial) territory, but that each party shall have the option of extending it to one or more of its colonies. One advantage of a colonial clause is that it enables the wishes of the inhabitants of the colony to be considered before the treaty is extended to the colony.

Treaties and third states
The general rule is that a treaty creates neither rights nor obligations for third states (that is, states which are not parties to the treaty). But there are exceptions to this general rule, which are laid down in detail in Articles 35-7 of the Convention.[1]

Application of successive treaties relating to the same subject-matter
It sometimes happens that a party to a treaty subsequently enters into another treaty relating to the same subject-matter, and that the provisions of the two treaties are mutually inconsistent; the position is complicated by the fact that the other party or parties to

[1] It is sometimes suggested that Article 2(6) of the United Nations Charter imposes obligations on states without their consent. What Article 2(6) actually says is that:

The Organization shall ensure that states which are not members of the United Nations act in accordance with these principles [that is, the principles of the United Nations, set out in Article 2 of the Charter] so far as may be necessary for the maintenance of international peace and security.

In reality, Article 2(6) does not even purport to impose obligations on non-members; it merely announces the policy which the United Nations will follow in its relations with non-members.

the second treaty may or may not also be parties to the first treaty. Article 30 of the Vienna Convention lays down detailed rules to deal with the resulting problems (see also Articles 39–41 on the amendment and modification of treaties, and Articles 58(1) and 59 on the termination or suspension of treaties).

Invalid Treaties

Article 42(1) of the Vienna Convention provides:

> The validity of a treaty or of the consent of a state to be bound by a treaty may be impeached only through the application of the present Convention.

This is to prevent states attempting to evade inconvenient treaty obligations by making far-fetched allegations that the treaty is invalid.

Provisions of municipal law regarding competence to conclude treaties

The constitutions of many countries provide that the head of state may not conclude (or, at least, may not ratify) a treaty without the consent of a legislative organ. What happens if the head of state disregards such a rule when entering into a treaty? Is the treaty valid or not? Opinion is divided. One school of thought says that the treaty is void, although this conclusion is sometimes limited to cases where the constitutional rule in question is well known – an imprecise qualification which would be difficult to apply in practice. Another school of thought considers that the treaty is valid, but some supporters of this school are prepared to make exceptions when one party to the treaty *knew* that the other party was acting in breach of a constitutional requirement. Most states favour the latter point of view, which is reflected in Article 46 of the Vienna Convention:

> 1. A state may not invoke the fact that its consent to be bound by a treaty has been expressed in violation of a provision of its internal law regarding competence to conclude treaties as invalidating its consent unless that violation was manifest and concerned a rule of its internal law of fundamental importance.
> 2. A violation is manifest if it would be objectively evident to any state conducting itself in the matter in accordance with normal practice and in good faith.

Treaties entered into by persons not authorised to represent a state

Article 46 is essentially concerned with the relationship between the executive and the legislature within a state. But it is one thing to say, as Article 46 in effect does, that the executive's act in making a treaty is binding on the state; it is another thing to decide which particular members of the executive are authorised to act in the name of the state – it would be absurd to suppose that a state could be bound by the acts of a junior clerk in the same way that it is bound by the acts of the minister for foreign affairs.

Accordingly, Article 7(1) of the Vienna Convention provides:

A person is considered as representing a state for the purpose of . . . expressing the consent of the state to be bound by a treaty if:
(*a*) he produces appropriate full powers;[1] or
(*b*) it appears from the practice of the states concerned or from other circumstances that their intention was to consider that person as representing the state for such purposes and to dispense with full powers.

Article 7(2) provides that heads of state, heads of government and ministers of foreign affairs are, in virtue of their functions and without having to produce full powers, considered as representing their state for the purpose of performing all acts relating to the conclusion of a treaty.

Article 8 provides:

An act relating to the conclusion of a treaty performed by a person who cannot be considered under Article 7 as authorized to represent a state for that purpose is without legal effect unless afterwards confirmed by that state.

Specific restrictions on authority to express the consent of a state
Although a person may be authorised to enter into a treaty on behalf of a state, in accordance with Article 7, it sometimes happens that a specific restriction is imposed on his authority, for example, he may be instructed not to enter into a treaty unless it contains a particular provision to which his state attaches importance. What happens if he disregards such a restriction? Article 47 provides:

If the authority of a representative to express the consent of a state to be bound by a particular treaty has been made subject to a specific restriction, his omission to observe that restriction may not be invoked as invalidating the consent expressed by him unless the restriction was

[1] Full powers are defined in Article 2(1)(*c*) as 'a document emanating from the competent authority of a state designating a person or persons to represent the state for negotiating, adopting or authenticating the text of a treaty, for expressing the consent of the state to be bound by a treaty, or for accomplishing any other act with respect to a treaty'.

notified to the other negotiating states prior to his expressing such consent.

Coercion of a representative of a state
Article 51 of the Vienna Convention provides:

> The expression of a state's consent to be bound by a treaty which has been procured by the coercion of its representative through acts or threats directed against him shall be without any legal effect.

Coercion of a state by the threat or use of force
Before the First World War, customary international law imposed no limitations on the right of states to go to war, and consequently a treaty procured by the threat or use of force against a state was as valid as any other treaty. Since the First World War there has been a growing tendency to regard aggression as illegal, and the corollary would seem to be that treaties imposed by an aggressor are void. Accordingly, Article 52 of the Vienna Convention provides:

> A treaty is void if its conclusion has been procured by the threat or use of force in violation of the principles of international law embodied in the Charter of the United Nations.

Article 52 is an accurate statement of the modern law (*Fisheries Jurisdiction* case, *ICJ Reports*, 1973, pp. 3, 14, *obiter*).

When Article 52 of the Vienna Convention speaks of 'the threat or use of force in violation of the principles . . . embodied in the Charter of the United Nations', it is obviously referring to Article 2(4) of the Charter, which prohibits 'the threat or use of force . . . in any . . . manner inconsistent with the purposes of the United Nations'. The communist states and the more militant Afro-Asian countries argue that 'force' in Article 2(4) covers economic and political pressure as well as military force, and that treaties imposed by economic or political pressure are void.[1] The Western countries disagree. The International Law Commission adopted a neutral attitude in its commentary on the law of treaties, saying that the meaning of 'force' 'should be left to be determined in practice by interpretation of the relevant provisions of the Charter'. However, it is submitted that the interpretation placed on the word 'force' by the communist states and the more militant Afro-Asian countries is an extremely strained interpretation.

---

[1] Such treaties are often called unequal treaties, although the term 'unequal treaties' is also used to describe treaties whose terms are unfair, regardless of the circumstances of their conclusion. States which argue that unequal treaties are void seldom define their terms.

Article 2(4) of the Charter gives effect to the principle, stated in the preamble to the Charter, that *'armed* force shall not be used, save in the common interest', and a Brazilian amendment to extend Article 2(4) to include economic and political coercion was rejected at the San Francisco conference, which drew up the United Nations Charter in 1945.

Despite occasional suggestions to the contrary by communist and militant Afro-Asian countries, the modern rules against force do not operate retroactively. In other words, if a treaty was procured by force at a time when force was not illegal, the validity of the treaty is not affected by subsequent changes in the law which declare that force is illegal and that treaties procured by force are void (see also below, pp. 150-1).

Other causes of invalidity

According to the Vienna Convention, a state's consent to be bound by a treaty can be invalidated by mistake (in certain circumstances, specified in Article 48), by the fraud of another negotiating state (Article 49), or by the corruption of its representative by another negotiating state (Article 50). It is uncertain whether these causes of invalidity existed in customary international law.

A treaty is void if it conflicts with *ius cogens* (Article 53; see above, pp. 40-1).

The consequences of invalidity

The consequences of invalidity vary according to the precise nature of the cause of invalidity. In cases covered by Articles 8 and 51-3 of the Vienna Convention, the treaty 'is void', or the expression of consent to be bound by the treaty is 'without legal effect', which comes to the same thing. In cases covered by Articles 46-50, however, the Vienna Convention says that a state may merely *invoke* the vitiating factor as invalidating the treaty, and the effect of this formula is that the treaty is probably voidable rather than void; the treaty is valid until a state claims that it is invalid, and the right to make such a claim may be lost in certain circumstances (Article 45). The vitiating factors mentioned in Articles 8 and 51-3 are more serious than those mentioned in Articles 46-50, so this distinction is logical; but it is doubtful whether it is as clearly established in customary law as the Vienna Convention suggests.

In both cases, however, Articles 65-8 of the Vienna Convention provide that a party challenging the validity of a treaty must notify the other parties to the treaty and give them time to make objections before it takes any action (although there are exceptions to this rule). If objections are made, and if the resulting dispute is not settled within twelve months, Article 66 confers jurisdiction on the International Court of Justice over disputes arising from Article 53 (*ius cogens*) and confers jurisdiction over other disputes on a special conciliation commission set up under an annex to the Convention. These provisions are obviously desirable in order to prevent abuse of the rules concerning causes of invalidity, but they represent an almost complete innovation when one compares them with the pre-existing customary law; in particular, under customary law, international courts and conciliation commissions do not have jurisdiction over *all* cases concerning claims that a treaty is invalid, but only over those cases which the parties *agree* to refer to the court or conciliation commission.

Termination of Treaties

Article 26 of the Vienna Convention provides:

> Every treaty in force is binding upon the parties to it and must be performed by them in good faith.

In other words, a state cannot release itself from its treaty obligations whenever it feels like it; if it could, legal relations would become hopelessly insecure. But the words 'in force' must not be overlooked; few treaties last for ever, and, unless some provision is made for the termination of treaties, the law will become hopelessly rigid. The rules of law concerning the termination of treaties try to steer a middle course between the two extremes of rigidity and insecurity. They work fairly well, because every state is a party to hundreds of treaties on a wide range of topics, and therefore has an interest in ensuring that the right balance between security and flexibility is maintained in practice. Article 42(2) of the Vienna Convention seeks to protect the security of legal relations by providing:

> The termination of a treaty, its denunciation or the withdrawal of a party, may take place only as a result of the application of the provisions of the treaty or of the present Convention. The same rule applies to suspension of the operation of a treaty.

Termination in accordance with the provisions of a treaty
Article 54 of the Vienna Convention provides:[1]

> The termination of a treaty or the withdrawal of a party may take place:
> (*a*)   in conformity with the provisions of the treaty . . .

[1] A similar rule applies to suspension of the operation of a treaty (Articles 57 and 58 (1)).

Indeed, the majority of modern treaties contain provisions for termination or withdrawal. Sometimes it is provided that the treaty shall come to an end automatically after a certain time, or when a particular event occurs; other treaties merely give each party an option to withdraw, usually after giving a certain period of notice.

Termination by consent of the parties

Article 54 of the Vienna Convention provides:[1]

> The termination of a treaty or the withdrawal of a party may take place:
> (a) . . .
> (b) at any time by consent of all the parties . . .

At one time it used to be thought that the treaty could only be terminated in exactly the same way as it was made; thus, a ratified treaty could be terminated only by another ratified treaty, and not by a treaty which came into force on signature alone. But this formalistic view is no longer accepted. Indeed, the International Law Commission thought that an agreement to terminate could even be *implied* if it was clear from the conduct of the parties that they no longer regarded the treaty as being in force.[2]

Implied right of denunciation or withdrawal

Article 56 of the Vienna Convention provides:

> 1. A treaty which contains no provision regarding its termination and which does not provide for denunciation or withdrawal is not subject to denunciation or withdrawal unless:
> (a) it is established that the parties intended to admit the possibility of denunciation or withdrawal; or
> (b) a right of denunciation or withdrawal may be implied by the nature of the treaty.
> 2. A party shall give not less than twelve months' notice of its intention to denounce or withdraw from a treaty under paragraph 1.

It follows from the wording of Article 56 that a right of denunciation or withdrawal can never be *implied* if the treaty contains an *express* provision concerning denunciation, withdrawal, or termination.

Treaties of alliance and certain types of commercial treaty are

---

[1] A similar rule applies to suspension of the operation of a treaty (Articles 57 and 58(1)).
[2] *American Journal of International Law*, vol. 61, 1967, p. 388. See also *S.E.* v. *G. and Gen.*, decided by the German Supreme Court in 1925; text in H. W. Briggs, *The Law of Nations*, 2nd ed., 1952, p. 902. The technical name for this method of termination is 'desuetude'. See also Article 59.

the main examples of the kind of treaty in which a right of denunciation or withdrawal can be inferred from the *nature* of the treaty, within the meaning of paragraph 1(*b*). International law is not unique in recognising such an implied right of denunciation; English law makes a similar inference in the case of contracts of employment, for instance.

Paragraph 2 is more precise than customary law, which merely requires reasonable notice to be given, without fixing any definite time-limit.

Termination or suspension of a treaty as a consequence of its breach (discharge through breach)
Article 60(1) of the Vienna Convention provides:

> A material breach of a bilateral treaty by one of the parties entitles the other to invoke the breach as a ground for terminating the treaty or suspending its operation in whole or in part.

The injured state's power to terminate or suspend a treaty is one of the main sanctions for breach of a treaty, but it is not the only one; there is nothing to prevent the injured state claiming compensation instead of, or in addition to, exercising its rights under Article 60(1).

The problem is more complicated if the treaty is multilateral. Obviously, breach by state A cannot entitle state B to denounce the treaty, because that would not be fair to states C, D, E, and so on. Accordingly, Article 60(2) provides:

> A material breach of a multilateral treaty by one of the parties entitles:
> (*a*) the other parties by unanimous agreement to suspend the operation of the treaty in whole or in part or to terminate it either:
>   (i) in the relations between themselves and the defaulting state, or
>   (ii) as between all parties:
> (*b*) a party specially affected by the breach to invoke it as a ground for suspending the operation of the treaty in whole or in part in the relations between itself and the defaulting state;
> (*c*) any party other than the defaulting state to invoke the breach as a ground for suspending the operation of the treaty in whole or in part with respect to itself if the treaty is of such a character that a material breach of its provisions by one party radically changes the position of every party with respect to the further performance of its obligations under the treaty.

An example of the type of treaty contemplated by paragraph 2(*c*) is a disarmament treaty. Clearly, breach of a disarmament treaty by one party constitutes a very serious threat to each of the other parties. But should this entitle one of the injured parties to create a similar threat to the other injured parties? Would it not be more appropriate to deal with the problem under paragraph 2(*a*)? It is in any case doubtful whether paragraph 2(*c*) really reflects customary law.

It is generally agreed that a right to terminate does not arise unless the breach is a material (that is, serious) one. Article 60(3) defines a material breach as:

(*a*) a repudiation of the treaty not sanctioned by the present convention; or

(*b*) the violation of a provision essential to the accomplishment of the object or purpose of the treaty.

This definition is defective, because it does not make clear that violation of an essential provision does not constitute a material breach unless it is a serious violation. If a state makes a treaty to deliver 5,000 tons of tin and delivers only 4,999 tons, a literal interpretation of Article 60(3) would imply that the other party could denounce the treaty because of this minor violation of an essential provision – which is repugnant to common sense.

Breach does not automatically terminate a treaty; it merely gives the injured party or parties an option to terminate or suspend the treaty, and, according to Article 45, an injured party loses the right to exercise this option:

if, after becoming aware of the facts:

(*a*) it shall have expressly agreed that the treaty . . . remains in force or continues in operation, as the case may be; or

(*b*) it must by reason of its conduct be considered as having acquiesced . . . in its [that is, the treaty's] maintenance in force or in operation, as the case may be.

Supervening impossibility of performance

Article 61 of the Vienna Convention provides:

1. A party may invoke the impossibility of performing a treaty as a ground for terminating or withdrawing from it if the impossibility results from the permanent disappearance or destruction of an object indispensable for the execution of the treaty. If the impossibility is temporary, it may be invoked only as a ground for suspending the operation of the treaty.

2. Impossibility of performance may not be invoked by a party as a ground for terminating, withdrawing from or suspending the operation of a treaty if the impossibility is the result of a breach by that party either of an obligation under the treaty or of any other international obligation owed to any other party to the treaty.

It is not hard to think of examples; for instance, a treaty providing that the waters of a particular river be used for irrigation would become impossible of performance if the river dried up. The Vienna Convention regards the impossibility not as automatically terminating the treaty, but as merely giving a party an option to terminate; this point was controversial at customary law.

Fundamental change of circumstances (rebus sic stantibus)
A party is not bound to perform a treaty if there has been a fundamental change of circumstances since the treaty was concluded. In previous centuries writers tried to explain this rule by saying that every treaty contained an implied term that it should remain in force only as long as circumstances remained the same (*rebus sic stantibus*) as at the time of conclusion. Such an explanation must be rejected, because it is based on a fiction, and because it exaggerates the scope of the rule. In modern times it is agreed that the rule applies only in the most exceptional circumstances; otherwise it could be used as an excuse to evade all sorts of inconvenient treaty obligations.

Article 62 of the Vienna Convention confines the rule within very narrow limits:

1. A fundamental change of circumstances which has occurred with regard to those existing at the time of the conclusion of a treaty, and which was not foreseen by the parties, may not be invoked as a ground for terminating or withdrawing from the treaty unless:
   (a)   the existence of those circumstances constituted an essential basis of the consent of the parties to be bound by the treaty; and
   (b)   the effect of the change is radically to transform the extent of obligations still to be performed under the treaty.
2. A fundamental change of circumstances may not be invoked as a ground for terminating or withdrawing from the treaty:
   (a)   if the treaty established a boundary; or
   (b)   if the fundamental change is the result of a breach by the party invoking it either of an obligation under the treaty or of any other international obligation owed to any other party to the treaty.
3. If, under the foregoing paragraphs, a party may invoke a fundamental change of circumstances as a ground for terminating or withdrawing from a treaty, it may also invoke the change as a ground for suspending the operation of the treaty.

In the *Fisheries Jurisdiction* case the International Court of Justice said that Article 62 'may in many respects be considered as a codification of existing customary law on the subject' (*ICJ Reports*, 1973, pp. 3, 18; see also the *Free Zones* case (1932), PCIJ, series A/B, no. 46, pp. 156-8).

Some writers consider that the change of circumstances automatically terminates the treaty; others hold that it merely gives a state an option to terminate. The Vienna Convention adopts the latter approach; moreover, the option to terminate may be lost in certain circumstances under Article 45 (see above, p. 137).

No doubt treaties often need to be altered, to bring them into line with changing conditions. But the *rebus sic stantibus* rule is an unsuitable method for achieving this end; it applies only in extreme cases, and, when it does apply, its effect is not to alter a treaty, but to terminate it. Alterations, as opposed to termination, can only be brought about by agreement, and not all states are prepared to agree to amendments which go against their interests; sometimes they fear that making concessions to one state will induce other states to demand similar changes in other treaties. But the desire of states to obtain the good will of other states often induces them to make the necessary concessions (this is particularly true of the 'super-powers' trying to obtain the good will of neutralist states). Moreover, the United Nations General Assembly has a power to recommend alterations of treaties, under Article 14 of the United Nations Charter, which provides:

the General Assembly may recommend measures for the peaceful adjustment of any situation, regardless of origin, which it deems likely to impair the general welfare or friendly relations among nations . . .

Emergence of a new peremptory norm (ius cogens)
Article 64 of the Vienna Convention provides:

If a new peremptory norm of general international law emerges, any existing treaty which is in conflict with that norm becomes void and terminates.

(The treaty does not, however, become void *retroactively*; see Article 71(2). On *ius cogens* generally, see above, pp. 40–1.)

Outbreak of war
The Vienna Convention does not deal with the effects of war on treaties, apart from stating that 'the provisions of the present convention shall not prejudge any question that may arise in regard to a treaty . . . from the outbreak of hostilities between states' (Article 73). The problem is extremely complicated. Originally, war was regarded as ending all treaties between belligerent states, but this rule has now been partly abandoned. Maybe it is not so much the rule which has changed, as the nature of the treaties to which the rule applies. It was sensible to say that war ended all treaties between belligerent states when most treaties were bilateral 'contract-treaties'; the rule has to be altered when many treaties are

multilateral 'law-making treaties', to which neutrals as well as belligerents are parties.

In any case, this tangled branch of the law is less important now than it used to be, for two reasons. First, when states are engaged in hostilities nowadays, they seldom admit that they are in a state of war in the technical sense; and, unlike war, hostilities falling short of war do not generally terminate treaties between the hostile states. Second, the peace treaty or other instrument which terminates a modern war usually provides what is to happen to prewar treaties (or at least bilateral treaties) between the belligerent states, so that it is unnecessary to apply the rules of customary law on this point.

Consequences of termination or suspension

Rules concerning the consequences of termination or suspension of a treaty are laid down in Articles 70, 71(2) and 72 of the Vienna Convention, which are too detailed to be discussed here.

Many of the rules in the Vienna Convention laying down the procedure to be followed when a treaty is alleged to be invalid also apply, *mutatis mutandis*, to termination or suspension; this is particularly true of Articles 65-8 (see above, pp. 133-4).

Suggestions for Further Reading

D. J. Harris, *Cases and Materials on International Law*, 3rd ed., 1983, ch. 10.
I. M. Sinclair, *The Vienna Convention on the Law of Treaties*, 1973.
T. O. Elias, *The Modern Law of Treaties*, 1974.
Lord McNair, *The Law of Treaties*, 1961.

Chapter 11

Acquisition of Territory

'Acquisition of territory' is an abbreviated way of describing acquisition of sovereignty over territory. Sovereignty, that much abused word, is here used in a specialised sense; sovereignty over territory means 'the right to exercise therein, to the exclusion of any other state, the functions of a state' (*Island of Palmas* case (1928), *UNRIAA* II 829, 838). But it is not necessarily unlimited. Other states may, by treaty or local custom, acquire minor rights over the territory, such as a right of way across it. Even the right of a state to transfer its territory to another state, which is often regarded as the acid test of sovereignty over territory, may be limited by treaty. For instance, by the State Treaty of 1955, Austria agreed not to enter into political or economic union with Germany. Again, under the Treaty of Utrecht of 1713, Great Britain agreed to offer Gibraltar to Spain before attempting to transfer sovereignty over Gibraltar to any other state.

Modes of Acquisition of Territory

The traditional view is that there are several distinct modes by which sovereignty can be acquired over territory. The classification of these modes was originally borrowed from the Roman law rules about the acquisition of property, which is not surprising, since sovereignty over territory bears some resemblance to ownership of property; and in the sixteenth and seventeenth centuries, when modern international law began to develop, the then current theories of absolute monarchy tended to regard a state's territory as the private estate of the prince. But there are several ways in which this use of private law concepts produces a distorted view of modern international law. In particular, it presupposes that transfers of territory take place between already existing states, just as transfers of property take place between already existing individuals. Nowadays, however, the most frequent form of transfer of territory occurs when a colony becomes independent; since territory is an essential ingredient of statehood, the birth of the state and the transfer of territory are inseparable – a state *is* its territory. In the pages which follow, an attempt will be made to fit the emergence of new states into the traditional list of modes of acquisition of territory; but it must be confessed that the emergence of new states does not fit very well into that list.

Another preliminary point to notice about modes of acquisition is that they are really only relevant when title to territory is uncertain. For instance, Devon has been part of the United Kingdom for so long that all states recognise it as part of the United Kingdom, and no one bothers to ask how the United Kingdom first acquired it.

Cession

Cession is the transfer of territory, usually by treaty, from one state to another. If there were defects in the ceding state's title, the title of the state to which the territory is ceded will be vitiated by the same defects; this is expressed by the Latin maxim, *nemo dat quod non habet*. For instance, in the *Island of Palmas* case (1928, *UNRIAA* II 829), Spain ceded the Philippine islands to the USA by the Treaty of Paris 1898; the treaty described the island of Palmas as forming part of the Philippines. But, when the United States went to take possession of the island of Palmas, they found it under Dutch control. In the ensuing arbitration between the USA and the Netherlands, the USA claimed that the island had belonged to Spain before 1898, and that the USA had acquired the island from Spain by cession. The arbitrator, Max Huber, held that, even if Spain had originally had sovereignty over the island (a point which he left open), the Netherlands had administered it since the early eighteenth century, thereby supplanting Spain as the sovereign over the island (see below, p. 145). Since Spain had no title to the island in 1898, the USA could not acquire title from Spain.

Granting independence to a colony may be regarded as a sort of 'quasi-cession', when the grant constitutes a single act and not a gradual process (cf. below, p. 145, on 'quasi-prescription').

See also below, pp. 146-8, on treaties of cession imposed by force.

Occupation

Occupation is the acquisition of *terra nullius*, that is, territory which, immediately before acquisition, belonged to no state. The territory may never have belonged to any state, or it may have been abandoned by the previous sovereign.[1] Nowadays there are very few parts of the world which are *terra nullius*, but many

---

[1] Abandonment requires not only failure to exercise authority over the territory, but also an *intention* to abandon the territory: *Clipperton Island* case (1932), *UN Reports of International Arbitral Awards* II 1105, 1110–11. This corresponds roughly to the distinction in municipal law between losing property and throwing it away.

modern disputes over territory have their roots in previous centuries, when territory was frequently acquired by occupation. In previous centuries European international lawyers were sometimes reluctant to admit that non-European societies could constitute states for the purposes of international law, and territory inhabited by non-European peoples was sometimes regarded as *terra nullius*.[1]

Territory is occupied when it is placed under effective control. The requirements of effective control have become increasingly stricter in international law, as unoccupied territory has become increasingly scarcer. In the sixteenth century, when large areas of unoccupied territory were being discovered, effective control was interpreted very liberally; indeed, mere discovery gave a state an 'inchoate title', that is, an option to occupy the territory within a reasonable time, and during that time other states were not allowed to occupy the territory. As time went on, international law demanded more and more in order to constitute effective control. However, even in modern times, effective control is a relative concept; it varies according to the nature of the territory concerned. It is, for instance, much easier to establish effective control over barren and uninhabited territory than over territory which is inhabited by savage tribes; troops would probably have to be stationed in the territory in the latter case, but not in the former case. Effective control is also relative in another sense, which was stressed by the Permanent Court of International Justice in the *Eastern Greenland* case (1933, PCIJ, series A/B, no. 53, at p. 46):

> Another circumstance which must be taken into account . . . is the extent to which sovereignty is claimed by some other power. In most of the cases involving claims to territorial sovereignty which have come before an international tribunal, there have been two competing claims to sovereignty, and the tribunal has had to decide which of the two is the stronger . . . In many cases the tribunal has been satisfied with very little in the way of actual exercise of sovereign rights, provided that the other state could not make out a superior claim. This is particularly true in the case of claims to sovereignty over areas in thinly populated or unsettled countries.

Some cases say that a state, in order to acquire territory by occupation, must not only exercise effective control, but must also have 'the intention and will to act as sovereign' (*Eastern Greenland* case, loc. cit., pp. 45–6; but see the criticism of this approach by Ian Brownlie, *Principles of Public International Law*, 3rd ed.,

---

[1] But such attitudes were rarer than is sometimes supposed; see the *Western Sahara* case, *ICJ Reports*, 1975, pp. 12, 39–40, and D. P. O'Connell, *International Law*, 2nd ed., 1970, Vol. 1, pp. 408–9.

1979, pp. 143–4). Consequently, 'the independent activity of private individuals is of little value unless it can be shown that they have acted in pursuance of . . . some . . . authority received from their governments or that in some other way their governments have asserted jurisdiction through them' (*Fisheries* case, *ICJ Reports*, 1951, pp. 116, 184, *per* Judge McNair).

Sometimes states may agree not to make claims to particular territory, so that the territory in effect remains *terra nullius*. Examples can be found in Article 2 of the Outer Space Treaty of 1967 (see below, p. 287) and in the Antarctica Treaty of 1959 (text in *American Journal of International Law*, 1960, p. 476). Before 1959 several states had laid claims to various areas of Antarctica, but the area claimed by one state sometimes overlapped with an area claimed by another state, and none of the areas was subject to effective control by the states concerned. The 1959 treaty has been ratified by all the states actively interested in Antarctica, and no state party to the treaty may withdraw from it during the first thirty years. The treaty provides for freedom of movement and scientific exploration throughout Antarctica; the parties agree to co-operate with one another and not to use Antarctica for military purposes. Existing claims to sovereignty in Antarctica are not affected by the treaty, but Article IV provides:

No acts or activities taking place while the present treaty is in force shall constitute a basis for asserting, supporting or denying a claim to territorial sovereignty in Antarctica or create any rights of sovereignty in Antarctica. No new claim, or enlargement of an existing claim, to territorial sovereignty in Antarctica shall be asserted while the present treaty is in force.

See Peterson, 'Antarctica: the last great land rush on Earth', *International Organization*, vol. 34, 1980, p. 377.

Prescription

Like occupation, prescription is based on effective control over territory (as in the case of occupation, effective control probably needs to be accompanied by 'the intention and will to act as sovereign'; see above, p. 143). The difference between prescription and occupation is that prescription is the acquisition of territory which belonged to another state, whereas occupation is acquisition of *terra nullius*. Consequently the effective control necessary to establish title by prescription must last for a longer period of time than the effective control which is necessary in cases of occupation; loss of title by the former sovereign is not readily presumed. In English law a 'squatter' acquires title to land after twelve years;

there is no fixed period in international law, but the time needed is almost certainly much more than twelve years.

Effective control by the acquiring state probably needs to be accompanied by acquiescence on the part of the losing state; protests can probably prevent acquisition of title by prescription (see below, pp. 294–5). This explains why, in the *Island of Palmas* case, the arbitrator emphasised the absence of Spanish protests against Dutch acts on the island (1928, *UNRIAA* II 829, 868).

Although occupation and prescription can be distinguished from one another in theory, the difference is usually blurred in real life, because often one of the very points in dispute is whether the territory was *terra nullius* or whether it was subject to the sovereignty of the 'first' state before the 'second' state arrived on the scene. For instance, the judgment in the *Island of Palmas* case does not make clear whether the island was under Spanish sovereignty before the Dutch began to exercise control. Many of the cases which textbooks classify as cases on occupation could equally well be regarded as cases on prescription, and vice versa. When faced with competing claims, international tribunals often decide in favour of the state which can prove the greater degree of effective control over the disputed territory, without basing their judgment on any specific mode of acquisition. For instance, in the *Eastern Greenland* case (see above, p. 143) the Permanent Court of International Justice gave judgment for Denmark because Denmark had exercised greater control than Norway over Eastern Greenland, but the Court did not specify the mode whereby Denmark had acquired sovereignty.

Acquisition of independence by a colony through a gradual process of constitutional development (as happened in the case of Australia, Canada and New Zealand) can be regarded as a sort of 'quasi-prescription'.

Operations of nature

A state can acquire territory through operations of nature, for example, when rivers silt up, or when volcanic islands emerge in a state's internal waters or territorial sea. Such events are rare and unimportant, and there is little point in discussing the detailed rules (see *The Anna* (1805), 165 E.R. 809; *Chamizal Arbitration* (1910), *UNRIAA* XI 316).

Adjudication

Adjudication is sometimes listed as a mode of acquisition, but its status is doubtful. In theory, a tribunal's normal task is to declare the rights which the parties already have, not to create new rights; in theory, therefore, adjudication does not give a state any

territory which it did not already own. On the other hand, it sometimes happens that states set up a boundary commission to mark
out an agreed boundary, but empower it to depart to some extent
from the agreed boundary (for example, to prevent a farm being
cut in two); however, this power of the boundary commission is
derived from the treaty setting it up, and the transfer of territory
may therefore be regarded as a sort of indirect cession.

Conquest

Normally a state defeated in a war used to cede territory to the
victor by treaty, but conquest alone, without a treaty, could also
confer title on the victor under the traditional law. However,
acquisition of territory by conquest was not lawful unless the war
had come to an end. If the defeated state entered into a peace
treaty which ceded territory to the victor, or which recognised the
victor's title, it was clear that the war had come to an end. In the
absence of a peace treaty, it was necessary to prove that the war
had come to an end in a different way, by producing clear evidence
that all resistance by the enemy state *and by its allies* had ceased;
thus the German annexation of Poland during the Second World
War was invalid, because Poland's allies continued the struggle
against Germany.[1] In addition, the conqueror only acquired
territory if he intended to do so; in 1945 the Allies expressly dis-
claimed the intention of annexing Germany, although they had
occupied all of Germany's territory and defeated all her allies.

In the nineteenth century, it was inevitable that international
law should allow states to acquire territory by conquest, because at
that time customary international law imposed no limit on the
right of states to go to war. During the twentieth century there has
been a growing movement, culminating in the United Nations
Charter, to restrict the right of states to go to war; as a general
rule, the use of force is now illegal, with certain exceptions such as
self-defence (see below, pp. 219–27). What effect has this
revolutionary change in the law had upon the possibility of acquiring territory by conquest?

We have already seen that the better view is that a treaty
imposed by an aggressor is now void (see above, p. 132). Since an
aggressor state cannot acquire territory by conquering another
state and forcing it to sign a treaty of cession, it must follow *a
fortiori* that an aggressor cannot acquire territory by conquest
alone. But, as long as the international community is not
determined to prevent aggressors from enjoying the fruits of their

---

[1] In law, Germany was merely the belligerent occupant of Poland, and her rights were
very much more limited than they would have been if the annexation had been valid. See L.
Oppenheim, *International Law*, Vol. 2, 7th ed., by H. Lauterpacht, 1952, pp. 432–56.

crimes, the idea that an aggressor cannot acquire a good title to territory is liable to produce a serious discrepancy between the law and the facts. Ideally, the facts should be brought into line with the law, but, if states are not prepared to take action to alter the facts, the only alternative is to bring the law into line with the facts, by means of recognition. An aggressor's title is invalid, simply because it is based on aggression, but its defects are cured when it is recognised *de jure* by other states. In this exceptional situation recognition has a constitutive effect (see above, p. 60 and below, p. 149).

What about the 'innocent' parties to a war? Can they still acquire territory by conquest? The Declaration on Principles of International Law concerning Friendly Relations and Co-operation among States in Accordance with the Charter of the United Nations, passed by the General Assembly in 1970, suggests that they cannot:[1]

> The territory of a state shall not be the object of military occupation resulting from the use of force in contravention of the provisions of the Charter. The territory of a state shall not be the object of acquisition by another state resulting from the threat or use of force.

In these words, the Declaration makes a significant distinction between military occupation and acquisition of territory. Military occupation[2] is unlawful only if it results from the use of force in contravention of the Charter; *any* threat or use of force, whether it is in contravention of the Charter or not, invalidates acquisition of territory.

After the Arab-Israeli hostilities of June 1967, the Security Council and General Assembly of the United Nations did not condemn either side for committing aggression: draft resolutions condemning Israel were defeated. But the General Assembly and the Security Council have repeatedly declared by overwhelming majorities that Israel is not entitled to annex any of the territory which Israel overran in 1967[3] – which provides further support for

---

[1] Text in Ian Brownlie, *Basic Documents in International Law*, 3rd ed.,1983, pp. 35, 39. For other relevant provisions of the Declaration, see below, pp. 149, no. 5, and 151, at n. 1.

[2] This is the same as belligerent occupation; see above, p. 146, n. 1.

[3] *Yearbook of the United Nations*, 1967, p. 221; ibid., 1977, pp. 323, 326; *UN Chronicle*, 1980, no. 1, p. 34, no. 7, pp. 20 and 30, and no. 8, pp. 13 and 18; ibid., 1981, no. 2, p. 11.

The General Assembly and the Security Council regard Israel as a belligerent occupant (see above, p. 146, n. 1), and therefore consider that the provisions concerning belligerent occupation laid down by the 1949 Geneva Convention on the Protection of Civilian Persons in Time of War apply to the territories occupied by Israel (*Yearbook of the United Nations*, 1977, p. 323). Article 49 of the Convention provides that 'the occupying power shall not . . . transfer parts of its own civilian population into the territory it occupies'; this is the basis on which the United Nations has condemned the establishment of Jewish settlements in the occupied territories (*UN Chronicle*, 1980, no. 1, p. 34; ibid., 1981, no. 2, pp. 16–17).

For further information on the territories under Israeli belligerent occupation, see *Round Table*, no. 280, October 1980, p. 443.

the view that the modern prohibition against the acquisition of territory by force applies to *all* states, and not merely to aggressor states. However, just as titles based on conquests by aggressors can be validated by *de jure* recognition by other states, so can titles based on conquests by non-aggressor states.

The modern rules prohibiting acquisition of territory by conquest are concerned only with international wars, not with civil wars. No breach of international law is therefore committed when part of a state's inhabitants succeed in setting up a new state by winning a civil war of secession, as happened in Algeria in 1956–62.

Acquiescence, Recognition and Estoppel

Acquiescence, recognition and estoppel play a very important role in the acquisition of territory, although they are not, strictly speaking, modes of acquisition. Where each of the rival claimants can show that it has exercised a certain degree of control over the disputed territory, an international tribunal is likely to decide the case in favour of the state which can prove that its title has been recognised by the other claimant or claimants. Such recognition may take the form of an express statement,[1] or it may be inferred from acquiescence, that is, failure to protest against the exercise of control by one's opponent. But in every case recognition or acquiescence by one state has little or no effect unless it is accompanied by some measure of control over the territory by the other state; failure to protest against a purely verbal assertion of title unsupported by any degree of control does not constitute acquiescence.[2]

It is sometimes said that recognition or acquiescence give rise to an estoppel. Estoppel is a technical rule of the English law of evidence; when one party makes a statement of fact and another party takes some action in reliance on that statement, the courts will not allow the first party to deny the truth of his statement if the party who acted in reliance on the statement would suffer some detriment in the event of the statement being proved to be false. Transposed into the context of international disputes over territory, this rule would mean that a state which had recognised another state's title to particular territory would be estopped from

---

[1] Recognition of a state does not necessarily entail recognition of all the territorial claims made by that state. However, if state A claims that *all* of state B's territory rightfully belongs to state A, but subsequently recognises state B *de jure*, the act of recognition must be interpreted as an abandonment of state A's claim.

[2] *Island of Palmas* case (1928), *UN Reports of International Arbitral Awards* II 829, 843.

denying the other state's title if the other state had taken some action in reliance on the recognition, for example, by constructing roads in the territory concerned, because the state constructing the roads would have been wasting its money if its title turned out to be bad. The attitude of international law towards estoppel is not always consistent. Sometimes international law insists on the English requirements of reliance and detriment;[1] at other times it does not.[2] Again, estoppel in international law sometimes has the effect of making it *impossible* for a party to contradict his previous statement, as in English law;[3] in other cases it is merely evidential, that is, its effect is simply to make it *difficult* for a party to contradict his previous statement.[4]

We have already seen that acquiescence and recognition play a crucial role in cases of prescription (see above, p. 145). But they are equally relevant to other modes of acquisition. For instance, in the *Eastern Greenland* case, Norway claimed to have acquired Eastern Greenland by occupation – a claim which presupposed that Eastern Greenland had been *terra nullius* before the Norwegian claim was made. Norway lost because Denmark had exercised more control over Eastern Greenland than Norway had done, and because Norway, by her actions, had recognised Denmark's title to the whole of Greenland (1933, PCIJ, series A/B, no. 53, at p. 68). Acquiescence and recognition can also be important in interpreting treaties of cession.

States are no longer allowed to acquire territory by conquest, but the invalidity of such acquisitions of territory can be cured by recognition.[5] But recognition is subject to special rules in this context. First, it must take the form of an express statement and cannot be implied (H. Lauterpacht, *Recognition in International Law*, 1947, pp. 395-6). Second, it cannot validate acquisition of territory by conquest unless it is *de jure*; if the recognising state says that it only recognises the conquest *de facto*, it is saying in effect that it regards the conqueror's title as defective, and such a statement obviously cannot give the conqueror a good title to the territory. Third, recognition by the victim of the conquest needs to be supplemented by recognition by third states, partly because the

---

[1] See Judge Fitzmaurice in the *Preah Vihear Temple* case, *International Court of Justice Reports*, 1962, pp. 6, 63-4.

[2] *Eastern Greenland* case (1933), Permanent Court of International Justice, series A/B, no. 53, at p. 68; McNair, *The Law of Treaties*, 1961, p. 485.

[3] *Preah Vihear Temple* case, above, n. 1; *Eastern Greenland* case, above, n. 2.

[4] *Minquiers and Ecrehos* case, *International Court of Justice Reports*, 1953, pp. 47, 71.

[5] See above, pp. 147-8. In an attempt to prevent such acquisitions being validated by recognition, the General Assembly has declared that 'no territorial acquisition resulting from the use or threat of force shall be recognized as legal' (text in Ian Brownlie, *Basic Documents in International Law*, 3rd ed., 1983, pp. 35, 39). But it remains to be seen whether states will withhold recognition indefinitely from such territorial acquisitions.

acquisition of territory by force is a matter of concern to the whole international community (Lauterpacht, op. cit., pp. 428–30), and partly because recognition by third states is needed to provide evidence that the victim granted recognition freely and without duress.[1]

Intertemporal Law

The rules governing acquisition of territory have changed over the centuries. This produces a problem of 'intertemporal law'; which century's law is to be applied to determine the validity of title to territory? The generally accepted view is that the validity of an acquisition of territory depends on the law in force at the moment of the alleged acquisition; this solution is really nothing more than an example of the general principle that laws should not be applied retroactively. See the *Western Sahara* case, *ICJ Reports*, 1975, pp. 12, 37–40.

But the generally accepted view has to some extent been undermined by the *Island of Palmas* case, where the arbitrator, Max Huber, said: 'A distinction must be made between the creation of rights and the existence of rights. The same principle which subjects the act creative of a right to the law in force at the time the right arises, demands that the existence of a right, in other words its continued manifestation, shall follow the conditions required by the evolution of law' (1928, *UNRIAA* II 829, 845–6). Therefore, as the requirements of the law for the acquisition of territory become stricter, a state has to do more and more in order to retain its title; it must run all the time in order to stay in the same place. Max Huber's decision was clearly right *on the facts*; increased Spanish action in the island of Palmas was necessary *to prevent the Dutch gaining a title by prescription*. But the wide terms in which Max Huber expressed himself virtually deny the effect of the rule that the validity of an acquisition of territory depends on the law in force at the time of the alleged acquisition.

This problem is particularly acute in the case of titles based on conquest. Nowadays conquest cannot confer title; in the past it could. Do old titles based on conquest now become void? If so, the results could be very startling; carried to its logical conclusion, this suggestion would mean that North America would have to be handed back to the Red Indians, and that the English would have to hand England back to the Welsh. It is therefore not surprising

---

[1] In the case of other modes of acquisition of territory, recognition by rival claimants is what counts, although recognition by third states does have a slight evidential value: R. Y. Jennings, *The Acquisition of Territory in International Law*, 1962, pp. 34–9, 42.

that the General Assembly declared in 1970 that the modern pro-hibition against the acquisition of territory by conquest should not be construed as affecting titles to territory created 'prior to the Charter régime and valid under international law'.[1] On the other hand, if state A conquered part of state B's territory in the nine-teenth century, state B may suffer from a sense of injustice and be tempted to break the law if it is told that it is not allowed to reconquer that territory now.

The Indian invasion of Goa in 1961 demonstrates the difficulties of doing justice in such a situation. Portugal acquired Goa by conquest in the sixteenth century, and India recognised the Portuguese title after becoming independent in 1947. However, in the Security Council debates which followed the invasion, India argued that Portugal's title was void because it was based on colonial conquest. Such a view is correct under twentieth-century notions of international law, but hardly under sixteenth-century notions. The sympathies of most of the members of the United Nations lay with India, and neither the Security Council nor the General Assembly condemned India's action. *But this does not necessarily mean that they thought that India's action was legally justified.* Where a rule of law works well in most cases but causes injustice in isolated cases, the best solution may be to turn a blind eye to violations of the rule in those isolated cases. In municipal law the police often exercise a good deal of discretion in deciding when to prosecute. The United Nations seems to have reacted in the same way to India's invasion of Goa.

India's invasion of Goa had an ironical sequel. A year later China invaded some areas held by India in the Himalayas, arguing that these areas had originally been seized from China by a colonial power (Britain), that Britain's title was invalid because it was based on colonial conquest, that the title which India had inherited from Britain was similarly invalid, and that China was entitled to use force to recover the territory in question, just as India had done in Goa (see the article by Arora in *Public Law*, 1963, p. 172). The argument that conquests in previous centuries are invalid is an argument which cuts both ways, and most states therefore do not accept this argument. Even communist China seems less interested in regaining lost territory than in securing admissions from her neighbours that the boundaries between them and China were established by imperialist aggression; once such an admission has been made (for example, by Pakistan and Burma), China has been prepared to negotiate a new boundary which is

---

[1] Text in Ian Brownlie, *Basic Documents in International Law,* 3rd ed., 1983, pp. 35, 39. The United Nations Charter entered into force on 24 October 1945.

almost indistinguishable from the old. If India and the Soviet Union had been prepared to make such an admission, they could probably have avoided their present boundary disputes with China.[1]

Legal and Political Arguments

In territorial disputes legal and political arguments are often used side by side – so much so that it is sometimes difficult to distinguish one from the other. There are good reasons for this; a state which relied solely on legal arguments might be suspected of having a weak case politically, and a state which relied solely on political arguments might be suspected of having a weak case legally. Besides, territorial disputes arouse extraordinary passions – people are prepared to fight and die rather than 'surrender an inch' of their territory, however useless the territory in dispute may be – and in these circumstances it is hardly to be expected that people will be able to distinguish between what the law is and what it ought to be. Sometimes the confusion is deliberate. 'If a political argument can be made to possess legal overtones, and the legal distinction between *meum* and *tuum* blurred, the claimant may be enabled to convey the impression to others and, perhaps more importantly, to himself that he already possesses a claim in the sense of a legal title.'[2]

The main political arguments which are used in territorial disputes are the principles of geographical contiguity, of historical continuity and of self-determination. The meaning and function of these principles can best be understood by considering briefly the position of Northern Ireland. It is generally agreed that Northern Ireland forms part of the United Kingdom from the point of view of international law; but the Republic of Ireland argues that Northern Ireland should be reunited with the Republic, because the two halves of Ireland form a natural geographical unit (geographical contiguity) and were administered as a political unit for centuries until 1922 (historical continuity); the United Kingdom replies that the majority of the population of Northern Ireland wishes to remain part of the United Kingdom (self-determination).

[1] On the Sino-Soviet boundary dispute, see *Revue générale de droit international public*, 1969, p. 1083. The Soviet attitude to the Sino-Soviet boundary is hard to reconcile with the Soviet position on 'unequal treaties' generally; see above, pp. 132–3.

[2] R. Y. Jennings, *The Acquisition of Territory in International Law*, 1962, p. 73. For instance, the Republic of Ireland often claims that Northern Ireland *already* forms part of the Republic, although the real purpose of these claims is to induce the United Kingdom to *transfer* Northern Ireland to the Republic.

Such principles cannot, by themselves, create a legal title to territory. In the *Island of Palmas* case, the arbitrator said of the principle of contiguity: 'it is impossible to show the existence of a rule of positive international law to the effect that islands situated outside territorial waters should belong to a state from the mere fact that its territory forms the *terra firma* (nearest continent or island of considerable size)'.[1] That does not mean, however, that such principles have no legal relevance. 'Contiguity is no more than evidence raising some sort of presumption of effective occupation – a presumption that may be rebutted by better evidence of sovereign possession by a rival claimant.'[2] In other words, the principle of contiguity can be taken into account by international tribunals in borderline cases. So, presumably, can the principles of self-determination and historical continuity; where there is genuine doubt about the effectiveness of a state's control over territory, the loyalties of the inhabitants, or the fact that the territory has traditionally formed part of a larger administrative unit, may constitute evidence of effective control by a claimant state. (On self-determination, see also below, pp. 253–6).

Minor Rights over Territory

So far we have been considering the situation where a state exercises full and exclusive sovereignty over territory. But there are also lesser rights over territory, which, although rare, deserve brief mention.

Two states may agree to exercise sovereignty jointly over a certain territory. This is known as a condominium, and resembles co-ownership in municipal law. The New Hebrides Islands in the Pacific were a Franco-British condominium before they became independent in 1980.

Occasionally a state leases part of its territory to another state; this is, in effect, a temporary transfer of sovereignty, because the state to which the territory is leased can exercise full sovereignty over the territory as long as the lease remains in force. Part of the British colony of Hong Kong is held by the United Kingdom under a lease from China which is due to expire in 1997.

A state may also, by treaty, be given the right to administer part of the territory of another state. For instance, the Treaty of Berlin 1878 gave the United Kingdom the right to administer the Turkish island of Cyprus (the subsequent British annexation of Cyprus in 1915 was recognised by Turkey in the Treaty of Lausanne 1923).

---

[1] *UN Reports of International Arbitral Awards* II 829, 854 (1928).

[2] Jennings, op. cit., p. 73. See also the *Eastern Greenland* case (1933), Permanent Court of International Justice, series A/B, no. 53, pp. 45–52.

Servitudes

A servitude is said to arise when territory belonging to one state is, in some particular way, made to serve the interests of territory belonging to another state. The state enjoying the benefit of the servitude may be entitled to do something on the territory concerned, for example, exercise a right of way, or take water for irrigation; alternatively, the state on whom the burden of the servitude is imposed may be under an obligation to abstain from certain action, for example, not to fortify or station forces on the territory in question. Servitudes are usually created by treaty, although they may also be derived from local custom (*Right of Passage* case, *ICJ Reports*, 1960, p. 6).

The term 'servitude' is borrowed from the Roman law of property, and many writers criticise its use in international law, on the grounds that so-called international servitudes are not subject to the same rules as servitudes in Roman law. The essential feature of servitudes in Roman law (and of equivalent institutions in modern systems of municipal law) was that they 'ran with the land', that is, all successors in title to the owner of the 'servient' land were subject to the burden of the servitude, and all successors in title to the owner of the 'dominant' land could claim the benefit of the servitude. Do the same rules apply to so-called international servitudes?

There are many cases of successor states being bound by territorial obligations entered into by predecessor states. For instance, in the *Free Zones of Upper Savoy and District of Gex* case, the Permanent Court of International Justice held that France was obliged to perform a promise made by Sardinia to maintain a customs-free zone in territory which France had subsequently acquired from Sardinia (1932, PCIJ, series A/B, no. 46).

Recorded examples of the *benefit* of an international servitude 'running with the land' in the same way are harder to find. But if obligations can 'run with the land', as in the *Free Zones* case, logic suggests that rights can also 'run with the land'. Moreover, it would be highly inconvenient if such rights did not survive changes in sovereignty; where the population of a particular area is economically dependent on obtaining water, for instance, from a neighbouring area, their livelihood ought not to be endangered by changes in sovereignty over either of the areas concerned.

International servitudes can sometimes exist, not for the benefit of a single state, but for the benefit of many states, or even for the benefit of all the states in the world. For instance, in 1856 Russia entered into a treaty obligation not to fortify the Aaland Islands in the Baltic; the islands lay near Stockholm, but Sweden was not a party to the treaty. In 1918 the islands became part of Finland, which started fortifying them. Sweden, feeling threatened by the fortifications, complained to the Council of the League of Nations. The Council appointed a Committee of Jurists to report on the legal issues involved. The Committee of Jurists advised the Council that Finland had succeeded to Russia's obligations, and that Sweden could claim the benefit of the 1856 treaty, although she was not a party to it, because the treaty was designed to preserve the balance of power in Europe, and could therefore be invoked by all the states which were 'directly interested', including Sweden (League of Nations, *Official Journal*, special supplement no. 3, 1920, pp. 18–19).

Servitudes are particularly important in connection with rivers and canals. In the eighteenth century states used to exclude foreign ships from using waterways within their territory. This caused great hardship, especially to landlocked states lying upstream, and since 1815 various treaties have been concluded, opening most of the major rivers of the world to navigation, either by the ships of all states, or by the ships of all riparian states, or by the ships of all states parties to the treaty (the treaties vary in their terms).

The Convention of Constantinople, signed in 1888 by Turkey and nine other states, declared the Suez Canal open to the ships of all nations. The same rule was applied to the Panama Canal by treaties concluded by the USA with the United Kingdom and Panama in 1901 and 1903. Egypt accepts that she has succeeded to Turkey's obligations under the 1888 Convention, and, after the nationalisation of the canal, she filed a declaration with the United Nations Secretariat in 1957, reaffirming her intention 'to respect the terms and the spirit of the Constantinople Convention', and agreeing to accept the jurisdiction of the International Court of Justice in all disputes between Egypt and the other parties to the Convention which might arise out of the Convention (text in *American Journal of International Law*, 1957, p. 673).

Duties Attached to the Possession of Territory

Every state is under an 'obligation not to allow knowingly its territory to be used for acts contrary to the rights of other states'.[1] For instance, a state must exercise reasonable care to prevent its inhabitants polluting the atmosphere of another state,[2] or using its territory as a base for subversive activities against another state (see below, p. 241–2).

[1] *Corfu Channel* case, *International Court of Justice Reports*, 1949, pp. 4, 22. (Albania was held liable because she *knew* that mines had been laid in her territorial sea; the mines damaged two British destroyers.)

[2] D. J. Harris, *Cases and Materials on International Law*, 3rd ed., 1983, pp. 204–9.

Suggestions for Further Reading

R. Y. Jennings, *The Acquisition of Territory in International Law*, 1962.

D. J. Harris, *Cases and Materials on International Law*, 3rd ed., 1983, ch. 5.

See also the appendix on the Falkland Islands dispute, pp. 291–8, below.

Chapter 12

Legal Consequences of Changes of Sovereignty over Territory (State Succession)

The term 'state succession' is used to describe that branch of international law which deals with the legal consequences of a change of sovereignty over territory. When one state acquires territory from another, how many of the rights and obligations of the 'predecessor state' pass to the 'successor state'? This problem is complicated because it can arise in several different forms. A state may lose part of its territory, or it may lose all. Similarly, the loss of territory may result in the enlargement of one or more existing states, or it may result in the creation of one or more new states. These distinctions are vital, because different rules of law apply to different types of situation; for instance, the legal effects of the creation of a new state are different from the legal effects of the enlargement of an existing state.

The importance of classifying the situation is exceeded only by the difficulty of doing so. For instance, is Yugoslavia a new state, or is it merely an enlargement of Serbia? – judicial decisions on the status of Yugoslavia vary. The only safe way of dealing with such problems is to ask, first, does the state concerned claim to be a new state, or does it claim to be a continuation of a previously existing state? and, second, how far have these claims been accepted by other states?

Treaties

The Vienna Convention on Succession of States in Respect of Treaties was signed in 1978 (text in *American Journal of International Law*, 1978, p. 971). It is not yet in force, but many of its provisions codify the customary law on the subject. The preliminary research and drafting were carried out by the International Law Commission, whose commentary (text in *Yearbook of the International Law Commission*, 1974, vol. 2, part 1, pp. 174–269) contains useful information about previous state practice.

In the case of 'dispositive' treaties (that is, treaties which deal with rights over territory), succession to rights and obligations always occurs. Such treaties 'run with the land' and are unaffected by changes of sovereignty over the territory (Articles 11 and 12 of the Vienna Convention 1978). Servitudes (see above, pp. 154–5) are one important example. Boundary treaties are another. If a treaty delimits a boundary between two states, and if the territory on one side of the boundary is acquired by a third state, the third state is bound by the boundary treaty. One consequence of this rule is that newly independent states inherit boundaries drawn by the former colonial powers; this consequence is accepted by almost all newly independent states, who have no wish to see their boundaries called into question. Colonial boundaries, particularly in Africa, are sometimes unnatural, disregarding tribal divisions and cutting through areas which form a natural economic unit, but, since the newly independent states cannot agree on a radical redrawing of boundaries, they are wise to avoid uncertainty and conflict by preserving their existing boundaries. (See Touval, 'The OAU and African borders', *International Organization*, vol. 21, 1967, p. 102, and see also above, pp. 150–2, on the effects of boundary treaties imposed by force.)

As regards other types of treaties, the rules vary according to the nature of the territorial change which has occurred.

When a state loses territory, it loses its rights and obligations under treaties, in so far as those treaties used to apply to the lost territory. Thus, if the United Kingdom grants independence to Nigeria, the United Kingdom is no longer bound by an Anglo-American extradition treaty to extradite criminals from Nigeria, nor does it have a right to require the extradition of criminals from the USA for crimes committed in Nigeria. (But treaties made by the United Kingdom will normally continue to apply to territory retained by the United Kingdom after it has granted independence to Nigeria.)

When an existing state acquires territory, it does not succeed to the predecessor state's treaties; but its own treaties normally become applicable to that territory. For instance, there are many decisions by French and Belgian courts holding that French treaties applied to Alsace and Lorraine after they were ceded to France in 1919. This rule is codified by Article 15 of the Vienna Convention 1978.

The real uncertainty concerns the position of the new state – a highly topical problem in an era of decolonisation.[1] The approach adopted by the Vienna Convention is as follows:

[1] As we have seen, colonies are frequently given a limited treaty-making power before they become independent (see above, p. 56). Treaties which they themselves make under such a power are not affected by independence. For instance, India joined the UN in 1945 and did not become independent till 1947; independence did not affect her membership of the UN (but Pakistan was regarded as a new state and had to apply to be admitted as a new member). Whether India succeeded to treaties made *by the United Kingdom*, however, is a much more difficult problem.

(1) A new state can succeed to a multilateral treaty, to which the predecessor state was a party, by notifying the depositary (cf. above, p. 123, n. 1) that it regards itself as succeeding to the treaty. (There are some exceptions to this rule; for instance, a new state cannot succeed to a multilateral treaty if that would be incompatible with the object and purpose of the treaty or with the intentions of the parties to the treaty.) A new state is under no obligation to succeed to a multilateral treaty if it does not want to do so (Article 17).

(2) A new state succeeds to a bilateral treaty, which the predecessor state made with another state, only if that other state and the new state both agree (Article 24). However, agreement can be inferred from conduct; for instance, if both sides claim rights, or grant rights to one another, on the basis of the treaty, they will be estopped from denying that succession has occurred (for the meaning of estoppel, see above, p. 148). Such implied agreements often occur, because both sides often find that it is in their mutual interests to continue to apply treaties made by the predecessor state.

These rules apply only if the new state was formerly a dependent territory (for example, a colony) of the predecessor state. A new state formed by secession from the metropolitan (that is, non-'colonial') territory of the predecessor state, or by the disintegration of the predecessor state's metropolitan territory into two or more new states, succeeds automatically to most of the predecessor state's treaties (Article 34). When a new state is formed by the merger of two or more existing states, treaties made by the predecessor states continue to apply to the territory to which they applied before the merger, subject to certain exceptions (Article 31).

Articles 17, 24 and 34 are the most controversial provisions of the Vienna Convention. They are supported by some, but by no means all, of the practice which has developed since 1945. Given the uncertainty of the existing law and the consequent difficulty of proving that customary law is *not* in accordance with the rules contained in the Convention, it is likely that future practice, even by states which are not parties to the Convention, will tend to follow the rules contained in the Convention. This is particularly true of Articles 17 and 24; these articles reflect the wishes of the newly independent states, which are becoming increasingly numerous and influential in the modern international community.

International Claims

International claims are regarded as being intensely 'personal', and no succession occurs to the rights of the claimant state or to the obligations of the defendant state. The claims are unaffected by expansion or contraction of the claimant state or of the defendant state; new states start off with a 'clean slate'; and extinction of either the claimant state or the defendant state results in extinction of the claim. This last proposition is exemplified by *Brown's* claim. Brown, a United States citizen, suffered a denial of justice in the South African Republic in 1895, but, before the claim was settled, the Boer War broke out and the Republic was annexed by the United Kingdom. The USA presented a claim against the United Kingdom, but the arbitrator held that the United Kingdom had not succeeded to the South African Republic's liabilities for international claims.[1]

Nationality

It is sometimes said that a change of sovereignty over territory means that the subjects of the predecessor state, who inhabit the territory, automatically lose their old nationality and acquire the nationality of the successor state. But what is meant by the 'inhabitants' of territory? Does birth on the territory suffice, or is residence to be taken as the criterion? Or are both birth and residence necessary? Or are they alternatives? If residence is taken into account, what are the critical dates or periods of time for determining whether someone is a resident? In practice, such problems can only be regulated by treaties or by municipal legislation.

Treaties sometimes allow the individuals concerned to choose whether they want to retain their old nationality or acquire the nationality of the successor state.

Public Property

When a state acquires all the territory of another state, it succeeds to all the public property of that state (that is, all property belonging to the state, as distinct from property belonging to its nationals or inhabitants), wherever that property may be situated (*Haile Selassie* v. *Cable & Wireless Ltd.*, [1939] Ch. 195).

On the other hand, if a state merely loses *some* of its territory,

---

[1] (1923), *UN Reports of International Arbitral Awards* VI 120. But the orthodox principle applied in this and other cases was not followed by the Permanent Court of Arbitration in the *Lighthouses Arbitration* (*International Law Reports*, vol. 23, 1956, pp. 81, 90-3).

the successor state succeeds to much less of the predecessor's public property. Most of the public property situated in territory retained by the predecessor state, or in third states, continues to belong to the predecessor state, while most of the public property situated in the transferred territory passes to the successor state (*Yearbook of the International Law Commission*, 1981, vol. 2, part 2, pp. 25–71; *Peter Pázmány University* case (1933), PCIJ, series A/B, no. 61, p. 237).

Private Property

Private property rights do not lapse automatically when territory is transferred. If the successor state subsequently wishes to expropriate privately owned property in the territory which it has acquired, the extent of its power to do so depends on the nationality of the owner. If the owner has (or has acquired) the nationality of the successor state, the successor state's right to expropriate his property is unlimited under customary international law (although it may be limited by treaties on human rights). On the other hand, if the owner is a national of the predecessor state or of a third state, the successor state must comply with the minimum international standard for the treatment of aliens, that is, expropriation must be for a public purpose and must be accompanied by compensation.[1]

Such, at any rate, are the traditional rules accepted by Western countries. Most Afro-Asian countries, however, have rejected these rules. Even when they are prepared to accept that the 'Western' rules are applicable to investments made in newly independent countries *after* independence, they maintain that different considerations apply to investments made *before* independence, at a time when those countries were unable to protect their own interests. Such investments, they argue, were often made on unequal terms and amounted to a form of colonialist exploitation. Some Western writers have tried to meet this point by suggesting that the rule requiring compensation in the event of expropriation is designed to prevent unjust enrichment, and that it is therefore logical, in certain cases, to reduce the amount of compensation payable for the act of expropriation, in order to take account of

[1] *United States* v. *Percheman* (1833), 32 U.S. 51, 86–8; *German Settlers'* case (1923), Permanent Court of International Justice, series B, no. 6; *Certain German Interests in Polish Upper Silesia* (1926), PCIJ, series A, no. 7, pp. 21–2; *Chorzów Factory* case (1928), PCIJ, series A, no. 17, pp. 46–8. In the last two cases the question was regulated by a treaty, but the Court said that the rules of customary law were the same as those contained in the treaty. On the minimum standard for the treatment of aliens, with special reference to expropriation, see above, pp. 89–96.

the extent to which the expropriated foreigner has unjustly enriched himself in the past (for example, Friedmann, *American Journal of International Law*, 1963, pp. 279, 295–9). Unfortunately words like 'unjust enrichment' and 'exploitation' are so subjective that there are bound to be constant disputes about the application of a rule drafted in such terms; enrichment which seems just to one party will seem unjust to the other. And Western investors are hardly likely to make new investments in newly independent countries if they feel that those countries have enriched themselves unjustly at the expense of old investments. It is therefore questionable whether a relaxation of the traditional rules would really be in the long-term interests of the newly independent countries.

Contractual rights

Even before the modern era of decolonisation, some authorities doubted whether a successor state succeeded to the contractual obligations of the predecessor state. For instance, in *West Rand Central Gold Mining Co.* v. *The King*, [1905] 2 K.B. 291, the English High Court held that the Crown did not succeed to the contractual liabilities of the South African Republic after it had been annexed by the United Kingdom. This case has been criticised, and it was not followed by the Permanent Court of International Justice in the *German Settlers'* case (1923, PCIJ, series B, no. 6).

It is sometimes said that the successor state cannot logically be bound by a contract to which it is not a party. But, if the alien has benefited the territory by spending money and effort in performing his contract, it is only fair that a state acquiring sovereignty over that territory should allow him to reap the rewards of his investment. On this analysis, the successor state's liability is probably not contractual but quasi-contractual – a term used to describe a situation where there is no contract, but where the law requires the parties to behave *as if* there were a contract, in order to prevent unjust enrichment. It does not matter much whether the successor state's liability is regarded as contractual or as quasi-contractual, because the results are the same in both cases – either the successor state must allow the alien to obtain the benefits due to him under the original contract, or, if it wishes to deprive him of some or all of those benefits, it must compensate him for expropriating his rights (but see below, p. 163, n. 1).

The problem of contractual rights has arisen chiefly in connection with concessions and the national debt. A concession is a right granted by a state to a company or individual to operate an undertaking on special terms defined in an agreement between the state and the concessionaire; the undertaking usually consists of extracting oil or other minerals, or of providing a public utility (supplying gas, water, or electricity, running a canal or railway, and so on). The concessionaire's rights are semi-proprietorial, semi-contractual. Practice is not entirely consistent, but the better view is that a successor state must pay compensation if it revokes a concession granted by the predecessor state (*Mavrommatis* case (1924), PCIJ, series A, no. 2, p. 28).[1]

The problems which arise in connection with the national debt are more complex, and can only be discussed in outline here. If state A annexes the whole of state B's territory, it succeeds to the obligations which state B owed to foreign creditors in respect of state B's national debt. If state B loses only part of its territory, it is right that the successor state or states should take over part of B's debt, otherwise B, with reduced territory and economic resources, might be unable to meet its debts.[2] Similarly, if state B loses all its territory as a result of being dismembered by several other states, it is only fair that responsibility for state B's debt should be split up among the successor states. The difficulty in these last two cases is deciding what *proportion* of the debt should be borne by each of the states concerned; in practice this problem can only be settled by treaty. See also *Yearbook of the International Law Commission*, 1981, vol. 2, part 2, pp. 72–113.

[1] This is the rule accepted by Western countries, but it is rejected by most Afro-Asian countries.

[2] When British colonies become independent, they are made liable for the debts raised by the local colonial administration, but not for any part of the British national debt (even while they are colonies they do not contribute towards the cost of the British national debt). See also *Yearbook of the International Law Commission*, 1981, vol. 2, part 2, pp. 91–105, on the legal position of former colonies in connection with national debts.

However, when the Irish Free State became independent in 1922, it took over part of the British national debt (D. P. O'Connell, *State Succession in Municipal Law and International Law*, 1967, vol. 1, p. 404); otherwise independence would have relieved taxpayers in the Irish Free State of their previous responsibility for paying interest on the national debt, and would have increased the burdens falling on taxpayers in the remaining parts of the United Kingdom.

Suggestions for Further Reading

International Law Commission, 'Draft Articles on Succession of States in Respect of Treaties', *Yearbook of the International Law Commission*, 1974, vol. 2, part 1, pp. 174–269 (summarised by Richard Kearney in the *American Journal of International Law*, 1975, pp. 591–602).
International Law Commission, 'Draft Articles on Succession of States in Respect of Matters Other Than Treaties', *Yearbook of the International Law Commission*, 1981, vol. 2, part 2, pp. 20–113.

Chapter 13

The United Nations

The United Nations Charter and the Problem of Interpretation

Like most international organisations, the United Nations was set up by a treaty – the United Nations Charter. The Charter defines the purposes for which the United Nations was set up, and confers certain powers on it. If the United Nations acts for other purposes, or attempts to exercise other powers, it is acting illegally.

It is no exaggeration to say that the whole history of the United Nations has been a series of disputes about the correct interpretation of the Charter. Language is inherently ambiguous, and there will often be disputes about the interpretation of rules of law which are expressed in words; laymen may be surprised by this fact, but lawyers take it for granted. However, there are several reasons why the United Nations Charter has given rise to an abnormally large number of problems of interpretation. It was drafted mainly by politicians, with little assistance from lawyers; often it is ambiguous, or fails to make provision for a certain problem (either by accident, or because no genuine agreement could be reached by the parties on the point at issue); often it sets up machinery which has not worked well in practice, so that other machinery has had to be improvised to fill the gap. There are five official texts, each of which is equally authentic – English, French, Spanish, Russian and Chinese. Negotiations at the San Francisco Conference, which drew up the United Nations Charter in 1945, were in English and French, and the other three texts were later translations of the English and French texts; but, even if one looks only at the English and French texts, there are differences between the two texts. One of the objects of interpretation is to reconcile such differences, but reconciliation is not always easy. It must also be remembered that neither English nor French was the native language of the majority of the delegates at San Francisco, so imprecise drafting was inevitable.

Various methods of interpretation are discussed below. But it must not be imagined that such methods provide a simple answer to all problems of interpretation. Interpretation is an art, not a science. In a sense, there are no rules of interpretation, only presumptions; and the presumptions very often conflict with one another. The choice between conflicting presumptions is almost bound to be influenced by political factors, however hard one tries to exclude them. And it is this intermixture of political factors with legal factors which explains why states are reluctant to refer disputes about the interpretation of the United Nations Charter to the International Court of Justice.

Literal interpretation

Literal interpretation may be described as a method of interpretation which looks exclusively at the words of a document, and which applies a number of different presumptions to determine the meaning of those words. For instance, words are presumed to be used in their ordinary meaning, unless it is clear from the context that a technical meaning is intended, in which case the technical meaning is applied; the document must be read as a whole, and it will be presumed that the same word used in different parts of the document will have the same meaning; if possible, a particular provision should not be interpreted so as to conflict with another provision, or to make another provision redundant, or to lead to a manifest absurdity.

This is the method of interpretation used most frequently by English judges when interpreting Acts of Parliament and other documents, and it is also used by international lawyers to interpret treaties. But in international law it does not always provide a clear answer, because treaties are usually drafted in less precise and less technical language than Acts of Parliament; this is particularly true of the United Nations Charter. The Charter was drawn up mainly by politicians, and often recalls the deliberate vagueness of an election manifesto. Different parts of the Charter were drawn up by different committees at the San Francisco Conference in 1945, and several amendments were made at the last minute; as a result, co-ordination between different provisions is sometimes poor.

Intention and travaux préparatoires

The intentions of the parties to a treaty may be discovered, not only by reading the treaty itself, but also by looking at the historical context in which the treaty was negotiated, and at the records of the negotiations themselves. Such records are called *travaux préparatoires* (preparatory work), and are often used as a subsidiary means of interpretation in international law.

But *travaux préparatoires* are used less for interpreting treaties setting up international organisations than for interpreting other kinds of treaty. Treaties setting up international organisations are intended to last longer than most other types of treaty, and recourse to *travaux préparatoires* would not always be appropriate in such circumstances, because it would mean looking at the (possibly distant) past, instead of looking at the present and the future; the intentions which states had in the 1940s may provide little guidance for solving the very different problems of the 1980s. Moreover, the fact that the majority of the members of the United Nations joined the United Nations after 1945 and were not represented at the San Francisco Conference makes it politically awkward to rely on the *travaux préparatoires* of the Charter.

Practice
The way in which states perform their obligations under a treaty can be evidence of what they originally intended when they drafted the treaty. This is particularly true of treaties setting up international organisations, because such treaties, by their very nature, are applied constantly over a number of years. In fact, one of the reasons why the United Nations Charter was loosely drafted was because the drafters wanted to leave room for flexibility in subsequent practice; unfortunately, the lack of trust between the member-states has not resulted in flexibility, but in constant disputes about interpretation.

When an organisation is empowered to take decisions by majority vote, it is inevitable that the practice supported by the majority of the member-states will come to be regarded as the practice of the organisation itself, and will be used as a means of interpreting the treaty setting up the organisation, despite the fact that the practice in question is opposed by a minority of the member-states. (Naturally, states forming the majority in an international organisation tend to rely heavily on practice as a means of interpreting the constituent treaty, while states in a minority favour a strict, literal interpretation, with more reliance on *travaux préparatoires*.)

Moreover, with the passage of time, it becomes a fiction to regard practice merely as evidence of the parties' original intentions. Practice acquires a force of its own, and may actually develop in the opposite direction to the parties' original intentions (for an example, see below, p. 169).

Practice may even develop in such a way as to run counter to the words of the treaty. Is such a practice illegal, or can it amend the treaty? There is little authority on this point, because the supporters of a particular practice usually defend it by saying that it is a mere interpretation of the treaty, not an amendment; but, if practice can terminate a treaty (see above, pp. 39 and 135), there is no logical reason why practice should not also be capable of amending a treaty. However, although the practice of the *majority* of member-states can be used to *interpret* a treaty setting up an international organisation, practice cannot be used to *amend* such a treaty unless it is *unanimously* accepted; all the parties must agree before a treaty can be amended. (The situation is different where the treaty itself provides for amendment by majority vote. For instance, Article 108 of the United Nations Charter provides that (express) amendments to the Charter 'shall come into force for all members of the United Nations when they have been adopted by a vote of two-thirds of the members of the General Assembly and ratified . . . by two-thirds of the members of the United Nations, including all the permanent members of the Security Council'. If this provision is applied by analogy to amendments implied from practice, it would seem that practice can amend the United Nations Charter provided it is accepted by two-thirds of the members, including all the permanent members of the Security Council.)

Effectiveness and implied powers
There is a presumption of interpretation in international law that a treaty should be interpreted so as to give full effect to its purposes. At first sight this presumption might seem to conflict with another presumption, that a treaty should be interpreted restrictively so as not to limit the sovereignty of states. In fact, however, the two presumptions are usually applied in different circumstances. The principle of restrictive interpretation is used most often to interpret treaties conferring jurisdiction on international tribunals, and treaties which place heavier burdens on one party than on the other party or parties (in such cases restrictive interpretation seeks to minimise the inequality of the parties). Conversely, the principle of effectiveness is used most often to interpret treaties placing identical burdens on all parties – such as treaties setting up international organisations.

The principle of effectiveness received a striking application in the *Reparation for Injuries* case, where the International Court of Justice advised that the United Nations possessed not only powers expressly conferred by the Charter, but also such implied powers as were necessary to enable it to achieve the purposes for which it was set up (*ICJ Reports*, 1949, pp. 174, 180, 182; see above, pp. 70–1).

However, it would be dangerous to regard the doctrine of implied powers as a solution to all problems of interpretation in international organisations. Most of the disputes about the interpretation of the United Nations Charter have concerned powers which were clearly conferred *expressly* on the organisation; the questions in dispute were – which *organ* should exercise the power? and in accordance with what *procedure*? The doctrine of implied powers provides little help in answering such problems, because it is concerned with the powers of the organisation as a whole, not with the internal distribution of powers within the organisation.

The Purposes of the United Nations

An international organisation acts illegally if it acts for purposes other than those for which it was created; and the purposes for which it was created must always be borne in mind when the constituent treaty of the organisation is being interpreted. This makes it particularly important to ascertain the purposes of the United Nations, which are stated in Article 1 of the Charter as follows:

1. To maintain international peace and security, and to that end: to take effective collective measures for the prevention and removal of threats to the peace, and for the suppression of acts of aggression or other breaches of the peace, and to bring about by peaceful means, and in conformity with the principles of justice and international law, adjustment or settlement of international disputes or situations which might lead to a breach of the peace;
2. To develop friendly relations among nations based on respect for the principle of equal rights and self-determination of peoples, and to take other appropriate measures to strengthen universal peace;
3. To achieve international co-operation in solving international problems of an economic, social, cultural or humanitarian character, and in promoting and encouraging respect for human rights and for fundamental freedoms for all without distinction as to race, sex, language, or religion; and
4. To be a centre for harmonizing the actions of nations in the attainment of these common ends.

Obviously the purposes are defined in very wide terms. Politicians in Western countries are sometimes too ready to assume that the main or only purpose of the United Nations is to preserve international security; but Afro-Asian countries attach equal importance, if not greater importance, to 'solving international problems of an economic . . . character' and to securing 'respect for the principle of equal rights and self-determination of peoples' (or at least of peoples under colonial rule).

Domestic Jurisdiction

One provision of the Charter which is, or could have been, a serious limitation on the powers of the United Nations is Article 2(7), which provides:

> Nothing contained in the present Charter shall authorize the United Nations to intervene in matters which are essentially within the domestic jurisdiction of any state or shall require the members to submit such matters to settlement under the present Charter; but this principle shall not prejudice the application of enforcement measures under Chapter VII.

Article 2(7) has given rise to more controversy than any other provision in the Charter, but in practice its interpretation is still as uncertain as ever. States which consider that Article 2(7) prohibits (or does not prohibit) the United Nations from taking a certain course of action in a particular case use all sorts of arguments to support their point of view, and the multiplicity of arguments used prevents the final decision from constituting an intelligible precedent.

The corresponding provision (Article 15(8)) of the Covenant of the League of Nations spoke of matters 'which *by international law*' were within a state's domestic jurisdiction. Domestic jurisdiction has a clear meaning in international law; it refers to those matters (for example, treatment by a state of its own nationals, until recently) where a state's discretion is not limited by obligations imposed by international law (*Nationality Decrees in Tunis and Morocco* (1923), PCIJ, series B, no. 4). But the San Francisco Conference deliberately rejected the idea that 'domestic jurisdiction' in the Charter should be defined by reference to international law, on the grounds that international law was vague. There is some truth in this criticism, since the Charter itself contains a number of references to human rights, self-determination, and so on, which are so vague that it is difficult to say what, if any, legal obligations they impose.

In the practice of the United Nations, a number of different tests are applied in order to determine whether a matter falls within a state's domestic jurisdiction. Thus, a matter is unlikely to be regarded as within a state's domestic jurisdiction if it amounts to a breach of international law, an infringement of the interests of other states, a threat to international peace, or a gross violation of human rights – or if it concerns progress towards self-determination in a colony. Political factors influence the votes cast by states, which are not always consistent. But in general the practice is to interpret 'domestic jurisdiction' narrowly – the opposite of what was intended by the drafters of the Charter.

Article 2(7) states that the principle of non-intervention in matters of domestic jurisdiction 'shall not prejudice the application of enforcement measures under Chapter VII'. Chapter VII is entitled: 'Action with respect to threats to the peace, breaches of the peace, and acts of aggression'. According to the recent practice of the United Nations, the proviso at the end of Article 2(7) is unnecessary, because a threat to the peace, breach of the peace, or act of aggression is nowadays automatically treated as not constituting a matter of domestic jurisdiction.

Membership

The founding members of the United Nations were the states which were on the Allied side in the Second World War. The admission of new members is governed by Article 4 of the Charter:

> 1. Membership in the United Nations is open to all other peace-loving states which accept the obligations contained in the present Charter, and, in the judgment of the Organization, are able and willing to carry out these obligations.
> 2. The admission of any such state to membership in the United Nations will be effected by a decision of the General Assembly upon the recommendation of the Security Council.

(This means that both the Security Council and the General Assembly must vote in favour of admission.) At present there are 158 member-states of the United Nations, of which only fifty-one were founding members. Almost all independent states in the world are now members of the United Nations.

A member-state against which enforcement action (see below, pp. 180–5) is being taken may be suspended from exercising the rights of membership (Article 5), and a member-state which has persistently violated the principles of the Charter may be expelled (Article 6); in each case the decision is taken by the General Assembly upon the recommendation of the Security Council. These provisions have never yet been applied, although many Afro-Asian states would like to expel South Africa. Expulsion, however, is not necessarily an effective sanction; some people might interpret it as a confession on the part of the organisation that it has failed to impose its will on the expelled member.

The Charter says nothing about withdrawal by member-states; the omission is deliberate, because the insertion of a right of withdrawal in the Covenant of the League of Nations had encouraged many member-states to withdraw, thereby seriously weakening the League. But the San Francisco Conference did recognise a right of withdrawal in exceptional circumstances, for example 'if . . . the organization was revealed to be unable to maintain peace or could do so only at the expense of law and justice', or if a member's 'rights and obligations as such were changed by Charter amendments in which it has not concurred and which it finds itself unable to accept, or if an amendment duly accepted by the necessary majority in the Assembly or in a general conference fails to secure the ratifications necessary to bring such amendment into effect' (text in *United Nations Conference on International Organization: Documents*, Vol. 7, pp. 328–9). This statement of opinion forms part of the *travaux préparatoires* of the Charter, and may therefore be used to interpret the Charter.

The question of withdrawal has arisen only once in practice. In January 1965 Indonesia purported to withdraw, in protest against the election of Malaysia (part of whose territory was claimed by Indonesia) as a non-permanent member of the Security Council. Although the election of Malaysia could hardly be regarded as an 'exceptional circumstance' within the meaning of the San Francisco statement, the Indonesian withdrawal was apparently accepted as valid by the Secretariat at the time. But in September 1966 Indonesia resumed participation in the United Nations. If her withdrawal had really been effective, she would have had to seek readmission under Article 4; instead, she simply resumed her seat, as if nothing had happened – which suggests that her withdrawal had been void. Logically, Indonesia should have had to pay all the arrears of her contributions as a member in respect of the period between January 1965 and September 1966, but, since she had derived no benefits from membership during that period, it was agreed that she should pay only 10 per cent of the arrears of her contributions.

The representation of China
The communists seized power in China at the end of 1949, but until 1971 China was represented at the United Nations by the nationalist government of Chiang Kai-shek. During that period one frequently heard people arguing that communist China should be 'admitted' to the United Nations; but, by treating the question as one of admission, they were unwittingly playing into the hands of the USA, which argued that communist China should not be 'admitted' because it did not fulfil the requirements of Article 4 (see above, p. 170) – it was not peace-loving, it was not willing to carry out the obligations of the Charter, and so on.

The correct analysis is that states, not governments, are members of the United Nations; the state of China is and always has been a member of the United Nations; the question is, which government should *represent* it at the United Nations? Although Article 4 could perhaps be applied by analogy to questions of representation, it seems more logical to hold that a member-state has a right to be represented by its *effective* government until that member-state is suspended or expelled; any other solution would be out of keeping with the general principles governing the relationship between states and governments in international law (see above, pp. 56–7). Although many states did not recognise the communist government of China until recently, it is undeniable that that government had been the effective government of China since the end of 1949.

The distinction between admission and representation is important in other respects, too. If communist China had been *admitted* as a new member-state, nationalist China could have remained a member of the United Nations (and a permanent member of the Security Council) even after the admission of communist China. If, however, the question is treated as one of *representation*, the arrival of communist representatives must inevitably be accompanied by the departure of nationalist representatives from all the organs of the United Nations, because a state cannot be represented simultaneously by two rival governments in an international organisation; and this is, in fact, what happened in 1971.

Moreover, questions concerning the admission of new members or the suspension or expulsion of existing members are treated as non-procedural questions, which means that the veto applies in the Security Council; questions concerning representation are treated as procedural questions, which means that the veto does not apply (see below, pp. 173–5).

The Organs of the United Nations

There are six principal organs of the United Nations: the General Assembly, consisting of all the member-states; the three Councils, which have more specialised functions and consist of a limited number of member-states – the Security Council, the Economic and Social Council and the Trusteeship Council; and two organs composed, not of member-states, but of individuals – the Secretariat and the International Court of Justice. There is also a vast number of subsidiary organs created by the principal organs.

The Security Council

The Security Council consists of fifteen member-states. Five are permanent members – China, France, the United Kingdom, the USA and the USSR. The other ten members of the Security

Council are non-permanent, elected for two years by the General Assembly. The number of non-permanent members was increased from six to ten on 1 January 1966, as a result of an amendment to the Charter; as the membership of the United Nations increased, it was considered that the membership of the Security Council should also be increased, in order to give more states an opportunity of sitting on the Security Council. The current practice is that five of the non-permanent places are filled by Afro-Asian states, two by Latin American states, one by an Eastern European state and two by Western European and other states (the 'other states' being principally the 'white' members of the Commonwealth).

Article 24(1) of the Charter provides:

In order to ensure prompt and effective action by the United Nations, its members confer on the Security Council primary responsibility for the maintenance of international peace and security, and agree that in carrying out its duties under this responsibility the Security Council acts on their behalf.

The Security Council's principal functions consist of making recommendations for the peaceful settlement of disputes (see below, pp. 202–4) and taking enforcement action to deal with threats to the peace, breaches of the peace and acts of aggression (see below, pp. 180–5).

Article 25 of the Charter provides:

The members of the United Nations agree to accept and carry out the decisions of the Security Council in accordance with the present Charter.

The Security Council thus has a power to take binding decisions, which member-states are under a legal obligation to obey (see below, pp. 182–4, 189–90, 203, 207 and 250).

Voting procedure in the Security Council is regulated by Article 27 of the Charter:

1. Each member of the Security Council shall have one vote.
2. Decisions of the Security Council on procedural matters shall be made by an affirmative vote of nine members.
3. Decisions of the Security Council on all other matters shall be made by an affirmative vote of nine members including the concurring votes of the permanent members; provided that, in decisions under Chapter VI . . . a party to a dispute shall abstain from voting.

(Before the membership of the Security Council was increased in 1966, decisions were taken by an affirmative vote of seven members (instead of nine), 'including the concurring votes of the permanent members' in the case of non-procedural questions.)

The effect of Article 27(3) is that each permanent member of the Security Council has a 'veto' on non-procedural questions, and each of them has used its veto on occasions, although the Soviet Union has used it more frequently than the other permanent members of the Security Council. The veto has often been criticised as a crippling limitation on the powers of the Security Council, but the existence of the veto recognises the realities of power politics; it is the price which must be paid for the unusually large powers conferred on the Security Council. It so happens that all the permanent members of the Security Council are nuclear powers; abolition of the veto would add little to the power of the United Nations, because it would still be virtually impossible for the United Nations to take enforcement action against a nuclear power.

In any case, some of the worst features of the veto have been softened in practice. A literal interpretation of Article 27(3) would produce the result that all permanent members would have to vote *for* a draft resolution in order for it to be passed; an abstention would constitute a veto. (This conclusion is spelt out even more clearly in the French text: 'Les décisions du Conseil de Sécurité sur toutes autres questions sont prises par un vote affirmatif de neuf de ses membres dans lequel sont comprises les voix de tous les membres permanents . . .') But, since the first years of the United Nations, there has been a consistent practice of not treating abstentions as vetoes, and this practice was recognised as lawful by the International Court of Justice in the *Namibia* case (*ICJ Reports*, 1971, pp. 16, 22).

The effect of absence by a permanent member is less certain, because the problem has really only arisen once. In 1950 the Soviet Union boycotted the Security Council in protest against the Council's refusal to seat the communist representatives of China. In June 1950, when North Korea invaded South Korea, the absence of the Soviet Union enabled the Security Council to pass a resolution recommending member-states to send forces to help South Korea. The Soviet Union challenged the legality of the resolution on the grounds that it had been passed in the absence of the Soviet Union. It is debatable whether the practice which has developed in relation to abstentions by a permanent member can be applied by analogy to the absence of a permanent member; but the Soviet boycott was itself probably a violation of the Soviet Union's obligations under Article 28 of the Charter:

The Security Council shall be so organized as to be able to function continuously. Each member of the Security Council shall for this purpose be represented at all times at the seat of the organization.

On this reasoning, the absence of a permanent member ought not to prevent the Security Council from taking a decision; otherwise the illegal act of one state would bring the whole work of the Security Council to a halt. At all events, the action taken by the Security Council in June 1950 has had one salutary effect – since then no permanent member has attempted to boycott the Security Council.

The veto does not apply to procedural questions. How does one decide whether or not a question is procedural? At the San Francisco Conference, the four powers which had convened the Conference (USA, USSR, UK and China) listed certain questions which would be regarded as procedural (for example, decisions under Articles 28–32 of the Charter, and questions relating to the agenda) and certain other questions which would be regarded as non-procedural (for example, recommendations for the peaceful settlement of disputes, and decisions to take enforcement action); in cases of doubt, which were expected to be rare, the preliminary question (that is, the question whether or not a particular question was procedural) would itself be a non-procedural question. This led to the 'double-veto'; a permanent member of the Security Council could veto any attempt to treat a question as procedural, and then proceed to veto any draft resolution dealing with that question. By means of the 'double-veto', the Soviet Union has sometimes tried to convert a number of questions, which were clearly listed as procedural in the four-power statement, into non-procedural questions. But the device of the presidential ruling can be used to prevent such abuse of the 'double-veto'. The post of president of the Security Council is held in turn by each member of the Security Council for a period of one month; if the president reacts to an attempted abuse of the 'double-veto' by ruling that the preliminary question is itself procedural, his ruling is final unless it is reversed by a (procedural) vote of the Security Council.

Article 27(3) of the Charter provides that in decisions under Chapter VI a party to a dispute shall abstain from voting. Chapter VI deals with the peaceful settlement of disputes – and also with the peaceful settlement of situations which might give rise to a dispute, and the distinction between disputes and situations is singularly imprecise. Moreover, it is often difficult to tell who is a party to a particular dispute; there are comparatively few states in the world, and many of them are linked together by alliances or other close ties, so that a dispute can affect the interests of many states to varying degrees. In the first few years of the United

Nations, there were arguments about the difference between disputes and situations, about the definition of parties to a dispute and about the precise scope of Chapter VI. Since about 1950 such legalistic arguments have become rarer, and in many cases the obligation to abstain from voting has been simply ignored – states have frequently taken part in votes about disputes to which they were parties, and objections have seldom been made by other states.

The General Assembly

The General Assembly consists of all the member-states of the United Nations. Some idea of the wide scope of the questions which it is competent to discuss may be obtained from examining the following provisions of the Charter:

> The General Assembly may discuss any questions or any matters within the scope of the present Charter or relating to the powers and functions of any organs provided for in the present Charter, and . . . may make recommendations to the members of the United Nations or to the Security Council or to both on any such questions or matters. (Article 10)

> The General Assembly may discuss any questions relating to the maintenance of international peace and security brought before it by any member of the United Nations, or by the Security Council, or by a state which is not a member of the United Nations . . . and . . . may make recommendations with regard to any such question to the state or states concerned or to the Security Council or to both . . . (Article 11(2))

> The General Assembly shall initiate studies and make recommendations for the purpose of:
> (a) promoting international co-operation in the political field and encouraging the progressive development of international law and its codification;
> (b) promoting international co-operation in the economic, social, cultural, educational and health fields, and assisting in the realization of human rights and fundamental freedoms for all . . . (Article 13(1))

> . . . the General Assembly may recommend measures for the peaceful adjustment of any situation . . . which it deems likely to impair the general welfare or friendly relations among nations . . . (Article 14)

In addition to these general powers, the General Assembly has certain more specific powers. For instance, it receives and considers reports from all the other principal organs of the United

Nations (Article 15). It approves the budget of the organisation and fixes the amounts of the budgetary contributions which each member-state must pay (Article 17; in practice, the amount which a state must pay is roughly related to the size of its gross national product). A member-state which is in arrears in the payment of its financial contributions to the organisation shall have no vote in the General Assembly if the amount of its arrears equals or exceeds the amount of the contributions due from it for the preceding two full years, although the General Assembly may waive this rule if it considers that failure to pay is caused by circumstances beyond the member-state's control (Article 19).

Voting procedure in the General Assembly is regulated by Article 18:

1. Each member of the General Assembly shall have one vote.
2. Decisions of the General Assembly on important questions shall be made by a two-thirds majority of the members present and voting. These questions shall include: recommendations with respect to the maintenance of international peace and security, the election of the non-permanent members of the Security Council, the election of members of the Economic and Social Council, the election of members of the Trusteeship Council in accordance with paragraph 1(c) of Article 86, the admission of new members to the United Nations, the suspension of the rights and privileges of membership, the expulsion of members, questions relating to the operation of the trusteeship system, and budgetary questions.
3. Decisions on other questions, including the determination of additional categories of questions to be decided by a two-thirds majority, shall be made by a majority of the members present and voting.

On certain questions concerning the internal running of the United Nations, the General Assembly may take decisions which are binding on member-states; budgetary resolutions are an obvious example. But, as regards other questions (for example, disputes between member-states, or questions of human rights), the General Assembly has no power to take binding decisions, nor does it have any power to take enforcement action; it can only make recommendations. In these respects its powers are much less than those of the Security Council, which explains why the veto exists in the Security Council but not in the General Assembly.

But, although General Assembly resolutions are not binding, they can have important legal effects. They may be evidence of customary law, or of the correct interpretation of the United Nations Charter. A resolution condemning a state for breaking international law is a useful means of putting pressure on that state to reconsider its position. A resolution condemning state A for committing aggression against state B implies that it is lawful for other states to go to state B's defence, and may therefore encourage them to do so.

The drafters of the Charter took some care to prevent conflicts arising between the Security Council and the General Assembly. Article 12(1) provides:

> While the Security Council is exercising in respect of any dispute or situation the functions assigned to it in the present Charter, the General Assembly shall not make any recommendations with regard to that dispute or situation unless the Security Council so requests.

Actually, Article 12(1) has turned out not to be a serious limitation for the General Assembly. Very often the Security Council is unable to reach a decision on a question because of the veto, and in such cases the Security Council has adopted the practice of removing the question from its agenda (this decision is procedural, so the veto does not apply), in order to leave the General Assembly free to deal with the question.

In the early years of the United Nations, the Western powers were keen to emphasise the powers of the General Assembly, where they had a majority; despite Soviet objections, there was a shift of power from the Security Council to the General Assembly. The shift of power has now been partially reversed; the decline in tension between East and West has made it easier for the great powers to reach agreement, and consequently the Security Council is paralysed by the veto less often than it used to be. The newly independent states of Africa and Asia are now the largest group of states in the General Assembly, and have become the chief supporters of an influential role for the General Assembly. By the same token the enthusiasm of the Western powers for the General Assembly has declined. Communist countries have now come to realise the value of the General Assembly as a forum for propaganda and discussion, but neither the Soviet Union nor China is prepared to entrust real power to a body where it does not have a veto.

When the Western powers dominated the General Assembly in the 1950s, they tried to develop it into a body which could take military action to preserve the peace of the world (see below, pp. 186-9). The Afro-Asian states, which dominate the General Assembly nowadays, have not tried to use the General Assembly in this way; they believe that the Security Council is the most appropriate body for taking military action, and they have preferred to use their position in the General Assembly to try to obtain respect for their views on economic questions, colonialism and apartheid (see below, pp. 195-9 and Chapter 17).

The Secretariat

The Secretary-General is appointed by the General Assembly upon the recommendation of the Security Council (this means that a candidate for the post of Secretary-General must secure the support both of the Security Council and of the General Assembly in order to be elected; the election is regarded as a non-procedural question (see above, pp. 173–5), and consequently the veto applies in the Security Council). The Secretary-General is the chief administrative officer of the organisation (Article 97), and performs such other functions as are entrusted to him by the General Assembly, the Security Council, the Economic and Social Council and the Trusteeship Council (Article 98). In addition, according to Article 99, he 'may bring to the attention of the Security Council any matter which in his opinion may threaten the maintenance of international peace and security'. Article 99 is important not only because of its actual terms, but also because of the light which it throws on the general nature of the Secretary-General's functions; he is not a mere servant of the political organs, but is expected to take political initiatives of his own. At any rate, that is the interpretation placed upon Article 99 by Western states; the Soviet Union, on the other hand, has always tried to minimise the power of the Secretariat.

Article 100 provides:

1. In the performance of their duties the Secretary-General and the staff shall not seek or receive instructions from any government or from any other authority external to the organization. They shall refrain from any action which might reflect on their position as international officials reponsible only to the organization.
2. Each member of the United Nations undertakes to respect the exclusively international character of the responsibilities of the Secretary-General and the staff and not to seek to influence them in the discharge of their responsibilities.

Article 100 has not always been observed; some states have tried to treat their nationals working in the Secretariat as if they were national agents or representatives. But the principles laid down in Article 100 are nevertheless indispensable if the Secretariat is to do its job properly.

The staff of the Secretariat, at present numbering more than 20,000, are appointed by the Secretary-General. Recruitment for posts in the Secretariat, other than manual and clerical posts, is subject to complicated rules about national quotas, which favour the nationals of smaller countries; obviously a certain degree of cosmopolitanism is essential if the Secretariat is to be genuinely international and impartial, but the rules about national quotas have sometimes resulted in the appointment of poorly qualified candidates. The terms of service of the staff are laid down mostly in Staff Regulations enacted by the General Assembly, and in Staff Rules issued by the Secretary-General under powers delegated to him by the Staff Regulations. Allegations by staff members that their terms of service have been infringed are heard by an Administrative Tribunal set up by the General Assembly; the Administrative Tribunal has applied a number of general principles of administrative law to fill gaps in the Staff Regulations and Rules. The existence of the Tribunal is really in the long-term interests of the organisation, because officials will not serve the organisation loyally, or resist pressures from member-states and other authorities outside the organisation, unless they are given guarantees of fair treatment and security of tenure.

Enforcement Action and United Nations Forces

After examining the Security Council, the General Assembly and the Secretariat, we can now turn to study enforcement action and United Nations forces – a complicated story involving all three of those organs. Chapter VII of the Charter, which contemplated action by the Security Council, has not worked well in practice, and states have sometimes (especially during the 1950s) turned to the General Assembly and the Secretariat to fill the gap. The Soviet Union has always opposed this trend, and since 1960 power has swung back to the Security Council (see above, p. 178). In the 1950s the General Assembly claimed the power to create a United Nations force, and actually exercised this power in 1956 (see below, pp. 186–9). From 1960 onwards all United Nations forces have been created by the Security Council, and no serious attempt has been made to get the General Assembly to create another United Nations force; the question whether the General Assembly has the legal power to create a United Nations force is no longer of much political importance, although it is still worth examining because it throws light on wider legal issues.

Chapter VII of the Charter
Chapter VII is entitled: 'Action with respect to threats to the peace, breaches of the peace, and acts of aggression'. The Charter does not try to define these terms (although it is fairly clear from the context that 'threats to the peace' and 'breaches of the peace' refer to *international* peace); instead, Article 39, the first Article in Chapter VII, provides: 'The Security Council shall determine the

existence of any threat to the peace, breach of the peace, or act of aggression and shall make recommendations, or decide what measures shall be taken in accordance with Articles 41 and 42, to maintain or restore international peace and security.' In other words, a threat to the peace is whatever the Security Council says is a threat to the peace.

This may seem startling, but it shows political realism. The Covenant of the League of Nations obliged member-states to apply sanctions against a member-state which had resorted to war in violation of its obligations under the Covenant, but every member-state was left to itself to decide whether another member-state had resorted to war in violation of its obligations under the Covenant; and naturally different states reached different decisions. Article 39 of the United Nations Charter was intended to prevent a repetition of that state of affairs. The omission of definitions from the Charter is equally realistic; there is a danger that definitions of aggression will merely leave loopholes which will be exploited by future aggressors.

On 11 November 1965 white settlers in the British colony of Rhodesia unilaterally declared Rhodesia independent, against the wishes of the United Kingdom and of the Africans who formed 94 per cent of the population of Rhodesia. On 16 December 1966 the Security Council decided that 'the present situation in . . . Rhodesia constitutes a threat to international peace', and ordered member-states to suspend trade in certain commodities with Rhodesia (*International Legal Materials*, 1967, p. 141; cf. below, p. 183–4).

Some right-wing politicians in the United Kingdom denied that the situation in Rhodesia constituted a threat to international peace; but Article 39 gives the Security Council a discretionary power to determine what constitutes a threat to the peace, and member-states cannot substitute their own opinion for that of the Security Council. Nor can it be said that the Security Council's decision was wholly unreasonable or an abuse of its discretionary power (in some systems of municipal law an administrative body's decisions are invalid if they are wholly unreasonable or an abuse of that body's discretionary power; but it is not certain whether a similar rule of international law applies to the Security Council). The whole purpose of the unilateral declaration of independence in Rhodesia was to preserve the political and economic dominance of the whites (numbering 6 per cent of the population) over the Africans (numbering 94 per cent of the population). There was obviously a risk that sooner or later the Rhodesian Africans would react violently against this state of affairs, and a risk that fighting between the Rhodesian Africans and the white régime might spill over into the territory of neighbouring states; indeed, both these risks became realities in the 1970s. If a situation is likely to lead to such results, it is not unreasonable to describe it as a threat to international peace.

Some people also criticised the Security Council action on Rhodesia on the grounds that Rhodesia was not a state (see above, pp. 54 and 63), and had not committed any breach of international law. (These two arguments were linked, because it was argued that Rhodesia could not have or break any obligations under international law unless it was a state.) But there is nothing in the Charter to suggest that a threat to the peace necessarily connotes action by a state or a breach of international law. Article 39 says that the Security Council's function is 'to maintain or restore international peace and security' – not to punish breaches of international law. Similarly, one can imagine many situations where international peace could be threatened by entities which are not states or subjects of international law – for instance, bandits, nomadic tribes, or even invaders from another planet.

(For further discussion of the legal problems raised by the Security Council action on Rhodesia, see Ralph Zacklin, *The United Nations and Rhodesia*, 1974, especially pt 2; R. Higgins, 'International law, Rhodesia, and the UN', *The World Today*, vol. 23, 1967, p. 94; J. E. S. Fawcett, 'Security Council resolutions on Rhodesia', *British Year Book of International Law*, vol. 41, 1965–6, p. 103; Harry Strack, *Sanctions: The Case of Rhodesia*, 1978, especially pp. 16–39. The Security Council revoked its resolutions on Rhodesia at the end of 1979, after the 'government' of Rhodesia had agreed to revoke the unilateral declaration of independence and to accept the principle of majority African rule; see *UN Chronicle*, 1980, no. 1, pp. 13–16.)

Article 40 of the United Nations Charter provides:

> In order to prevent an aggravation of the situation, the Security Council may, before making the recommendations or deciding upon the measures provided for in Article 39, call upon the parties concerned to comply with such provisional measures as it deems necessary or desirable. Such provisional measures shall be without prejudice to the rights, claims, or position of the parties concerned. The Security Council shall duly take account of failure to comply with such provisional measures.

A typical example would be a resolution calling for a ceasefire.

The words 'call upon', used in Article 40, cause some problems of interpretation. They are often used in United Nations resolutions as a synonym for 'recommend' (for instance, see below, p. 183, n. 1), but member-states seem to agree that the words, when used in Article 40, mean 'order'; this interpretation is reinforced when Article 40 is read in conjunction with Article 25 (see above, p. 173). For instance, on 15 July 1948 the Security Council passed a ceasefire resolution calling upon the Arabs and Israelis to stop fighting, and this resolution was clearly understood to be mandatory, that is, it was an order which created a legal obligation to obey.

In general, however, the Security Council has made sparing use of its powers under Article 40. Most ceasefire resolutions are phrased as recommendations, not as orders (for example, the resolutions addressed to the Arabs and Israelis during the Six Days' War in June 1967). The reason is probably that members of the Security Council would feel morally obliged to take enforcement action against states which disobeyed an order, and they are reluctant to take enforcement action against states which are their own allies or *protégés*. Even when phrased as recommendations, however, ceasefire resolutions have often succeeded in stopping the fighting; states are reluctant to continue fighting in defiance of the great powers and of world opinion generally.

Enforcement action *stricto sensu* (that is, action to deal with a threat to the peace, breach of the peace, or act of aggression) can take two forms; Article 41 provides for non-military enforcement action and Article 42 provides for military enforcement action.

Article 41 reads as follows:

The Security Council may decide what measures not involving the use of armed force are to be employed to give effect to its decisions, and it may call upon the members of the United Nations to apply such measures. These may include complete or partial interruption of economic relations and of rail, sea, air, postal, telegraphic, radio, and other means of communication, and the severance of diplomatic relations.

Once again the words 'call upon' are used, and again they mean 'order'. But the Security Council has been even more sparing in using its powers under Article 41 than it has been in using its powers under Article 40. For instance, the first resolution on Rhodesia, passed immediately after the unilateral declaration of independence in November 1965, in effect merely *recommended* member-states to suspend trade in certain commodities with Rhodesia;[1] it was not until December 1966 that the 'sanctions' were made mandatory. Indeed, the Rhodesia resolution of 1966 repre-

[1] Text in *American Journal of International Law*, vol. 60, 1966, p. 924; *International Legal Materials*, vol. 5, 1966, p. 167. Despite the use of the words 'call upon' in the resolution, it was not mandatory; see *British Practice in International Law*, 1965, pp. 101, 176–8.

sents the first clear occasion on which the Security Council has given an order under Article 41. Apart from Rhodesia, an order has been issued under Article 41 on only one occasion; the Security Council imposed a mandatory ban on exports of arms to South Africa in 1977 (*UN Monthly Chronicle*, December 1977, p. 10). An attempt to apply Article 41 against Iran in January 1980, in order to compel Iran to release the United States diplomats being held as hostages in Tehran, was defeated by a Soviet veto (*UN Chronicle*, 1980, no. 2, pp. 18-26).

Article 42 provides:

Should the Security Council consider that measures provided for in Article 41 would be inadequate or have proved to be inadequate, it may take such action by air, sea, or land forces as may be necessary to maintain or restore international peace and security. Such action may include demonstrations, blockade, and other operations by air, sea, or land forces of members of the United Nations.

Article 42 must be read in conjunction with Article 43, which provides:

All members of the United Nations . . . undertake to make available to the Security Council, on its call and in accordance with a special agreement or agreements, armed forces, assistance, and facilities, including rights of passage, necessary for the purpose of maintaining international peace and security . . . The agreement or agreements shall be negotiated as soon as possible on the initiative of the Security Council. They shall be concluded between the Security Council and members [of the United Nations] . . .

A state is not obliged to take part in military operations under Article 42 unless it has concluded a 'special agreement' under Article 43. The Security Council cannot *order* a state to take part in military enforcement action in the same way that it can order a state to take part in non-military enforcement action.[1]

In fact, no agreements have been concluded under Article 43. This has not prevented the United Nations from assembling forces by other means. Such forces were, for instance, sent to the Middle East in 1956 and to the Congo in 1960. The Soviet Union argued that these two forces were illegal, because they had not been set up

[1] But the Security Council can *authorise* a state to use force, even in circumstances where force would normally be illegal. Article 42 empowers the Security Council to use force in such circumstances, and therefore may be interpreted *a fortiori* as enabling the Security Council to authorise states to do the same. For an example, see the resolution of 9 April 1966 authorising the UK to search ships on the high seas to see whether they were carrying oil destined for Rhodesia (text in *American Journal of International Law*, vol. 60, 1966, p. 925; *International Legal Materials*, vol. 5, 1966, p. 534).

in accordance with Article 43. The International Court of Justice replied that the forces in question were not designed to take enforcement action, and that Article 43 applied only to forces designed to take enforcement action; consequently, failure to comply with the procedure of Article 43 did not invalidate the creation of the forces (*Expenses* case, *ICJ Reports*, 1962, pp. 151, 166, 171–2, 177).

It seems, however, that the International Court did *not* intend to imply that failure to comply with the procedure of Article 43 *would* have invalidated the creation of a force designed to take enforcement action (ibid., p. 167). When Article 42 says that 'action by . . . [United Nations] forces . . . *may include* . . . operations by . . . forces of members of the United Nations', it clearly implies that there is more than one way in which United Nations forces may be recruited.

The purpose of Article 43 was to *facilitate* action by the Security Council; it would be wholly alien to that purpose to argue that the absence of agreements under Article 43 should *prevent* action by the Security Council. In other words, Article 43 provides a procedure by which the Security Council *may* act, but it does not prevent the Security Council from choosing an alternative procedure.

The United Nations force in Korea

When North Korea invaded South Korea ('the Republic of Korea') in June 1950, the Security Council, profiting from the absence of the Soviet representative (see above, pp. 174–5), passed a resolution recommending member-states to 'furnish such assistance to the Republic of Korea as may be necessary to repel the armed attack and to restore international peace'; later it passed another resolution recommending them to place their forces in Korea under a unified command to be appointed by the USA (texts in *Yearbook of the United Nations*, 1950, pp. 222 and 230).

It is doubtful whether the forces in Korea constituted a United Nations force in any meaningful sense. They were always called a United Nations force, they were authorised by the Security Council to fly the United Nations flag and they were awarded United Nations medals by the General Assembly. But all the decisions concerning the operations of the forces were taken by the USA (sometimes after consulting the other states which had sent forces to Korea), and the Commander took his orders from the USA, not from the United Nations; the decision to dismiss the original Commander, General MacArthur, and to replace him by a new Commander, was taken unilaterally by the USA. Moreover, when the fighting ended and a conference met at Geneva in 1954 to try to reunify Korea, the 'Allied side' at the conference did not consist of representatives of the United Nations, but of representatives of the individual states which had sent forces to Korea.

The states which sent forces to Korea might be regarded as exercising a right of collective self-defence under Article 51 of the Charter (see below, pp. 221-5); alternatively, they might be regarded as acting under an authorisation conferred by the Security Council (if the Security Council can use force itself, it can *a fortiori* authorise member-states to do the same – see above, p. 184, n. 1). But the forces were probably national forces, not United Nations forces.

The Uniting for Peace resolution

The Security Council had been able to act in Korea because the Soviet Union had been boycotting the Security Council; and it was unlikely that Soviet boycotts would recur in the future. After the outbreak of the Korean war, Western states therefore tried to strengthen the General Assembly, in order that it might be able to act when the Soviet veto prevented the Security Council from acting. Article 24 of the Charter gave the Security Council '*primary* responsibility for the maintenance of international peace and security', and it was argued that this did not preclude the General Assembly from exercising a secondary or residual responsibility – an argument which was approved by the International Court of Justice in the *Expenses* case (*ICJ Reports*, 1962, pp. 151, 162-3). On 3 November 1950 the General Assembly passed the Uniting for Peace resolution, in order to increase its ability to exercise this secondary or residual responsibility (text in *Yearbook of the United Nations*, 1950, pp. 193-5).

Unlike the Security Council, which is 'so organized as to be able to function continuously' (Article 28 of the United Nations Charter), the General Assembly only meets 'in regular annual sessions and in such special sessions as occasion may require' (Article 20). Consequently, the General Assembly might find it difficult to deal with trouble which occurred when it was not in session. To remedy this defect, the Uniting for Peace resolution streamlined the procedure for calling special sessions of the General Assembly. This was an exercise of the General Assembly's power to 'adopt its own rules of procedure' (Article 21); even the communist countries, which challenged the legality of the resolution in 1950, have made use of this procedure when requesting special sessions of the General Assembly (for example, at the time of the Suez invasion in 1956).

The Uniting for Peace resolution also states that, if the Security Council fails in its primary responsibility for maintaining international peace and security, the General Assembly shall consider the matter immediately with a view to making recommendations for collective measures, including the use of armed force where necessary; and it recommends members to maintain contingents in their armed forces which could be made available 'for service as a United Nations unit . . . upon recommendation by the Security Council or General Assembly'. Needless to say, the communist countries opposed this part of the resolution with especial vehemence; and its legality is certainly open to doubt. Article 11(2) of the Charter says that 'any . . . question on which action is necessary shall be referred to the Security Council by the General Assembly . . .', and it is fairly clear that this gives the Security Council a monopoly of 'action'. In the *Expenses* case, the International Court of Justice interpreted 'action' to mean 'enforcement action', and said that the United Nations Emergency Force in the Middle East, created by the General Assembly in 1956, was not contrary to Article 11(2) because it was not designed to take enforcement action (*ICJ Reports*, 1962, pp. 151, 165, 171–2); the Court clearly implied that the General Assembly would have acted illegally if it had set up a force designed to take enforcement action.

On the other hand, states have a right of collective self-defence under Article 51 of the Charter, and there is nothing to prevent the General Assembly recommending them to exercise this right in order to defend the victim of an aggression; but in this case it is difficult to describe the forces of the states concerned as 'a United Nations unit'.

The first United Nations Emergency Force in the Middle East (UNEF)

At the end of October 1956 Israel, France and the United Kingdom attacked Egypt. But within a few days the states concerned agreed to a ceasefire, and on 5 November 1956 the General Assembly set up a United Nations Emergency Force (UNEF) 'to secure and supervise the cessation of hostilities' (*Yearbook of the United Nations*, 1956, p. 36). Later, when Israel, France and the United Kingdom had withdrawn their troops, UNEF was sent to patrol the Israeli–Egyptian armistice line, in order to encourage 'the scrupulous maintenance of the armistice agreement of 1949' (ibid., p. 61).

The Force consisted of contingents of national armies, made available under agreements between the contributing states and the Secretary-General. The General Assembly appointed the Commander of the Force, and authorised the Secretary-General to enact regulations setting out the rights and duties of soldiers serving in it. The Force was paid by the United Nations, and it took its orders solely from the General Assembly and the Secretary-General. Consequently, although certain questions such as promotion were still dealt with by the contributing states, the Force was a United Nations force in a much more real sense than the forces in Korea.

The Force was founded very largely on the principle of consent. No state was obliged to provide a contingent unless it consented to do so. The Force could not enter the territory of any state without that state's consent; thus it operated solely on Egyptian territory and not on Israeli territory, because Israel, unlike Egypt, did not consent to its presence.

The Force was authorised to fight in order to defend itself, but it was not expected to resist large-scale invasions across the armistice line; indeed, the fact that it never numbered more than 6,000 men would have made such a role impracticable. Its function was to patrol the armistice line and to report troop movements taking place near the line; it also used to arrest individuals trespassing near the armistice line and hand them over to the Egyptian police. For over ten years until it was withdrawn in 1967, its presence helped to create a peaceful atmosphere in which there were very few guerilla raids across the armistice line.

The legal basis for the creation of the Force was uncertain. The communist countries, which abstained in the vote setting up the Force, said that the use of *any* type of United Nations force constituted enforcement action, which could only be taken by the Security Council. In the *Expenses* case, the International Court of Justice said that the operations of UNEF did not constitute enforcement action because they were not directed against any state without that state's consent.[1] But it is one thing to show that there is no provision in the Charter *forbidding* the creation of the Force; it is another thing to find a provision *authorising* its creation. The International Court suggested that the force might have been based either on Article 11 or on Article 14 of the Charter.[2] The trouble with these Articles is that they merely empower the General Assembly to *recommend* measures to be taken by somebody else; they do not empower it to *take* measures. But the practice of the General Assembly suggests that the fact that the General Assembly can only make recommendations does not prevent it setting up subsidiary bodies to carry out those

---

[1] *ICJ Reports*, 1962, pp. 151, 171–2. See also pp. 184–5, above. Most commentators have described UNEF as a 'peace-keeping force'. The concept of peace-keeping forces, and the distinction between peace-keeping and enforcement action, are not mentioned in the Charter, but have been developed by practice.

[2] ibid., p. 172. For the text of these Articles, see above, p. 176.

recommendations, provided that the consent of the states concerned is obtained (*International Court of Justice: Pleadings, Oral Arguments, Documents: Effect of Awards of Compensation made by the UN Administrative Tribunal*, 1954, pp. 295–301).

The United Nations force in the Congo (ONUC)

On 30 June 1960 Belgium granted independence to the Belgian Congo. But little had been done to prepare the Congo for independence, and almost immediately the Congolese army mutinied and began attacking Europeans resident in the Congo. Belgium, which had retained military bases in the Congo, deployed troops to protect the Europeans, and the Congolese government appealed to the United Nations for military assistance against 'Belgian aggression'. On 14 July 1960 the Security Council authorised the Secretary-General to provide the Congo with military assistance (*Yearbook of the United Nations*, 1960, p. 97); the Secretary-General had announced in advance that he would interpet this resolution as authorising him to create a force modelled on UNEF, and the action which he took to set up the force was approved unanimously by the Security Council eight days later (ibid.). Despite the circumstances in which the force was set up, it was not intended to take military action against Belgian troops; its function was to help the Congolese government to maintain law and order, and thus to create a situation in which the Belgian government would realise that Europeans in the Congo did not need protection by the Belgian army. The force was modelled on UNEF, but a number of differences soon began to appear.

In the first place, the Security Council was prevented by the veto from giving clear instructions to the Secretary-General, and consequently the Secretary-General had to take all sorts of decisions which, in the case of UNEF, had been taken by the General Assembly (for example, appointing the Commander of the force).

Second, although the force was intended to operate with the consent of the Congolese government, this principle became difficult to observe when the Congolese government disintegrated into warring factions. Another departure from the principle of consent can be seen in the Security Council resolution passed on 9 August 1960, which referred to earlier resolutions about the Congo and reminded member-states that they were under a legal obligation, by virtue of Article 25 of the Charter (see above, p. 173), 'to accept and carry out the decisions of the Security Council' (*Yearbook of the United Nations*, 1960). One of the earlier decisions referred to in the resolution of 9 August 1960 was the resolution of 22 July 1960, which *inter alia* requested 'all states to refrain from any action which might . . . impede the restoration of law and order . . . and also to refrain from any action which might undermine the territorial integrity and political independence . . . of the Congo'. This request, which was transformed into an order by the resolution of 9 August 1960, was ignored by certain Western financial interests, which assisted the secessionist activities of Moïse Tshombe in Katanga, and by the Soviet Union, which supported the Prime Minister, Patrice Lumumba, in his struggle against President Kasavubu.

Third, although the force was originally intended to fight only in order to defend itself, it was subsequently authorised to fight in other circumstances as well – in order to prevent civil war, and in order to expel foreign mercenaries. In the end the force found itself engaged in extensive military operations against the secessionist movement in Katanga.

The legal basis for the creation of the force is obscure and controversial. The Soviet Union argued that the creation of the force was illegal for a number of reasons, including the fact that the force was virtually under the control of the Secretary-General, instead of being under the control of the Security Council, as it ought to have been. But there is no reason why the Security Council should not delegate its powers to the Secretary-General under Article 98 of the Charter, which provides that 'the Secretary-General . . . shall perform such . . . functions as are entrusted to him by' the Security Council. In any case, the Soviet position is hard to reconcile with the fact that the Soviet Union voted for the resolutions creating the force.

In the *Expenses* case the International Court of Justice said that the operations of the force did not constitute enforcement action.[1] But one of the resolutions concerning the force was phrased in mandatory terms (see above, pp. 189–90); several commentators have suggested that the creation of the force constituted 'provisional measures' within the meaning of Article 40, and this view has received some support from the United Nations Secretariat.[2]

Reliance on Article 40 implies that the situation in the Congo must have amounted to (at least) a threat to international peace.

---

[1] *ICJ Reports*, 1962, pp. 151, 177; and see above, pp. 184–5. This statement by the Court is rather surprising, considering the scale of the military operations in Katanga. However, commentators have generally described the operations of the force as 'peace-keeping action', as opposed to 'enforcement action'; see above, p. 188, n. 1.

[2] For the text of Article 40, see above, p. 182. Although Article 40 appears in Chapter VII, it would seem that 'provisional measures' under Article 40 do not constitute 'enforcement action'; otherwise, a state which had been called upon to comply with provisional measures could be suspended from exercising the rights and privileges of membership under Article 5 (see above, p. 170), which would be incompatible with the principle, laid down in Article 40, that 'provisional measures shall be without prejudice to the rights . . . of the parties concerned'.

Although there was no express finding to that effect by the Security Council, it is obvious that the danger of civil war in the Congo was a threat to international peace in the same way that the danger of civil war in Rhodesia was a threat to international peace.[1] Indeed, the situation in the Congo was much more serious, because there was a risk of the Soviet Union and the USA taking sides in the civil war. The United Nations action did not entirely succeed in averting that risk, but, if it had not been for the United Nations action, the two super-powers might have found themselves dragged against their will into a war of Vietnamese proportions in the Congo. Each super-power was therefore probably glad that the United Nations filled the vacuum in the Congo and thus prevented the Congo falling under the control of the other super-power.

The Expenses case
When the United Nations forces in the Middle East and the Congo were set up, the General Assembly decided that member-states were under a legal duty to pay for the forces. However, the forces were not financed out of the ordinary budget, but out of separate accounts (one for each force); and a different scale of contributions was used, which reduced the size of the contributions payable by the poorest member-states. These facts led some states to argue that the expenses of the forces were so different from the ordinary expenses of the United Nations that member-states were under no obligation to pay for the forces. The communist countries also argued that there was no duty to pay for the forces because the forces had been created illegally. Soon it became clear that the United Nations was facing a major financial crisis, and shortage of money forced the United Nations to reduce the force in the Congo in 1963 and to withdraw it altogether in 1964.

Consequently the General Assembly asked the International Court of Justice to advise whether the expenses of the two forces were expenses of the United Nations within the meaning of Article 17(2) of the Charter, which provides that 'the expenses of the organisation shall be borne by the members as apportioned by the General Assembly'. On 20 July 1962 the Court answered this question in the affirmative, by 9 votes to 5 (*ICJ Reports*, 1962, p. 151). The question put to the Court was not *directly* concerned with the legality of the creation of the forces, and the Court's brief remarks about the legality of their creation were somewhat inconclusive; it limited itself to saying that the creation of the forces was *probably* legal, and to indicating those provisions of the Charter

[1] See above, pp. 181–2. A determination by the Security Council that the situation constituted a threat to the peace is probably implicit in the decision to act under Article 40.

which it regarded as *probably* constituting the legal justification for their creation.

The Court's opinion, being an advisory opinion, was not binding, and, although some of the states which had previously defaulted began to pay after the Court had delivered its opinion, the Soviet bloc and France remained adamant in their refusal to pay. The USA and its allies threatened to invoke Article 19 of the Charter, which deprives a defaulting state of its right to vote in the General Assembly 'if the amount of its arrears equals or exceeds the amount of the contributions due from it for the preceding two full years'. The Soviet Union retorted by threatening to leave the organisation if it was deprived of its vote in the General Assembly. Eventually, in August 1965, the USA and its allies gave way and agreed not to invoke Article 19; in return, the Soviet Union promised to make a voluntary contribution towards the expenses of the two forces.

The United Nations force in Cyprus (UNFICYP)

When Cyprus became independent in 1960, it had a complicated constitution designed to protect the interests of the Turkish-speaking minority; in a Treaty of Guarantee 1960 Cyprus agreed not to alter the basic provisions of the constitution, and gave each of the other parties to the treaty (Greece, Turkey and the United Kingdom) a right to take unilateral 'action' (a word which was probably deliberately ambiguous) in order to uphold the constitution. In 1963 President Makarios of Cyprus declared that the constitution was unworkable and would be altered. This led to fighting between the Greek and Turkish communities in Cyprus, and British troops arrived, with the consent of all the interested parties, to keep the peace between the two communities. Keeping the peace turned out to be a harder task than the British had expected, and so the British asked the United Nations to send a peace-keeping force to the island.

There was clearly a danger that war between Greece and Turkey could develop out of clashes between the Greek and Turkish communities in Cyprus. The Security Council therefore decided unanimously on 4 March 1964 to set up a United Nations force for the purpose of preventing a recurrence of fighting between the two communities in Cyprus (*Yearbook of the United Nations*, 1964, p. 165).

The force was largely modelled on UNEF, but with some significant differences. First, it was financed by voluntary contributions. Second, as in the case of the force in the Congo, the composition and the size of the force were to be decided by the Secretary-General, and the Commander was to be appointed by him. On the other hand, a certain distrust of the Secretary-General was shown by the fact that the force was only set up for three months; since then the Secretary-General has had to ask the Security Council to prolong the existence of the force for successive periods of three or six months.

The Secretary-General instructed the force to be impartial and to fight only in order to defend itself. These restrictions have not limited the usefulness of the force as much as one might have expected. The force patrols territory separating areas held by the rival communities, and escorts people from one community across areas held by the other community; if it is fired upon when carrying out these functions, it fires back in self-defence. It also investigates and reports outbreaks of fighting, and tries to persuade the parties to cease fire when such outbreaks occur. However, it was not intended to impose a political settlement on the parties, who have still not yet reached agreement about the constitutional future of Cyprus. Nor was it intended to take part in large-scale hostilities, and consequently it did not attempt to resist the invasion of northern Cyprus by Turkey in 1974. (For further information about the functions of the force, see the paper by A. J. Rodriguez Carrión in *United Nations Peace-Keeping* (edited by A. Cassese), 1978, pp. 158–60, 163–9.)

As usual, the resolution setting up the force does not specify the Articles of the Charter justifying its creation. Some commentators have suggested that it is based on Chapter VI of the Charter (peaceful settlement of disputes – see below, pp. 202–4) rather than on Chapter VII (enforcement action). The preamble to the resolution setting up the force says that 'the present situation with regard to Cyprus is *likely* to threaten international peace and security', which echoes the language of Chapter VI ('dispute or situation . . . *likely* to endanger the maintenance of international peace and security'), rather than the language of Chapter VII (Chapter VII applies only when there is *already* an *actual* threat to the peace, breach of the peace, or act of aggression). Unlike Chapter VII, the relevant provisions of Chapter VI do not authorise the Security Council to address *orders* to states, but that does not matter in the present context, because the resolution setting up the force in Cyprus was not phrased in mandatory terms. A more serious limitation to Chapter VI is that, interpreted literally, it does not authorise the Security Council to *do* anything; it merely empowers the Security Council to *recommend* states to do certain things. But, if the General Assembly could set up UNEF on the basis of Articles 11 or 14 (see above, p. 188), there is no reason why the Security Council should not set up a similar force on the basis of Chapter VI.

New forces in the Middle East

Further fighting broke out between Egypt and Israel in October 1973. The Security Council called for a ceasefire and set up a second United Nations Emergency Force (UNEF II) to supervise the ceasefire. Later, Egypt and Israel entered into two disengagement agreements, which provided that UNEF II should occupy a buffer zone between the Egyptian and Israeli forces, and should carry out periodic inspections to ensure that Egypt and Israel were complying with the terms of the disengagement agreements which limited the forces which each state was allowed to keep in the areas adjacent to the buffer zone (*International Legal Materials*, 1973, pp. 1528–30, 1537–40; ibid., 1975, pp. 1450 ff.; on the first United Nations Emergency Force, cf. above, p. 187).

In May 1974 Israel entered into a disengagement agreement with Syria, under which Israel withdrew from some of the Syrian territory which it had occupied in 1967 and 1973, and the Security Council set up a Disengagement Observer Force (UNDOF), which performs the same type of functions as UNEF II performed under the disengagement agreements between Egypt and Israel (*UN Monthly Chronicle*, June 1974, pp. 26–8). But UNDOF consists of only about 1,250 men, compared with 7,000 in UNEF II.

In March 1978 Israel invaded Lebanon, as a reprisal against raids by Palestinian terrorists from Lebanon against Israel. The Security Council called on Israel to withdraw its forces from Lebanon, and decided 'to establish a United Nations Interim Force for Southern Lebanon [UNIFIL] for the purpose of confirming the withdrawal of Israeli forces, restoring international peace and security and assisting the government of Lebanon in ensuring the return of its effective authority in the area' (*UN Monthly Chronicle*, April 1978, pp. 5–22, 75–6). Despite the presence of UNIFIL, fighting has continued in southern Lebanon between right-wing Lebanese Christians (armed and paid by Israel) and their Palestinian opponents; both of these rival factions refuse to accept the authority of the Lebanese government, and have attacked UNIFIL from time to time.

UNEF II, UNDOF and UNIFIL have many things in common. They were created by the Security Council, but the relevant resolutions and debates do not indicate which provisions of the Charter provided the legal basis for the Forces. One possibility is that the Forces were based on Article 40 of the Charter (cf. above, p. 190); another possibility is that they were based on Chapter VI (cf. above, p. 193). However, it is clear that all three of these Forces were intended to be peacekeeping forces; they were authorised to fight only in order to defend themselves. Each of the Forces was created originally for six months, and since then their mandates have been renewed by the Security Council for successive periods varying between three and twelve months; when the mandate of UNEF II expired for the last time in July 1979, it was not renewed because the Soviet Union had threatened to veto any attempt to renew it (*International Relations*, May 1981, pp. 1044–7). The Secretary-General appointed the Commander of each Force, with the consent of the Security Council, and selected contingents (from states willing to provide them) in consultation with the Security Council. The General Assembly decided that members of the United Nations were under a legal obligation to pay for the Forces, but the contributions which members were required to pay were based, not on the scale used for the ordinary budget, but on a special scale, which increased by more than 15 per cent the proportion which the permanent members of the Security Council were required to pay, and reduced by 80 or 90 per cent the proportion which the developing countries were required to pay; however, some states have refused to pay their contributions (see *UN Monthly Chronicle*, January 1974, pp. 72–4; ibid., May 1978, pp. 5–17, 44–8; ibid., December 1978, pp. 59–60; ibid., January 1979, pp. 73–4; *UN Chronicle*, 1980, no. 2, pp. 84–6).

Economic and Social Co-operation

Article 55 of the United Nations Charter provides:

With a view to the creation of conditions of stability and well-being which are necessary for peaceful and friendly relations among nations based on respect for the principle of equal rights and self-determination of peoples, the United Nations shall promote:
(a) higher standards of living, full employment, and conditions of economic and social progress and development;
(b) solutions of international economic, social, health, and related problems; and international cultural and educational co-operation; and
(c) universal respect for, and observance of, human rights and fundamental freedoms for all without distinction as to race, sex, language, or religion.

Article 56 provides:

All members pledge themselves to take joint and separate action in co-operation with the organization for the achievement of the purposes set forth in Article 55.

The extent to which Articles 55 and 56 create legal obligations for member-states has already been discussed (see above, p. 75).

'Responsibility for the discharge of the functions set forth in' Articles 55 and 56 is 'vested in the General Assembly and, under the authority of the General Assembly, in the Economic and Social Council' (Article 60).

The Economic and Social Council

The Economic and Social Council consists of fifty-four members of the United Nations; eighteen are elected each year by the General Assembly to serve for three years (Article 61). Decisions of the Council are taken by a majority of the members present and voting (Article 67). The Council may make or initiate studies and reports, make recommendations, prepare draft conventions and organise international conferences (Article 62); like the General Assembly, its terms of reference are wide, but its powers are limited, in the sense that it cannot take decisions which are binding on member-states. It also assists the Security Council at the Security Council's request (Article 65), and performs such other functions as are assigned to it by the General Assembly; with the approval of the General Assembly, it may also perform services at the request of members of the United Nations or at the request of specialised agencies (Article 66).

The Economic and Social Council may arrange for consultation with non-governmental organisations which deal with matters within its competence (Article 71). Such arrangements have been made with hundreds of non-governmental organisations, giving them the right to send observers to the Council's meetings and (in some cases) to make written or oral statements to the Council. So far, these arrangements have not produced very impressive results, but they do provide a useful channel of communication between the United Nations and public opinion.

The specialised agencies

One of the main functions of the Economic and Social Council is to co-ordinate the activities of the 'specialised agencies', which are defined as organisations 'established by intergovernmental agreement and having wide international responsibilities . . . in economic, social, cultural, educational, health and related fields'. Such an organisation becomes a specialised agency when it is 'brought into relationship with the United Nations' by means of an agreement made by the agency with the Economic and Social Council and approved by the General Assembly. The terms of the agreements vary from agency to agency, but certain features are common to most agreements. For instance, each of the two parties (the United Nations and the specialised agency in question) is usually given a right to send representatives (without voting rights) to meetings of certain organs in the other organisation. Most of the specialised agencies agree to consider recommendations made by the General Assembly, and to transmit regular reports to the Economic and Social Council; many of them are given a right to request opinions from the International Court of Justice on questions falling within their competence. Provision is also usually made for the mutual exchange of information and documents, and for the enactment of similar Staff Regulations and Staff Rules by each of the organisations concerned.

The Economic and Social Council is empowered by Article 63(2) of the Charter to 'co-ordinate the activities of the specialized agencies through consultation with and recommendations to such agencies and through recommendations to the General Assembly and to the members of the United Nations'. The General Assembly may 'examine the administrative budgets of . . . specialized agencies with a view to making recommendations to the agencies concerned' (Article 17(3)). There is also an Administrative Committee on Co-ordination, composed of the Secretary-General of the United Nations and the administrative heads of the specialised agencies, which co-ordinates operations at the administrative level.

So far, the following international organisations have become specialised agencies of the United Nations – the Food and Agriculture Organisation (FAO), the Inter-Governmental Maritime Consultative Organisation (IMCO), the International Civil Aviation Organisation (ICAO), the International Labour Organisation (ILO), the International Bank for Reconstruction and Development (IBRD or World Bank), the International Fund for Agricultural Development (IFAD), the International Monetary Fund (IMF), the International Telecommunications Union (ITU), the United Nations Educational Scientific and Cultural Organisation (UNESCO), the Universal Postal Union (UPU), the World Health Organisation (WHO), the World Intellectual Property Organisation (WIPO) and the World Meteorological Organisation (WMO). Some of these agencies are considerably older than the United Nations; for instance, ITU was founded in 1865 and UPU in 1874.

Most of the specialised agencies have no power to take decisions binding on their members, but their constituent treaties often provide for interesting means of putting pressure on member-states to act in a particular way. For instance, ILO, UNESCO and WHO can draw up recommendations and draft conventions; member-states are not obliged to accept the recommendations and draft conventions, but they must make periodic reports to the relevant organisation about their law and practice in the fields covered by the recommendations and draft conventions in question, and in some cases they must state their reasons for not accepting them. On certain topics WHO can adopt regulations, which are binding on every member-state which does not 'opt out' of the regulations concerned. These are useful means of overcoming the inertia of states, and of inducing them to act together.

Relations between rich states and poor states
Article 1(3) of the United Nations Charter declares that one of the purposes of the United Nations is 'to achieve international co-operation in solving international problems of an economic . . . character', and the poorer states in the world have often used meetings of United Nations organs as an occasion for urging the richer states to help the poorer states to develop their economies. On such questions United Nations organs have no power to take decisions which are binding on member-states; they can only make recommendations. Poorer states often become exasperated by the meagre response of richer states to such recommendations; for instance, the British government spends more than thirteen times as much on defence as it spends on overseas aid. But the fact that it has become standard practice for richer states to give aid to poorer states is quite a remarkable development, when one remembers that before the Second World War no government provided aid to help the economic development of other states on a continuing basis (as opposed to temporary relief after earthquakes, famines and similar disasters). There are also other ways in which richer states have tried to help the poorer states. Some of them, particularly member-states of the EEC, have reduced or abolished their tariffs on exports (including exports of manufactured goods) from poorer states. They have also entered into agreements with the poorer states to stabilise the prices of various raw materials which constitute the main exports of many poorer states. Most of these developments have taken place outside the institutional framework of the United Nations (for instance, governments usually prefer to give aid on a government-to-government basis, instead of channelling it through international organisations), but it is likely that many of them would never have occurred at all if it had not been for the constant pressure exerted through debates and resolutions at the United Nations.

The quadrupling of the price of oil in late 1973 aggravated the economic problems of most of the poorer states, but it strengthened their political position because the newly rich oil-exporting states supported the demands of the poorer states against the richer industrialised states. The General Assembly passed a series of resolutions urging radical changes to the world's economic system for the benefit of the poorer states (for example, *International Legal Materials*, 1974, p. 720; ibid., 1975, p. 251). These resolutions do not claim to be declaratory of existing law; they recommend a *change* in the law, the establishment of a *new* economic order. It remains to be seen whether the richer industrialised states will co-operate in setting up a new economic order in practice; indeed, there is a danger that the demands of the poorer states will simply be ignored by the richer industrialised states if those demands are pitched too high. In particular, the richer industrialised states dislike the attempts by the General Assembly resolutions on the new international economic order to create a legal obligation for richer states to help poorer states; although the richer industrialised states are continuing to help the poorer states in many ways, they are usually reluctant to recognise or undertake any legal obligation to do so.

See Andrew Farran, 'The changing economic order and international law', *Australian Outlook*, vol. 34, 1980, p. 179.

Conclusion

Many people, especially in Western countries, feel that the United Nations has achieved very little. Unfortunately, such people often have very exaggerated ideas about what the United Nations set out to achieve; they tend to imagine that the United Nations was intended to be a sort of embryonic world government. It is true that the provisions of the United Nations Charter concerning enforcement action give the United Nations one or two of the powers of a world government, and it is also true that those provisions have not worked well. But taking enforcement action is only one of the functions of the United Nations. The United Nations has had far more success in performing its other functions – economic and social co-operation (see above, pp. 195–9), peaceful settlement of disputes (see below, pp. 202–4) and decolonisation (see below, pp. 250–3). These other functions have one thing in common – they involve co-operation by states, and not coercion by the United Nations. Indeed, experience shows that the United Nations achieves most when it works with the consent of states, rather than when it tries to work without their consent; United Nations peacekeeping forces, for instance, which operate with the consent of the states concerned, have been more successful than the United Nations' attempts to take enforcement action.

Obviously, states would co-operate with one another to some extent even if there were no United Nations. But the existence of the United Nations increases the readiness of states to co-operate with one another; debates and votes at the United Nations exert political influence which often induces the minority to act in accordance with the wishes of the majority. For instance, the colonial powers would probably not have granted independence to their colonies so fast, or on such a wide scale, if it had not been for the political influence exerted by and through the United Nations.

But, in the last analysis, the effectiveness of the United Nations depends on the willingness of member-states to co-operate, and no amount of changes in the structure of the United Nations will guarantee its effectiveness unless member-states are willing to co-operate with the United Nations and with one another. To a large extent, the United Nations is a mirror of the world in which we live, and there cannot be a perfect United Nations in an imperfect world.

Suggestions for Further Reading

Evan Luard, *The United Nations*, 1979.

Andrew Boyd, 'The United Nations thirty years on', *International Affairs*, vol. 52, 1976, p. 67.

H. G. Nicholas, *The United Nations as a Political Institution*, 5th ed., 1975.

Leland M. Goodrich, *The United Nations in a Changing World*, 1974.

Inis L. Claude, *Swords into Plowshares*, 4th ed., 1971.

Joyce Gutteridge, *The United Nations in a Changing World*, 1969.

Chapter 14

Peaceful Settlement of Disputes between States

Non-Judicial Methods of Settlement

The vast majority of disputes between states are settled by *negotiation*. International law is not unique in this respect; the vast majority of disputes in any legal system are settled by negotiation. When a municipal lawyer is negotiating the settlement of a dispute, he can always threaten to go to court if the other side will not give way; such a threat can seldom be made in international law, where the jurisdiction of tribunals is dependent on the consent of states. But we have already seen that states have other motives for obeying international law, motives which have nothing to do with fear of litigation (see above, pp. 8–11). Moreover, most states have legal advisers who know enough about international law to recognise a valid claim when they see one, and who can usually be relied upon to advise their own state to give way when its legal position is weak. But negotiation is not always a good method of settling international disputes. There is no guarantee that a state will listen to its legal advisers. In addition, third parties seldom take part in negotiations, and this means that there is no impartial machinery for resolving disputed questions of fact. It also means that there is little to restrain a disputing state from putting forward extreme claims, especially where its bargaining power is very strong.

Sometimes third states, or international organisations, may try to help the disputing states to reach agreement. Such help can take two forms – *good offices* and *mediation*. A state is said to offer its good offices when it tries to persuade disputing states to enter into negotiations; when the negotiations start, its functions are at an end. A mediator, on the other hand, actually takes part in the negotiations and suggests terms of settlement to the disputing states. Obviously a mediator has to enjoy the confidence of both sides, and it is often difficult to find a mediator who fulfils this requirement.

Disputing states may sometimes agree to appoint an impartial body to carry out an *inquiry*; the object of the inquiry is to produce an impartial finding of disputed facts, and thus to prepare the way for a negotiated settlement. Many international disputes turn solely on disputed questions of fact, and an impartial inquiry is an excellent way of reducing the tension and the area of disagreement between the parties. The parties are not obliged to accept the findings of the inquiry, but almost always do accept them.

Conciliation is a combination of inquiry and mediation. The conciliator, who is appointed by agreement between the parties, investigates the facts of the dispute and suggests the terms of a settlement. But conciliation is more formal and less flexible than mediation; if a mediator's proposals are not accepted, he can go on formulating new proposals, whereas a conciliator usually only issues a single report. (However, the conciliator usually has discussions with each of the parties behind the scenes, with a view to finding an area of agreement between them, before issuing his report.) The parties are not obliged to accept the conciliator's terms of settlement; but, apart from that, conciliation often resembles arbitration, particularly when the dispute involves difficult points of law; in order to make a good impression on the conciliator, states are forced to rephrase their case in more moderate language, as they would before an arbitrator.

Settlement of Disputes under the United Nations Charter

Article 1(1) of the United Nations Charter states that it is one of the purposes of the United Nations 'to bring about by peaceful means, and in conformity with the principles of justice and international law, adjustment or settlement of international disputes or situations which might lead to a breach of the peace'. Article 2(3) obliges member states to 'settle their disputes by peaceful means in such a manner that international peace and security, and justice, are not endangered'.

Apart from the International Court of Justice (see below, pp. 206–210), the two most important organs of the United Nations for the peaceful settlement of disputes are the Security Council and the General Assembly.

A dispute may be brought before the Security Council:

(i)   by a member of the United Nations, whether or not it is a party to the dispute (Article 35(1) of the Charter);

(ii) by a state which is not a member of the United Nations, provided that it is a party to the dispute and 'accepts in advance, for the purposes of the dispute, the obligations of pacific settlement provided in the . . . Charter' (Article 35(2));

(iii)   by the General Assembly, which 'may call the attention of the Security Council to situations which are likely to endanger international peace and security' (Article 11(3) – and see also Articles 10 and 11(2), above, p. 176);

(iv)   by the Secretary-General, who 'may bring to the attention of the Security Council any matter which in his opinion may threaten the maintenance of international peace and security' (Article 99).

However, a state, the General Assembly, or the Secretary-General can only *request* the Security Council to consider a dispute; it is for the Security Council to decide whether to accede to that request by placing the dispute on its agenda. Similarly, a dispute can be removed from the Security Council's agenda only by the Security Council, and not by the parties to the dispute; the wisdom of this practice was shown a few days after the Soviet invasion of Czechoslovakia in August 1968, when the Security Council refused to accept a request from Czechoslovakia (which was, of course, acting under Soviet pressure) to remove the question of the invasion from its agenda. Decisions concerning the agenda are procedural decisions, and therefore the veto does not apply.

Chapter VI empowers the Security Council to make various types of recommendation for the peaceful settlement of disputes; the Security Council also has certain powers of investigation. According to the letter of the Charter, the circumstances in which the Security Council may recommend *terms* of settlement are different from the circumstances in which it may recommend *procedures* for settlement; but the circumstances in question are defined in very imprecise terms. Fortunately the Security Council usually disregards these complexities in practice and makes all sorts of recommendations, without citing any articles of the Charter, and without bothering about the tortuous and imprecise distinctions made in Chapter VI. But it must be emphasised that recommendations made by the Security Council under Chapter VI do not create legal obligations (see below, p. 207), although they often exercise great political influence. As regards voting procedure, recommendations under Chapter VI are non-procedural, that is, the veto applies.

The General Assembly may also deal with disputes under Articles 10, 11(2), 12 and 14 of the Charter (see above, pp. 176 and 178). Any member-state of the United Nations may bring a dispute before the General Assembly; and so may a non-member-state, provided it is a party to the dispute in question and accepts in advance, for the purposes of that dispute, the obligations of pacific settlement contained in the Charter. The practice concerning the agenda is the same in the General Assembly as it is in the Security Council. The General Assembly may make recommendations and appoint fact-finding missions; states are under no legal obligation to comply with such recommendations or to co-operate with fact-finding missions, although General Assembly recommendations often exercise great political influence.

The functions of the Security Council and the General Assembly in connection with the settlement of disputes represent a mixture of good offices, mediation, inquiry and conciliation. But the Security Council and the General Assembly are not, and were never intended to be, judicial bodies. Although they take legal factors into account, they also take political factors into account, and political considerations often overshadow legal considerations in their deliberations. Moreover, members of the Security Council and the General Assembly are not always impartial; members of an alliance tend to support one another, and small neutralist states try to avoid giving offence to the two super-powers. If a dispute between two members of the same alliance is brought to the United Nations, enemies of the alliance may try to *aggravate* the dispute (instead of encouraging the parties to settle it), in the hope of disrupting the alliance. In view of these factors, the absence of a power to take binding decisions should be regarded as a necessary safeguard for member-states, and not as a defect in the system.

Normally states take disputes to the United Nations in order to put political pressure on their opponents, by mobilising world opinion against them. Sometimes, however, recourse to the United Nations may serve another purpose; a state which is under pressure from its own domestic opinion to take a 'strong line' against another state may try to satisfy domestic opinion by making fierce speeches at the United Nations, as a substitute for action of a more damaging character. In such cases, the United Nations forms a safety valve, which enables states to 'let off steam'. But the frequency with which the United Nations is used for this purpose explains why states sometimes regard it as an unfriendly act to complain to the United Nations against another state.

Arbitration and Judicial Settlement

The differences between arbitration and judicial settlement are much less in international law than they are in municipal law:

(1) In municipal law arbitrators are appointed by the disputing parties (or by someone nominated by the disputing parties), and judges are not. This difference is more or less valid in international

law (but see below, p. 206, concerning *ad hoc* judges in the International Court of Justice).

(2) In municipal law jurisdiction is conferred on an arbitrator by agreement, and on a judge by the general law (although the jurisdiction of a court may sometimes be *extended* by agreement). In international law this difference does not exist; no arbitrator or judge has jurisdiction unless the disputing parties agree to confer jurisdiction on him.

(3) In municipal law the parties can agree that an arbitrator shall apply rules other than those of the ordinary law; such an agreement is impossible in the case of a court. In international law there is nothing to prevent the parties authorising a court to apply rules other than those of the ordinary law, although such authorisations are given more frequently to arbitrators than to courts.

A frequent pattern in arbitration treaties is for each of the two parties to appoint an arbitrator; the two arbitrators thus appointed agree on the choice of the third arbitrator (or umpire); the arbitral tribunal consequently consists of three men, who can decide by majority vote. In the nineteenth century there was a tendency for arbitrators appointed by the parties to regard themselves as representatives of the state which had appointed them, rather than as impartial dispensers of justice. Fortunately, such attitudes are now rare (or maybe more skilfully concealed).

The Permanent Court of Arbitration was set up by the Hague Convention for the Pacific Settlement of International Disputes 1899. The name of this 'Court' is misleading. Each state party to the Convention may nominate four persons to serve on a panel of arbitrators, and disputing states may select arbitrators from this panel in the traditional way. In reality, therefore, the 1899 Convention did not create a court; it merely created machinery for setting up arbitral tribunals. The composition of the 'Court' varies so much from case to case that it cannot develop a coherent case-law. The Permanent Court of Arbitration decided twenty cases between 1900 and 1932; since then it has been overshadowed by the Permanent Court of International Justice and the International Court of Justice, and has heard very few cases.

The constituent treaty (or 'Statute') of the Permanent Court of International Justice was signed in 1920 and came into force in 1921. The judges of the Court were not chosen by the parties to each dispute, but were elected by the League of Nations. It is unnecessary to describe the Court in detail, because it was dissolved at the same time as the League of Nations in 1946; besides, it is very similar to its successor, the International Court of Justice.

The International Court of Justice

The International Court of Justice is one of the six principal organs of the United Nations, and its Statute, which closely resembles the Statute of the PCIJ, is annexed to the United Nations Charter, so that all members of the United Nations are automatically parties to the Statute. However, in certain circumstances, states which are not members of the United Nations may appear before the Court, and may even become parties to its Statute.

The Court consists of fifteen judges; five are elected every three years to hold office for nine years. The election procedure is complicated, but can be summed up by saying that election requires an absolute majority of votes in both the Security Council and the General Assembly. In 1981 the Court consisted of judges from the United Kingdom, Nigeria, Senegal, France, Poland, the USSR, India, Argentina, West Germany, Japan, Italy, Egypt, Brazil, Syria and the USA. If a state appearing before the Court does not have a judge of its own nationality on the Court, it may appoint an *ad hoc* judge for the particular case. The institution of the *ad hoc* judge is a survival of the traditional method of appointing arbitrators, and may be necessary to reassure litigants that the Court will not ignore their views; but it is hard to reconcile with the principle that judges are impartial and independent, and are not representatives of their national governments.

Only states may be parties in contentious proceedings before the Court (Article 34 of the Statute of the ICJ; on the difference between contentious proceedings and advisory proceedings, see below, pp. 209–210). Jurisdiction in contentious proceedings is dependent on the consent of states; many of the smaller states represented at the San Francisco Conference in 1945 wanted to provide for compulsory jurisdiction in the Charter, but the opposition of the great powers prevented the adoption of any such provision.

The consent of a state to appear before the Court may take several forms.

Article 36(1) of the Statute provides:

The jurisdiction of the Court comprises all cases which the parties refer to it and all matters specially provided for in the Charter of the United Nations or in treaties and conventions in force.

The words 'all cases which the parties refer to it' require some explanation. The word 'parties' is in the plural, and implies that all the parties to the dispute must agree that the case should be referred to the Court. Normally the parties refer the dispute to the

Court jointly, but there is no reason why each party should not make a separate reference at a separate time. The Court has held that a defendant state may accept the jurisdiction of the Court *after* proceedings have been instituted against it; such acceptance may take the form of an express statement,[1] or it can be implied if the defendant state defends the case on the merits without challenging the jurisdiction of the Court.[2]

States can agree by treaty to confer jurisdiction on the Court; that is what Article 36(1) of the Statute means when it refers to 'matters specially provided for . . . in treaties'. But the mention of 'matters specially provided for in the Charter of the United Nations' raises a problem. Article 36(3) of the Charter, dealing with the peaceful settlement of disputes, empowers the Security Council to recommend that the parties to a legal dispute should refer it to the Court, and in the *Corfu Channel* case the United Kingdom argued that such a recommendation, addressed to the United Kingdom and Albania, was sufficient to give the Court jurisdiction to hear a British complaint against Albania. The Court held that Albania had agreed to accept the Court's jurisdiction, and most of the judges therefore found it unnecessary to comment on the British argument about the effects of the Security Council resolution recommending Albania and the United Kingdom to go to the Court. But seven of the judges added a separate opinion in which they said that the British argument was wrong, since recommendations of the Security Council were not binding.[3] If the opinion of the seven judges is right, as it is generally accepted to be, one must conclude that there are *no* 'matters specially provided for in the Charter of the United Nations'. The explanation of this paradox is that Article 36(1) of the Statute of the Court was drafted at a time when it looked as if the Charter would provide for compulsory jurisdiction; the San Francisco Conference subsequently rejected proposals to provide for compulsory jurisdiction in the Charter, but forgot to delete the cross-reference in the Statute.

Paragraphs 2 and 3 of Article 36 provide as follows:

2. The states parties to the present Statute may at any time declare that they recognize as compulsory *ipso facto* and without special agreement, in relation to any other state accepting the same obligation, the jurisdiction of the Court in all legal disputes . . .

[1] *Corfu Channel* case, *International Court of Justice Reports*, 1947–8, pp. 15, 27–8.
[2] *Rights of Minorities in Upper Silesia* (*Minorities Schools*), Permanent Court of International Justice, series A, no. 15, pp. 20–5 (1928).
[3] *International Court of Justice Reports*, 1947–8, pp. 15, 31–2. On the Albanian acceptance of the Court's jurisdiction, see above, n. 1.

3. The declarations referred to above may be made unconditionally or on condition of reciprocity on the part of several or certain states, or for a certain time.

This optional clause, as it is called, emerged as a compromise between the advocates and the opponents of compulsory jurisdiction. At present forty-seven states (that is, about 30 per cent of the states parties to the Statute) have accepted the jurisdiction of the Court under the optional clause.

States which accept the jurisdiction of the Court under the optional clause do so, according to paragraph 2, only 'in relation to any other state accepting the same obligation'. This is known as the principle of reciprocity.[1] A state cannot enjoy the benefits of the optional clause unless it is prepared to accept the obligations of the optional clause. If state A has accepted the optional clause and state B has not, state A cannot be sued by state B. If the claimant state has accepted the optional clause subject to reservations, the defendant state can rely upon the claimant state's reservations by way of reciprocity.

Article 36(3) permits reservations relating to reciprocity and reservations relating to time. In practice, reservations of many other types are also made and have always been accepted as valid.[2] There is, however, a possible exception in the case of 'automatic reservations', that is, reservations whose scope is to be determined by the reserving state – for instance, a reservation excluding the Court's jurisdiction over 'all matters within the domestic jurisdiction of state X, *as determined by state X*'. In the *Norwegian Loans* case, the British judge, Sir Hersch Lauterpacht, said that such a reservation was invalid, because it was contrary to Article 36(6) of the Statute, which provides: 'In the event of a dispute as to whether the Court has jurisdiction, the matter shall be settled by the decision of the Court'; moreover, since the reservation could

---

[1] The provision in paragraph 3, which allows states to accept the optional clause 'on condition of reciprocity on the part of several or certain states', might appear to be redundant, in view of the words quoted from paragraph 2. But, according to the *travaux préparatoires*, paragraph 3 uses the word 'reciprocity' in a different sense; the effect of paragraph 3 is that a state may add a reservation to its acceptance of the optional clause, stating that its acceptance is not to come into force until states X and Y have also accepted the optional clause. Until states X and Y have accepted the optional clause, the state making such a reservation cannot be sued by *any* state. In fact, no reservations of this sort have been made.

[2] In particular, many states have made reservations permitting them to withdraw their acceptance at any time. (Unless such a reservation is made, acceptance of the optional clause is irrevocable; the optional clause is, in effect, a treaty, which cannot be denounced at will.) If a state withdraws its acceptance, in accordance with such a reservation, it prevents the Court trying future cases against it, but it does not deprive the Court of jurisdiction over cases which have already been started against it: *Nottebohm* case, *ICJ Reports*, 1953, pp. 111, 122–3.

not be severed from the rest of the acceptance, the nullity of the reservation entailed the nullity of the whole acceptance (*ICJ Reports*, 1957, pp. 9, 43–66). However, most of the judges left Lauterpacht's argument open; they applied the reservation, since neither of the litigants had pleaded that it was invalid (ibid., p. 27). A piquant feature of the *Norwegian Loans* case was that the automatic reservation was contained in the acceptance filed by the claimant state, France, and was successfully invoked by the defendant state, Norway. This application of the principle of reciprocity, coupled with judicial criticisms of automatic reservations, led to the abandonment of such reservations by several states which had previously inserted them in their acceptances (for example, India, Pakistan and the United Kingdom). But automatic reservations are still retained by Liberia, Malawi, Mexico, the Philippines, the Sudan and the USA (which had been the first state to make an automatic reservation, in 1945).

Before it can examine the merits of the case, the Court usually has to consider several preliminary objections. Defendant states often plead, by way of a preliminary objection, that the Court lacks jurisdiction to try the case, but preliminary objections can take many other forms; for instance, if the claimant state is making a claim on behalf of one of its nationals, there may be preliminary objections based on the rules concerning nationality of claims or exhaustion of local remedies (see above, pp. 97–100). Preliminary objections are usually dealt with separately in a preliminary judgment, but sometimes the Court 'joins them to the merits', that is, deals with them together with the merits in a single judgment.

Judgments of the Court are binding (and so are the judgments of all international courts and arbitral tribunals). Article 94 of the United Nations Charter authorises the Security Council to 'make recommendations or decide upon measures to be taken to give effect to the judgment', although these powers have not yet been used. Actually, the problem of enforcement is not as serious as one might imagine; if a state is willing to accept the jurisdiction of the Court, it is *usually* willing to carry out the Court's judgment; the real difficulty lies in persuading a state to accept the Court's jurisdiction in the first place.

In addition to its power to decide disputes between states (contentious jurisdiction), the Court also has a power to give advisory opinions (advisory jurisdiction). Article 96 of the United Nations Charter provides:

1. The General Assembly or the Security Council may request the International Court of Justice to give an advisory opinion on any legal question.

3. Other organs of the United Nations and specialized agencies, which may at any time be so authorized by the General Assembly, may also request advisory opinions of the Court on legal questions arising within the scope of their activities.

Unlike judgments, advisory opinions are not binding. But they carry political weight and are complied with in most cases; some advisory opinions have significantly altered the course of the development of international law (see, for instance, pp. 70-1 and 128, above).

Reasons for the unpopularity of arbitration and judicial settlement
Only 30 per cent of the states parties to the Statute of the International Court of Justice have accepted the optional clause. Over half of the non-communist states in Europe have accepted it, and so have the USA, Australia, Canada and New Zealand. Half of the Latin American states have accepted it, but only two of them are in South America (as opposed to Central America and the Caribbean islands). Less than a quarter of the Afro-Asian states have accepted the optional clause; half of them are members of the Commonwealth. Only two Arab states have accepted the optional clause (in very limited terms), and none of the communist states has accepted it.

Moreover, most of the states which have accepted the optional clause have inserted reservations of one sort or another in their acceptances.

Some of the reasons for the reluctance of states to accept the optional clause are fairly straightforward. For instance, a state which has just become independent may hesitate for a time before accepting unfamiliar commitments. Again, states may be reluctant to go to the International Court of Justice because they prefer other tribunals which are smaller (and therefore cheaper and faster) or more specialised. For every dispute between states which has been brought before the International Court of Justice since 1945, approximately four such disputes have been brought before other international tribunals.

But the reluctance of states to appear before the International Court of Justice also has a more fundamental significance; it is symptomatic of a distrust which states feel for arbitration and judicial settlement in general. They are reluctant to appear before international courts,[1] either as plaintiffs or as defendants. Despite cynical views to the contrary, the reluctance is seldom *caused* by a desire to be able to break international law with impunity; still, it

---

[1] In the remainder of this chapter, the words 'court' and 'judge' are used to include arbitral tribunals.

must be confessed that the absence of a competent court may sometimes have the *effect* of tempting a state to break international law. The rule that the jurisdiction of international courts is dependent on the consent of states is therefore a defect in international law. But it is not a fatal defect. International courts hardly existed before the nineteenth century, but international law managed to work without them; even today, the communist states remain opposed to international courts on principle, although they do not deny the binding force of international law (see above, pp. 16–19, especially p. 18). Courts are probably an indispensable part of municipal legal systems, because fear of sanctions imposed by courts is one of the main reasons why people obey municipal law; international law is different, because states have other reasons for obeying international law, reasons which have no counterpart in municipal systems (see above, pp. 8–11). We must resist the temptation to condemn international law as deficient whenever it fails to resemble municipal law; international law and municipal law work in different ways, but that does not mean that one works less effectively than the other.

There are two reasons why it is instructive to consider the reasons which induce states to distrust international courts. First, such an examination will serve to refute the conclusion that distrust of international courts necessarily connotes disrespect for international law. Second, if an international lawyer is going to persuade states to overcome their distrust of international courts, he will need to have a very clear understanding of the fears felt by states before he can hope to show that those fears are exaggerated or unfounded.

The main reason why states are reluctant to accept the jurisdiction of an international court is because they believe that judicial decisions are often *unpredictable*. It is not that international law in general is uncertain; but, since most states have competent legal advisers and are fairly law-abiding, the fact that a dispute cannot be settled by negotiation often indicates that the relevant law or the facts of the case are uncertain. And it is these 'unpredictable' cases which are most likely to come before an international court.

States can also point to the prevalence of dissenting opinions as evidence of the unpredictability of judicial decisions; when several members of a court dissent from the judgment given by the majority, it is easy to argue that the case would have been decided the other way if the court had been differently constituted. If different judges are likely to reach different decisions, it is clear that the outcome of litigation is often a matter of pure chance.

Where the law is uncertain, a judge is likely to be influenced, consciously or unconsciously, by political considerations. This casts doubt on his impartiality; and states may be forgiven for thinking that political decisions should be taken by states and not by courts.

The element of unpredictability in judicial decisions may be tolerable in minor cases, but not when important political issues are at stake. This explains why a state like the USA, which has participated in hundreds of arbitrations about *specific* questions, refuses to accept a *general* commitment to appear before international courts, even though its refusal takes the disguised form of an automatic reservation to its acceptance of the optional clause (see above, p. 208). Automatic reservations are the modern equivalent of those clauses in pre-1914 arbitration treaties which excluded the obligation to arbitrate in cases affecting the honour or vital interests of the states concerned. Before 1914 writers tried to explain these clauses by saying that 'political' disputes (which were defined in different ways by different writers) were, *by their very nature*, incapable of judicial settlement. This view is now discredited. But the fact that disputes affecting the vital interests of a state could *in theory* be decided by an international court does not alter the fact that states usually refuse to submit such disputes to international courts *in practice*.

An additional factor is that the effects of a court's decision are not limited to the facts of a particular case; it is also a precedent for future cases. Some states distrust the International Court of Justice because they think that its decisions have changed the law too much. Indeed, when a case turns on a point of law about which the parties *honestly* hold opposing views, the losing party will *always* feel that the court has changed the law. States create law for themselves through treaties and custom, and are jealous of rival sources, such as judicial precedents; if changes in the law are needed, states prefer to retain the power of deciding for themselves what the new rules should be.

Conversely, other states distrust international courts because they think that international courts are too conservative. When a customary rule is changing, or a state has reasons to hope that the rule is about to change, a judgment reaffirming the old rule may, through its effect as a precedent, delay or prevent the change. It is significant that the rich states, who may be presumed to be satisfied with the *status quo*, are much readier to accept the International Court's jurisdiction under the optional clause than the poor (and presumably dissatisfied) states. Besides, it is only recently that the number of Afro-Asian judges on the Court has begun to respond to the increase in the number of independent Afro-Asian states.

Although courts sometimes change the law indirectly, their main function is to apply the existing law; consequently, to expect a court to be able to settle an international dispute, when one side is demanding a change in the law, is rather like trying to settle a wage claim by telling the workers that wages are fixed by the contract of employment and that contracts can be altered only by mutual agreement.[1] But the difference between claims for the application of the law and claims for changes in the law is not always clear. The law itself may be uncertain, and it is always bad tactics for a state to concede that its position is legally untenable; consequently, states often make claims in negotiations without indicating whether their claim is based on the existing law or whether it amounts to a demand for a change in the law. There is also the paradox caused by the element of *opinio iuris* in the formation of new rules of customary law (see above, pp. 29–31); because a new rule sometimes cannot *become* law until it is regarded as being *already* part of the law, claims for changes in the law are often disguised as claims for the application of the existing law. As a result, many cases which appear suitable for judicial settlement are not so in fact.

Finally, there are also a number of minor reasons for the reluctance of states to use international courts for the settlement of disputes. To start judicial proceedings against another state is sometimes regarded as an unfriendly act; states fear that they will lose face if the court's decision goes against them. Moreover, the reluctance of states to go to court produces a vicious circle, in the sense that the large number of preliminary objections raised by defendant states before international courts causes great complexity in the law and makes litigation very expensive and time-consuming; and these consequences in turn intensify the reluctance of states to appear before international courts, either as plaintiff or as defendant.

What happens to disputes which states are unwilling to refer to international courts? Most of them are eventually settled by some political means of settlement, such as negotiation or mediation; indeed, the creation of international organisations like the United Nations has increased the chances of political settlement, by adding to the number of available means of political settlement. Very often the settlement takes the form of a compromise (for example, global settlements in cases of expropriation – see above,

---

[1] Idealists sometimes suggest that international courts of law should be complemented by an international court of equity, which would possess the power to change the law when the law is unfair. But a body with a general power to change the law is a legislature, not a court, and states are not yet prepared to accept an international legislature (cf. the refusal of states to authorise the International Court of Justice to decide *ex aequo et bono*: see above, p. 39). States distrust courts because they regard judicial decisions as unpredictable; it is easy to imagine what their attitude would be to a body whose decisions would inevitably be a hundred times more unpredictable and subjective.

p. 94), or of a 'package deal', in which one state makes concessions in one dispute in return for concessions by the other state in another, more or less unrelated, dispute.

Alternatively, the dispute can simply result in a stalemate; states are immortal and can afford to wait until a change in the law or in the balance of power enables them to negotiate a settlement on more favourable terms. Disputes over title to territory, in particular, tend to drag on for centuries, because of the virtually indestructible character of territory; moreover, the complexity and uncertainty of the facts in most territorial disputes makes judicial decisions particularly unpredictable, and the strong emotional attachment felt by peoples for every inch of their territory, however useless the territory in dispute may be, increases the unpopularity of international courts as a means of settling such disputes.

In the nineteenth century a strong state might take military action to compel a weak state to accept arbitration; nowadays, changes in the law and in popular attitudes concerning the use of force make such action unthinkable, and stalemate has replaced war as the main alternative to judicial settlement. However, the fact that many disputes lead to stalemate instead of being settled by a court results in an unnecessary prolongation of international tension. What is even more serious is that the absence of compulsory judicial settlement sometimes enables states to break international law with apparent impunity, and thus produces gross injustice (and cynicism about the effectiveness of international law).

How well-founded are the reasons which induce states to distrust international courts? At one extreme, states are clearly right in thinking that a court cannot effectively settle a dispute which is concerned with demands for a *change* in the law. At the other extreme, the idea that litigation is an unfriendly act, and necessarily complex, expensive and time-consuming, is correct only because states have chosen to approach litigation in this spirit; if states accepted litigation as a normal and desirable means for settling disputes, and did not try to obstruct international courts, litigation would become a simple, quick, cheap and amicable process.

As for the central problem of judicial unpredictability, the fears of states are to some extent well-founded, but only in certain cases; in other cases it is easy to predict the decision of the court. Similarly, as regards the related problem of vital interests, states sometimes have an exaggerated idea of what is vital; interests which states regarded as vital (and therefore non-justiciable) sixty years ago are now seen not to be vital after all, and there is no logical reason why this process of contraction should not continue. Again, the fear of judicial precedents as a source of law is also probably exaggerated; in international law judicial precedents are merely persuasive, not binding, and in any case the effect of an unpopular precedent can always be eliminated by a treaty or by subsequent developments in customary law (for examples, see below, pp. 270–2 and 277–8).

Finally, one or two suggestions can be made for overcoming the distrust which states feel for international courts. In the first place, if states do not want to submit certain categories of disputes to a court, they should try to define those categories precisely and accept the court's jurisdiction over all other categories of disputes; this would avoid the present situation, where a reluctance to accept a court's jurisdiction over certain categories of disputes often results in a failure to accept the court's jurisdiction at all – or results in an acceptance coupled with vague and unnecessarily wide reservations. Second, more care should be exercised in selecting judges. The ideal international judge is a man who understands the political aspirations of different states, and who, if he is forced to make a political decision, will do so consciously and wisely, in an attempt to reach a solution which is acceptable to both parties. The judge who is loudest in professing his attachment to the letter of the law and his refusal to be swayed by political considerations often turns out to be basing his judgments on preconceived political ideas of which he is not even conscious. Judges of the latter type have been common in the past. But that is no reason for condemning international courts in general. The solution is to choose better judges in future, and, if necessary, to set up new courts to function side by side with the old.

Suggestions for Further Reading

David Davies Memorial Institute of International Studies, *International Disputes: The Legal Aspects*, 1972.
R. P. Anand, *Studies in International Adjudication*, 1969.
Prott, 'The future of the International Court of Justice', *Year Book of World Affairs*, 1979, p. 284.
Higgins, 'The place of international law in the settlement of disputes by the Security Council', *American Journal of International Law*, vol. 64, 1970, p. 1.
Merrills, 'The justiciability of international disputes', *Canadian Bar Review*, vol. 47, 1969, p. 241.

Chapter 15

International Wars

Lawful and Unlawful Wars

Developments before 1945

For many centuries Western European attitudes towards the legality of war were dominated by the teachings of the Roman Catholic Church. One of the first theologians to write on the subject was St Augustine (354–430), who said:

> Just wars are usually defined as those which avenge injuries, when the nation or city against which warlike action is to be directed has neglected either to punish wrongs committed by its own citizens or to restore what has been unjustly taken by it. Further, that kind of war is undoubtedly just which God Himself ordains.

These ideas continued to be accepted for over 1,000 years. War was regarded as a means of obtaining reparation for a prior illegal act committed by the other side (the reparation sought had to be proportional to the seriousness of the illegality). In addition, wars against unbelievers and heretics were sometimes (but not always) regarded as being commanded by God.

In the late sixteenth century the distinction between just and unjust wars began to break down. Theologians were particularly concerned with the state of a man's conscience, and admitted that each side would be blameless if it genuinely believed that it was in the right, even though one of the sides might have been objectively in the wrong (this was known as the doctrine of probabilism). Moreover, the category of just wars began to be dangerously extended. Although seventeenth-century writers like Grotius made some attempt to re-establish traditional doctrines, the eighteenth and nineteenth centuries produced an almost complete abandonment of the distinction between legal and illegal wars. Wars were said to be justified if they were fought for the defence of certain vital interests, but each state remained the sole judge of its vital interests, which were never defined with any attempt at precision. Indeed, the whole doctrine of vital interests probably constituted, not a legal criterion of the legality of war, but a source of political justifications and excuses, to be used for propaganda purposes.

The most realistic view of the customary law of that period is that it placed *no* limits on the right of states to resort to war.

Some modern writers have suggested that a legal system which made no distinction between the legal and illegal use of force was not worthy of the name of law. Certainly this would be true of a system of municipal law which made no such distinction. Human beings are particularly vulnerable to physical attack; even the strongest man has to sleep sometimes, and, while he is asleep, anyone can kill him in a split second, with a fair chance of escaping detection. Consequently a law against murder is indispensable for any society composed of human beings. In the international society of states the position is different. States derive protection from the fact that they are few in number and are composed of territory and population. Because states are few in number, an attack on one state threatens the interests of the other states, which are therefore likely to come to its help. Similarly, the fact that states are composed of territory and population means that they cannot be overpowered instantaneously; until tanks and aircraft were invented, the time required for a hostile army to penetrate far into another state was usually long enough for the victim to mobilise resistance and to obtain help from its allies.

Alliances were, indeed, of crucial importance in the nineteenth century – the classic period of the balance of power. Despite Alexander Pope's cynical comment:

> Now, Europe balanced, neither side prevails;
> For nothing's left in either of the scales –

the balance of power system was fairly successful in making wars rare. The expense, destructiveness and long duration of wars, and the risks of defeat, meant that wars were not worth fighting unless a state could hope to gain a large amount of territory by going to war; but a state which seized too much territory threatened the whole of Europe because it upset the balance of power, and states were usually deterred from attempting to seize large areas of territory by the knowledge that such an attempt would unite the rest of Europe against them.

When studying comparative law, one often comes across a topic which is regulated by law in one country and regulated by extra-legal factors in another country. For instance, in West Germany relations between trade unions and employers are regulated by law, but in the United Kingdom, where the whole history of industrial relations is radically different, they are regulated in a more informal, extralegal way, which (despite popular beliefs) is only slightly less successful, as a means of preserving industrial peace, than the German method of doing things. Similarly, in the nineteenth century, the prevention of violence, which in municipal societies was largely secured by rules of law, was achieved at the international level by extralegal factors such as the balance of power.

Where necessary, the balance of power system could be supplemented by law (in the form of treaties), to deal with special cases. For instance, treaties of 1815 and 1839 guaranteed Switzerland and Belgium against attack. Later, the Latin American states persuaded several other states to sign the second Hague Convention of 1907, which prohibited the use of force to recover contract debts, unless the debtor state refused to go to arbitration or refused to carry out the arbitral award. The third Hague Convention of 1907 required war to be preceded by a formal declaration of war or by an ultimatum containing a conditional declaration of war.

The unprecedented suffering of the First World War caused a revolutionary change in attitudes towards war. Nowadays people (at least in Europe) are accustomed to regard war as an appalling evil. We find it hard to realise that during the eighteenth and nineteenth centuries most people (except for a few pacifists) regarded war in much the same way as they regarded a hard winter – uncomfortable, certainly, but part of the settled order of things, and providing excellent opportunities for exhilarating sports; even the wounded soldier did not regard war as wrong, any more than the skier with a broken leg regards skiing as wrong. All this changed after 1914, but the law took some time to catch up with public opinion. The Covenant of the League of Nations, signed in 1919, did not prohibit war altogether; instead, Article 12(1) provided:

> The Members of the League agree that, if there should arise between them any dispute likely to lead to a rupture, they will submit the matter either to arbitration or judicial settlement or to inquiry by the Council, and they agree in no case to resort to war until three months after the award by the arbitrators or the judicial decision, or the report by the Council.

(The three months' period of delay was intended to allow time for passions to die down; if states had observed a three months' delay after the assassination of the Archduke Franz Ferdinand in 1914, it is probable that the First World War could have been averted.) In addition, members of the League agreed not to go to war with members complying with an arbitral award or judicial decision (Article 13(4)) or with a *unanimous* report by the Council (Article 15(6)).

During the 1920s various efforts were made to fill the 'gaps in the Covenant', that is, to transform the Covenant's partial prohibition of war into a total prohibition of war. These efforts culminated in the General Treaty for the Renunciation of War (otherwise known as the Kellogg–Briand Pact or the Pact of Paris), signed in 1928. Almost all the states in the world became parties to this treaty, which provided:

> The High Contracting Parties solemnly declare . . . that they condemn recourse to war for the solution of international controversies, and renounce it as an instrument of national policy in their relations with one another.

> The High Contracting Parties agree that the settlement or solution of all disputes or conflicts of whatever nature or of whatever origin they may be which may arise among them, shall never be sought except by pacific means.

The United Nations Charter

Article 2(4) of the United Nations Charter provides:

> All members shall refrain in their international relations from the threat or use of force against the territorial integrity or political independence of any state, or in any other manner inconsistent with the purposes of the United Nations.

This rule is of universal validity; even the few states which are not members of the United Nations accept it as a rule of customary law.

Article 2(4) is well drafted, in so far as it talks of 'the threat or use of *force*', and not of 'war'. 'War' has a technical (but imprecise) sense in international law, and states often engage in hostilities while denying that they are technically in a state of war; such hostilities can range from minor border incidents to extensive military operations, such as the Anglo-French attempt to occupy the area surrounding the Suez Canal in 1956. The distinction between war and hostilities falling short of war may appear to be a very fine distinction, but it can have important consequences; for instance, war automatically terminates diplomatic relations and certain categories of treaties between the belligerent states, but hostilities falling short of war do not; similarly, a technical state of war can have special effects in municipal law, for example, as regards trading with the enemy and internment of enemy subjects. Article 2(4) applies to all force, regardless of whether or not it constitutes a technical state of war.

On the other hand, Article 2(4) is badly drafted, in so far as it prohibits the threat or use of force only 'against the territorial integrity or political independence of any state or in any other manner inconsistent with the purposes of the United Nations'. The words quoted open up the possibility of arguing that force used for a wide variety of purposes (for example, to protect human rights,[1] or to enforce any type of legal right belonging to a state) is legal because it is not aimed 'against the territorial integrity or political independence of any state'. But the reference to territorial integrity or political independence should not distract our attention from the words 'or in any other manner inconsistent with the purposes of the United Nations'. Although Article 1 of the Charter, which deals with the purposes of the United Nations, makes a passing reference to justice and international law, which could be used to support the argument that force used in the interests of justice and international law is not illegal, the over-riding purpose mentioned in Article 1 is 'to maintain international *peace* and security' – which must surely indicate that *any* breach of international peace is automatically contrary to the purposes of the United Nations (for the text of Article 1 of the United Nations Charter, see above, p. 168).

This extensive interpretation of Article 2(4) is reinforced by an examination of other provisions of the Charter. The preamble says that 'the peoples of the United Nations [are] determined to save succeeding generations from the scourge of war, which twice in our lifetime has brought untold sorrow to mankind'; and Article 2(3) obliges members to 'settle their international disputes by *peaceful* means in such a manner that *international peace and security*, and justice, are not endangered' (italics added).

The view that Article 2(4) should be broadly interpreted is also supported by the *Corfu Channel* case (*ICJ Reports*, 1949, pp. 4, 35). In that case, British warships had been struck by mines while exercising a right of innocent passage in Albanian territorial waters, and the United Kingdom sent some more warships to sweep the minefield ('Operation Retail'). Minesweeping is not included in the right of innocent passage, but the United Kingdom argued that it had a right to intervene in order to make sure that the mines were produced as evidence before an international tribunal. The International Court of Justice rejected this argument:

> The court can only regard the alleged right of intervention as the manifestation of a policy of force, such as has in the past given rise to most serious abuses and such as cannot, whatever be the present defects in international organization, find a place in international law.

The Court went on to say:

> The United Kingdom Agent . . . has further classified 'Operation Retail' among methods of self-protection or self-help. The Court

---

[1] On the alleged right of humanitarian intervention, see Hedley Bull (ed.), *Intervention in World Politics,* 1984, ch. 7.

cannot accept this defence either. Between independent states, respect for territorial sovereignty is an essential foundation of international relations.

No doubt it may be galling for a strong state to be prohibited from using force against a weak state which infringes its legal rights; but the Charter is based on the belief that international law should not be enforced at the expense of international peace. As the General Assembly declared in 1970: 'Every state has the duty to refrain from the threat or use of force . . . as a means of solving international disputes' (Ian Brownlie, *Basic Documents in International Law*, 3rd edn., 1983, p. 38).

It is submitted, therefore, that Article 2(4) should be interpreted as totally prohibiting the threat or use of force. However, there are other provisions of the Charter which contain exceptions to the principle, and these exceptions must now be examined.

(1) *Action taken or authorised by the United Nations*. This has already been considered (see above, pp. 184–95).
(2) *Self-defence* is another exception, although its extent is controversial. Article 51 of the Charter, which is the legal basis for NATO, the Warsaw Pact and similar alliances, provides:

> Nothing in the present Charter shall impair the inherent right of individual or collective self-defence if an armed attack occurs against a member of the United Nations, until the Security Council has taken the measures necessary to maintain international peace and security. Measures taken by members in the exercise of this right of self-defence shall be immediately reported to the Security Council and shall not in any way affect the authority and responsibility of the Security Council under the present Charter to take at any time such action as it deems necessary in order to maintain or restore international peace and security.

There is disagreement about the circumstances in which the right of self-defence may be exercised. The words 'if an armed attack occurs', interpreted literally, imply that the armed attack must have already occurred before force can be used in self-defence; there is no right of anticipatory self-defence against an imminent danger of attack. (It is true that the French text uses the words 'dans le cas où un membre . . . est l'objet d'une agression armée', and a state can be the object of an attack before the attack occurs. But the Spanish text ('en caso de ataque armada') is closer to the English text.)

However, supporters of a right of anticipatory self-defence claim that Article 51 does not limit the circumstances in which self-defence may be exercised; they deny that the word 'if', as used in Article 51, means 'if and only if'.[1] The difficulty about this approach is that it is hard to imagine why the drafters of the Charter bothered to stipulate conditions for the exercise of the right of self-defence unless they intended those conditions to be exhaustive. Supporters of a right of anticipatory self-defence try to meet this objection in two ways. First, they argue that the conditions stated in Article 51 cannot be treated as exhaustive, otherwise the words 'if an armed attack occurs *against a member*' would have the absurd result of preventing members from protecting *non-members* against attack.[2] Second, they point out that Article 51 describes self-defence as an 'inherent right', and they suggest that it would be inconsistent for a provision simultaneously to restrict a right and to recognise that right as inherent.

It is submitted, however, that anticipatory self-defence is incompatible with the Charter. Article 51 is an exception to Article 2(4), and it is a general rule of interpretation that exceptions to a principle should be interpreted restrictively, so as not to undermine the principle. Article 53 of the Charter provides that parties to regional arrangements may take enforcement action against a 'renewal of aggressive policy' (a term which is much wider than 'aggression') on the part of former enemy states, and this provision would be unnecessary if Article 51 permitted anticipatory self-defence. It is also significant that the North Atlantic Treaty and similar treaties based on Article 51 provide only for defence against armed attacks, and not for defence against imminent dangers of armed attacks. Unlike many academic writers, the USA did not invoke a right of anticipatory self-defence in order to justify the 'quarantine' imposed on Cuba during the Cuban missiles crisis (see below, p. 227). The USA realised that such an attitude would have created a precedent which the Soviet Union

[1] This argument sometimes takes the extreme form of saying that a state may use force in defence of a large range of interests, even when there is neither an actual armed attack nor an imminent danger of one (for example, D. W. Bowett, *Self-Defence in International Law*, 1958, chs 5 and 6). This view, which is reminiscent of nineteenth-century ideas of vital interests (see above, pp. 216–17), is generally discredited. See Ian Brownlie, *International Law and the Use of Force by States*, 1963, pp. 250–7, 281–301; Rosalyn Higgins, *The Development of International Law through the Political Organs of the United Nations*, 1963, pp. 216–21. General Assembly Resolution 3314 (XXIX), after defining aggression in very wide terms, declares in Article 5 that 'no consideration of whatever nature, whether political, economic, military or otherwise, may serve as a justification for aggression' (text in *American Journal of International Law*, 1975, p. 480).

[2] In practice, members do claim a right to protect non-members against attack; one of the main purposes of NATO is to protect West Germany, although West Germany did not become a member of the United Nations until 1973.

In 1945 it was expected that virtually all states in the world would soon become members of the United Nations, and therefore the failure of the Charter to mention attacks on non-members was probably due to an oversight.

could have used against American missile sites in Europe; indeed, on the same reasoning, virtually every state in the world could have claimed to be threatened by a build-up of arms in a neighbouring state and could have resorted to preventive war. It is true that the facts of the Cuban missiles crisis are not a good example of the typical situation contemplated by supporters of the doctrine of anticipatory self-defence, because a communist attack was probably not imminent; but the question whether an attack is imminent is inevitably a question of opinion and degree, and any rule founded on such a criterion is bound to be subjective and capable of abuse. To confine self-defence to cases where an armed attack has actually occurred, on the other hand, has the merit of precision; the occurrence of an armed attack is a question of fact which is usually capable of objective verification.

From the practical point of view, the exclusion of a right of anticipatory self-defence deprives the 'innocent' state of the military advantage of striking the first blow (although the advantage of striking the first blow in hostilities between states is almost never as decisive as it can be in a fight between individuals). But the trouble about anticipatory self-defence is that a state can seldom be absolutely certain about the other side's intentions; in moments of crisis, there is seldom time to check information suggesting that an attack is imminent. Is a nuclear power entitled to destroy most of mankind simply because a radar system mistakes a flight of geese for enemy missiles? (Radar systems have actually made such mistakes in the past.) Fortunately, neither the USA nor the Soviet Union now needs to rely on anticipatory self-defence, since each has acquired a second-strike capacity (that is, a capacity to make a crippling nuclear counter-attack on the other side, even after suffering the effects of a previous all-out nuclear attack launched by the other side).

Three further points should be noted concerning the circumstances in which force may be used in self-defence. First, the attack which gives rise to the right of self-defence need not necessarily be directed against a state's *territory*;[1] Article 6 of the North Atlantic Treaty 1949 provides for collective self-defence against 'an armed attack on the territory of any of the parties in Europe or North America, . . . on the occupation forces of any party in Europe, on the islands under the jurisdiction of any party in the North Atlantic area . . . or on the vessels or aircraft in this

---

[1] In most circumstances it is unlawful to attack territory which is in the possession of another state, even though that state does not have sovereignty over the territory: Ian Brownlie, *International Law and the Use of Force by States*, 1963, pp. 382-3, and *Basic Documents in International Law*, 3rd ed., 1983, p. 38. In such cases the state in possession of the territory is entitled to use force in self-defence against such an attack.

area of any of the parties', and in the *Corfu Channel* case the International Court of Justice held that British warships, attacked while exercising a right of innocent passage in foreign territorial waters, were entitled to return fire (*ICJ Reports*, 1949, pp. 4, 30–1). But most states and most writers agree that attacks on a state's nationals resident abroad do not entitle the state to use force in order to defend its nationals (Hedley Bull (ed.), *Intervention in World Politics*, 1984, pp. 99–116). Second, self-defence does not include a right of armed reprisals; if terrorists enter one state from another, the first state may use force to arrest or expel the terrorists, but, having done so, it is not entitled to retaliate by attacking the other state. The Security Council has frequently condemned Israel for carrying out armed reprisals against her neighbours, and in 1970 the General Assembly declared that 'states have a duty to refrain from acts of reprisal involving the use of force' (Ian Brownlie, *Basic Documents in International Law*, 3rd ed., 1983, p. 38). Third, and most important, force used in self-defence must be proportional to the seriousness of the armed attack. This is a matter of common sense; otherwise a minor frontier incident could be made a pretext for starting an all-out war.

Finally, there is a controversy concerning the scope of *collective* self-defence. Article 51 of the Charter speaks of 'individual or collective self-defence', and Dr Bowett has argued that a right of collective self-defence is merely a combination of individual rights of self-defence; states may exercise collectively a right which any of them might have exercised individually. The corollary, according to Dr Bowett, is that no state may defend another state unless each state could have legally exercised a right of *individual* self-defence in the same circumstances; thus, Greece could not defend Peru against attack, because an attack on Peru does not affect the rights or interests of Greece (D. W. Bowett, *Self-Defence in International Law*, 1958, ch. 10).

This view is based partly on analogies drawn from English law. At the time when Dr Bowett was writing, English law did not allow one person to use force in defence of another person unless there was a close relationship (for example, a family relationship) between the two persons concerned. However, English law on this point has now been altered by the Court of Appeal's decision in *R. v. Duffy*, which recognised a right to use force in defence of *any* person.[1]

---

[1] [1967] 1 Q.B. 63. French law is equally wide; Article 328 of the Code pénal authorises 'légitime défense' of oneself or of a third party, and French courts have never placed any limitation on the categories of third parties who may be protected. Note that the French text of Article 51 uses the same term, 'légitime défense', which avoids the contradiction inherent in speaking about 'self-defence' of another person.

State practice lends no support to Dr Bowett's views. Under the North Atlantic Treaty and similar treaties, each party undertakes to defend every other party against attack, and this undertaking is not limited to circumstances where an attack on one party threatens the rights or interests of another party.

(3) *Action against former enemy states*. Article 107 of the Charter provides:

> Nothing in the present Charter shall invalidate or preclude action, in relation to any state which during the second world war has been an enemy of any signatory to the present Charter, taken or authorized as a result of that war by the governments having responsibility for such action.

Article 53(1) provides:

> The Security Council shall, where appropriate, utilize . . . regional arrangements or agencies for enforcement action under its authority. But no enforcement action shall be taken under regional arrangements or by regional agencies without the authorization of the Security Council, with the exception of measures against any [former] enemy state . . . provided for pursuant to Article 107 or in regional arrangements directed against renewal of aggressive policy on the part of any such state, until such time as the organization may, on request of the governments concerned, be charged with the responsibility for preventing further aggression by such a state.

Immediately after the Second World War the Soviet Union concluded bilateral treaties of alliance with other Eastern European countries; these treaties were ostensibly aimed against a renewal of German aggression, and were thus probably based by implication on Articles 53 and 107. They were replaced in 1955 by the multilateral Warsaw Pact, which is expressly based on Article 51, but the Soviet Union has continued to invoke Articles 53 and 107 from time to time. For instance, references to Articles 53 and 107 frequently appeared in Soviet justifications of the invasion of Czechoslovakia in 1968; the Soviet Union tried to argue that the liberalising movement in Czechoslovakia was in some unexplained way a result of West German subversion.

The view of the Western powers is that Articles 53 and 107 were only intended to cover the immediate postwar period and are now obsolete. This may be true of Article 107, which appears in a chapter headed 'transitional security arrangements', but the temporary character of Article 53 is much less clear. In any case, most of the acts which the Soviet Union has attempted to justify by means of Articles 53 and 107 were not aimed against former enemy states, but against the Soviet Union's wartime allies, such as Czechoslovakia (for example, the invasion of Czechoslovakia in 1968) or the USA, the United Kingdom and France (for example, the Berlin blockade in 1948-9). Since such acts are clearly not justified by Articles 53 and 107, it is unnecessary to decide whether or not those articles are obsolete.

In 1970 West Germany and the Soviet Union signed a treaty in which the Soviet Union by implication renounced its rights under Articles 53 and 107 to use force against West Germany (text in *International Legal Materials*, 1970, p. 1026). Poland, Czechoslovakia and East Germany have also made similar treaties with West Germany.

(4) *Actions by regional agencies*. Article 52(1) of the Charter provides:

Nothing in the present Charter precludes the existence of regional arrangements or agencies for dealing with such matters relating to the maintenance of international peace and security as are appropriate for regional action, provided that such arrangements or agencies and their activities are consistent with the purposes and principles of the United Nations.

In the 1960s the USA and most of the Latin American countries tried to place an extensive interpretation on the powers of the Organisation of American States (OAS) and of other regional agencies. In this context, Article 53 of the Charter, which provides that 'no enforcement action shall be taken . . . by regional agencies without the authorization of the Security Council', constituted a serious obstacle, which the USA and its allies tried to overcome in a number of ways.

In 1960 the OAS imposed economic sanctions against the right-wing dictatorship of General Trujillo in the Dominican Republic, which was accused of fomenting subversion in other Latin American countries. At the beginning of 1962 similar action was taken against the Castro régime in Cuba, for the same reasons. The Soviet Union argued in the Security Council that such economic sanctions constituted enforcement action, which was illegal without Security Council authorisation. But the majority of the members of the Security Council considered that economic sanctions did not constitute enforcement action within the meaning of Article 53, and did not require authorisation by the Security Council, because the OAS was merely doing collectively what any of its members could have done individually; for, under customary law, every state is at liberty to sever its economic relations with another state (Akehurst, 'Enforcement action by regional agencies', *British Year Book of International Law*, 1967, pp. 175, 185–97).

The use of force, however, is another matter. During the Cuban missiles crisis, the USA, acting in accordance with an OAS authorisation, searched merchant ships approaching Cuba and forced them to turn back if they were found to be carrying arms; this 'quarantine', as it was called, clearly entailed a threat to use force against any ship which refused to comply. The USA put forward a number of unconvincing arguments to reconcile this action with Article 53. For instance, it said that the failure by the Security Council to condemn the OAS amounted to acquiescence, and therefore to implied authorisation. But this argument is contrary to the plain meaning of Article 53 (Akehurst, loc. cit., pp. 197–203 and 216–19).

However, even if we accept that the action taken during the Cuban missiles crisis was illegal, there is still a lesson to be learned from that crisis. Why did the USA base its case on Article 53, rather than on Article 51? The explanation seems to be that reliance on an extensive interpretation of Article 51 would have created an unfortunate precedent, which could have been abused by many other states (see above, pp. 222–3); reliance on Article 53 was not open to the same objection, because there are very few regional agencies similar to the OAS; moreover, a regional agency cannot act or authorise action by its members unless the majority of its members are in favour of the proposed action, and consequently an extensive interpretation of the powers of regional agencies creates a smaller risk of irresponsible action than an extensive interpretation of the right of self-defence would have done. The Cuban missiles crisis is a classic example of the paradoxical way in which international law can influence the behaviour of states even when they break it (Akehurst, loc. cit., pp. 221–7).

The effectiveness of the modern rules against the use of force

For over thirty years since 1945 the world has been relatively free from *international* wars, despite the existence of acute political tensions which would almost certainly have led to war in previous ages. Such fighting as has occurred has mostly taken the form of *civil* wars, although there is always a danger that civil wars will escalate into international wars (for example, Vietnam). It would be foolish to suggest that international law is the main cause of the infrequency of wars; the destructiveness of modern war is a much more potent factor. The popular revulsion against the destructiveness of modern war gave rise to rules of law against the use of force; but those rules have in turn served to augment popular revulsion against war (similarly laws against homicide are simultaneously a consequence and a cause of popular revulsion against homicide).

The biggest defect in the modern rules is that they are often imprecise. Practice has done little to reduce the imprecision. Many states want to retain the possibility of using force in certain circumstances, but they know that an interpretation which allowed them to do so would also allow other states to use force against them; so they 'keep their options open' by failing to adopt a clear attitude towards the problem of interpretation in question. In moments of crisis a state will be tempted to exploit such uncertainties in the law; its sense of objectivity will be lost, and it may genuinely come to believe that a doubtful interpretation which suits its interests is well-founded. In theory the organs of the United Nations ought to strengthen and clarify the rules by deciding whether they have been broken in particular cases. But sometimes the member-states of the United Nations which consider that a particular state has acted legally are as numerous as those which consider that it has acted illegally, and in such cases the United Nations is unable to reach any decision (for instance, it was for this reason that the United Nations adopted a 'neutral' attitude to the fighting between Israel and her neighbours in 1967 and 1973). Sometimes, moreover, a state may hope to escape censure at the United Nations if it uses force on a small scale (for example, the Indonesian 'confrontation' of Malaysia in 1963-6), or if it achieves a quick victory which presents the world with a *fait accompli* (for example, the Six Days' War in June 1967).

But although there are cases where the rules are unclear, and where the United Nations adopts an ambiguous attitude, there are also other cases where the law is perfectly clear; the rules may be blurred around the edges, but they have a hard core of certainty. And in cases of this second type the law exercises a real restraining influence on the actions of states.

Lawful and Unlawful Means of Waging War

The eighteenth and nineteenth centuries, which saw the abandonment of any attempt by international law to restrict the right of states to go to war, also saw the growth of rules regulating the way in which wars should be fought. Nor was this a coincidence; in the days when the theory of the just war had been dominant, each side had usually considered that the other side's cause was unjust, and it had therefore tended to treat the other side as mere bandits, lacking any right to fair treatment.

To many people it seems a paradox that war, the ultimate break-down in law and order, should be fought in accordance with rules of law; why should a nation fighting for survival allow its struggle to be impeded by legal restrictions? Part of the answer lies in the fact that nations did not regard themselves as fighting for survival in the eighteenth and nineteenth centuries. Wars were seldom fought for ideological reasons and tended not to rouse the same intensity of passion as twentieth-century wars. In an age when governments interfered little with the lives of their subjects, a change of sovereignty over territory had little effect on the way of life of the inhabitants, who consequently tended to be philo-sophical about the prospect of defeat in war. In any case, the balance of power system deterred the territorial aggrandisement of states and therefore limited the territorial changes which would otherwise have resulted from wars. The balance of power system also necessitated flexibility in political alignments and meant that a state's enemy today might be its ally tomorrow; this naturally had a restraining effect on the degree of brutality practised in wars, because states did not want to arouse undying bitterness among potential allies.

Even more important than these political considerations was the fact that the laws of war were designed mainly to prevent *unnecessary* suffering. 'Unnecessary suffering' meant suffering which would produce no military advantage, or a military advant-age which was very small in comparison with the amount of suffer-ing involved.[1] Violations of the laws of war were therefore rare, because the military advantage to be gained by breaking those laws was almost always outweighed by disadvantages such as reprisals, loss of neutral good will, and so on.

Wars in the eighteenth and nineteenth centuries were wars between armed forces, rather than wars between peoples. 'The destruction of the enemy's military force is the foundation-stone of all action in war', wrote Clausewitz, the greatest of nineteenth-century military writers. It was therefore easy for international law to protect civilians.[2] Moreover, Clausewitz explains that 'destruction of the enemy's military power' means that 'the military power must be . . . reduced to such a state as not to be able to prosecute the war'; 'the aim of all action in war is to *disarm* the enemy'. Consequently, rules grew up to protect even members of

[1] However, there were a few exceptions to this general rule; for instance, it was and still is forbidden to torture prisoners in order to obtain information, although the military advantage could be enormous in certain cases.

[2] But the protection was never absolute; for instance, an army besieging a town was entitled to hasten the fall of the town by preventing food from entering the town and by preventing civilian inhabitants from leaving. In other words, the army compelled the town to surrender by starving the civilian inhabitants.

the armed forces who were *hors de combat* – the sick and wounded, prisoners of war, and so on. Although Clausewitz said that the laws of war were 'almost imperceptible and hardly worth mentioning', the reason for their imperceptibility was that they accorded so perfectly with the limits of military necessity; 'if we find civilized nations do not put their prisoners to death, do not devastate towns and countries, this is because their intelligence . . . has taught them more effectual means of applying force than these rude acts of mere instinct'.

In the second half of the nineteenth century states began to issue manuals of military law, containing a restatement of the laws of war, for use by their commanders in the field; this led to greater respect for the laws of war, as well as more precision in their formulation. At the same time, the laws of war, which had hitherto been derived almost entirely from customary law, began to be codified and extended by treaties. The chief treaties were the Geneva Conventions of 1864 and 1906, protecting sick and wounded soldiers, and the three Hague Conventions of 1899 and the thirteen Hague Conventions of 1907, which dealt with most of the remaining aspects of the laws of war. Although these treaties were of course only binding on the states which became parties to them, nearly all of them stated rules which either were already part of customary law or subsequently came to be accepted as new customary law.

Since the First World War further treaties on the laws of war have been concluded from time to time. The London Treaty of 1930 and the Protocol of 1936 sought to regulate the use of submarines; the Geneva Protocol of 1925 prohibited the use of gas and bacteriological warfare; a convention was signed at The Hague in 1954 for the protection of cultural property (for example, works of art) in the event of armed conflict; a convention of 1972 prohibited the use and possession of bacteriological (biological) and toxin weapons; a convention of 1976 prohibited the military use of environmental modification techniques; and a convention and three protocols were signed in 1981 to limit the use of cruel or indiscriminate non-nuclear weapons, such as incendiary weapons (for example, napalm), land-mines and booby-traps, particularly their use against civilians. More important, however, are the three Geneva Conventions of 1929 for the protection of sick and wounded soldiers, of sick and wounded sailors and of prisoners of war, and the four Geneva Conventions of 1949 for the protection of sick and wounded soldiers, of sick and wounded sailors, of prisoners of war and of civilians, together with the First Protocol of 1977 which supplements the 1949 Conventions. The scope of the Civilians' Convention is much less than its name implies; it is mainly concerned with protecting only two classes of civilians – those who find themselves in enemy territory at the outbreak of war, and those who inhabit territory which is over-run and occupied by the enemy during the war. But the Convention does contain some provisions which apply to all civilians, wherever they may be; for instance, it prohibits attacks on civilian hospitals. Articles 48–60 of the First Protocol of 1977 (text in *International Legal Materials*, 1977, p. 1391) go much further in protecting civilians against attacks, but in 1983 only 33 states (mostly from the 'Third World') were parties to the First Protocol, compared with 154 states parties to the Geneva Civilians' Convention of 1949.

The creation of new law by treaties has tended to lag far behind the development of military technology. For instance, until the First Protocol of 1977 there was no treaty dealing with the bombing of civilians. This would not have mattered much if the customary law on the subject had been clear, but it was not. State practice concerning the laws of war occurs mainly during wartime, and therefore lacks continuity; major wars are infrequent, and nowadays technological changes occur so rapidly that each war differs radically from the previous war. It is also difficult to establish an *opinio iuris*, because states seldom give legal reasons for what they do in wartime. Nor do war crimes trials do much to clarify the law. For instance, not a single German was prosecuted after the Second World War for organising mass bombing raids; it is understandable that the Allies were reluctant to prosecute Germans for doing what the Allies had also done, but the result is that there is no judicial pronouncement on the legality of bombing.

Meanwhile, the Hague Conventions of 1899 and 1907 are still technically in force, but the fact that many of their provisions are manifestly inappropriate to modern conditions has often tempted states to break them.

There are two further factors which have encouraged violations of the laws of war during the twentieth century. In the first place, the First and Second World Wars produced more bitter feelings than previous wars; they were fought for ideological reasons, and for virtually unlimited objectives – belligerent states no longer sought to achieve a delicate adjustment to the balance of power, but adopted a policy of unconditional surrender, which naturally spurred the other side on to fight to the death. Second, economic and technological changes vastly increased the military advantage to be gained by breaking the laws of war. (There are exceptions, of course; for instance, killing prisoners of war still produces little military advantage, and the relevant rules of law therefore stand a good chance of surviving.) In particular, the distinction between the armed forces and civilians is largely illusory, now that the whole of a country's economy is geared to the war effort. Destruction of factories, and even the killing of factory workers, produce a military advantage which would have been inconceivable a century ago; and the invention of the aircraft has given belligerent states the means to carry out such acts.

Nuclear weapons

In 1961 the United Nations General Assembly passed a resolution declaring that the use of nuclear weapons was illegal (*Yearbook of the United Nations*, 1961, pp. 30–1). Fifty-five states (consisting mainly of communist and Afro-Asian countries) voted in favour of the resolution, twenty states (consisting mainly of Western countries) voted against, and twenty-six states (consisting mainly of Latin American countries) abstained. The divergence between the positions of the communist and Western countries is explained by the fact that the Soviet superiority in conventional (that is, non-nuclear) forces in Europe is so great that the Western countries would be compelled to use nuclear weapons in order to defend themselves against an invasion of Western Europe by Soviet conventional forces; consequently, the Western countries argue that the use of nuclear weapons is not contrary to international law. The Soviet Union, on the other hand, can afford to win Afro-Asian good will by subscribing to the view that the use of nuclear weapons is illegal, because it knows that it will not need to be the first state to use them; if Western countries use them first, the Soviet Union will be able to justify its own use of nuclear weapons by means of the doctrine of reprisals (see below, pp. 236–7).

A General Assembly resolution of this type is, at the most, merely evidence of customary law; but the voting figures for this resolution show the absence of a generally accepted custom. The Western powers, at any rate, are probably entitled to claim that the resolution has no legal effect on them, since they have consistently repudiated the ideas stated in it.

Certain rules of international law might be extended by analogy to deal with nuclear weapons. For instance, Article 23(*a*) of the Hague Regulations 1907 declares that it is forbidden 'to employ poison or poisoned weapons', and the Geneva Gas Protocol 1925 prohibits 'the use in war of asphyxiating, poisonous or other gases, and of all analogous liquids, materials or devices'. It is arguable that the fall-out caused by nuclear weapons resembles poison, but the analogy is not close enough to be absolutely compelling; fall-out is only a *side-effect* of nuclear weapons, whereas poisoning is the *main* (if not the sole) effect of using poison gas.

Alternatively, nuclear weapons could be compared with the mass bombing raids of the Second World War; but there was no treaty prohibiting those raids, and it would be difficult to argue that they were contrary to customary law, in the light of the extensive use of them by both sides in the Second World War.[1]

There remains the underlying principle that acts of war should not cause unnecessary suffering, that is, suffering out of all proportion to the military advantage to be gained from those acts. Nuclear weapons cause enormous suffering, but they can also produce an enormous military advantage; if nuclear weapons had not been used against Japan in 1945, the war against Japan might have lasted at least another year. It would therefore be unwise to conclude that the use of nuclear weapons is unlawful in all circumstances.

But, even if we accept that the use of nuclear weapons is sometimes lawful, this does not mean that the laws of war restricting the use of 'conventional' weapons are obsolete. To drop a nuclear bomb on a city may be lawful because the military advantage gained by destroying military installations, factories, means of communication, and so on, outweighs the suffering; but to drop a 'conventional' bomb deliberately on a school or hospital in the same city would be illegal, because there would be no military advantage to outweigh the suffering.

Economic uses of maritime warfare

The sea has always been used for the transport of merchandise, and for centuries one of the main objects of naval warfare has been to cripple the enemy's economy. Enemy merchant ships may be seized at sea; the rules of naval warfare are thus different from the rules of land warfare, which prohibit (or used to prohibit) the seizure of private enemy-owned property, subject to certain exceptions. In addition, neutral merchant ships can be seized if they try to carry contraband to the enemy, or if they try to run (that is, break through) a blockade. (Neutral shipowners who carry contraband or who run a blockade are not acting illegally (nor is their national state acting illegally by permitting them to behave in this way); but they run the risk of confiscation if they are caught.)

---

[1] If Articles 48–60 of the First Protocol of 1977 had been in force during the Second World War, they would have prohibited many of the bombing raids which occurred during that war. But the USA, when signing the First Protocol in 1977, placed on record its 'understanding . . . that the rules established by this Protocol were not intended to have any effect on and do not regulate or prohibit the use of nuclear weapons' (*American Journal of International Law*, 1978, p. 407). Similar statements were made by the British and French governments.

On the legality or illegality of non-nuclear bombing, see the article by Blix in the *British Year Book of International Law*, 1978, p. 31.

In the eighteenth and nineteenth centuries goods were divided into three classes – absolute contraband, conditional contraband and free goods. Neutral ships carrying absolute contraband (that is, goods having an obvious military use, such as gunpowder) to an enemy country were always liable to seizure; neutral ships carrying free goods (for example, luxuries such as silk) to an enemy country were never liable to seizure; neutral ships carrying other goods (that is, conditional contraband, such as food or cloth) were liable to seizure if the goods were intended for the enemy government, but not if they were intended for private individuals in the enemy country. The distinctions between the three categories were never very precise, and belligerent states had a certain discretion in deciding what constituted absolute or conditional contraband. In the First and Second World Wars the whole economy of each of the belligerents was geared to the war effort, in a way unknown in previous wars, and consequently virtually all goods came to be listed as absolute contraband, even though they had been treated as conditional contraband or free goods in previous wars.

In the eighteenth and nineteenth centuries belligerent states were also entitled to *blockade* an enemy coastline, that is, to send warships to sail up and down near the enemy coastline in order to prevent other ships reaching or leaving enemy ports. Neutral ships which tried to run (that is, break through) a blockade were liable to seizure; but the right of seizure arose only if the blockade reached a certain degree of effectiveness. During the First World War German mines and submarines made it impossible for Allied warships to operate near the German coast; instead, the Allies instituted a 'long-distance blockade', stopping neutral vessels hundreds of miles from the German coast and seizing them if they were found to be carrying goods destined for Germany. Neutral states protested against this extension of the concept of blockade, and against the changes in the practice relating to contraband; but, after the entry of the USA into the war, neutral states were too few and weak to secure respect for their views.

Belligerent warships are entitled to stop and search neutral merchant ships (except in neutral territorial waters), to see whether they are carrying contraband or trying to run a blockade; if the search confirms the suspicion, the merchant ship is taken into port to be condemned as a 'lawful prize' by a Prize Court set up for this purpose by the captor state. However, during the First and Second World Wars this practice was altered in several respects. In particular, it became more common to sink merchant ships instead of capturing them. Before 1914 there was controversy about the circumstances in which it was lawful to sink merchant ships, but on one point there was agreement – the warship had to rescue the crew of the sunk merchant ship. All this changed with the invention of the submarine. The German policy of sinking merchant ships at sight, without rescuing their crews, provoked the USA into declaring war on Germany in 1917, but both sides adopted a similar policy in the Second World War. The Nuremberg Tribunal held that this policy was unlawful, but did not punish the German leaders for following it, because the Allies had done the same (*Annual Digest and Reports of Public International Law Cases*, vol. 13, 1946, pp. 203, 219–20).

Possible future developments

Writers often assume that the erosion of the traditional laws of war, which took place during the First and Second World Wars, will continue in future wars. It is possible, however, that the development of nuclear weapons will have the indirect and paradoxical effect of re-establishing some of the traditional rules which fell into decline during the two world wars. (Different considerations apply to civil wars, or to wars which are 'semi-civil' and 'semi-international', like the war in Vietnam; see below, pp. 246–7.)

Since 1945 fear of nuclear war has prevented nuclear powers from entering into even the most limited conflict with one another (apart from skirmishes on the Soviet–Chinese border), and it is likely that this state of affairs will continue. In future wars, therefore, at least one of the two sides will probably not possess nuclear weapons. The corollary is that there are likely to be a large number of states, including one or more nuclear powers, who will be neutral in future wars, even though their sympathies may lie with one side or another. As a result, belligerent states will have to pay far more attention to neutral opinion than they did during the two world wars. Disregard of the rights of neutral shipping was by no means the only violation of the laws of war during the two world wars which was facilitated by the fact that neutrals were few and weak. If neutrals outnumber belligerents in future wars, the position will be very different. The parties involved in the wars in 'Biafra' and Vietnam were very sensitive to allegations that they had committed atrocities, and this sensitivity shows the influence which can be exercised by public opinion in neutral countries.

Even if nuclear powers get involved in 'conventional' hostilities with one another, fear that the fighting may escalate into a nuclear war is likely to induce them to conduct the hostilities cautiously, on a limited scale and for limited objectives. In other words, the hostilities will bear more resemblance to the 'limited wars' of the eighteenth and nineteenth centuries than to the 'total war' of the two world wars; and it is not unreasonable to hope that the respect for the laws of war, which characterised the wars of the eighteenth and nineteenth centuries, will be revived in such hostilities. ·

If the United Nations, and the rules in the United Nations Charter concerning the use of force, continue to operate semi-effectively, as at present, there will be three further developments.

First, fear of intervention by the United Nations will probably cause hostilities to be brief or on a limited scale. In the two world wars, the embittering effect of years of total war led to a *gradual* abandonment of the laws of war; with luck, such a process will not recur in the future.

Second, fear of intervention by the United Nations will probably induce states to understate the extent of the hostilities in which they are involved; in particular, they will deny that a technical state of war exists. This gives rise to the problem whether the laws of war apply to hostilities falling short of war. It is fairly clear that they do. But an exception may exist as far as relations with neutral states are concerned; in the past, neutrals were reluctant to allow their ships to be seized for carrying contraband or running a blockade unless a technical state of war existed.

Third, there is the problem whether the benefits of the laws of war may be withheld from a state because it violated the United Nations Charter by starting the hostilities. The answer is probably no. The laws of war are designed to prevent unnecessary suffering, and it is unjust that soldiers and civilians should be made to suffer unnecessarily for the acts of leaders over whom they have little or no control. Moreover, if each side considered that the other side was in the wrong, and denied it the benefits of the laws of war, the suffering would be appalling.

On the other hand, the legality of a war may affect the application of the rules of neutrality (cf. below, pp. 241–2). Under Chapter VII of the Charter, the Security Council may order or authorise member-states to depart from the ordinary rules of neutrality. But, even in the absence of such action by the Security Council, there is authority for the view that states may now adopt a policy of 'qualified neutrality', which involves breaking some of the traditional duties of neutrality by discriminating against the aggressor. This is what the USA did when it supplied warships to the United Kingdom under the 'lend-lease' scheme in 1940–1, before entering the Second World War.

Reprisals

Reprisals are one of the main means of forcing states to obey the laws of war – and indeed of forcing them to obey international law in general. A reprisal is an act which would normally be illegal but which is rendered lawful by a prior illegal act committed by the state against which the reprisal is directed; it is a form of retaliation against the prior illegal act. Reprisals may be used only when other means of redress (for example, protests, warnings, and so on) have failed (and see above, p. 6).

Reprisals have an undoubted deterrent effect; it was fear of reprisals which prevented gas being used during the Second World War. But reprisals often cause hardship for innocent persons, and consequently the four Geneva Conventions of 1949 forbid reprisals against the persons, buildings, vessels, equipment and property protected by those Conventions.

War crimes trials

War crimes trials are another means of forcing states to obey the laws of war. For centuries, members of the armed forces and other persons who commit breaches (or, at any rate, serious breaches) of the laws of war have been liable to prosecution. Theoretically any state may try them, but in practice jurisdiction is usually exercised by a state on the opposite side in the relevant war. There is obviously a danger that war crimes trials may sometimes degenerate into a mere instrument of revenge, but abolition of a state's right to try enemy nationals for war crimes would mean that many guilty men would escape punishment. It is rare to find a state trying its own nationals for war crimes, although such trials do sometimes occur, and are usually used to create a favourable impression on neutral public opinion; for instance, in November 1968 Nigeria tried a Nigerian officer for shooting a 'Biafran' prisoner, and executed him in front of BBC television cameras.

Defendants in war crimes trials often put forward the defence that they were carrying out the orders of a superior, but this defence rarely succeeds. The general view is that superior orders are not a defence, but that they may be taken into account to reduce the level of punishment imposed. A few cases, however, treat superior orders as a valid defence to minor charges.

War criminals should be distinguished from 'unprivileged belligerents', such as spies. Unprivileged belligerents are not entitled to be treated as prisoners of war, and may be shot upon capture, provided that their status as unprivileged belligerents is proved by a fair trial. But unprivileged belligerents, and the states which employ them, are not guilty of violating the law of war; the state employing them is under no obligation to pay compensation for their activities, as it would have been if those activities had been contrary to international law. Similarly, a spy who returns to his own forces cannot subsequently be punished for spying; there is no similar rule of international law extinguishing a war criminal's liability.

The Nuremberg Tribunal, which was set up by an inter-Allied

agreement at the end of the Second World War, tried the German leaders not only for war crimes, but also for crimes against peace and crimes against humanity.

Crimes against peace were defined in the Tribunal's Charter as:

> planning, preparation, initiation or waging of a war of aggression, or a war in violation of international treaties. . . .

This provision in the Tribunal's Charter was criticised by some people as retroactive legislation. Clearly a war of aggression was illegal, after the Kellogg–Briand Pact (see above, p. 219), but there was nothing in the Kellogg–Briand Pact to indicate that aggression was a crime,[1] or that the Pact imposed obligations on individuals. However, a number of unratified treaties and League of Nations resolutions dating from the 1920s,[2] which can be regarded as evidence of customary law, did declare specifically that aggression was a *crime*.

As for the question of individual liability, pre-existing types of 'international crimes', such as war crimes, entailed individual liability, and it was therefore reasonable to apply the principle of individual liability by analogy to the new international crime of aggression.

The accusation about retroactive legislation is closer to the truth as regards crimes against humanity. These were defined in the Tribunal's Charter as follows:

> murder, extermination, enslavement, deportation and other inhumane acts committed against any civilian population before or during the war, or persecutions on political, racial or religious grounds in execution of or in connection with any crime within the jurisdiction of the Tribunal, whether or not in violation of the domestic law of the country where perpetrated.

In some respects, crimes against humanity are wider than war crimes; they can be committed before a war as well as during a war, and they can be directed against 'any civilian population', including the wrong-doing state's own population. The prohibition of 'crimes against humanity' thus constituted an exception to the old rule that a state was entitled to treat its nationals as it pleased; and it is fairly clear that this prohibition was not accepted as part

---

[1] Many acts are illegal (for example, torts and breaches of contract in municipal law) without being crimes.

[2] They are quoted in the Tribunal's judgment: *American Journal of International Law*, vol. 41, 1947, pp. 172, 219–20.

It should be noted that liability for crimes against peace falls only on the leaders of the state, and not on the ordinary soldiers who take part in a war of aggression. In this respect crimes against peace differ from war crimes (and from crimes against humanity).

of international law before 1945. However, the Tribunal restricted the scope of crimes against humanity by stressing the words 'in execution of or in connection with any crime within the jurisdiction of the Tribunal', and by interpreting the words 'any crime' to mean 'any *other* crime within the jurisdiction of the Tribunal', that is, war crimes and crimes against peace. In other words, an act can constitute a crime against humanity only if it is 'in execution of or in connection with' a war crime or crime against peace. Thus, confiscation of Jewish property in Germany before the Second World War would have constituted a crime against humanity if the property had been used to finance a war of aggression, but not if it had been used to finance the Olympic Games. (But this restriction on the scope of crimes against humanity was not followed in some of the other postwar war crimes trials: see the *Eichmann* case (1961), *International Law Reports*, vol. 36, pp. 5, 48–9.)

Even if certain provisions in the Charter of the Nuremberg Tribunal constituted retroactive legislation, there is no general rule in international law against retroactive legislation. It is true that retroactive legislation can lead to injustice in certain cases, but anyone who thinks that justice demanded the acquittal of the men convicted at Nuremberg has a very peculiar idea of justice. In any case, there can be no complaints about retroactive legislation in future cases; the judgment of the Nuremberg Tribunal constitutes a precedent for the future, and the principles laid down in the Charter and judgment of the Tribunal were later approved by the General Assembly and by the International Law Commission.

Suggestions for Further Reading

Ian Brownlie, *International Law and the Use of Force by States*, 1963.
Rosalyn Higgins, *The Development of International Law through the Political Organs of the United Nations*, 1963, pt 4.
L. Oppenheim, *International Law*, 7th ed., H. Lauterpacht (ed.), Vol. 2, 1952.
Julius Stone, *Legal Controls of International Conflict*, rev. impression with supplement, 1959.
R. E. Osgood and R. W. Tucker, *Force, Order and Justice*, 1967.
Geoffrey Best, *Humanity in Warfare*, 1980.
See also the appendix on the Falkland Islands dispute, pp. 297–8, below.

Chapter 16

Civil Wars

Most of the wars fought since 1945 have been civil wars; and even many of the international wars since 1945 have had their roots in civil wars (for instance, the conflict between the Arab states and Israel developed out of hostilities which had occurred between the Jewish and Arab communities in Palestine during the last years of the British mandate). In the modern world, states seldom try to enlarge their territory by sending their armies to over-run the territory of other states; instead, they increase their influence by encouraging factions sharing their own ideology to seize or retain power in other states. The existence of ideologies transcending national frontiers not only makes civil wars more frequent; it also increases the dangers of civil wars developing into international wars, because the rules of international law concerning participation in civil wars by foreign states are not as clear as the rules prohibiting international wars.

A civil war may be fought for the control of the government of a state; or it may be caused by the desire of part of the population to secede and form a new state. The legal problems which arise in each case are so similar that it is convenient to study both types of civil war simultaneously.

The individuals who wish to set up a new government or a new state are often called insurgents, and it is proposed to use that term in the present work; it has the merit of being less emotive than other words, such as 'rebels' or 'revolutionaries'. The party on the other side is often called the *de jure* government, or the *de jure* authorities, but in the present work it is proposed to use the more neutral expression 'established authorities'; the words '*de jure*' are misleading, because they introduce irrelevant overtones from the law of recognition, and because they imply that international law is on the side of the established authorities – which is not wholly true.

The Legality of Civil Wars

There is no rule in international law against civil wars. Article 2(4) of the United Nations Charter prohibits the use or threat of force in *international* relations only. It is possible that each side will regard the other side as traitors from the point of view of municipal law, but neither the insurgents nor the established authorities are guilty of any breach of international law.

There may, however, be one exception to this principle. The use of force to frustrate the exercise of a legal right of self-determination is generally regarded as illegal nowadays, but it is uncertain whether such wars (wars of national liberation) should be classified as international wars or as civil wars (see below, pp. 256-7).

Participation by Other States: General Problems

With the possible exception of the use of force to frustrate the exercise of a legal right of self-determination, there is no rule of international law prohibiting civil wars. That does not necessarily mean, however, that other states are at liberty to participate in the civil war by giving help to one or other of the sides. But it is advisable to be clear at the outset what we mean when we talk about 'giving help to one or other of the sides'. For instance, a state is not obliged to prevent its nationals selling or giving food to either side. In the present chapter the word 'help' will be used in a more limited sense, to refer to those forms of help which, if given by a neutral state to a belligerent state during an international war, would constitute a breach of the obligations imposed by international law on neutral states. This definition necessitates a slight digression concerning the rules of neutrality in international wars.

Obviously, neutral states must refrain from fighting in an international war. In addition, they must not supply either side with arms or money (although this rule has been violated so often in the last forty years that it may perhaps be obsolete); they must not allow their territory to be used by either side for the movement of troops or military supplies, for the training of troops, or as a base for military operations; and they must not allow either side to open recruiting offices in their territory.

On the other hand, a neutral state is not obliged to prevent private individuals within its territory from helping either side. In particular, it is under no duty to prevent individuals from leaving its territory in order to join the forces of one of the belligerent states, and it is under no duty to prevent individuals from supplying money or arms to the belligerent states. (There is, however, one exception – neutral states must prevent individuals from constructing or adapting warships for a belligerent state.) Any restrictions imposed by the neutral state on the acts of individuals must be imposed impartially; a neutral state would be acting illegally if it allowed its inhabitants to sell weapons to one side and prevented them from selling weapons to the other side (but see above, p. 236).

Participation by Other States: Help for the Insurgents

As a general rule, foreign states are forbidden to give help (as defined above) to the insurgents in a civil war. For instance, General Assembly resolution 2131 (XX) declares that 'no state shall organize, assist, foment, finance, incite or tolerate subversive, terrorist or armed activities directed towards the violent overthrow of the régime of another state, or interfere in civil strife in another state' (*Yearbook of the United Nations*, 1965, p. 94; the resolution was passed by 109 votes to nil). The rule stated in this resolution has been repeated in later resolutions; see, for instance, Ian Brownlie, *Basic Documents in International Law*, 3rd ed., 1983, pp. 39, 40, and *International Legal Materials*, 1980, p. 534, para. 7.

An exception to this rule probably exists when the established authorities are receiving foreign help. In these circumstances, states sympathetic to the insurgents often claim a right to help the insurgents, in order to counterbalance the help obtained by the established authorities from other states. For instance, after the Soviet intervention in Afghanistan at the end of 1979, Egypt started providing military training and weapons for the Muslim insurgents against the Soviet-backed government, and Saudi Arabia gave money to the insurgents (*Keesing's Contemporary Archives*, 1980, pp. 30364, 30385). This right of counter-intervention, as it is sometimes called, is often supported by the argument that counter-intervention is necessary to protect the independence of the country where the civil war is taking place, on the grounds that the established authorities have lost popular support and have become puppets controlled by their foreign supporters.

A more controversial exception to the prohibition against giving foreign help to the insurgents concerns wars of national liberation; see below, pp. 257-9.

Participation by Other States: Help for the Established Authorities

The theory that help for the established authorities is legal
States have often argued that help given to the established authorities in a civil war is always legal.[1] The theory underlying

[1] Supporters of this 'rule' admit the existence of one exception to it: when the insurgents have been recognised as belligerents, the rules of neutrality come into operation, and foreign help for the established authorities is no longer lawful. This exception is of no practical importance nowadays; recognition of belligerency occurred in some nineteenth-century civil wars, especially the American civil war of 1861-5, but has virtually never occurred in any civil war during the twentieth century. See H. Lauterpacht, *Recognition in International Law*, 1947, pp. 175-269, and C. Rousseau, *Droit international public*, Vol. 3, 1977, pp. 596-604.

this argument is that the government is the agent of the state, and that therefore the government, until it is definitely overthrown, remains competent to invite foreign troops into the state's territory and to seek other forms of foreign help, whatever the effect which that help may have on the political future of the state.

The theory that help for the established authorities is illegal

The traditional view, that help for the established authorities is legal, is open to abuse; for instance, during the Spanish civil war, Germany and Italy tried to legitimise their help to the nationalists (insurgents) by prematurely recognising the nationalists as the *de jure* government of Spain. Even apart from such obvious instances of abuse, there may be situations where it is genuinely hard to say who are the established authorities and who are the insurgents. Thus, shortly after the Congo became independent in 1960, the President (Kasavubu) and the Prime Minister (Lumumba) came into conflict with each other, and each purported to dismiss the other; in such circumstances it is dangerously easy for foreign states to argue that their own protégés are the established authorities, and that the other side are the insurgents.

But the traditional view is also open to an even more fundamental objection. It is based on the idea that the government of a state is competent to act in the name of the state until it is overthrown. This idea is a fallacy; the competence of the government to act in the name of the state is the very thing which is called into question by the outbreak of a civil war. As Hall puts it:[1]

> the fact that it has been necessary to call in foreign help is enough to show that the issue of the conflict would without it be uncertain, and consequently there is doubt as to which side would ultimately establish itself as the legal representative of the state.

The idea that foreign states should not intervene on either side in a civil war is a wise one, otherwise help given by some states to the established authorities runs the risk of provoking other states into helping the insurgents (see above, p. 242, on counter-intervention). It was for this reason that many European states adopted a policy of non-intervention in the Spanish civil war 1936-9; the policy failed, but only because the fascist and communist dictatorships refused to abide by it. Non-intervention has received some support as a rule of law in subsequent state practice; in 1963 the United Kingdom stated that it 'considered that, if civil

---

[1] A. Pearce Higgins, *Hall's International Law*, 8th ed., 1924, p. 347. Similarly, the outbreak of a secessionary revolt renders uncertain the status of the territory concerned and therefore suspends the right of the established authorities to seek foreign help in order to maintain their control over that territory.

war broke out in a state and the insurgents did not receive outside help or support, it was unlawful for a foreign state to intervene, even on the invitation of the régime in power, to assist in maintaining law and order' (*British Practice in International Law*, 1963, p. 87).

Collective self-defence against subversion

The United Kingdom's statement of support for the rule of non-intervention was made subject to a condition – 'if . . . the insurgents did not receive outside help or support'. Virtually every state considers itself entitled to defend an ally against foreign subversion (subversion may consist of helping to start a revolt, or of helping a revolt which has *already* started).

The USA argued that its participation in the fighting in Vietnam between 1965 and 1973 was justified on the grounds that it was defending South Vietnam against subversion from North Vietnam. North Vietnam had in fact been sending men and weapons to help the insurgents in South Vietnam for several years before United States troops entered the war in 1965; but, long before North Vietnam started helping the insurgents, the USA had been providing the established authorities in South Vietnam with money, weapons and military instructors from 1954 onwards. (The USA claimed that the revolt was organised by North Vietnam from the beginning, but most of the evidence suggests that the insurgents received no help from North Vietnam during the first year or so of the revolt in the late 1950s.) Consequently it could be argued that the North Vietnamese help for the insurgents was justified by the prior American help for the established authorities.[1]

Help against subversion can probably be regarded as a form of collective self-defence under Article 51 of the United Nations Charter. Article 51 applies only if there has been an armed attack (or, more doubtfully, if there is an imminent threat of an armed attack). It has sometimes been doubted whether subversion constitutes an armed attack; for instance, the Organisation of American States has in practice dealt with subversion under Article 6 of the Rio de Janeiro Treaty 1947, which speaks of 'aggression which is not an armed attack', rather than under Article 3, which speaks of armed attacks. But a state which carries out subversion against another state does commit an armed attack

[1] See above, p. 242, on counter-intervention. Even so, it could be argued that counter-intervention must be proportionate to the original intervention (cf. below, p. 245), and that the North Vietnamese supply of troops was a disproportionate reaction to the United States supply of money, weapons and military instructors during the 1950s.

On the Vietnam War generally, including the question whether South Vietnam and North Vietnam were separate states or merely temporarily divided zones of a single state, see R. A. Falk (ed.), *The Vietnam War and International Law*, 4 vols., 1968-76.

indirectly, through the insurgents whom it helps in their armed rebellion.

It is true that there are certain dangers in permitting a right of collective self-defence against subversion. The right can easily be abused, because it is easier to make allegations of subversion than it is to verify them; in this respect subversion differs from the more orthodox type of armed invasion, which can usually be verified without too much difficulty. As controversy over Vietnam shows, it is often difficult for commentators to agree whether a particular movement is composed of genuine insurgents or whether it is the product of foreign subversion; and there is a danger that states will try to legitimise help for friendly governments by pinning the label of foreign subversion on all sorts of genuine insurgent movements. On the other hand, the possibility that collective self-defence against subversion may be abused should not disguise the fact that it meets a real need when it is properly used. If there were no collective self-defence against subversion, states would not be deterred from subverting their neighbours. There are sound policy reasons for interpreting Article 51 of the United Nations Charter restrictively, but restrictive interpretation should not be carried to the point of facilitating evasion of the rule against aggression – for that, after all, is what subversion is (see Article 3(g) of the definition of aggression adopted by the General Assembly in 1974 (text in *American Journal of International Law*, 1975, p. 480)). There would have been little point in prohibiting direct attacks by one state against another, or in providing for collective self-defence against direct attacks, if indirect attacks (that is, subversion) remained lawful or if international law prohibited a state to defend its allies against indirect attacks.

Very often an insurgent movement depends partly on internal support and partly on foreign help. Can the right of collective self-defence be exercised against such a movement? In theory the answer would appear to be yes, provided that the foreign help given to the established authorities is proportionate to the foreign help given to the insurgents; force used in individual or collective self-defence must be proportionate to the force used by the other side (see above, p. 224). Moreover, disproportionately large foreign help for the established authorities might be inexpedient in such circumstances, because it would probably provoke a massive increase in help for the insurgents from the other foreign state, and thus add to the dangers of the civil war escalating into an all-out international war. However, it must be confessed that there is something artificial in talking about proportionality in such circumstances, because it will probably be impossible to calculate the exact quantum of foreign help received by the insurgents.

Conclusion
It seems to be generally agreed that a state may help the established authorities of another state against foreign subversion; as regards similar help to the established authorities against genuine insurgents, state practice is inconsistent. It is not that some states follow one practice and other states follow another practice; rather, each state follows one practice one year and another practice another year. However, since 1945 there has been a tendency for states to try to justify their participation in foreign civil wars by saying that they are defending the established authorities against external subversion. This is certainly true of the United States interventions in the Lebanon (1958), the Dominican Republic (1965) and Vietnam (1965–73), and of Cuba's intervention in the Ogaden (1977–8); even the Soviet Union made a half-hearted attempt to justify its invasions of Hungary (1956), Czechoslovakia (1968) and Afghanistan (1979) by arguing that it was defending those countries against Western subversion. The fact that such 'justifications' are often contrary to the facts is beside the point; the significant thing is the frequency with which such 'justifications' are used (or abused) – it is almost as if states were implying that intervention in other circumstances would be illegal.

It is true that British and Soviet arms supplies to the Nigerian government during the Nigerian civil war in the late 1960s indicate that foreign states are sometimes prepared to help the established authorities against genuine insurgents, as well as against external subversion; but the arms supplies to Nigeria differed from the interventions listed in the previous paragraph in one crucial respect – they did not involve the use of the *troops* of one state in the territory of another. It may be, therefore, that we are witnessing the emergence of a new rule of customary law, which will permit states to supply the established authorities with money and arms during every type of civil war, but which will forbid states to send troops to help the established authorities except when foreign subversion is occurring.

Rules Governing the Conduct of Civil Wars

Under customary international law, it was uncertain whether the laws of war protecting civilians, the sick and wounded, prisoners of war, and so on, applied to civil wars. The appalling brutality of the Spanish civil war showed how unsatisfactory this position was, and Article 3 of each of the four Geneva Conventions of 1949 tried to remedy the situation by extending some of the more basic laws of war to civil wars (text in H. W. Briggs, *The Law of Nations*, 2nd ed., 1952, p. 1009). The Second Protocol to the 1949 Conventions, signed in 1977, goes further than Article 3 of the 1949 Conventions, by extending more (but not all) of the laws of war to civil wars. Article 1(4) of the First Protocol to the 1949 Conventions, also signed in 1977, goes further still by classifying 'armed conflicts in which peoples are fighting against colonial domination and alien occupation and against racist régimes in the exercise of their right of self-determination' as *international* wars for the purposes of applying the rules contained in the First Protocol (and also perhaps, by implication, for the purposes of applying the laws of war in general; on this latter point, see also *Yearbook of the United Nations*, 1973, pp. 549–50, 552–3). At present 154 states are parties to the 1949 Conventions, but only 33 and 27 states (mostly from the 'Third World') are parties to the First and Second Protocols respectively (texts in *International Legal Materials*, 1977, pp. 1391 and 1442).

Article 3 has not worked well in practice, and it remains to be seen whether the 1977 Protocols will enjoy more success. In a civil war each side tends to regard the other side as traitors, which does not create a favourable climate for the application of the laws of war. Moreover, civil wars are often fought by guerrillas or other irregular forces, which makes it difficult to distinguish between combatants and civilians. Even when a civil war is 'internationalised' by the participation of foreign troops, experience in Vietnam between 1965 and 1973 indicates that the likelihood of compliance with the laws of war is not noticeably increased. However, fear of reprisals and fear of war crimes trials have sometimes secured a certain amount of compliance with Article 3. Desire to make a favourable impression on foreign public opinion has also often acted as a restraining influence (for examples, see above, pp. 235 and 237).

Suggestions for Further Reading

R. A. Falk (ed.), *The International Law of Civil War*, 1971.
D. E. T. Luard (ed.), *The International Regulation of Civil War*, 1972.
T. J. Farer, 'The regulation of foreign intervention in civil armed conflict', *Recueil des cours de l'Académie de droit international de La Haye*, vol. 142, 1974, p. 291.
J. N. Moore (ed.), *Law and Civil War in the Modern World*, 1974.
D. P. Forsythe, 'Legal management of internal war: the 1977 Protocol on Non-International Armed Conflict', *American Journal of International Law*, vol. 72, 1978, p. 272.
D. Schindler, 'The different types of armed conflicts according to the Geneva Conventions and Protocols', *Recueil des cours de l'Académie de droit international de La Haye*, vol. 163, 1979, p. 125.

Chapter 17

Self-Determination

The right of self-determination is the right of a people living in a territory to determine the political and legal status of that territory, for example, by setting up a state of their own or by choosing to become part of another state. Before 1945 this right was conferred by a few treaties on the inhabitants of a few territories (for instance, the Treaty of Versailles 1919 provided for a plebiscite in Upper Silesia, to determine whether it should form part of Germany or of Poland); but there was probably no legal right of self-determination in the absence of such treaty provisions. Since 1945 resolutions passed by the United Nations General Assembly have attributed a wider scope to the right of self-determination, and have brought about major changes in international law.

Mandated Territories, Trust Territories and Non-Self-Governing Territories

Mandated territories
After the First World War, some of the Allies wanted to annex Germany's colonies and certain Arabic-speaking areas of the Turkish Empire; but their plans were opposed by President Wilson, who wished to secure recognition for the ideal of self-determination. Eventually a compromise was reached; each of the territories in question was to be administered by one of the Allies, under the supervision of the League of Nations. This was known as the mandate system. Article 22 of the League of Nations Covenant implied that the peoples inhabiting the mandated territories would be allowed to exercise a right of self-determination at some time in the future, but it did not fix a date for the exercise of that right (*Namibia* case, *ICJ Reports*, 1971, pp. 16, 28–32).

Trust territories
The United Nations Charter provides for a trusteeship system, modelled on the League's mandate system (Articles 75–91). In 1955 there were eleven trust territories, administered by seven different

states. Now only one remains – a group of islands in the Pacific, originally held by Japan under a League of Nations mandate and now administered by the USA. The others have become independent or have chosen to merge with other states.

South West Africa

Of the territories administered under the League of Nations mandate system, all but one became independent before or shortly after the dissolution of the League in 1946, or were placed under the United Nations trusteeship system. The exception was South West Africa, a former German colony administered by South Africa. The status of South West Africa has given rise to a prolonged dispute between South Africa and the United Nations, and to four advisory opinions and two judgments from the International Court of Justice.

In its first advisory opinion, the Court said that South Africa was not obliged to place South West Africa under the trusteeship system. However, unless she did so, South Africa remained bound by the obligations contained in the mandate, and the General Assembly succeeded to the supervisory powers which the League had exercised under the mandate (*ICJ Reports*, 1950, p. 128). In two further advisory opinions the Court dealt with the procedure to be followed by the General Assembly when exercising its supervisory powers (ibid., 1955, p. 67, and 1956, p. 23).

These expressions of judicial opinion, being advisory opinions, were not binding, and South Africa refused to act in accordance with them, arguing that international supervision of her administration of South West Africa had lapsed when the League was dissolved in 1946. In 1960 Liberia and Ethiopia, two former members of the League, instituted contentious proceedings against South Africa before the International Court of Justice; they asked the Court to declare that South Africa had violated the mandate by introducing apartheid into South West Africa. If the Court had decided for Liberia and Ethiopia, its judgment, unlike the earlier advisory opinions, would have been binding upon South Africa – that is the big difference between advisory and contentious proceedings.

However, in 1966 the Court decided that South Africa's obligations under the mandate, in so far as they related to the treatment of the inhabitants of South West Africa, had been owed to the League, and not to individual members of the League; the Court therefore dismissed the cases brought by Ethiopia and Liberia, holding that Ethiopia and Liberia were not entitled to enforce rights which did not belong to them (*ICJ Reports*, 1966, p. 6).

The Court's judgment was severely criticised, particularly by

Afro-Asian states, because the ground on which the Court decided the case was very similar to an argument which the Court had rejected in 1962, when it had handed down a preliminary judgment rejecting various pleas by South Africa that it had no jurisdiction to try the case (*ICJ Reports*, 1962, p. 319). As a result of changes in the composition of the Court, the judges who had been in a minority in 1962 found themselves in a majority in 1966, and proceeded to reverse the effect of the Court's earlier judgment.

Later in 1966 the General Assembly passed a resolution declaring 'that South Africa has failed to fulfil its obligations in respect of the administration of the mandated territory . . . and has, in fact, disavowed the mandate', and deciding 'that the mandate . . . is therefore terminated, that South Africa has no . . . right to administer the territory and that henceforth South West Africa comes under the direct responsibility of the United Nations' (*Yearbook of the United Nations*, 1966, p. 606).

The International Court handed down a further advisory opinion in 1971 (*Namibia* case, *ICJ Reports*, 1971, p. 16), in which it said that the General Assembly had succeeded to the League's supervisory powers (pp. 27–45) and had acted lawfully when terminating the mandate (pp. 45–50); the Court also advised that South Africa was under a duty to withdraw from South West Africa (or Namibia, as it had been renamed by the General Assembly), and that other states were obliged, by a binding resolution passed by the Security Council, to refrain from any dealings with South Africa which were inconsistent with the termination of the mandate (pp. 51–8).

In 1978 South Africa announced that it was willing in principle to allow elections to be held in Namibia under United Nations supervision, which would lead to independence for Namibia. However, South Africa has not yet reached agreement with the United Nations and with the guerilla movement in Namibia about safeguards to ensure that there will be no intimidation during the proposed elections, and in the meantime South Africa continues to administer Namibia in defiance of the United Nations. See Michael Spicer, 'Namibia – elusive independence', *The World Today*, October 1980, p. 406.

Non-self-governing territories

Article 73 of the United Nations Charter provides:

> Members of the United Nations which have . . . responsibilities for the administration of territories whose peoples have not yet attained a full measure of self-government recognize the principle that the interests of the inhabitants of these territories are paramount, and accept as a

sacred trust the obligation to promote to the utmost . . . the well-being of the inhabitants of these territories, and, to this end:

(a) to ensure, with due respect for the culture of the peoples concerned, their political, economic, social, and educational advancement, their just treatment and their protection against abuses;

(b) to develop self-government, to take due account of the political aspirations of the peoples, and to assist them in the progressive development of their free political institutions, according to the particular circumstances of each territory and its peoples and their varying stages of advancement;

(c) to further international peace and security;

(d) to promote constructive measures of development . . .;

(e) to transmit regularly to the Secretary-General for information purposes, subject to such limitation as security and constitutional considerations may require . . . information . . . relating to economic, social, and educational conditions in the territories for which they are respectively responsible . . .

Article 73 applies to colonies and to territories which resemble colonies. According to resolution 1541 (XV) of the General Assembly, there is a presumption that Article 73 applies to every territory 'which is geographically separate and is distinct ethnically and/or culturally from the country administering it'; this presumption is strengthened if the territory is in a position of 'subordination' to the administering power (*Yearbook of the United Nations*, 1960, p. 509). Thus the General Assembly considered that Article 73 applied to Portugal's territories in Africa, even though Portugal claimed that these territories were not colonies but overseas provinces of Portugal. On the other hand, the General Assembly has never regarded Northern Ireland as a non-self-governing territory; Northern Ireland is geographically close to the rest of the United Kingdom, there is little cultural or ethnic difference between the population of Northern Ireland and the population of the rest of the United Kingdom, and Northern Ireland is not in a position of subordination to the United Kingdom, since it is represented in the United Kingdom Parliament.

Article 73 imposes fewer obligations than the provisions dealing with the trusteeship system; in particular, it does not provide for supervision by the United Nations. But in practice, and despite opposition from the colonial powers, the General Assembly has asserted considerable powers of supervision, by placing an extensive interpretation on the administering powers' duty to submit reports under Article 73(e). Anticolonialist feeling has increased in the General Assembly as more and more newly independent states have joined the United Nations.

An important landmark in the anticolonialist trend is resolution 1514 (XV), passed by the General Assembly on 14 December 1960, by 89 votes to nil, with 9 abstentions (*Yearbook of the United Nations*, 1960, p. 49). This resolution declares:

1. The subjection of peoples to alien subjugation and exploitation constitutes a denial of fundamental human rights, is contrary to the Charter of the United Nations and is an impediment to . . . world peace and co-operation.
2. All peoples have the right to self-determination; by virtue of that right they freely determine their political status and freely pursue their economic, social and cultural development.
3. Inadequacy of political, economic, social or educational preparedness should never serve as a pretext for delaying independence.
4. All armed action or repressive measures of all kinds directed against dependent peoples shall cease in order to enable them to exercise peacefully and freely their right to complete independence, and the integrity of their national territory shall be respected.
5. Immediate steps shall be taken, in the trust and non-self-governing territories or all other territories which have not yet attained independence, to transfer all power to the peoples of those territories . . . in accordance with their freely expressed will . . . in order to enable them to enjoy complete independence and freedom.
6. Any attempt aimed at the partial or total disruption of the national unity and the territorial integrity of a country is incompatible with the purposes and principles of the Charter of the United Nations.

To put it mildly, the resolution is a bold interpretation of Article 73 of the Charter. However, even the (mainly Western) states which had abstained when the resolution was adopted in 1960, had by 1970 come to accept it as an accurate statement of modern international law, a view which was echoed by the International Court of Justice in the *Namibia* and *Western Sahara* cases (*ICJ Reports*, 1971, pp. 16, 31; ibid., 1975, pp. 12, 31–3, 121).

Self-determination normally leads to independence, but resolution 1541 (XV) recognises that the people of a non-self-governing territory may choose integration with an independent state, or free association with an independent state, as an alternative to independence (*Yearbook of the United Nations*, 1960, p. 509). 'Integration' means that the territory becomes part of an independent state, as Alaska and Hawaii did when they became part of the USA. 'Association' means that the associated state has internal self-government, while the independent state with which it is associated is responsible for foreign affairs and defence. Resolution 1541 (XV) says that the people of each non-self-governing territory should be allowed to choose freely between independence, integration and association, but in practice the General

Assembly has shown a bias in favour of independence as opposed to other forms of self-determination. (See James Crawford, *The Creation of States in International Law*, 1979, pp. 367–77.)

In the case of very small territories (colonial enclaves) adjoining another state, most members of the United Nations regard union with the adjoining state as the appropriate method of decolonisation, regardless of the wishes of the inhabitants, who are regarded as too few to constitute a separate people. This approach is applied only to very small territories. The General Assembly regarded Western Sahara and East Timor as too large to be treated as colonial enclaves. It is true that Morocco and Mauritania annexed Western Sahara (a former Spanish colony) without the consent of the inhabitants, and that Indonesia annexed East Timor (a former Portuguese colony) without the consent of the inhabitants, but Morocco, Mauritania and Indonesia sought to justify their actions by pretending that the inhabitants had consented; Morocco, Mauritania and Indonesia admitted that the inhabitants of Western Sahara and East Timor had a legal right to self-determination, and the dispute between them and their many critics at the United Nations was limited to the question of fact whether that right had been respected or violated. (See, generally, James Crawford, *The Creation of States in International Law*, 1979, pp. 377–84; and see the *Yearbook of the United Nations*, 1975 onwards, and *UN Chronicle*, January 1981, pp. 18–20, for discussions of Western Sahara and East Timor at the United Nations.)

Double Standards?

The legal right of self-determination clearly applies to non-self-governing territories, trust territories and mandated territories (see paragraph 5 of resolution 1514 (XV), and the *Namibia* case, *ICJ Reports*, 1971, pp. 16, 31). Whether it also applies to other territories is uncertain. On the one hand, paragraph 2 of resolution 1514 (XV) says that *all* peoples have the right to self-determination; on the other hand, paragraph 6 of resolution 1514 (XV) forbids secession (or maybe only foreign assistance to secessionary movements). In 1970 the General Assembly declared that the principle of self-determination did not authorise 'any action which would dismember . . . independent states conducting themselves in compliance with the principle of . . . self-determination of peoples . . . and thus possessed of a government representing the whole people . . . without distinction as to race, creed or colour' (text in Ian Brownlie, *Basic Documents in International Law*, 3rd ed.,

1983, p. 43); this implies that action to dismember an independent state *is* permitted if the government does *not* represent the whole people.

In practice, however, organs of the United Nations have shown little concern for self-determination in territories other than non-self-governing territories, trust territories and mandated territories. Many people in the West have accused the United Nations of applying double standards, but these double standards are inherent in the Charter; Article 73, dealing with non-self-governing territories, is far more specific than the vague general references to self-determination in Articles 1(2) and 55, which are so vague that it is doubtful whether they create any legal obligation at all (for the text of Articles 1(2) and 55, see above, pp. 168 and 195).

Many General Assembly resolutions say that the inhabitants of South Africa are entitled to self-determination (see, for instance, *UN Monthly Chronicle*, January 1969, p. 94; ibid., December 1976, pp. 38–45 and 79). Since 1970 the General Assembly has frequently declared that the Palestinians are also entitled to self-determination (see, for instance, ibid., January 1971, pp. 47–8; ibid., December 1974, pp. 36–44; ibid., December 1978, pp. 52–3, 81–2); none of these resolutions specifies the territories whose status is affected by self-determination for the Palestinians – self-determination for the Palestinians could be interpreted as limited to the West Bank and Gaza, which have been under Israeli military occupation since 1967 but are not legally part of Israel (see above, p. 147), or it could be interpreted as implying the total replacement of Israel by a Palestinian state.

The Palestinians and the inhabitants of South Africa are the only 'non-colonial' peoples whose right to self-determination has been expressly recognised by the General Assembly. Several states opposed the resolutions dealing with the Palestinians and the inhabitants of South Africa, and some Western states explained their opposition by arguing that the right of self-determination did not apply outside the 'colonial' context.[1] Some Afro-Asian states try to meet this point by arguing that South Africa and Israel are 'neo-colonialist'; most of the whites living in South Africa are the descendants of colonial settlers, and most of the Jews living in Israel when Israel became independent in 1948 had entered Palestine as immigrants while it was being administered by the United Kingdom under a League of Nations mandate. But, whatever the previous status of South Africa and Palestine may have been, South Africa and Israel are now independent states, and it is

---

[1] But in 1980 the member-states of the EEC recognised that the Palestinians were entitled to self-determination; see *Keesing's Contemporary Archives*, 1980, p. 30635.

illogical to treat them differently from other independent states. The General Assembly's extension of the right of self-determination to the Palestinians and the inhabitants of South Africa, coupled with its failure to extend that right to other 'non-colonial' peoples, has increased rather than reduced the problem of double standards.

Consequences of Violations of the Right of Self-Determination

Violation of the right of self-determination creates a situation which has repercussions on many areas of international law. The effects of the interaction between the new rule of self-determination and various older rules of international law are often unclear, and the conclusions suggested below must be treated as tentative.

Creation of new states
Traditionally, secession was not regarded as creating a new state until the secessionary movement had established permanent control over the territory in question (see above, pp. 53-4). Has this rule been altered by the right of self-determination? Can a national liberation movement claim to be the government of a new state before it has established permanent control over the territory in question? The answer is probably no. It is true that the General Assembly passed a resolution recognising Guinea-Bissau as an independent state in 1973, while it was still struggling for independence against Portugal, but many of the states which voted for this resolution argued that the national liberation movement controlled most of the territory of Guinea-Bissau (*Yearbook of the United Nations*, 1973, pp. 143-7); the resolution on Guinea-Bissau thus represents an application of the traditional test of control (even though the test was probably not applied as stringently as it usually is), and not the abandonment of the test of control in favour of some other criterion. In any case, the resolution on Guinea-Bissau is unique; no other national liberation movement has ever been recognised by the United Nations as the government of an independent state while it was still struggling for independence.

On the other hand, a state established in violation of the right of self-determination is probably a nullity in the eyes of international law. Since 1976 South Africa has purported to confer independence on a number of black states ('Bantustans') established on South African territory in pursuance of the South African policy of apartheid. The General Assembly regards apartheid as a violation of the right of self-determination (see above, p. 254); the creation of 'Bantustans' is equally illegal and invalid, according to the General Assembly, because it represents the implementation of apartheid. The General Assembly urged states not to recognise the Bantustans, and no state (except South Africa) has so far recognised any of them. (See James Crawford, *The Creation of States in International Law*, 1979, pp. 103–6 and 219–27; *UN Chronicle*, January 1980, p. 26).

Title to territory

A state administering a colony is under a legal duty to allow the inhabitants of that colony to exercise their right of self-determination. Does the state automatically lose sovereignty over the colony if it fails to carry out that duty? Opinions differ (James Crawford, *The Creation of States in International Law*, 1979, pp. 363–4), but in 1960 the International Court of Justice decided the *Right of Passage* case on the tacit assumption that this question should be answered in the negative (*ICJ Reports*, 1960, pp. 6, 39). It is submitted that that assumption is correct. Self-determination usually leads to independence, but, as we have just seen, peoples under colonial rule are not usually regarded as forming a new state until their struggle for independence has been successfully completed. The view that the colonial power no longer has sovereignty over its colony would mean that *no* state would have sovereignty over the territory in question while the inhabitants were still struggling for independence – a conclusion which raises all kinds of practical and theoretical difficulties. These difficulties can be avoided if we accept that the colonial power retains sovereignty until it has allowed the people to exercise their right of self-determination.

Wars of national liberation

If the inhabitants of a particular territory are regarded by international law as possessing a legal right of self-determination but the state administering that territory refuses to let them exercise their right of self-determination, they may need to fight a war of national liberation in order to achieve self-determination in practice.

Western states regard wars of national liberation as civil wars, but communist states and Afro-Asian states regard them as international wars; this difference of classification affects the application of the laws of war (see above, p. 247), but for other purposes it has little practical importance.

There is general agreement that peoples who have a legal right to self-determination are entitled to fight a war of national liberation. Even Western states do not dissent from this view, if only because there is no rule in international law against rebellion (see above, pp. 53, 60 and 240–1), although they consider that General

Assembly resolutions *encouraging* wars of national liberation are *politically* undesirable.

The use of force to *prevent* the exercise of self-determination is probably unlawful. Paragraph 4 of General Assembly resolution 1514 (XV) states that 'all armed action or repressive measures of all kinds directed against dependent peoples shall cease in order to enable them to exercise . . . their right to complete independence' (*Yearbook of the United Nations*, 1960, p. 49). Even the Western states, after initial opposition in the early 1960s, have now accepted that there is a legal duty not to use force to frustrate the exercise of a legal right to self-determination. However, there is still disagreement between Western states and other states about the basis of this rule. Western states regard it as derived solely from the right of self-determination, and not from Article 2(4) of the United Nations Charter, because Article 2(4) prohibits the use of force in international relations only and Western states do not regard the use of force by a state against its own nationals (including its colonial subjects) as a use of force in international relations; most Afro-Asian states regard the rule as derived from Article 2(4) as well as from the right of self-determination. See the chapter by Ronzitti in *Current Problems of International Law* (edited by A. Cassese), 1975, pp. 319–53.

If a state is acting unlawfully when it uses force to prevent the exercise of a legal right of self-determination, it would seem to follow, as a matter of logic, that other states are acting equally unlawfully if they help that state in its struggle to frustrate self-determination.

There is still disagreement between Western states and other states as regards the legality or illegality of help given by foreign states to national liberation movements. Paragraph 10 of General Assembly resolution 2105 (XX), passed on 20 December 1965 by 74 votes to 6 with 27 abstentions, 'recognises the legitimacy of the struggle by peoples under colonial rule to exercise their right to self-determination and independence and invites all states to provide material and moral assistance to the national liberation movements in colonial territories' (*Yearbook of the United Nations*, 1965, pp. 554–5). But this view is not accepted by Western states, which abstained or voted against the resolution. Later resolutions (for example, Article 7 of the General Assembly's definition of aggression – text in *American Journal of International Law*, 1975, p. 480) speak of the right of peoples struggling against colonial rule to receive 'support' from other states; but this formula is simply an attempt to paper over the disagreement between the communist and Afro-Asian states, which interpret 'support' to include material support (for example, weapons), and the Western states, which think that support must be limited to moral and diplomatic support (*American Journal of International Law*, 1971, pp. 730–3, and 1977, pp. 233–7).

The General Assembly considers that the right of self-determination applies not only to peoples under colonial rule, but also to the Palestinians and the inhabitants of South Africa (see above, p. 254). Despite Western opposition, the General Assembly has passed resolutions urging states to provide material assistance to the Palestinians and the inhabitants of South Africa in their armed struggle for self-determination (see, for instance, *UN Monthly Chronicle*, December 1974, pp. 36–44; ibid., December 1976, pp. 38–45 and 79; ibid., December 1978, pp. 52–3 and 81–2; *UN Chronicle*, January 1980, pp. 24 and 79).

It is difficult to reconcile these resolutions with the general rule against giving help to insurgents in civil wars (see above, p. 242). It is true that violation of the right of self-determination is a violation of international law. But breaches by a state of other rules of international law (for example, the rules protecting human rights) are not treated as justifying help given to insurgents against that state, and there is no logical reason for treating violations of the right of self-determination differently from other breaches of international law.

Alternatively, if wars of national liberation are classified as international wars and not as civil wars, the General Assembly resolutions urging states to help national liberation movements in colonial territories, Palestine and South Africa are hard to reconcile with the rules of international law concerning international wars. The use of force in international relations is normally prohibited by international law; there are some exceptions to this rule, but the only one which has any possible relevance to wars of national liberation is collective self-defence against armed attack.[1] Accordingly, intervention by foreign states in wars of national liberation would be lawful only if it could be shown that the national liberation movement (or the people whom it

[1] See above, pp. 219–27, especially pp. 221–5. This assumes that the rules of self-defence, which apply in the event of an armed attack against a *state*, can be extended by analogy to an armed attack against a people who are not yet a state – an assumption which many lawyers in the West are unwilling to make.

Foreign states seldom send their armed forces to help national liberation movements; instead, they usually confine themselves to providing weapons, bases, military training, and so on. But that makes no difference to the legal position. In an international war, a state which is not at war is bound by the rules of neutrality, which prohibit the supply of weapons, bases, or military training to either side (see above, p. 241). The only exception to the rules of neutrality is that it is probably lawful to give help to the victims of aggression (see above, p. 236), but, for reasons which are explained in the main text above this footnote, it is submitted that national liberation movements cannot be regarded as the victims of aggression.

claims to represent) was the victim of an armed attack. But wars of national liberation usually start with an armed attack *by* (not *against*) the national liberation movement, in order to overthrow the rule of the government which had previously been administering the territory peacefully. Some Afro-Asian writers and diplomats try to get round this objection by looking at the issue in a longer historical perspective and by arguing that the original acquisition of colonies by European states involved the use of force and that colonialism therefore constitutes a form of permanent or continuing aggression. But not all colonies were acquired by conquest; some were acquired by cession from native rulers, or by other peaceful means. Even when colonies were acquired by conquest, the conquest was lawful under the rules of international law which existed at the time (see above, pp. 146 and 150–2) and was completed a long time ago. It is absurd to suggest that a right of collective self-defence can be exercised today against an attack which was successfully and lawfully completed centuries ago; one might as well argue that the United Kingdom can now reopen the hostilities with France which began with the Norman Conquest in 1066. See the article by Dugard in the *International and Comparative Law Quarterly*, 1967, p. 157.

Suggestions for Further Reading

A. Rigo Sureda, *The Evolution of the Right of Self-Determination*, 1973, especially chs 2–5.

James Crawford, *The Creation of States in International Law*, 1979, pp. 84–118, 219–27, 257–68, 335–84.

See also the appendix on the Falkland Islands dispute, pp. 296–7, below.

Chapter 18

The Law of the Sea

For legal purposes the sea is divided into three different zones, each of which is subject to different rules. Moving outwards from land, these zones are (*a*) internal waters, (*b*) territorial sea and (*c*) high seas. In recent years the position has been complicated by the tendency of coastal states to claim limited rights over areas of the high seas adjacent to their territorial sea (contiguous zones, exclusive fishery zones, exclusive economic zones and the continental shelf).

The law of the sea was to a large extent codified by the United Nations conference at Geneva in 1958, which drew up four conventions: the Convention on the Territorial Sea and the Contiguous Zone, the Convention on the High Seas, the Convention on Fishing and Conservation of the Living Resources of the High Seas, and the Convention on the Continental Shelf (texts in Ian Brownlie, *Basic Documents in International Law*, 3rd ed., 1983, pp. 85–121). By 1981 these conventions had been ratified or acceded to by forty-five, fifty-six, thirty-five and fifty-three states respectively; the United Kingdom and the USA are parties to all four conventions, and the USSR is a party to all of them except the Convention on Fishing and Conservation. Most of the provisions of the first two conventions, and some of the provisions of the Convention on the Continental Shelf, codify customary law. Consequently, although the conventions as such are binding only on states which are parties to them, many of their provisions can be used as evidence of customary law even against states which are not parties to them.

The 1958 conference failed to reach agreement on a number of questions (especially the question of the width of the territorial sea; a second conference in 1960 also failed to reach agreement on this question). Moreover, some states became dissatisfied with various rules which were laid down in the 1958 Conventions; and technological advances created a need for new rules. Consequently a *third* United Nations Conference on the Law of the Sea (UNCLOS III) was convened in 1973, to draw up a new comprehensive convention on the law of the sea. After meeting intermittently for nine years, the Conference finally adopted the text of the United Nations Convention on the Law of the Sea in 1982 (text in *International Legal Materials*, 1982, p. 1261). One reason for the slow progress made at the Conference was that so many of the issues were inter-related; states were often willing to support a proposal on one issue only if other states were willing to support another proposal on another issue, and the result was that deadlock on one issue tended to produce deadlock on many other issues. Moreover, whenever possible, the third United Nations Conference on the Law of the Sea (unlike the two previous conferences) tried to take decisions by consensus, and not by majority vote; and this caused further delays.

The 1982 Convention will, according to its Article 308 (1), 'enter into force twelve months after the date of deposit of the sixtieth instrument of ratification or accession', and this is not likely to occur for several years, especially since many Western states refuse to sign or ratify the Convention because they are dissatisfied with some of its provisions about exploitation of the deep seabed (see below, p. 282). Much of the uncertainty which surrounded many parts of the law of the sea before 1982 is likely to continue until the 1982 Convention comes into force.

Some of the provisions of the 1982 Convention codify the customary international law of the sea; this is particularly true of those provisions of the 1982 Convention which are identical to those provisions of the 1958 Conventions which codified customary law. But most of the provisions of the 1982 Convention represent a departure from the pre-existing customary law. It is possible that future state practice, even by states which are not parties to the 1982 Convention, will imitate provisions of the 1982 Convention, thus creating new rules of customary law (for an example of a case where this has happened already, see below, pp. 270–2), but there is no certainty that all of the provisions of the 1982 Convention will pass into customary law in this way. At the moment, most of the provisions of the 1982 Convention probably do not represent existing law; rather, they indicate the directions in which the law may evolve in the future.

Internal Waters

Internal waters consist of ports, harbours, rivers, lakes and canals (and also water on the landward side of the baselines used for measuring the width of the territorial sea; see below, p. 269). Internal waters are scarcely mentioned in the 1958 or 1982 Conventions on the law of the sea; the relevant rules are to be found mainly in customary international law.

A MODERN INTRODUCTION TO INTERNATIONAL LAW

A coastal state is entitled to prohibit entry into its ports by foreign warships. It is uncertain whether a coastal state has a similar right to forbid foreign merchant ships to enter its ports; but most states are keen to build up a flourishing trade, and therefore welcome foreign ships to their ports. The important question is not whether a ship has a right of entry to a port, but its legal status once it has got there. Here, as in virtually every branch of the law of the sea, a distinction must be made between merchant ships and warships.

Broadly speaking, the coastal state may apply and enforce its laws in full against foreign merchant ships in its internal waters. This principle is subject to a number of exceptions, most of which are more apparent than real:

(1) The jurisdiction of the coastal state's courts is not exclusive. The courts of the flag-state may also try people for crimes committed on board the ship.

(2) The coastal state will not interfere with the exercise of disciplinary powers by the captain over his crew.

(3) If a crime committed by a member of the crew does not affect the good order of the coastal state or any of its inhabitants, the coastal state will usually allow the matter to be dealt with by the authorities of the flag-state, instead of trying the criminal in its own courts. This abstention from exercising jurisdiction is probably a matter of grace and convenience, rather than obligation.

(4) Ships in distress (for example, ships fleeing from a tempest, or ships which are severely damaged) possess some degree of immunity: for instance, the coastal state cannot profit from their distress by imposing harbour duties and similar taxes which exceed the cost of services rendered.

The powers of the coastal state over foreign warships are much less than its powers over foreign merchant ships. A foreign warship is expected to observe the coastal state's laws about navigation and health regulations, but the authorities of the coastal state cannot even set foot on the ship, or carry out any act on board, without the permission of the captain or of some other authority of the flag-state. Members of the crew are immune from prosecution by the coastal state for crimes committed on board the ship – and for crimes committed on shore, if they were in uniform and on official business at the time of the crime. However, the flag-state may waive their immunity.

Territorial Sea

The territorial sea (alias territorial waters, or the maritime belt) extends for an uncertain number of miles beyond internal waters. The width of the territorial sea is one of the most controversial questions in international law and, before studying it, it will be helpful to examine what rights the coastal state and other states have over the territorial sea. In this way it will be possible to understand the conflict of interests which has arisen between states concerning the width of the territorial sea; for it is this conflict of interests which is at the root of the legal controversies.

The right of innocent passage

Article 1 of the Geneva Convention on the Territorial Sea 1958 says that the coastal state exercises sovereignty over its territorial sea. But the coastal state's sovereignty is subject to a very important limitation – foreign ships have a right of innocent passage through the territorial sea.

Passage is innocent so long as it is not prejudicial to the peace, good order, or security of the coastal state; fishing vessels must comply with laws enacted by the coastal state to prevent them fishing, and submarines must navigate on the surface and show their flag (Article 14 of the Geneva Convention on the Territorial Sea 1958; see also R. R. Churchill and A. V. Lowe, *The Law of the Sea*, 1983, pp. 64–8, and Article 19 of the 1982 Convention). The coastal state must not hamper innocent passage, and must give warning of known dangers to navigation in the territorial sea (Article 15 of the Geneva Convention on the Territorial Sea 1958). It may prevent non-innocent passage; and it may also, for security reasons, temporarily suspend innocent passage in specified areas of its territorial sea, provided that the areas do not constitute 'straits which are used for international navigation between one part of the high seas and another part of the high seas or the territorial sea of a foreign state' (Article 16). No charges may be levied upon foreign ships except for specific services rendered (Article 18).

'Western' states maintain that the right of innocent passage extends to warships, but this is denied by communist countries and by some other countries. In the *Corfu Channel* case (*ICJ Reports*, 1949, pp. 4, 29–30) the International Court of Justice held that warships have a right of passage through international straits, but did not decide the wider question of the territorial sea in general. In the Geneva Convention, the rules mentioned in the previous paragraph (with the exception of the prohibition against levying charges) appear under the heading 'rules applicable to all ships', which includes warships by implication; but a number of states made reservations to the Convention, denying the right of innocent passage for warships.

Rights of the coastal state over the territorial sea

The coastal state's sovereignty over the territorial sea includes the following rights:

(1) An *exclusive* right to fish, and to exploit the resources of the seabed and subsoil of the territorial sea.

(2) Exclusive enjoyment of the air space above the territorial sea; unlike ships, foreign aircraft have no right of innocent passage.

(3) The coastal state's ships have the exclusive right to transport goods and passengers from one part of the coastal state to another (cabotage).

(4) If the coastal state is neutral in time of war, belligerent states may not fight, or capture merchant ships, in the coastal state's territorial sea.

(5) The coastal state may enact regulations concerning navigation, health, customs duties and immigration, which foreign ships must obey.

(6) The coastal state has certain powers of arrest over merchant ships exercising a right of innocent passage, and over persons on board such ships (Articles 19 and 20 of the Geneva Convention on the Territorial Sea 1958). No similar powers of arrest exist in relation to warships, which are regarded, for certain purposes, as if they were floating islands of the flag-state; but, according to Article 23 of the Geneva Convention, 'if any warship does not comply with the regulations of the coastal state concerning passage through the territorial sea and disregards any request for compliance which is made to it, the coastal state may require the warship to leave the territorial sea'. In other words, the floating island may be told to go and float somewhere else.

(7) In *R.* v. *Keyn* (1876), 2 Ex. D. 63, the English Court of Crown Cases Reserved held that English courts had no jurisdiction to try people for crimes committed on board foreign merchant ships in the English territorial sea; but this decision, which was based on a gap in English law rather than on any prohibition by international law, was reversed two years later by the Territorial Waters Jurisdiction Act 1878. Unless the Act is to be regarded as going beyond what is permitted by customary international law, it would seem that coastal states have a general power to try crimes committed on foreign merchant ships in the territorial sea. (The flag-state has a concurrent jurisdiction, however.)

Members of the crew of foreign warships may be tried by the

courts of the flag-state for crimes committed on the warship while it was in the territorial sea, but are immune from the jurisdiction of the coastal state's courts, unless the flag-state waives immunity (*Chung Chi Cheung* v. *R.*, [1939] A.C. 160).

The width of the territorial sea

In the sixteenth and seventeenth centuries, states made extravagant claims to large areas of the sea. But these claims were gradually discredited, and in the eighteenth century it came to be generally accepted that the width of the territorial sea should be the same as the range of a cannon (the cannon-shot rule). During the Napoleonic wars the practice grew up of regarding the territorial sea as being 3 miles wide. (The nautical mile is equivalent to 1,000 fathoms, 6,080 feet or 1,853 metres). The three-mile rule is popularly thought of as a rationalisation of the cannon-shot rule, but it was more probably a new rule substituted for the cannon-shot rule; the disagreement is academic, because no one has ever suggested that the three-mile rule should be automatically altered to keep pace with improvements in artillery.

In the nineteenth century the three-mile rule was accepted by most states, although the Scandinavian states claimed 4 miles of territorial sea and Spain and Portugal claimed 6. During the twentieth century there has been a progressive abandonment of the rule. The states supporting the rule were in the majority at the unsuccessful codification conference organised by the League of Nations in 1930, but the rule was accepted by only twenty-one of the eighty-six states attending the Geneva conference in 1958. At the end of 1983, twenty-three states (including the USA and the UK) claimed 3 miles, two states claimed 4 miles, four states claimed 6 miles, eighty-five states claimed 12 miles, eleven states (mostly in Africa) claimed between 15 and 150 miles, and fourteen states (all in Latin America and Africa) claimed 200 miles.

Why have so many states abandoned the three-mile rule? And why has agreement on a new rule been so hard to reach? The answer to both questions is that a wide territorial sea is in the interests of some states, but against the interests of other states.

The most obvious conflict of interests concerns fishing. Areas of the sea close to shore are particularly rich in fish, and modern improvements in trawling techniques, coupled with the development of refrigeration, have made it possible for fishing vessels from one state to catch huge quantities of fish near the coasts of distant countries. Nowadays states are entitled to claim exclusive fishery zones beyond their territorial seas (see below, pp. 270–2), but this rule is of recent origin; until about 1960, the only way in which a state could extend its exclusive fishing limits was by extending its territorial sea. Consequently, poor states which were dependent on *local* fisheries (because they could not afford the large trawlers and refrigerating equipment which are needed for fishing in *distant* waters) sought to extend their territorial seas in order to exclude foreign fishing vessels, particularly when there was a danger of over-exploitation by foreign fishing vessels causing exhaustion of local fishing stocks. On the other hand, rich states with large and technologically advanced fishing fleets, such as the UK, the USA and Japan, favoured a narrow territorial sea; the losses which they suffered by allowing other states to fish near their coasts were outweighed by the gains which they made by fishing off the coasts of other states.

The economic interests which affect the attitudes of states are not confined to fisheries; for instance, since aircraft have no right of innocent passage through the air space above the territorial sea, an extension of the territorial sea is opposed by some states on the grounds that it would force aircraft to make expensive detours.

But, apart from fishing, the main clash of interests relates to questions of security. Some Afro-Asian states want a wide territorial sea because they are afraid that the three-mile rule would enable a great power to exert psychological pressure at moments of crisis by an ostentatious display of naval force just beyond the three-mile limit. On the other hand, Western states, which are traditionally dependent on sea-power and on sea-borne trade, fear that an extension of the territorial sea, especially if coupled with a denial of innocent passage for warships, would restrict the freedom of movement of their fleets, and thus place them at a strategic disadvantage. They also fear that extensive neutral territorial seas could be used as a sanctuary by enemy (that is, Russian) submarines in wartime. (Such use would be illegal vis-à-vis the neutral state, but the neutral state might be too weak to stop it.)

Since 1945 very many new states have come into being; most of them are economically and militarily weak, and therefore favour an extension of their territorial seas.

At the Geneva Conference of 1958 the United Kingdom suggested, as a compromise, that the width of the territorial sea should be fixed at 6 miles. This suggestion was later withdrawn in favour of a United States proposal for a six-mile territorial sea, with a further six-mile zone in which the coastal state would have exclusive fishing rights, subject to the right of other states to fish in the outer zone without limit of time if they had fished there regularly during the previous five years. Other states suggested that the width of the territorial sea should be fixed at 12 miles. No agreement was reached; the United States proposal received more support than any other proposal (with 45 votes in favour, 33 against and 7 abstentions), but fell short of the two-thirds majority required by the rules of the conference. Another conference met at Geneva in 1960 to try to solve the deadlock, and the American proposal of 1958 was amended in the hope of obtaining more support; the 'traditional' fishing rights of other states in the outer six-mile zone were now not to last indefinitely, but only for ten years. The amended proposal received 54 votes in favour, with 28 against and 5 abstentions – narrowly missing the required two-thirds majority.

Given the diversity of state practice, and the failure of the conferences of 1958 and 1960 to reach agreement on this point, it is difficult to say what the customary law is concerning the width of the territorial sea. Almost all states agree that international law imposes a limit on the width of the territorial sea (a Peruvian proposal at the 1958 conference that each state should be allowed to claim whatever it considered reasonable (that is, in effect, to claim as much territorial sea as it liked) received so little support that it was never put to the vote); but states disagree as to what that limit is. The law is obviously in a state of flux, and it may be several years before a new consensus emerges. However, although the legality of claims in the 4 to 12 miles range is controversial, it is generally agreed that claims of more than 12 miles are invalid; at least, that is what the International Law Commission said when it was doing the preparatory research before the Geneva Conference of 1958. Moreover, Article 24 of the Geneva Convention on the Territorial Sea and Contiguous Zone 1958 says that the contiguous zone cannot extend more than 12 miles from the baselines from which the territorial sea is measured; since the contiguous zone is an area of the high seas stretching beyond the territorial sea, it follows *a fortiori* that the territorial sea itself cannot extend more than 12 miles. Even today, few states claim more than 12 miles (see above, p. 265); whenever such a claim is made, some other states protest that it is illegal (for the significance of such protests, see above, p. 29). Finally, Article 3 of the 1982 Convention says that 'every state has the right to establish the breadth of its territorial sea up to a limit not exceeding twelve nautical miles'.

However, major maritime powers such as the USA and the UK made it clear, at the third United Nations Conference on the Law of the Sea, that they would not accept Article 3 of the 1982 Convention unless a special régime was adopted for international straits. Extension of the territorial sea to 12 miles would mean that many international straits (for example, the Straits of Dover), which were previously high seas, would fall within the territorial seas of the coastal states. The normal rule is that foreign aircraft have no right to fly over the territorial sea, but the major maritime powers wanted an exception to this rule to be made in the case of international straits. They also wanted the rules governing passage of foreign ships through international straits to be more favourable to foreign ships than the normal rules concerning innocent passage through the territorial sea. For instance, they wanted submarines to be allowed to go through an international strait under water – something which is normally forbidden in the territorial sea. Articles 34–45 of the 1982 Convention go a long way towards meeting the wishes of the major maritime powers on these points, apart from an ambiguous silence on the question of submarines. See *American Journal of International Law*, 1980, pp. 48-121, and *International Relations*, May 1981, pp. 1047-9.

The line from which the territorial sea is measured
The normal baseline from which the width of the territorial sea is measured is the low-water line (that is, the line on the shore reached by the sea at low tide), and this rule is reaffirmed in Article 3 of the Geneva Convention on the Territorial Sea 1958.

But in certain geographical circumstances it is permissible to draw straight lines across the sea on a map, from headland to headland, or from island to island, and to measure the territorial sea from those straight lines. Article 4 of the Geneva Convention provides:

1. In localities where the coastline is deeply indented and cut into, or if there is a fringe of islands along the coast in its immediate vicinity, the method of straight baselines joining appropriate points may be employed in drawing the baseline from which the breadth of the territorial sea is measured.
2. The drawing of such baselines must not depart to any appreciable extent from the general direction of the coast . . .
3. . . . .
4. Where the method of straight baselines is applicable under the provisions of paragraph 1, account may be taken, in determining particular baselines, of economic interests peculiar to the region concerned, the reality and the importance of which are clearly evidenced by a long usage.

Article 4 restates the principle laid down by the International Court of Justice in the *Fisheries* case (*ICJ Reports*, 1951, p. 116), but attributes less importance than the Court did to the coastal region's economic interests. At the time, the Court's decision was regarded as an innovation, but the principle laid down in Article 4 has come to be generally accepted, and since 1964 the United

Kingdom (which was the losing party in the *Fisheries* case) has used straight baselines off the west coast of Scotland.

Article 5 of the Convention provides:

1. Waters on the landward side of the baseline . . . form part of the internal waters of the state.
2. Where the establishment of a straight baseline in accordance with Article 4 has the effect of enclosing as internal waters areas which previously had been considered as part of the territorial sea or of the high seas, a right of innocent passage . . . shall exist in those waters.

Bays are restrictively defined and regulated in great detail by Article 7 of the Convention. Long before the *Fisheries* case, it had been customary to draw straight baselines across the mouth of a bay and to measure the width of the territorial sea from such lines. But there was controversy about the maximum permissible length of such lines. After considerable argument, the Geneva Conference laid down 24 miles as the maximum length.

The provisions of Article 7 are stated not to apply to historic bays, that is, bays which the coastal state claims to be entitled to treat as internal waters, not by virtue of the general law, but by virtue of a special historic right. For instance, Canada claims historic rights over Hudson's Bay, which has an area of 580,000 square miles and is 50 miles wide at the entrance. The Geneva Conference did not deal with historic bays, which is not surprising; the trouble about historic bays is that everything tends to turn on the facts of specific cases, rather than on general principles.

Article 10(2) states that 'the territorial sea of an island is measured in accordance with the provisions of these articles'. The British government regards this as an implied condemnation of the practice (followed by the Philippines and Indonesia) of measuring the territorial sea from straight baselines drawn round the outer edge of an archipelago. In fact, however, the 1958 conference evaded the question of archipelagos for the same reason that it evaded the question of historic bays – discussion tended to turn too much on the facts of specific cases, rather than on general principles. Articles 46–54 of the 1982 Convention accept the claims made by states such as the Philippines and Indonesia, subject to certain conditions (for example, concerning transit by ships and aircraft of other states), but the position under customary international law is still uncertain; see R. R. Churchill and A. V. Lowe, *The Law of the Sea*, 1983, chapter 6.

As regards *boundaries between areas of sea claimed by two or more states*, see below, pp. 283–5.

The contiguous zone
At various periods of history different states have claimed limited
rights in areas of the high seas adjacent to their territorial seas, or
have claimed different widths of territorial sea for different
purposes. Between the two world wars the French writer Gidel
propounded the theory of the contiguous zone as a means of
rationalising the conflicting practice of states. At that time the
British government attacked the contiguous zone as a surreptitious
means of extending the territorial sea, and failure to agree about
the contiguous zone was one of the main reasons for the failure of
the League of Nations Codification Conference in 1930. However,
opposition has faded away since then, and Article 24 of the Geneva
Convention on the Territorial Sea and the Contiguous Zone 1958
provides:

1. In a zone of the high seas contiguous to its territorial sea, the coastal
state may exercise the control necessary to:
(*a*)   prevent infringement of its customs, fiscal, immigration or
sanitary regulations within its territory or territorial sea;
(*b*)   punish infringement of the above regulations committed within
its territory or territorial sea.
2. The contiguous zone may not extend beyond twelve miles from the
baseline from which the breadth of the territorial sea is measured.

Article 33(2) of the 1982 Convention provides that 'the contiguous zone may not extend beyond twenty-four nautical miles
from the baselines from which the breadth of the territorial sea is
measured'; in other words, if a state has a territorial sea of 12 miles,
it will be entitled to a contiguous zone of a further 12 miles.

See Churchill and Lowe, *The Law of the Sea*, 1983, ch. 7.

Exclusive Fishery Zones and Exclusive Economic Zones

Since about 1960 there has been a tendency for states to claim
exclusive fishery zones beyond their territorial seas. In the *Fisheries
Jurisdiction* case between the United Kingdom and Iceland, the
International   Court of Justice held in 1974 that a rule of
customary law had developed since 1960 which permitted states to
claim exclusive fishery zones of 12 miles (this width of 12 miles
included the territorial sea; thus, if a state claimed a territorial sea
of 3 miles, it was entitled to an exclusive fishery zone of a further 9
miles). The Court also held that a coastal state had a *preferential*
right over fish in adjacent areas of sea beyond the twelve-mile
limit, at least if the coastal state was (like Iceland) economically
dependent on local fisheries, but that the coastal state could not
wholly exclude other states from fishing in such areas, especially if

they had traditionally fished there and if part of their population was economically dependent on fishing there (*ICJ Reports*, 1974, pp. 3, 23–9).

However, it soon became apparent that the third United Nations Conference on the Law of the Sea would approve a territorial sea of 12 miles, with an exclusive economic zone extending for a further 188 miles, making a total of 200 miles. Article 56(1)(*a*) of the 1982 Convention gives the coastal state sovereign rights over all the economic resources of the sea, seabed and subsoil in its exclusive economic zone; this includes not only fish, but also minerals beneath the seabed (see also below, pp. 278–81). To some extent the word 'exclusive' is misleading, because Articles 62 and 69–71 of the 1982 Convention provide that a coastal state which cannot exploit the fish or other living resources of its exclusive economic zone to the full should make arrangements to share the surplus with other states; however, it can require payment for allowing foreign vessels to fish in its exclusive economic zone (Article 62(4)(*a*)). The coastal state will also have limited powers to prevent pollution and to control scientific research in its exclusive economic zone (Articles 211(5) and (6), 220 and 246–55). But foreign states will enjoy freedom of navigation and overflight, and the right to lay submarine cables and pipelines, in the coastal state's exclusive economic zone (Article 58).

Since 1976 most states have anticipated the outcome of the conference by claiming exclusive fishery zones or exclusive economic zones of 200 miles. In 1979, out of 133 coastal states, 92 claimed exclusive fishing rights for 200 miles (14 claimed a territorial sea of 200 miles, 45 claimed an exclusive economic zone of 200 miles and 33 claimed an exclusive fishery zone of 200 miles); about 17 other states claimed a territorial sea, exclusive fishery zone, or exclusive economic zone exceeding 12 miles but less than 200 miles. The states claiming an exclusive fishery zone of 200 miles include the USA, the USSR, Japan and the EEC countries (including the UK), which had previously opposed wide fishery zones. Most states which claim exclusive fishing rights for 200 miles have made treaties permitting other states to fish there, but only if those other states are prepared to offer something in return (see *Annuaire français de droit international*, 1978, pp. 851, 858–65, or Barston and Birnie, *The Maritime Dimension*, 1980, pp. 45–6; on the Common Fisheries Policy of the EEC, see *Journal of Common Market Studies*, December 1980, p. 123).

The practice of claiming exclusive fishing rights for 200 miles, although recent, is now so widespread that it can probably no longer be regarded as illegal. In other words, the rules laid down by the International Court of Justice in 1974 (see above, pp. 270–1) have now been replaced by a new rule of customary international law permitting states to claim exclusive fishing rights for 200 miles.

The High Seas

'The term "high seas" means all parts of the sea that are not included in the territorial sea or in the internal waters of a state' (Article 1 of the Geneva Convention on the High Seas 1958; but see also Article 86 of the 1982 Convention). The high seas may be used freely by the ships of all nations; Article 2 of the Geneva Convention on the High Seas 1958 states that freedom of the high seas comprises, *inter alia*, freedom of navigation, freedom of fishing, freedom to lay submarine cables and pipelines, and freedom to fly over the high seas. (Some of these freedoms are limited where a coastal state claims an exclusive fishery zone, an exclusive economic zone, or a contiguous zone – see above, pp. 270–1). These freedoms may also be enjoyed by land-locked states, which are given the right to sail ships under their own flags on the high seas (Article 4); states lying between land-locked states and the sea should negotiate agreements with land-locked states in order to give the latter the right to use their ports and rights of transit through their territory (Article 3).

As a general rule, a ship on the high seas is subject only to international law and to the laws of the flag-state. This makes it important to know which state is the flag-state. The 'flag state' really means the state whose nationality the ship possesses; it is nationality which creates the right to fly a country's flag, and not vice versa. The nationality of warships does not give rise to any problems, but the same is not true of merchant ships. Apart from very small ships, the nationality of merchant ships is determined in virtually all countries by registration; a ship has French nationality, for instance, if it is registered in France.[1] The conditions which states lay down before placing a ship on their register vary from state to state. The traditional shipowning countries like the United Kingdom lay down stringent requirements about the nationality of the shipowners, the nationality of the crew, or the place of construction. Other states – the so-called 'flags of convenience' countries – are prepared to register virtually any ship in return for payment of a fee.

---

[1] Article 6 of the Geneva Convention on the High Seas 1958 provides: 'Ships shall sail under the flag of one state only . . . A ship may not change its flag . . . save in the case of a real transfer of ownership or change of registry. A ship which sails under the flags of two or more states, using them according to convenience, may not claim any of the nationalities in question with respect to any other state, and may be assimilated to a ship without nationality.'

Flags of convenience are mainly used as a means of avoiding payment of taxes and statutory wage-rates. But they can also be used for more sinister purposes. A vast amount of the law of the sea is contained in treaties – dealing with such matters as ships' lights, safety regulations, the slave trade, compulsory insurance, 'pirate' radio stations, pollution and the conservation of fisheries – which, of course, are only binding on states parties to them. It is dangerously easy for shipowners to avoid compliance with such treaties by registering their ships in states which are not parties to them.

The popularity of flags of convenience is shown by the fact that Liberia has been the largest shipowning nation (in terms of registered tonnage) since 1967. Most countries with flags of convenience are developing countries, but in recent years the majority of developing countries have demanded the abolition of flags of convenience. Opinion among developed countries is equally divided; France is strongly opposed to flags of convenience, but the USA is not; as long as American shipowners are prepared to let the United States government requisition their ships in time of war, the government does not care where the ships are registered, and many of the ships concerned would operate at a loss if their owners were forced to pay American wage-rates.

Flags of convenience were an explosive issue at the Geneva Conference of 1958. Article 5 of the High Seas Convention emerged as an ambiguous compromise: 'There must exist a genuine link between the [flag] state and the ship; in particular, the state must effectively exercise its jurisdiction and control in administrative, technical and social matters over ships flying its flag.' Obviously, the fact that a ship is owned by foreigners does not necessarily prevent a flag-state exercising control in administrative, technical and social matters over the ship; but the Convention uses the words 'in particular', and it may therefore be that exercise of such control is not enough by itself to constitute a genuine link.

What happens if there is no genuine link between the ship and the flag-state? Is the nationality valid or void? Here again, Article 5 is badly drafted, because it provides no answer to this question.

For further discussion of the nationality of ships and of flags of convenience, see R. R. Churchill and A. V. Lowe, *The Law of the Sea*, 1983, pp. 178–83.

Interference with ships on the high seas

As a general rule, no one but the flag-state may exercise jurisdiction (in the sense of powers of arrest or other acts of physical interference) over a ship on the high seas (Articles 5, 8 and 9 of the Geneva Convention on the High Seas 1958).

As regards interference with warships, there is only one exception, which was too obvious to be mentioned in the Convention – in time of war, a warship of a belligerent state is liable to be attacked by enemy warships.

In the case of merchant ships, the same general rule applies; but there are a large number of exceptional cases where a warship of one state may interfere with a merchant ship of another state:

(1) *Exclusive fishery zones, exclusive economic zones and contiguous zones.* Foreign ships which violate the rights of a coastal state in its exclusive fishery zone or exclusive economic zone (see above, pp. 270-1) may be arrested by the coastal state. The coastal state also has certain powers of arrest in its contiguous zone (see above, p. 270).

(2) *Stateless ships.* Since the high seas are open to the ships of all *nations,* the Privy Council held in the *Asya,* [1948] A.C. 351, that it was lawful to seize a *stateless* ship on the high seas. Although the decision was probably correct on the facts of the case, the Privy Council's reasoning should not be carried to its logical conclusion; it is possible that arbitrary confiscation or destruction of a stateless ship would entitle the national state of the shipowners to make an international claim.

(3) *Hot pursuit.* As we have seen, the coastal state has certain powers of arrest over foreign merchant ships in its internal waters, territorial sea and contiguous zone. The right of hot pursuit is designed to prevent the ship avoiding arrest by escaping to the high seas. It is regulated in some detail by Article 23 of the Geneva Convention on the High Seas 1958, the most important provisions of which read as follows:

1. The hot pursuit of a foreign ship may be undertaken when the competent authorities of the coastal state have good reason to believe that the ship has violated the laws and regulations of that state. Such pursuit must be commenced when the foreign ship or one of its boats is within the internal waters or the territorial sea or the contiguous zone of the pursuing state, and may only be continued outside the territorial sea or the contiguous zone if the pursuit has not been interrupted . . . If the foreign ship is within a contiguous zone, as defined in Article 24 of the Convention on the Territorial Sea and the Contiguous Zone, the pursuit may only be undertaken if there has been a violation of the rights for the protection of which the zone was established.

2. The right of hot pursuit ceases as soon as the ship pursued enters the territorial sea of its own country or of a third state.

3. . . . . The pursuit may only be commenced after a visual or auditory

signal to stop has been given at a distance which enables it to be seen or heard by the foreign ship.

4. The right of hot pursuit may be exercised only by warships or military aircraft, or other ships or aircraft on government service specially authorized to that effect.

Hot pursuit may also begin in the coastal state's exclusive fishery zone if the foreign ship was illegally fishing there (*American Journal of International Law*, 1976, p. 95). Article 111 (2) of the 1982 Convention lays down a similar rule for the exclusive economic zone.

According to the *I'm Alone* case (1935, *UN Reports of International Arbitral Awards* III 1609, 1615), the right of hot pursuit does not include the right to sink the pursued vessel deliberately; but accidental sinking in the course of arrest may be lawful.

(4) *The right of approach.* The general rule is that merchant ships on the high seas are subject to control only by warships of the flag-state. If a merchant ship is doing something which it ought not to be doing, it may try to escape the control of warships from its own state, by flying a foreign flag or no flag at all. Consequently, if a warship encounters a merchant ship on the high seas and has reasonable grounds for suspecting that the merchant ship is of the same nationality as the warship, it may carry out investigations on board the merchant ship in order to ascertain its nationality. This power is reaffirmed in Article 22 of the Geneva Convention on the High Seas 1958.

(5) *Treaties* often give the contracting parties a reciprocal power of arrest over one another's merchant ships. Examples may be found in treaties for the conservation of fisheries, or for the protection of submarine cables. Such provisions used to be particularly common in treaties for the suppression of the slave trade; but Article 22 of the Geneva Convention on the High Seas 1958 suggests that the power to search foreign ships suspected of engaging in the slave trade has now become a rule of customary law.

It is important to note that states, in such cases, only have a reciprocal power of *arrest*; after arrest, the offenders must be handed back to their flag-state for trial. (Theoretically a treaty could provide for reciprocal powers of trial, as well as reciprocal powers of arrest; examples are rare, but see Articles 109 and 110(1)(c) of the 1982 Convention, which deal with unauthorised broadcasting.)

(6) *Piracy* is dealt with at length in Articles 14–22 of the Geneva Convention on the High Seas 1958. According to Article 15, piracy consists of any of the following acts:

(1) Any illegal acts of violence, detention or any act of depredation,

committed for private ends by the crew or the passengers of a private
ship or a private aircraft,[1] and directed:

(a)   on the high seas, against another ship or aircraft, or against
       persons or property on board such a ship or aircraft;

(b)   against a ship, aircraft, persons or property in a place outside the
       jurisdiction of any state.

(2) Any act of voluntary participation in the operation of a ship or of
an aircraft with knowledge of facts making it a pirate ship or aircraft.

(3) Any act of inciting or of intentionally facilitating an act described
in sub-paragraph (1) or sub-paragraph (2) of this Article.

If a warship has reasonable grounds for suspecting that a
merchant ship is engaged in piracy, it may board her on the high
seas for purposes of investigation, regardless of the merchant
ship's nationality (Article 22). If the suspicions are justified, the
merchant ship may be seized and the persons on board may be
arrested and tried (Article 19). Every state is entitled to arrest *and
to try* a pirate, without being limited by any of the rules which are
often regarded as restricting the jurisdiction of municipal courts in
criminal cases (see above, pp. 103–4).

Laymen often use the word 'piracy' loosely to include all sorts of
acts which international law does not regard as piracy, for
example, broadcasts by 'pirate' radio stations. Such acts may be
crimes under the laws of certain countries (indeed, in the laws of
some countries they are even described as piracy); but, since they
are not piracy within the meaning of *international* law, a ship
being used for such purposes may be arrested on the high seas only
by the flag-state and not by other states (unless there is a treaty
authorising arrest by other states).

(7) *Belligerent rights.* In time of war a warship belonging to a
belligerent state may seize enemy merchant ships and also, in
certain circumstances, neutral merchant ships trading with the
enemy (see above, pp. 233–6).

(8) *Self-defence.* Even when there is no war, states sometimes
claim a right to interfere with foreign merchant ships on the
grounds of self-defence, but the law on this point is uncertain. For
instance, France cited self-defence as a justification for seizing
foreign merchants ships carrying arms to the rebel movement in
Algeria in the 1950s, but such seizures were condemned as illegal
by some of the flag-states concerned (M. M. Whiteman, *Digest of
International Law*, vol. 4, 1965, pp. 513–14). On the other hand,
when a foreign merchant ship has been involved in an accident on
the high seas which creates an imminent threat of massive oil

[1] This includes a warship, government ship, or government aircraft whose crew has
mutinied and taken control of the ship or aircraft (Article 16).

pollution on neighbouring coasts, it is possible that the coastal state is entitled to seize or destroy the ship in order to prevent pollution (Hague Academy of International Law, *Colloquium*, 1973, pp. 39–50); thus the Liberian government did not protest in 1967 when the United Kingdom bombed the *Torrey Canyon*, a Liberian oil tanker which had run aground on a reef in the English Channel. Perhaps the distinction lies in the differing degrees of urgency in the two situations; France could have waited until the ships carrying arms entered the French territorial sea before arresting them, whereas *immediate* destruction of a wrecked oil tanker is often the *only* way to prevent pollution of coasts. See also Article 221 of the 1982 Convention.

(9) *Action authorised by the United Nations.* See above, pp. 181–4, especially p. 184, n. 1.

Jurisdiction of municipal courts over crimes committed on the high seas

Apart from the special case of piracy, the ordinary rules of international law concerning criminal jurisdiction apply to crimes committed on the high seas (see above, pp. 103–4 and 276). For this purpose, a ship is treated as if it were the territory of the flag-state. For instance, if an Englishman on a French ship fires a fatal shot at someone on a German ship, he can be tried in England (nationality principle), France (subjective territorial principle) and Germany (objective territorial principle).

However, controversies have arisen in connection with criminal liability for collisions at sea. In the *Lotus* case, a French ship, the *Lotus*, collided with a Turkish ship on the high seas, and, as a result, people on the Turkish ship were drowned; when the *Lotus* reached a Turkish port, Lieutenant Demons, who had been steering the *Lotus* at the time of the collision, was arrested and prosecuted for manslaughter. France complained that this exercise of jurisdiction by Turkey was contrary to international law, but the Permanent Court of International Justice held that Lieutenant Demons could be tried, not only by his own flag-state, France, but also by Turkey, because the effects of his actions had been felt on the Turkish ship (1927, PCIJ, series A, no. 10). This decision, based on the objective territorial principle, produced alarm among seafaring men, and a long campaign against the rule in the *Lotus* case culminated in Article 11(1) of the Geneva Convention on the High Seas 1958 which provides:

In the event of collision or of any other incident of navigation concerning a ship on the high seas, involving the penal [that is, criminal] or disciplinary responsibility of the master or of any other person in the service of the ship, no penal or disciplinary proceedings may be instituted against such persons except before the judicial or administrative authorities either of the flag state or of the state of which such person is a national.

This reverses the effect of the *Lotus* decision, in so far as the *Lotus* decision dealt with collisions and other 'incidents of navigation'. But the wider principles laid down in the *Lotus* case, concerning the objective territorial principle, jurisdiction in general, and the nature of customary law, remain valid. It is as if the British Parliament passed an Act saying that it was not a tort to put snails in ginger-beer bottles; *Donoghue* v. *Stevenson* would no longer be good law on its peculiar facts, but the general principles laid down in that case about the duties of manufacturers would remain valid.

The Continental Shelf

Before 1945 the freedom of the high seas meant, among other things, that every state had the right to exploit the seabed and subsoil of the high seas. This right was shared with all other states; no state could claim an *exclusive* right to any part of the seabed or subsoil of the high seas.

However, the law began to change when it became technologically and economically feasible to exploit oil deposits beneath the sea by means of off-shore oil wells. In 1945 President Truman of the USA issued a proclamation that the USA had the exclusive right to exploit the seabed and subsoil of the continental shelf off the coasts of the USA. (This term, 'the continental shelf', requires some explanation. In most parts of the world the seabed slopes gently away from the coast for quite a long distance before it slopes steeply down to the great ocean depths. This offshore part of the seabed, covered by shallow water, is called the continental shelf by geologists, and in prehistoric times was dry land. For the purposes of President Truman's proclamation, the continental shelf was defined as being those offshore areas of the seabed which were not more than 100 fathoms deep.)

President Truman's proclamation was copied by certain other states, and offshore drilling for oil and natural gas became common in the Caribbean and the Persian Gulf. No protests were made by other states, except when Chile and Peru made claims which went far beyond the scope of President Truman's proclamation. Chile and Peru have no continental shelf in the geological sense; the seabed off their coasts drops sharply down to the great ocean depths. Therefore, instead of claiming a continental shelf, they claimed sovereignty over the seabed and subsoil for a distance of 200 miles from their coasts; and they also claimed sovereignty over the superjacent waters and air space, which had been expressly excluded from the proclamations issued by the USA and other countries.

The history of the continental shelf in the years after 1945 is a classic example of the formation of a new rule of customary law. The action of the USA created a precedent which other states followed – and in some cases tried to extend. Claims to exclusive rights to exploit the seabed and subsoil were copied, or at least not challenged, by other states, and thus gave rise to a new rule of customary law; claims to sovereignty over superjacent waters did not give rise to a new rule of customary law, because they met with protests from other states. (Even the 200-mile exclusive economic zone, a concept of much more recent origin (see above, p. 271), gives the coastal state fewer rights than the sovereignty over superjacent waters claimed by Chile and Peru.)

Before 1958 customary law on the continental shelf was still rather vague and controversial; the Geneva Convention on the Continental Shelf 1958 added more precision and detail to the rules.

Article 1 defines the continental shelf as:

the seabed and subsoil of the submarine areas adjacent to the coast but outside the area of the territorial sea, to a depth of 200 metres, or, beyond that limit, to where the depth of the superjacent waters admits of the exploitation of the natural resources of the said areas . . .

Article 2 provides:

1. The coastal state exercises over the continental shelf sovereign rights for the purpose of exploring it and exploiting its natural resources.
2. The rights referred to in paragraph 1 of this Article are exclusive in the sense that if the coastal state does not explore the continental shelf or exploit its natural resources, no one may undertake these activities, or make a claim to the continental shelf, without the express consent of the coastal state.
3. The rights of the coastal state over the continental shelf do not depend on occupation, effective or notional, or on any express proclamation.
4. The natural resources referred to in these Articles consist of the mineral and other non-living resources of the seabed and subsoil together with living organisms belonging to sedentary species, that is to say, organisms which, at the harvestable stage, either are immobile on or under the seabed or are unable to move except in constant physical contact with the seabed or the subsoil.

Article 3 provides that 'the rights of the coastal state over the continental shelf do not affect the legal status of the superjacent waters as high seas, or that of the air space above those waters'.

Article 5 provides that the exploration and exploitation of the continental shelf must not cause unreasonable interference with navigation, fishing, conservation of fisheries, or scientific research (paragraph 1). Subject to paragraph 1, the coastal state may construct installations for the purposes of exploiting the natural resources of the continental shelf. The installations may protrude above the surface of the sea, but they do not have the legal status of islands (for example, they have no territorial sea), although the coastal state may establish safety zones with a radius of 500 metres round each installation. There are further provisions to prevent the installations being dangerous, for example, there must be an adequate system of warning of their presence, and they must be dismantled when disused.

The Deep Seabed

What are the outer limits of the continental shelf for legal purposes? Does it have any outer limits at all, or do the coastal state's exclusive rights over the seabed and subsoil extend to mid-ocean, regardless of the depth of the ocean? This is a vital question, because in the near future the deep seabed (or ocean floor) is going to be of great economic importance. The ocean floor in many areas is covered with manganese nodules, averaging about 4 cm in diameter and containing up to 50 per cent manganese, with significant traces of copper, nickel, cobalt and other metals. It is estimated that there are 1,500,000,000,000 tons of these nodules on the floor of the Pacific alone, sometimes in concentrations of up to 100,000 tons per square mile.

Article 1 of the Geneva Convention on the Continental Shelf 1958 speaks of exploitability as a criterion for fixing the outer limit of the continental shelf. This might suggest that the continental shelf could, for legal purposes, extend to mid-ocean; but such an interpretation is unsound, for several reasons. The Geneva Convention defines the continental shelf as 'submarine areas *adjacent* to the coast', and areas in mid-ocean cannot be regarded as adjacent to any of the coastal states. Again, the International Court of Justice emphasised in the *North Sea Continental Shelf* case (*ICJ Reports*, 1969, pp. 3, 31, 47, 53) that the continental shelf was a prolongation of land territory – and the deep seabed is too deep, and too far from shore, to be regarded as a prolongation of land territory. Finally, the continental shelf is a geological concept as well as a legal concept, and, from the geological point of view, to say that the deep seabed forms part of the continental shelf is as absurd as saying that Africa forms part of Australia.

Article 76(1) of the 1982 Convention provides:

The continental shelf of a coastal state comprises the seabed and subsoil of the submarine areas that extend beyond its territorial sea throughout the natural prolongation of its land territory to the outer edge of the continental margin, or to a distance of 200 nautical miles from the baselines from which the breadth of the territorial sea is measured where the outer edge of the continental margin does not extend up to that distance.

Article 76 also contains complicated and controversial provisions for delineating the outer edge of the continental margin. The continental margin consists not only of the continental shelf, but also of the continental slope, a steeply sloping area beyond the continental shelf, and the continental rise, a gently sloping area between the continental slope and the deep seabed. (The minimum limit of 200 miles was copied from the provisions on the exclusive economic zone; see above, p. 271.)

Resolution 2749 (XXV), passed by the General Assembly on 17 December 1970 by 108 votes to nil with 14 abstentions, declared that the deep seabed was the common heritage of mankind, and laid down various principles to govern the future exploitation of its resources (text in Ian Brownlie, *Basic Documents in International Law*, 3rd ed., 1983, p. 122). These principles are elaborated in detail in Articles 133–91 and Annexes III and IV of the 1982 Convention. According to the 1982 Convention, control of the deep seabed (that is, the seabed beyond the continental shelf, as defined in Article 76) will be vested in an International Seabed Authority, which will exploit the deep seabed and its subsoil or grant licences for such exploitation to states or commercial companies. (The powers of the Authority will apply only to the seabed and subsoil; Article 135 of the 1982 Convention declares that the provisions of the 1982 Convention concerning the deep seabed and the Authority shall not affect the legal status of the superjacent waters (high seas) or the airspace above those waters.) The International Seabed Authority will also receive part of the revenue from the exploitation of the continental shelf beyond the 200-mile limit; the coastal state will receive the remainder of such revenue (Article 82). Revenue, royalties and profits received by the Authority will be used for the benefit of mankind as a whole, taking into particular consideration the needs of developing countries, whether coastal or landlocked.

The developing countries hope to benefit financially from the

International Seabed Authority. But the developed countries, which are the only countries with the advanced technology and huge amounts of capital needed to exploit the resources of the seabed, hope to get a fair return on the money and effort which they will put into exploiting those resources. This clash of interests affects many provisions of the 1982 Convention concerning the functions, powers, structure and voting procedure of the International Seabed Authority and the relations between mining companies and the Authority. Until 1981 it seemed likely that the UN Conference on the Law of the Sea would reach agreement on a compromise between the interests of the developed states and the interests of the developing states (see the 1980 draft of the 1982 Convention in *International Legal Materials*, 1980, p. 1129). But in 1981 President Reagan of the USA demanded that some amendments should be made to the provisions of the 1980 draft concerning the deep seabed and the Authority, in order to make them more favourable to the developed states. The Conference made a few changes to the text of the 1980 draft in order to make it more acceptable to the developed states (R. R. Churchill and A. V. Lowe, *The Law of the Sea*, 1983, pp. 171–3), but most Western states (including the USA and the UK) remained unsatisfied and refused to sign or ratify the 1982 Convention.

Even before President Reagan took office in 1981, the USA had become so impatient with the disagreements and delays at the conference that it passed a law authorising United States companies to start exploiting the deep seabed (text in *International Legal Materials*, 1980, p. 1003). Similar laws have also been passed by some other developed states, such as West Germany and the United Kingdom. There is a tacit understanding among the states which have passed such laws that companies from one 'reciprocating state' (to use the terminology of the law passed by the USA) will be forbidden to operate in an area covered by a licence issued by another 'reciprocating state'. The laws in question do not purport to create rights over any part of the deep seabed which will be exclusive vis-à-vis non-reciprocating states; moreover, the laws are intended to apply only during the period before the International Seabed Authority is set up, and they provide that all or part of the revenue received by the government concerned from the exploitation of the seabed will be subsequently transferred to the International Seabed Authority after that Authority is set up. In spite of that, these laws have been condemned by developing countries as a violation of General Assembly resolution 2749 (XXV). See *American Journal of International Law*, vol. 73, 1979, pp. 30–8, or *Tulane Law Review*, vol. 53, 1979, pp. 492–520.

Maritime Boundaries

Many disputes have arisen in recent years over the location of boundaries between areas of sea claimed by one state and areas of sea claimed by another state.

Article 12(1) of the Geneva Convention on the Territorial Sea 1958 provides as follows:

Where the coasts of two states are opposite or adjacent to each other, neither of the two states is entitled, failing agreement between them to the contrary, to extend its territorial sea beyond the median line every point of which is equidistant from the nearest points on the baselines from which the breadth of the territorial seas of each of the two states is measured. The provisions of this paragraph shall not apply, however, where it is necessary by reason of historic title or other special circumstances to delimit the territorial seas of the two states in a way which is at variance with this provision.

The same rules are laid down in Article 15 of the 1982 Convention.

In the case of the contiguous zone, Article 24(3) of the Geneva Convention on the Territorial Sea lays down the same rule as Article 12(1), except that it omits the final sentence of Article 12(1). The 1982 Convention contains no provision for delimiting contiguous zones claimed by opposite or adjacent states.

Article 6(1) of the Geneva Convention on the Continental Shelf 1958 provides as follows:

Where the same continental shelf is adjacent to the territories of two or more states whose coasts are opposite each other, the boundary of the continental shelf appertaining to such states shall be determined by agreement between them. In the absence of agreement, and unless another boundary line is justified by special circumstances, the boundary is the median line, every point of which is equidistant from the nearest points of the baselines from which the breadth of the territorial sea of each state is measured.

Article 6(2) applies the same rules 'where the same continental shelf is adjacent to the territories of two adjacent states'.

Articles 12(1) and 24(3) of the Geneva Convention on the Territorial Sea place primary emphasis on the equidistance principle. By contrast, Article 6 of the Geneva Convention on the Continental Shelf places primary emphasis on delimitation by agreement. Both Article 12(1) of the Geneva Convention on the Territorial Sea and Article 6 of the Geneva Convention on the Continental Shelf provide for a 'special circumstances' exception to the equidistance principle, but in practice the 'special circumstances' exception is likely to be invoked more often in delimiting the continental shelf than in delimiting the territorial sea, because continental shelves stretch further than territorial seas; maritime boundaries based on the equidistance principle are often distorted by the presence of islands or by curvatures on the coast, and the effect of such distortions increases as one moves further out to sea (*ICJ Reports*, 1969, pp. 16–18). Such distortions may be tolerable if they enable one state to extend its territorial sea at the expense of another state by a few miles, but not if they enable one state to extend its continental shelf at the expense of another state by hundreds of miles.

In the *North Sea Continental Shelf* case the International Court of Justice held that the rules contained in Article 6(2) of the Geneva Convention on the Continental Shelf were not rules of customary law, and were therefore not binding on West Germany, which was not a party to the Convention. Instead, the Court said that the relevant rule of customary law required the parties (West Germany, Denmark and the Netherlands) to negotiate in good faith in order to reach an agreement on an equitable delimitation (*ICJ Reports*, 1969, p. 3, especially pp. 46–54). However, the arbitral award in a later case between the United Kingdom and France, concerning the delimitation of the continental shelf in the English Channel, suggests that the difference between customary law and Article 6 of the Geneva Convention on the Continental Shelf is slight; the United Kingdom and France were both parties to the Convention, but the arbitrators held that the position of the Channel Islands and of the Isles of Scilly constituted 'special circumstances' within the meaning of Article 6 of the Convention and that the boundary should be based on equitable considerations (which involved departing from the median (equidistance) line) wherever such special circumstances existed (*International Law Reports*, vol. 54, pp. 6, 8–10, 54–9, 101–3, 123–4; see the case-notes by Bowett in the *British Year Book of International Law*, 1978, p. 1, and by Colson in the *American Journal of International Law*, 1978, p. 95, and see also Blecher, 'Equitable delimitation of the continental shelf', *American Journal of International Law*, 1979, p. 60).

The down-grading of the equidistance principle has been carried a stage further by Article 83(1) of the 1982 Convention which provides:

The delimitation of the continental shelf between states with opposite or adjacent coasts shall be effected by agreement on the basis of international law, as referred to in Article 38 of the Statute of the International Court of Justice, in order to achieve an equitable solution.

Article 74(1) of the 1982 Convention applies the same rule to the delimitation of exclusive economic zones (for the text of Article 38(1) of the Statute of the International Court of Justice, see above, p. 23; for the text of Article 38(2), see above, p. 39, n. 1). Articles 83(1) and 74(1) are vague, but that is inevitable; the whole question of delimitation was a source of acute controversy at the third United Nations Conference on the Law of the Sea. Judicial and arbitral decisions in the future will probably clarify the concept of 'an equitable solution', but that is bound to be a slow process; what is equitable in one geographical situation will not be equitable in other geographical situations, and there is therefore a danger that each decided case will be unique and incapable of serving as a precedent for other cases.

See also D. W. Bowett, *The Legal Régime of Islands in International Law*, 1979, especially pp. 249–81 on the dispute between Greece and Turkey concerning the continental shelf of the Aegean Sea.

Article 121(3) of the 1982 Convention provides that 'rocks which cannot sustain human habitation or economic life of their own shall have no exclusive economic zone or continental shelf'. This innovation is regarded as desirable by most states (but presumably not by the United Kingdom, which claims an exclusive fishery zone of 200 miles around Rockall, an uninhabitable rock 180 miles west of the Hebrides). However, Article 121 implies that such rocks will continue to possess a territorial sea and a contiguous zone.

Suggestions for Further Reading

R. P. Barston and P. Birnie, *The Maritime Dimension*, 1980, especially chs 1, 5, 8 and 9.

D. J. Harris, *Cases and Materials on International Law*, 3rd ed., 1983, ch. 7.

C. J. Colombos, *The International Law of the Sea*, 6th ed., 1967.

G. J. Mangone, *Law for the World Ocean*, 1981.

R. R. Churchill and A. V. Lowe, *The Law of the Sea*, 1983.

'The Law of the Sea – Where Now?', *Law and Contemporary Problems*, vol. 46, no. 2, Spring 1983.

Chapter 19

Air Space and Outer Space

Air Space

Between 1900 and 1914 academic lawyers proposed various theories about the legal status of air space. But from 1914 onwards it was clear that states would be content with nothing less than complete sovereignty over their air space, unlimited by any right of innocent passage; and a new rule of customary law to that effect arose very quickly. The military potential of aircraft for bombing and reconnaissance, demonstrated during the First World War, meant that any other rule would have been unacceptable to states, on security grounds. (In fact, it was the neutral states which were most insistent on their right to exclude foreign aircraft during the First World War, in order to prevent aerial battles taking place over their territory.)

Since then, the customary rule has been that aircraft from one state have a right to fly over the high seas, but not over the territory or territorial sea of another state. It is a serious breach of international law for a state to order its aircraft to violate the air space of another state. In May 1960, when a United States U2 reconnaissance aircraft was shot down over the Soviet Union, the Soviet Union cancelled a summit conference with the United States in protest against the violation of its air space (see *American Journal of International Law*, 1960, p. 836, and 1962, p. 135; *Columbia Law Review*, 1961, p. 1074).

Apparently the United States did not protest against the shooting down of the U2. But that does not mean that states have an unlimited right to attack intruding aircraft in all circumstances. In 1953 Lissitzyn (*American Journal of International Law*, 1953, pp. 559, 586) suggested that the following rule of customary law could be inferred from state practice: 'In its efforts to control the movements of intruding aircraft the territorial sovereign must not expose the aircraft and its occupants to unnecessary or unreasonably great danger – unreasonably great, that is, in relation to the reasonably apprehended harmfulness of the intrusion . . . .'. This is a very flexible principle. It implies that a state must not attack an intruding aircraft unless it has reason to suspect that the aircraft constitutes a real threat to its security (military aircraft are obviously more likely to present such a threat than civil aircraft); it also implies that a warning to land or change course should be given before the aircraft is attacked, unless there is reason to suspect that the aircraft constitutes an immediate and very serious threat to the security of the state, or unless it is impracticable to give such a warning.

In 1981 the International Civil Aviation Organisation (a specialised agency of the United Nations – see above, pp. 196–8) recommended to its member states that 'intercepting aircraft should refrain from the use of weapons *in all cases* of interception of *civil* aircraft' (*International Legal Materials*, 1983, pp. 1185, 1187; italics added). In 1983 the Soviet Union shot down a South Korean civil airliner which had entered Soviet air space; in the United Nations Security Council a draft resolution condemning the Soviet action (ibid., p. 1148) received nine votes in favour, but was vetoed by the Soviet Union (Poland also voted against, and China, Guyana, Nicaragua and Zimbabwe abstained). The preamble to the draft resolution contained a paragraph 'reaffirming the rules of international law that prohibit acts of violence which pose a threat to the safety of international civil aviation', which implies that attacks on *civil* aircraft are *never* permitted (the position is obviously different if *military* aircraft enter the air space of another state). This 'absolute' rule was supported by statements made by the United States, South Korea, Australia, Togo, Ecuador and Portugal (ibid., pp. 1110, 1114, 1118, 1129, 1133–4 and 1139), while Canada, Zaire, West Germany and Fiji echoed Lissitzyn's more flexible approach by saying that the Soviet reaction was *disproportionate* in the circumstances (ibid., pp. 1117, 1120 and 1133). Even the Soviet Union did not claim that it had an unlimited right to shoot down intruding aircraft; instead, it claimed that it had mistaken the South Korean airliner for a United States military reconnaissance aircraft, and that the South Korean airliner had acted suspiciously and had ignored Soviet orders to land (ibid., pp. 1126–8; cf. p. 1074). (For discussion of some similar incidents in earlier years, see D. W. Greig, *International Law*, 2nd ed., 1976, pp. 356–60.)

Lissitzyn's flexible approach is probably still an accurate statement of the law in the case of *military* aircraft which enter the air space of another state without that state's consent. However, as we have just seen, there is some disagreement about the action which can be taken against *civil* aircraft which enter the air space of another state without that state's consent; some states still seem to support the application of Lissitzyn's flexible approach to civil aircraft (as well as to military aircraft), but other states (and the International Civil Aviation Organisation) believe that civil aircraft must *never* be attacked in such circumstances. On the other hand, civil aircraft which enter the air space of another state without that state's consent can be ordered to leave or to land, and the state whose air space has been violated can protest to the state in which the aircraft are registered if such orders are ignored; the rule (if it is a rule) that trespassing civil aircraft must not be attacked does not mean that they have a legal right to trespass.

Air transport from one state to another is rendered possible by a network of bilateral treaties, by which one state gives aircraft from another state the right to fly through its air space (usually in return for a similar concession from the other state in favour of the first state's aircraft). Between the beginning of 1945 and the end of 1960 the United Kingdom concluded no less than 182 bilateral treaties concerning civil air transport.

Many of the rules governing aircraft have been copied from the rules governing ships. For instance, the nationality of aircraft is based on registration, and an aircraft cannot be registered in two or more states at the same time; the problem of flags of convenience, which has caused so much controversy in connection with merchant ships, has scarcely arisen in the context of aircraft – maybe because most airlines are owned or subsidised by governments. Similarly, the rules concerning the power to try crimes committed on aircraft resemble the rules concerning the power to try crimes committed on ships. For the purposes of the territorial principle of jurisdiction, a civil aircraft in flight may be treated as if it were a part of the state of registration (a sort of 'flying island', so to speak), but it may also be regarded as present within the subjacent state, so that both the state of registration and the subjacent state may try the offender. This resembles the concurrent jurisdiction exercised by the flag-state and the coastal state over crimes committed on foreign merchant ships in internal waters or the territorial sea. (See also Akehurst, 'Hijacking', *Indian Journal of International Law*, 1974, pp. 81–9.)

Outer Space

The first artificial satellite went into orbit around the earth on 4 October 1957, and since then artificial satellites have passed over the territory of other states on innumerable occasions; for many years no state ever protested that this constituted a violation of its air space. The conduct of the states launching satellites, coupled with the acquiescence of other states, gave rise to a new permissive rule of customary international law; states are entitled to put satellites in orbit over the territory of other states. The rule concerning outer space is thus different from the rule concerning air space (see above). The precise location of the point where air space ends and outer space begins is uncertain but unimportant, because the minimum height at which satellites can remain in orbit is at least twice the maximum height at which aircraft can fly.

Much of the present law on outer space is contained in the Outer Space Treaty of 1967 (text in Ian Brownlie, *Basic Documents in International Law*, 3rd ed., 1983, p. 204; in 1981 eighty states, including the USA, USSR and UK, were parties to the treaty). The treaty provides that outer space is free for exploration and use by all states (Article 1) and cannot be annexed by any state (Article 2). The exploration and use of outer space must be carried out for the benefit of all countries (Article 1) and in accordance with international law (Article 3). Activities in outer space must not contaminate the environment of the earth or of celestial bodies, and must not interfere with the activities of other states in outer space (Article 9). States must disclose information about their activities in outer space (Articles 10–12). Activities of non-governmental entities in outer space require governmental authorisation, and the state concerned is responsible for all activities which it authorises (Article 6). A state which launches (or authorises the launching of) an object into outer space is liable for any damage caused by that object (Article 7). States must assist astronauts in distress; an astronaut from one state who makes a forced landing in another state must be returned to the former state (Article 5). Ownership of objects launched into outer space is not altered by their presence in outer space or by their return to earth; if found, such objects must be returned to the state of origin (Article 8). The rules in Articles 7, 5 and 8 were subsequently laid down in greater detail by the Convention on Liability for Damage Caused by Objects Launched into Outer Space (text in *International Legal Materials*, 1971, p. 965) and by the Agreement on the Rescue of Astronauts, the Return of Astronauts and the Return of Objects Launched into Outer Space (text in *American Journal of International Law*, 1969, p. 382).

Article 4 of the Outer Space Treaty provides that the moon and other celestial bodies 'shall be used . . . exclusively for peaceful purposes'. However, as regards spacecraft orbiting around the earth, Article 4 merely provides that nuclear weapons and other weapons of mass destruction must not be placed in orbit around the earth. This difference between the rules applicable to spacecraft in earth orbit and the rules applicable to celestial bodies justifies the inference that spacecraft in earth orbit may be used for military purposes which do *not* involve nuclear weapons or other weapons of mass destruction; in particular, they may be used for purposes of reconnaissance. During the negotiations leading up to the conclusion of the Outer Space Treaty, the Soviet Union (which, as a 'closed society', had most to lose from being observed by satellites) argued that the use of satellites for reconnaissance purposes was illegal and should be prohibited by the treaty; but the USA disagreed. One advantage of the use of reconnaissance satellites is that they will provide an efficient means of verifying compliance with disarmament treaties in the future; in the past, avoidance of inspection has always been a major obstacle to disarmament.

Suggestions for Further Reading

Darwin, 'The Outer Space Treaty', *British Year Book of International Law*, vol. 42, 1967, p. 278.

Goedhuis, 'The changing legal régime of air and outer space', *International and Comparative Law Quarterly*, vol. 27, 1978, p. 576.

Cheng, 'The Moon Treaty', *Current Legal Problems*, vol. 33, 1980, p. 213.

Appendix

The Falkland Islands Dispute

The Falkland Islands dispute between the United Kingdom and Argentina is a good example of the way in which an international dispute can involve several different areas of international law.

Title to Territory – The Position Before 1833

The Falkland Islands consist of two large islands, East Falkland and West Falkland, and many smaller islands. They are situated about 300 miles from the mainland of South America, and their total area is about 4700 square miles. In 1980 their population was 1813, of whom 1723 were United Kingdom nationals.

The Falkland Islands were discovered in the sixteenth century; it is uncertain whether the first discovery was made by the Portuguese, the Spanish, the English or the Dutch. However, before 1764 no government attempted to exercise control over the islands, which remained uninhabited and *terra nullius* (the technical term for territory which is not under the sovereignty of any state).

In 1764 France established a settlement on the east coast of East Falkland. In 1767 Spain forced France to sell that settlement to Spain, and the Spanish settlement remained until 1811. Spain can therefore be regarded as having acquired sovereignty over East Falkland, either by cession from France (see above, p. 142) or by occupation (see above, pp. 142–4). Moreover, Spain's title probably survived the departure of the Spanish in 1811, because there is no evidence that Spain intended to abandon sovereignty; physical departure from territory does not lead to loss of sovereignty over that territory unless it is accompanied by an intention to abandon sovereignty (see above, p. 142, n. 1).

Argentina, which declared its independence from Spain in 1816, succeeded to Spain's title. It is a rule of international law that a newly independent state which was formerly a colony succeeds to all the territory within the former colonial boundaries. This rule, known to Latin American lawyers as the principle of *uti possidetis*, is not peculiar to Latin America; it has also been applied by former colonies in Africa and Asia (see above, p. 158).

Argentina established settlements on East Falkland in the 1820s, and these settlements remained until the settlers were evicted by the United Kingdom in 1833. So, even if Spain's title to East Falkland had lapsed in 1811, with the result that East Falkland became *terra nullius* again, Argentina could claim that she had acquired sovereignty over East Falkland by occupation, by establishing her own effective control over East Falkland.

In 1766 the United Kingdom established a settlement on Saunders Island, a small island off the north coast of West Falkland. Spain evicted the British settlers in 1770, which nearly led to war between the United Kingdom and Spain. In 1771 Spain agreed to let the British settlers return, but stated that this agreement 'cannot . . . affect the question of the prior right of sovereignty' over the Falkland Islands (in other words, Spain and the United Kingdom agreed to differ about the question of sovereignty over the Falkland Islands). Some historians (particularly Julius Goebel, *The Struggle for the Falkland Islands*, 1927, ch. 7) claim that the United Kingdom gave a secret oral promise to Spain in 1771 to withdraw the British settlement after anti-Spanish sentiment in the United Kingdom had died down, but others deny that any such promise was ever given (see the article by Northedge in *International Relations*, 1982, p. 2167). Even Goebel's version of the events of 1771 does not make clear whether the United Kingdom promised to abandon sovereignty or whether the United Kingdom merely promised to carry out a physical withdrawal (for the significance of this distinction, see above, p. 142, n. 1). At all events, when the United Kingdom did withdraw from Saunders Island in 1774, it said it was doing so only in order to save money, and it left a plaque on Saunders Island claiming sovereignty over the Falkland Islands. It is thus clear that the United Kingdom did not intend to abandon sovereignty over Saunders Island in 1774. On the other hand, after 1774 the United Kingdom took no further interest in the Falkland Islands until 1829, when it protested against Argentinian claims to the islands, and it is possible that an intention to abandon sovereignty could be inferred from this long period of apathy.

Before 1833 no state had established a settlement on West Falkland, but Spain and Argentina exercised some degree of control over West Falkland; Spain visited West Falkland from time to time to make sure that foreigners had not settled there, and later Argentina tried to prevent foreign ships fishing near West Falkland (and also East Falkland). Argentina could invoke these acts to support a claim that Spain or Argentina had acquired sovereignty to West Falkland by occupation (see above, pp. 142–4). On the other hand, the United Kingdom could invoke the proximity of West Falkland to the British settlement on Saunders Island, to support a claim to British sovereignty over West Falkland. (West Falkland is 48 miles from the Spanish and Argentinian settlements on the east coast of East Falkland, but less than a mile from Saunders Island – Saunders Island is so close to West Falkland that it can almost be regarded as part of West Falkland). 'Geographical proximity . . . is . . . not . . . an independent source of title', but is 'relevant . . . as a fact assisting the determination of the limits of an effective occupation' (Waldock, in *British Year Book of International Law*, 1948, p. 342); it raises 'some sort of presumption of effective occupation – a presumption that can be rebutted by better evidence of sovereign possession by a rival claimant' (R. Y. Jennings, *The Acquisition of Territory in International Law*, 1962, p. 73).

In the *Eastern Greenland case* (see above, p. 143) the Permanent Court of International Justice said:

> In most of the cases involving claims to territorial sovereignty which have come before an international tribunal, there have been two competing claims to sovereignty, and the tribunal has had to decide which of the two is the stronger . . . In many cases the tribunal has been satisfied with very little in the way of actual exercise of sovereign rights, provided that the other state could not make out a superior claim. This is particularly true in the case of claims to sovereignty over areas in thinly populated or unsettled countries.

So the United Kingdom's claim to sovereignty over West Falkland was weak but would probably have been valid if Spain and Argentina had never taken any interest in West Falkland, and the claims by Spain and Argentina to sovereignty over West Falkland were weak but would probably have been valid if the United Kingdom had not established a settlement on Saunders Island. But the position is different when (as in this case) two or more states make competing claims. As far as West Falkland is concerned, the correct conclusion is probably that the weak claim by the United Kingdom and the weak claims by Spain and Argentina cancelled each other out, so to speak, with the result that West Falkland remained *terra nullius*.

To sum up, the position immediately before 1833 was that East Falkland was probably under Argentinian sovereignty, Saunders Island was probably either under British sovereignty or *terra nullius*, and West Falkland was probably *terra nullius*.

Title to Territory – The Position After 1833

In 1833 the United Kingdom returned to the Falkland Islands and evicted the Argentinian settlers from East Falkland. In the years following 1833 the United Kingdom established settlements all over the Falkland Islands, and since then the islands have been administered as a British colony.

If West Falkland was *terra nullius* immediately before 1833, the establishment of British settlements on West Falkland after 1833 enables the United Kingdom to claim sovereignty over West Falkland by occupation. But if East Falkland was under Argentinian sovereignty immediately before 1833, the United Kingdom could not have acquired title to it by occupation. Could the United Kingdom have acquired title to East Falkland by some other means? The United Kingdom has never invoked conquest (see above, pp. 146–8) as the basis of its title to any part of the Falkland Islands, but it has invoked prescription (see above, pp. 144–5) as a possible basis of title.

A state, in order to acquire title to territory from another state by prescription, must exercise effective control over that territory for a long period. The United Kingdom has clearly satisfied that requirement as regards the Falkland Islands. But international lawyers, with very few exceptions, consider that effective control is not enough on its own; it has to be accompanied by acquiescence on the part of the 'losing' state (I. Brownlie, *Principles of Public International Law*, 3rd ed., 1979, pp. 160–3). There is some disagreement among international lawyers about the meaning of acquiescence; some say that protests are enough to negative acquiescence, while others say that protests need to be supported by further steps such as breaking off diplomatic relations or offering to refer the dispute to arbitration (ibid., p. 161).[1] This controversy is of little importance as far as the present dispute is concerned, because Argentina's protests against the United Kingdom's presence on the Falkland Islands have been accompanied by further steps. In 1884 Argentina offered to refer the dispute to arbitration (but the United Kingdom did not accept the offer); later Argentina refused to recognise the British nationality of the islanders and tried to conscript them into the Argentinian army when they visited Argentina; in recent years Argentina has taken the dispute to the United Nations General Assembly.

The real uncertainty arises from the fact that for long periods (1849–1884, 1888–1908) Argentina remained silent, without protesting or taking other steps to manifest her disapproval of the United Kingdom's presence on the Falkland Islands. Normally, in cases of prescription, a state which remains silent for a long time is

---

[1] Brownlie rejects the latter view: 'if acquiescence is the crux of the matter . . . one cannot dictate what its content is to be . . .' (ibid., p. 161). In other words, *any* act or statement which demonstrates a lack of acquiescence prevents loss of territory by prescription. For this purpose, a protest is as effective as any other act or statement which demonstrates a lack of acquiescence; a protest does not need to be accompanied by other kinds of action.

regarded as acquiescing and therefore as losing its title to the territory in dispute. However, immediately before Argentina fell silent in 1849, she sent a note to the British government in which she said that she did not intend to protest any more because she felt humiliated when the United Kingdom paid no attention to her protests; but she added that her silence should not be interpreted as acquiescence. The legal effect of this note is most uncertain. On the one hand Argentina could argue that she was making clear that she did not acquiesce, and the United Kingdom could therefore not acquire title by prescription; on the other hand the United Kingdom could argue that Argentina's silence between 1849 and 1884 enabled the United Kingdom to acquire title by prescription, because protests or other acts or statements demonstrating a lack of acquiescence need to be *repeated* after a number of years, otherwise they will have only a temporary effect – when that temporary effect has expired, prescription will take place unless the protest is repeated. It is impossible to predict how an international court would decide this issue.

In the past, both the United Kingdom and Argentina have been willing to admit *in private* that the legal status of the Falkland Islands is uncertain. In 1911 and 1935–6 officials and lawyers in the British Foreign Office wrote minutes admitting that there were some weaknesses in the United Kingdom's claim to the Falkland Islands, and that there was no certainty that an arbitrator would decide in favour of the United Kingdom (see the article by Beck in the *Journal of International Studies* (*Millennium*), 1983, p. 6). Conversely, in 1927 the Argentinian Foreign Minister told the British Foreign Secretary that he thought the British claim to the Falkland Islands was 'exceedingly strong' (Paul Eddy and others (the *Sunday Times* Insight Team), *The Falklands War*, 1982, p. 41).

In fact, the position is even more uncertain than the necessarily brief and over-simplified version given in the present book suggests. Other writers have put forward a bewildering variety of opinions on sovereignty over the Falkland Islands. See, for example, Julius Goebel, *The Struggle for the Falkland Islands* (1927) and the articles by Metford (*International Affairs*, 1968, p. 463), Cohen-Jonathan (*Annuaire français de droit international*, 1972, p. 235), Northedge (*International Relations*, 1982, p. 2167), Calvert (*International Affairs*, 1983, p. 405), Hope (*Boston College International and Comparative Law Review*, 1983, p. 391) and Reisman (*Yale Law Journal*, vol. 93, 1983–4, p. 287). On the entirely separate disputes between the United Kingdom and Argentina over the Falkland Island Dependencies such as South Georgia, see the article by Waldock in the *British Year Book of International Law*, 1948, p. 311 (the United Kingdom offered to refer the disputes over the

Falkland Islands Dependencies to the International Court of Justice in 1947, but Argentina refused; since 1884 neither the United Kingdom nor Argentina has been willing to refer the dispute over the Falkland Islands to arbitration or judicial settlement).

Self-determination

During United Nations debates on the Falkland Islands, the United Kingdom has argued that the principle of self-determination supports the British position, because the Falkland Islanders want to remain under British rule. It is only recently that self-determination has become a legal principle as well as a political principle, and many aspects of self-determination are still controversial; the dividing line between politics and law is not always clear. To suggest that self-determination on its own can provide a legal title to territory is rather a novel proposition (see above, pp. 152–3 and 256), and it may be that the British government was invoking self-determination, not as a basis for the United Kingdom's *legal* title to the Falkland Islands, but as a *political* argument for permitting the islands to remain under British rule in the future.

Be that as it may, there are a number of objections which some states invoke to counter the British argument about self-determination.

First, Argentina claims that the United Kingdom never acquired a valid title to the Falkland Islands, and that the British inhabitants are therefore illegal immigrants (or the descendants of illegal immigrants) whose wishes should not be allowed to determine the future status of the islands.

Second, self-determination means self-determination of *peoples*. At the time of the last census in 1980, the population of the Falklands was 1813, of whom 1723 were United Kingdom nationals. Can a population as small as this be said to constitute a separate people?

Third, many members of the United Nations regard colonialism as illegal, even when the inhabitants of the colony want to remain under colonial rule. (This view is not shared by Western states.)

Fourth, paragraph 6 of General Assembly resolution 1514 (XV) condemns the 'disruption of the national unity and the territorial integrity of a country' (see above, p. 252). Argentina argues that the British seizure of the Falkland Islands in 1833 disrupted the national unity and territorial integrity of Argentina, and that therefore the appropriate method of decolonisation is to restore the islands to Argentina, regardless of the inhabitants' wishes. (The British view is that paragraph 6 condemns *future* disruptions and is not designed to undo *past* disruptions.)

General Assembly resolutions on the Falkland Islands have steered a middle course between the British and Argentinian positions on self-determination. On the one hand, the General Assembly has not accepted the Argentinian argument that paragraph 6 of resolution 1514 (XV) should be applied to the Falkland Islands (although it has accepted the Spanish argument that paragraph 6 should be applied to Gibraltar – see *Yearbook of the United Nations*, 1967, pp. 675–6). On the other hand, the General Assembly has never said that the Falkland Islanders are a 'people' or that they are entitled to self-determination; instead, it has passed resolutions recommending the United Kingdom and Argentina to enter into negotiations to settle the dispute about sovereignty over the Falkland Islands, 'bearing in mind . . . the interests [not wishes] of the inhabitants' (*Yearbook of the United Nations*, 1965, pp. 578–9, and 1973, pp. 713–14; *United Nations Chronicle*, 1983, no. 1, pp. 4–5). These resolutions also call for the termination of the colonial situation in the Falkland Islands. But termination of the colonial situation in the Falkland Islands need not necessarily take the form of integration or association with Argentina; it could also take other forms (see above, p. 252), such as independence, or integration or association with the United Kingdom.

Use of Force

On 2 April 1982 Argentina invaded the Falkland Islands. On the following day the Security Council passed resolution 502 which, after reciting that the Security Council was deeply disturbed at reports of an invasion by Argentina, determined that there existed a breach of the peace in the region of the Falkland Islands (for the significance of this determination, see above, pp. 180–3). The Security Council demanded an immediate cessation of hostilities and an immediate withdrawal of all Argentinian forces from the Falkland Islands, and called on Argentina and the United Kingdom to seek a diplomatic solution to their differences. (For the text of resolution 502, see *International Legal Materials*, 1982, p. 679; it was passed by ten votes to one (Panama), with four abstentions (China, Poland, Spain and the USSR).)

Resolution 502 constituted an implied condemnation of Argentina's use of force. Argentina argued that she was entitled to use force to recover possession of territory which rightfully belonged to Argentina. This argument was supported by some Latin American countries, but was rejected by most member States of the United Nations. Article 2 (3) of the United Nations Charter requires member States to settle their disputes by peaceful means, and this obligation applies as much to territorial disputes as to any other class of dispute; the General Assembly's Friendly Relations Declaration of 1970 says that 'every state has the duty to refrain from the threat or use of force . . . as a means of solving international disputes, including territorial disputes . . .' (I. Brownlie, *Basic Documents in International Law*, 3rd ed., 1983, p. 38). In the Security Council debates on Argentina's invasion of the Falkland Islands, Jordan and Uganda supported Argentina's claim to the islands but nevertheless condemned Argentina's use of force as illegal. (For further details of the Security Council debates, see *United Nations Chronicle*, 1982, no. 5, pp. 5–10, and D. J. Harris, *Cases and Materials on International Law*, 3rd ed., 1983, pp. 661–7.)

If Argentina's invasion of the Falkland Islands was unlawful, the United Kingdom was entitled to use force in self-defence. It is generally accepted, even by Latin American states, that a state in possession of territory is entitled to use force in self-defence against invasion by a rival claimant, even though the rival claimant may have a better title to the territory than the state in possession (D.W. Bowett, *Self-Defence in International Law*, 1958, pp. 34–6; I. Brownlie, *International Law and the Use of Force by States*, 1963, pp. 382–3). The implied condemnation of Argentina's invasion by resolution 502, and Argentina's refusal to obey that resolution, added further strength to the United Kingdom's claim to be entitled to use force in self-defence; and the United Kingdom also argued that, if Argentina's invasion was allowed to succeed, other states all over the world would be encouraged to use force in support of territorial claims against their neighbours.

Table of Cases

Index